The Failed Experiment

The Failed Experiment

Was Hamilton Right

Mart Grams

Print information available on the last page.

Rev. date: 02/12/2018

To order additional copies of this book, contact:
Xlibris
1-888-795-4274
www.Xlibris.com
Orders@Xlibris.com
773429

CONTENTS

DEDICATION

T HIS BOOK IS dedicated to my late wife, Linda. Right now, all I have is an empty soul, and crushed heart. I slept next to her for over three decades, other than when she birthed our two sons, or I was away from home for business. Less than a handful of times, did I not smell, hear, feel, know her next to me. He gets her now. I watched her take His hand and I let go. She promised me she'd wait for me. God's math is 1+1=1, My other 1/2 is waiting for this 1/2, soon to be full again. It is an honor to have known you; I hope this book would measure up to your standards.

Love, Mart

ACKNOWLEDGMENTS

IT IS ALWAYS hard when completing any project to attribute thanks to all that helped. Putting in a pond in your yard, shovel maker, advise from books on food and type of fish, sons who helped dig and hauled away soil, and the hose maker remind me of Leonard Reed's "I, Pencil." The same is true here. I cannot name all that helped here. Robert Murphy, who, a decade ago, sent me a crate full of books and said, "Read and we'll discuss," began my conversion to Austrian economics and anarcho-capitalism and opened my eyes to what was in front but I could not see. Thomas Woods and his Liberty Classroom and presenters, podcasts, and daily newsletter kept me on fire! FEE. org, Mises.org, Ron Paul Institute for Peace and Prosperity, Rutherford Institute, and the Institute for Justice, to name a few think tanks from which I reaped (stole) many of the ideas.

My students who over the years kept challenging me with "This can't be right. Mr. Cunningham said . . ." and "Mrs. Smith said not to listen to you!" Their questions spurred these answers. Frederick Douglass is supposedly to have said—more apocryphal than citable, "It's easier to build strong children than to repair broken men." Our job as parents, families, and teachers is to build strong children. Giving them the right answers, even if you're the lone voice in the wilderness, will save those that hear and listen. Many I still am in contact with; many of their children and grandchildren I have taught. Thanks for making me teach, not merely indoctrinate.

And most importantly, my idealism and optimism for the American Republic have been renewed as I see the next generation, my grandchildren. The plan of action at the end is for them and your children and grandchildren. As Christ said, when your son asks for a fish, you don't give him a serpent; when your daughter asks for bread, don't give her a stone. As Calvin Coolidge said, "To live under the American Constitution is the greatest political privilege that was ever accorded to the human race." Let's give our children, our posterity, a rebirth of freedom and finish that unfinished work that we let crumble—the great experiment of the AMERICAN REPUBLIC.

PREFACE

Tyler Cowen from "The Complacent Class" video on MRUniversity.edu

D O WE STILL live in a world of wonder, or have we become too complacent and too set in our ways? And if so, how and why? To consider this question, let's go back to one of the great wonders of American history. In 1893, Chicago hosted the World's Fair; over twenty-five million awestruck visitors came to an artificially constructed city with over two hundred custom-made buildings surrounded by man-made canals and lagoons. Twenty-five million—that was more than a third of the entire US population at that time. Imagine that Americans in 1893 were far from wealthy, yet even without cars or planes, so many of them found their way to Chicago. This far exceeds the attendance at modern events such as the Olympics, our World Cup, or even the yearly traffic at Disney World.

Now why would so many make such a trip? To get a glimpse of the future. The world was changing fast, and that glimpse could be breathtaking and unprecedented. Just imagine what that experience must have been like as a grown adult to take your first drive on a Ferris wheel or to be transported along the first moving sidewalk or to watch genius inventors such as Nikola Tesla demonstrate what they had created. The first experience of the dishwasher or try Wrigley's gum. For many who had only kerosene lamps, the thousands of glowing bulbs of various shapes and colors would be their very first glimpse of electric light.

And all this innovation was not unique to Chicago's fair. At the Philadelphia fair, you could experience the wonder at first hearing human voice through a telephone. Or at the Buffalo fair, you would be shocked at seeing what's beneath your skin via an x-ray machine. All the while tasting your first hot dog or ice cream cone. These fairs are just a glimpse at an earlier American pioneer culture that drove dramatic economic growth of what's been called "a hockey stick of human prosperity." Early American pioneers transformed the country and indeed the broader world through a dramatic series of grand projects.

Change didn't slow as the twentieth century dawned; in some ways, it accelerated. They added radio and then TV, the first cars and airplanes, vaccines and antibiotics, a bit later nuclear power, all the while fighting and winning two World Wars; even computers date from that era. And we weren't done; what about carving an interstate highway system throughout most of the United States? Sure, walking on the moon. OK, no problem.

Then something happened in the 1970s and beyond. Incremental improvements continued, but there was really only one grand epic project for the history books: this [cell phone]. There was nothing resembling this fifty years ago; nothing that so easily enabled human beings to communicate with each other or to access the world's information so readily. However, beyond computers and communication devices, most of the physical world we see today, it's not that different from the 1960s. While our virtual world has been booming and changing, our physical world has been surprisingly static for hundreds of years. We dramatically increased our ability to travel across longer distance and at ever-higher speeds; but now, the speed of travel is stagnating or even slowing because of traffic or degraded mass transit system. We scrapped supersonic travel, and we still rely heavily on a plane designed in the late 1960s.

This is just a few examples. In general, we seem to be more content with slamming the brakes on dramatic upheaval; we prefer safety and comfort to change. Rather than seek dynamism, we so often want to be protected from it, and so complacency has spread. The shift in the American attitude from the pioneering spirit to the complacent can be seen in many ways. Our ancestors packed their wagons and ventured into unknown lands often in the face of pretty high risk.

Today the trend is toward staying put, whether in terms of where you live or where you work. Our kids have gone from taking dodge balls to the face as I once did in sixth grade to not being allowed to play tag or maybe even go outside at all with or without sunscreen. We've gone from the counterculture and Russian novels and Nietzsche to a culture of education focusing on safe spaces and trigger warnings. The 1960s and '70s had massive marches for civil rights and against the war in Vietnam. Change was demanded often regardless of the risk; today you need to hire a protest planner, file for permits, and be confined to control demonstration zones. We've bureaucratized so much of our culture including its very acts of protest. Our public spaces are barricaded and restricted from any kind of possibly disorderly public demonstration; again, we prefer safety and control over change.

This complacency shows through in our economic performance. Rates of productivity growth, wages, geographic mobility, and indeed economic growth, they're all down. The millennials measure as being the least entrepreneurial generation in recent history. For much of the economy, change has been replaced by partial stasis. So maybe you ask, "Well, what's wrong with stasis? Things are pretty comfortable and safe up here on top of the hockey stick!" It is arguably the golden age on TV gaming and podcasts; online education too. "Can't we just enjoy it all?"

Well, we're seeing some trouble some mornings that this lack of change is not sustainable forever. Societies require dynamism to refresh and renew their ideas, to restimulate their economic growth, to make it possible to pay the bills in the future. And so without enough dynamism and indeed a crisis is brewing, it's likely that some big changes are coming along down the road in a way we can no longer limit our control. I call that the Great Reset.

This also brings up a broader and more fundamental question—is it possible for humanity to progress steadily, for this hockey stick blade to continue stretching upward, or is there something inherently cyclical about human history whereby very good periods tend to be followed by something rather worse?

In an interview with Ana Swanson for the *Washington Post*, December 2016, Tyler Cowen talked about the *complacent class*. He argued that a new kind of cultural segregation has handcuffed the American dream. This division benefits a select class, leaving behind the rest of the nation. "The U.S. population has sorted out not only along political lines, but also by education, race, income, social status and even technological ability. Along the way, the country has become more polarized, less dynamic and less fair."

What many called the 1 percent versus the 99 percent, Cowen sees an educated urban elite not only enjoying the fruits of a new world of globalized trade, derivatives, international capital markets, but also increasingly isolated from other parts of the country. This 1 percent doesn't see the need for change, though more and more of the country is left behind and becoming more and more dissatisfied.

Technology may be one issue that expresses the contradiction of a world closer together yet tearing itself in two.

> I think of matching and segregation as two sides of the same coin. On the positive side, so many of the gains in our well-being over the last 20 years have come from better matching, rather than traditional forms of economic growth. These days, if I buy music, I know in advance I like it. In the old days, you would buy an album, and you might not like most of the songs. Or if you look at couples, their ability to find a compatible partner is much greater because of the Internet. People who are good at using matching technologies are really much better off.

> But there are two downsides. One is many people don't have these technologies or use them well, because of the digital divide. Secondly, matching is also a kind of segregation. People who are of the same political views, the same education, same cultural tastes, similar income levels, they're much more likely to be living together than before. It has very real benefits for some people, but in my opinion, it is not overall a good thing. This came up as an issue in the election.

> People of high socio-economic status and particular political views are much more likely these days to be matched into parts of New York, California, Washington D.C., and a group of smaller but high-status towns, like Ann Arbor, Santa Barbara, and so on. This means those people are actually somewhat insulated from the "real America." When you run that experiment in politics, all of a sudden,

it's possible to get this big divergence between the popular vote, which went for Hillary Clinton, and the electoral college vote, which went solidly for Donald Trump.

The most literal meaning is well-educated, upper middle class to upper class professionals. They've dug themselves in and have more or less impregnable positions with high income. They're highly qualified for their jobs, and they could get another great job at will.

But the trend of complacency goes beyond that. Even among people of lower educational backgrounds or lower incomes, there's a much greater willingness to accept the status quo. If you look at the 1960s, with the riots, the discontent, the crime rates, there was a sense of urgency—which was actually mostly disruptive, I'm not advocating we go back to that—but it was the other side of the coin of greater dynamism. And now, even people who are significant losers from the current arrangement are less likely to do something disruptive. This may just now be changing, though.

The benefits of today are very real—lower risk, higher safety, a greater sense of calm. Even if you don't belong to a minority group that was badly oppressed back then, life is generally much better today. The problem is, we can't just keep the status quo forever. When everyone tries to dig in and tries to become super safe, ultimately dynamism dwindles, you run out of the ability to pay the bills, and you can't maintain all those protective barriers. The more you try to control risk in the micro sense, the more you lose your ability to hold the really big risks at bay.

Well, we just had a big one this November. Trump's election was something many people thought couldn't happen, and it did. It's very hard to predict exactly what the Trump administration will do, but it's already proven highly disruptive.

You write that "Some of the places that are the most segregated are the parts of America where people feel very good about themselves"—places like New York and

California, liberal cities and college towns. You say that segregation in these places is not mostly the result of overt racism anymore, but when you have segregation by education, by income, by social status, does the effect end up being largely the same?

A lot of the effects are similar. There are plenty of people who would never dream of thinking of themselves as racist, yet they will choose where they buy their home based on getting into "the best school district possible," and that will have a segregating effect. In absolute terms, many of the most segregated school systems are in the north, in places like New York state. It's nice that there is no racist intent, it's still a positive thing. But at the end of the day, the mixing that boosts mobility is in danger. And the fact that it's not so explicitly racist in some ways makes it harder to combat. Because who could object to someone wanting a better school district for their kids? Of course, that's natural.

Have we become complacent, have we become the fear of Franklin that the Republic created in the summer of '87 in Philadelphia would be lost? Was Washington correct that only a moral, civically virtuous people could rule themselves? Have we lost that virtue, the civic knowledge necessary to understand how to rule ourselves? In recent years, it appears we've lost the self-restraint of playing politics with temper tantrums in the streets when policies or elections go a direction away from our own. Yet, in relation to restraint, it is an assertion; do we have the courage to stand for what is right, to exercise our rights, to NOT do what is wrong, to fill the jails as Martin Luther King Jr. said?

In addition to civic knowledge, self-restraint, and self-assertion, citizens must be self-reliant. For citizens to be free, they must be able to take care of themselves and their families. Those unable to care for themselves must be cared for; the leviathan state becomes the surrogate family. Self-reliant citizens are free, live longer, and are more secure in their rights and their own value.

In addition to civic knowledge, self-restraint, and self-assertion, citizens must possess the civic virtue of self-reliance. Many say that Thomas Jefferson said it, though no evidence substantiates it, but according to Gerald Ford addressing Congress in 1974, "A government big enough to give you everything you want, is a government big enough to take away everything that you have." It makes sense. In the late eighteenth century, the idea that a national government would provide roads or collect income tax was simply unimaginable. I don't think in their wildest dreams any of the Founders imagined their federal or state governments could ever grow to the size that it could give every citizen what they wanted.

At the end of *The Federalist 55*, James Madison wrote, "Republican government presupposes the existence of [civic virtue] in a higher degree than any other form." The Framers had learned through experience that political freedom requires limited government—that is, government should leave people alone, for the most part, in their private associations such as family, religion, education, and business. But they, like Franklin, knew limited government is tenuous at best, dangerous at the extreme. Ron Paul, the leader of a new "revolution of liberty," like Franklin, believes liberty and a republic are not easy to achieve or maintain. When people are left alone, they might use that freedom to violate the rights of others; or they might simply live irresponsibly, depending on others with money and resources to care for them. Thus, limited government requires a certain kind of citizen, not complacent to innovation or assertion of God-given rights, not ignorant of her history or governmental workings, not reliant on others or the government for his survival, but most importantly an active participant in the Great Experiment of America.

But, and this is a difficult statement for me to write, many are doubting this experiment in self-rule. As far back as Alexander Hamilton, a Framer, a writer of the many of Federalist essays, did not believe the average citizen was competent to rule. That the best, the richest, the elites, the educated, should rule. Debate over recent changes to the tax code December 2017 found a twenty-first-century paraphrase when Iowa senator Charles Grassley gave his rationale for eliminating the death (inheritance) tax. "I think not having the estate tax recognizes the people that are investing, as opposed to those that are just spending every darn penny they have, whether it's on booze or women or movies." iowastartingline.com I think sums up the ideology of the deep state of Hamilton.

It's difficult to think of a more condescending, elitist worldview—that if you're not ultra-wealthy, it's clearly because you're wasting all your money on alcohol, frivolous fun and prostitutes (I assume that's what he meant when he said women). Certainly it couldn't be because people are struggling to find decent-paying jobs, are straddled with debt from the college education they need to attain better jobs, or are paying outrageous sums for health insurance and medical bills. Nope, it must be because they're all getting hand jobs from hookers in the back of a dark movie theater while downing a bottle of Jack Daniel's.

Hamilton's plan, his curse according to Tom DiLorenzo, was to build a nation of power, corporate leaders would finance the government, holding millions, today trillions, in treasury debts. They would not rebel as the Founders did; they'd lose a fortune, and taxpayers would pay ever-increasing interest payments on the unpayable debts. By buying the debt, these few would control elected offices with bribes, extortion, and contracts. DiLorenzo reminds us "ideas have consequences," and Hamilton's have had the terrible consequences for freedom.

Hamilton was a statist, mercantilist, and nationalist. He purposely confused his readers to sound like a Federalist when in fact he is the father of Henry Clay's American system of high tariffs, many regulations, and protecting the 1 percent over the majority. Today's Democratic Party is the Whigs of the twenty-first century.

Art Carden for FEE, in reviewing Tom's book *Hamilton's Curse,* sums up today's deep state very accurately, unfortunately.

Hamilton's vision for the nation included a strong sense of nationalism, zealous protectionism, enthusiasm for central banking, and methods of constitutional interpretation like the doctrine of "implied powers" that essentially stripped away the Constitution's restraints on the central government. DiLorenzo depicts Hamilton and his intellectual followers as technocrats who view society as a lump of clay for them to fashion with their expert hands. They couldn't grasp the spontaneous order of the free market.

To borrow a phrase from Adam Smith, Hamilton was the quintessential "man of system." In his ideal society he and others who were blessed with inside knowledge of "the common good" would arrange things just so, thereby creating the ideal society. DiLorenzo points out explicit parallels between Hamilton's thinking and Rousseau's idea of "the general will," under which government officials would "force people to be free." Individual liberty holds no importance for such people.

The debt would be financed and serviced by the many as taxpayers. They would be convinced by intellectuals to hold up the vision of the state and economy or through force. Hamilton believed in a strong-standing army to enforce recalcitrant thinkers, such as he did in the Whiskey Rebellion of the early Republic.

Hamilton would be proud of what we've become, a world empire controlled by a deep state of corporations, military-industrial contractors supported by Silicon Valley's information control—"too big to fail," protectionism, the imperial presidency (see Arthur Schlesinger's work on this), eminent domain, and Progressive regulations. Presidents are at best CEOs, at worst rubber stamps. Reagan was used in Iran-Contra to sell weapons, the same weapons, many times over, even though banned by Congress. Bill Clinton, as his wife, Hillary, almost would later, surrounded his administration with money men from Goldman Sachs, Lehman Brothers, and others. Bill Clinton would repeal Glass-Steagall allowing derivatives, CDOs, and later collapse and loss of nearly $20 trillion in 2008. He continues to gain after 2001 when he left office with $23 million in "speaking fees" in the financial sector. Bush, the younger, was controlled and kept out of the loop by Dick Cheney, a master of the Hamiltonian deep state. Barack Obama would be used to bolster the insurance industry under the guise of Progressive health care "reform." And lately, even the outsider, swamp-draining Donald Trump sided with darkness in bombing Syria.

Mike Lofgren in his *Deep State: The Fall of the Constitution and the Rise of a Shadow Government*, reminds we idealists "for all the preening, grandstanding, and money grubbing of the presidential race, the politicians we elect have as little ability to shift policy as Communist Party apparatchiks in the old Soviet Union."

Washington DC has become a circus of distraction from conspiracy theories to screaming for special prosecutors every time one loses a vote. But what the Constitution requires, the duties of presidents and congresses get done behind the scenes by invisible unelected bureaucrats in a vast web of freelance agencies deciding our financial policy, defense policy, and security decisions. Why did the Obama administration and the Bush administration look so similar? Tom Woods has a series of "rules" he goes by to explain the politics of today. Rule number two is no matter Hillary, Jeb, Trump, you get John McCain. Real power lies not in We, the People, or in the Constitution, or in the values or ideals of the Declaration, but in a Hamiltonian deep state, a power elite few of whom we will ever know about. This elite owns the US debt, is controlled by large corporate interests, and is dependent on Silicon Valley, whose data-collecting systems allow them to control the masses' every swipe and click.

Barack Obama, elected for "Hope and Change," was an enigma. He was the most reluctant but most efficient chairman of the deep state. He allowed the Cold War to rebubble talking "smack" to Putin of Russia yet did little; "pulled out of the Middle East" yet surged in Afghanistan, created insurgents (ISIS, or ISIL) a cancer in the Middle East; paid enemies of America, who were even bigger enemies of our enemies, in Libya, Syria, Yemen. The director of the CIA, John Brennan, said that Obama did "not have an appreciation" of national security when he came into office, but with training by himself and others of the system, he [Obama] "has gone to school and understands the complexities."

In 2016, I saw a slight hope, a light, a change. Donald Trump, a billionaire, nonpartisan, nonelite, and disdained by the elite, artists, both political parties, and Hollywood, defeated the appointed heir Hillary Clinton. The deep state with its controlled media, all intellectuals, knew, KNEW! She was the next president; she was "due." She had been preened, programmed, to win, control, and allow the 1 percent to benefit. With fake news, rigged primaries, buying off all contenders, million spent to convince We, the People that Trump was the antichrist, Hitler, Stalin, the devil, and even Pee-wee Herman, the election brought an unbuyable forty-fifth presidency. Maybe the chains will be broken and the failed experiment will be the great experiment again.

Many say it is too late; "they" have us all under surveillance, metadata, the threat of tax audits, the deep state is just that deep! But my last book, *Economics for the Remnant*, was in remembrance of an article I read a while back by Albert Nock, "Isaiah's Job."

> In the year of Uzziah's death, the Lord commissioned the prophet to go out and warn the people of the wrath to come. "Tell them what a worthless lot they are." He said, "Tell them what is wrong, and why and what is going to happen unless they have a change of heart and straighten up. Don't mince matters. Make it clear that they are positively down to their last chance. Give it to them good and strong and keep on giving it to them. I suppose perhaps I ought to tell you," He added, "that it won't do any good. The official class and their intelligentsia will turn up their noses at you and the masses will not even listen. They will all keep on in their own ways until they carry everything down to destruction, and you will probably be lucky if you get out with your life."
>
> Isaiah had been very willing to take on the job—in fact, he had asked for it—but the prospect put a new face on the situation. It raised the obvious question: Why, if all that were so—if the enterprise were to be a failure from the start—was there any sense in starting it? "Ah," the Lord said, "you do not get the point. There is a Remnant there that you know nothing about. They are obscure, unorganized, inarticulate, each one rubbing along as best he can. They need to be encouraged and braced up because when everything has gone completely to the dogs, they are the ones who will come back and build up a new society; and meanwhile, your preaching will reassure them and keep them hanging on. Your job is to take care of the Remnant, so be off now and set about it."

Hopefully, this book will be read by more than the Remnant, and as Tom Woods says, Nock was wrong, our job is to grow the Remnant.

When Trump won the recent 2016 presidential election, many people all over the global and the political spectrum were stunned. But even more shocking was the discovery of a cryptic online quote posthumously attributed to Kurt Cobain on Donald Trump, made a year before Cobain's death:

> In the end I believe my generation will surprise everyone. We already know that both political parties are playing both sides from the middle and we'll elect a true outsider when we fully mature.
>
> I wouldn't be surprised if it's not a business tycoon who can't be bought and who does what's right for the people. Someone like Donald Trump as crazy as that sounds.

INTRODUCTION

If one rejects laissez faire on account of man's fallibility
and moral weakness, one must for the same reason
also reject every kind of government action.
—Ludwig von Mises, *Planning for Freedom*

T HERE ARE SEVERAL reasons I decided to take my students' text and edit it for the purposes of explaining to the general population our system of government. Without an active understanding of the foundations of the American experiment, the ideal the Framers and Founders of this nation will perish. As Abraham Lincoln stated, "The philosophy of the classroom today will be the philosophy of government tomorrow." We have gone drastically off track in teaching the ideas and ideals of the past, the realities of a free market, and the complexities of a free social organization. Human prosperity and social cooperation develop spontaneously in societies that protect private property rights and encourage voluntary trade. It is the duty of government to protect life, liberty, and property. We have in the last decades seen the decline of this ideal in academia, and recent students, today's and tomorrow's voters, might accidentally, or purposively if ill instructed, crash this train of freedom.

First, I'd like to talk a bit about the foundations of the Framers' thoughts when creating this experiment. They took what they knew of human nature and honestly and coherently structured a system around these ideas. The philosophical background of the Constitution from the Greeks and Romans, through the medieval period, and the explosion of Enlightenment ideas are so intertwined in the minds of these radicals, yes, radicals, that to ignore the past, we may not have a future. Be aware that this discussion has not yet been decided; as Ben Franklin stated, we have "a Republic, if you can keep it."

But, like students, we are not born free thinkers. The freedom of the market is quite frankly somewhat contrary to the raising of children. Mothers provide all, food, clothing, and shelter when we are infants. Parents feed, care for, and shelter from the real world while children grow and mature. Then, as we have seen recently (last eighty years), government has become the nanny state where success and failure are absent. Mediocrity is the norm; children are taught to share and fit in rather than excel. Thus, we must teach the reality of freedom, the success of the individual, and the prosperity of the free market. Ronald Reagan stated it as succinctly as any:

> Freedom is never more than one generation away from extinction. We didn't pass it to our children in the bloodstream. It must be fought for, protected, and handed on for them to do the same, or one day we will spend our sunset years telling our children and our children's children what it was once like in the United States where men were free. Ronald Reagan

Without the philosophical foundations, many continue to achieve little and become a member of the herd, and as Rome fell, we will see the end of this great experiment, and we may add ourselves to the pile of history as the failed experiment. Both Thomas Jefferson of the eighteenth century and H. L. Mencken of the twentieth gave reasons. I must write this apology, a defense of the experiment, both for ourselves and the success and hope of our children and children's children. This book is my attempt for your understanding of your individual and our national purposes.

> To give to every citizen the information he needs for the transaction of his own business; To enable him to calculate for himself, and to express and preserve his ideas, his contracts and accounts, in writing; To improve, by reading, his morals and faculties; To understand his duties to his neighbors and country, and to discharge with competence the functions confided to him by either; To know his rights; to exercise with order and justice those he retains; to choose with discretion the fiduciary of those he delegates; and to notice their conduct with diligence, with candor, and judgment; And, in general, to observe with intelligence and faithfulness all the social relations under which he shall be

placed (Thomas Jefferson, Report of the Commissioners for the University of Virginia, 1818).

> The most dangerous man to any government is the man who is able to think things out without regard to the prevailing superstitions and taboos. Almost inevitably he comes to the conclusion that the government he lives under is dishonest, insane, intolerable, and so if he is romantic, he tries to change it. And even if he is not romantic personally he is very apt to spread discontent among those who are (H. L. Mencken)

I will try to explain as I would to my students as simply and succinctly as I am able; any errors are mine, not the past's. Let's start with the historical and philosophical foundations of our country's ideas about constitutional government. Then a brief look at the mechanics of the Constitution and organization the national government. Brief? Yes, others have done better. Check out the Heritage Foundation's *Guide to the Constitution*, second edition 2014, for the best analysis, clause by clause. In looking at the development of the Constitution, meaning of the various rights guaranteed in the Bill of Rights, expansion of rights during the last two hundred years, we will see the decay of many aspects of the original plan: Federalism, division of power, and checks and balances. Last, my greatest concern is the roles that many citizens have ignored, even rejected in the experiment of the American Republic.

Full disclosure, I am a retired economics and government instructor with a more than Libertarian, freedom-loving lean. I have lived under a dozen presidents, having voted for only two of them. I will tell you up front so that you may dispose of this evil text, not burning, rummage sale, or back to the bookstore: Ronald Reagan and Donald Trump. Yet my favorites are no one this century, or the last. They include those that swore and oath to the Constitution and followed that oath. They include John Tyler, Grover Cleveland, James K. Polk (as the only one to carry out his campaign promise), Thomas Jefferson, and Andrew Johnson. These are men, human failing creatures, but they are the nearest thing to a Constitutional executive we have had. Now James Garfield and William Henry Harrison also are in my "liked" category, though for crass reasons.

My hope is that by the time you finish, you will be as well informed as any of your fellow citizens about your country's system of government (and more informed than most). Don't worry about what you don't know. Appreciating what you have yet to learn will help you make the most of your reading and discussion of the lessons.

Throughout, I have included "Critical Thinking"; these exercises give you an opportunity to stop, analyze, and discuss a problem or issue related to the subject. These exercises are intended not only to increase your understanding of the material but also to develop those skills that will prove useful to you as citizens. These are for self-learning, only you, or if doing a reading club, your group will see your thoughts. As I said, as retired instructor, I do not want to grade your ideas, penmanship (a very lost art), or even your understanding. As the Founders and Framers believed, a republic is a discussion; we're not angels or all-knowing. To start, get an empty notebook and write out your thoughts on these five exercises.

Looking at the Declaration of Independence

Let us see how much you already know about the meaning of this document. What do you know about the Declaration of Independence? The Declaration of Independence, drafted by Thomas Jefferson and adopted by the Continental Congress in July 1776, is our country's founding document. The words and ideas contained in that document will be referred to frequently throughout this text.

The Declaration of Independence appears in the reference section at the back of the book. Or online on numerous sites. I am biased to print copies, harder to alter for future readers. Read very carefully the first two paragraphs of the Declaration and then try to answer the following questions:

What is the main purpose of the document? For whom is it written, and what is it trying to explain?

What sort of action is the Declaration attempting to justify? Why do you think the Declaration regards this action as a very serious and unusual one?

What does the Declaration suggest in the relationship between a government and the people it governs? On what conditions is all-legitimate government based? What justifies the ending of that relationship?

Per the Declaration, what is the primary purpose of government?

The Declaration speaks of "truths," which are "self-evident." What are these "truths"? Why are they called "truths"? What makes them "self-evident"?

What do you know about the Constitution? If the Declaration of Independence is America's founding document, the Constitution is its rule book of government. Drafted in 1787 and ratified by the American people the following year, it established the system of government with which the nation has lived for over two hundred years.

The Preamble to the Constitution

The Constitution is also included in the reference section. Read carefully the preamble to that document and then try to answer the following questions:

Per the preamble, what is the purpose of the Constitution? Explain the meaning of each of its stated purposes.

By what authority is it "ordained and established"?

What is the connection between the stated goals of the Constitution and the purposes of government as outlined in the Declaration of Independence?

What do you know about the Bill of Rights?

What about the Bill of Rights?

The first ten amendments to the Constitution are known as the Bill of Rights. This document was drafted and approved by Congress in 1789 from lists developed by the states, sorted down by James Madison to a dozen, and ten ratified by the people in 1791 as the Bill of Rights. It contains some of the basic rights of individuals that the government is prohibited from violating. When the Framers wrote our Constitution and, later, the Bill of Rights, they were careful to include written protections of what they thought were many of the basic rights of a free people. Do not refer to the Bill of Rights itself or any other reference material.

What is a "right"?

What rights are protected by the Bill of Rights?

From whom does the Bill of Rights protect you?

Does the Bill of Rights provide all the protections you need for your life, liberty, and property? Explain your answer.

Now let's provide you an opportunity to reconsider some of your original ideas about the Bill of Rights. Read carefully the copy of the Bill of Rights in the Reference Section. Revise your answers in light of what you have learned. Find at least three rights in the Bill of Rights you did not list in response to your first list. What appear to be the purposes of these rights? Review your answers to the other questions and make any changes or additions to them you think should be made.

Thinking about, not just saying, the Pledge of Allegiance

What do you know about the rights and responsibilities of citizenship? My primary purpose is not to fill your head with a lot of facts about American history and government. Knowledge of these facts is important but only insofar as it deepens your understanding of the American constitutional system and its development. For Americans, the most familiar expression of citizenship is taking the Pledge of Allegiance. The pledge is something you have recited countless times and probably know by heart:

> I pledge allegiance to the flag of the United States of
> America and to the Republic for which it stands, one nation,
> under God, indivisible, with liberty and justice for all.

The original draft of the Pledge of Allegiance was written by James B. Upham in 1888 and revised slightly four years later by Francis Bellamy, who included it in the four hundredth anniversary celebration of Columbus's first voyage to the New World. The phrase "under God" was added to the Pledge of Allegiance by Act of Congress in 1954.

What is involved in pledging allegiance? What does allegiance mean? What does the taking of the pledge say about your relationship to government?

Why do we pledge allegiance to the American flag? Why not to the president of the United States, our members of Congress, or the justices of the Supreme Court?

Do we have the right to withhold our allegiance? What would be the consequences of doing that? If you were born here, when and how do you decide to be an American citizen? If you were not born an American citizen, how do you become one? How is a citizen different from someone else living in this country?

What is a "republic"? Does the pledge define what that word means? How does a republic differ from a democracy?

Analyzing Judge Hand's statement

Where can the most important protections of rights be found? A written constitution or a bill of rights does not mean that citizens have these rights. Laws passed by our national, state, and local governments don't guarantee that citizens' rights won't be violated by the very laws that are supposed to protect them. Some people who have observed the common violations of individual rights in our own society and in others have argued that the most important protection of rights lies in the hearts and minds of ordinary citizens.

Learned Hand, a great American judge in 1941, delivered a commencement address at Yale University; in 1944, he gave another speech in New York City, titled "The Spirit of Liberty." Both speeches were nearly identical, but the ideas were so important, twice may not have been enough. What are the main or points in Judge Hand's argument?

> I often wonder whether we do not rest our hopes too
> much upon constitutions, upon laws and courts. These are
> false hopes; believe me, these are false hopes. Liberty lies in
> the hearts of men; when it dies there, no constitution, no
> law, no court can save it; no constitution, no law, no court
> can even do much to help it. While it lies there it needs
> no constitution, no law, no court to save it. What are your
> responsibilities as a citizen that he expects?

Do you agree with the Judge? Why, or Why not?

Based on Judge Hand's idea about where liberty lies, do you think that constitutions and bills of rights are unnecessary?

So why then a book on Hamilton? Well, as Brion McClanahan in his new study, *How Alexander Hamilton Screwed up America*, I also believe it is because of Hamilton's duplicity that we now live in a nation with a government the Founders and Framers would be considered traitors, or at least a hindrance to the deep state. Now I'm not going to ruin Brion's great exposition on the big four of the destruction of the American Revolution, maybe the end of the great experiment had begun immediately by these four early Lincoln-type pre-Progressives, though I hope not: John Marshall, Joseph Story, Hugo Black, and Alexander Hamilton. They were Anti-Federalism, not to be confused with the Anti-Federalists that were actually Federalists; the states were to be mere administrative districts, corporations of the national state. They supported a loose to nearly nonexistent Constitution; if it ain't denied, it must be allowed. High debt, high protective tariffs, one law for every possible contingency in every state.

Hamilton, like the others following him, believe in empire, economic and political, large standing armies, a strong independent presidency, a submissive and compiling legislature, and a judicial system that gave legitimacy to it all. All of this, this Hamiltonian System, later under Henry Clay, the American system, later the Progressives added public school indoctrination, national family regulations through abortion, welfare, same-sex marriage, the end of any religion not protecting and sanctifying the state, large military, industrial, and governmental entanglements, were and are contrary to everything the Founding Fathers and Framers understood as the American Republic, the Constitution, the great experiment. Even all they were told by the Federalists including Hamilton during the ratification conventions confirms this was to be a federal republic, not the nationalistic centralized state we inhabit today.

Thus, while many admire the *Hamilton* of Broadway, he is the source of the deep state, surveillance, high taxes, heavy regulations, a failed banking system, loss of most civil liberties, and the Framers and great patriots throughout the last 250 years had and have hoped to be avoided. The true Hamilton, today's Progressives, has succeeded beyond his dreams. Richard Evelyn Byrd Sr., speaker of the Delaware House of Delegates in 1910, one hundred years ago, saw the deep state of the twenty-first century:

> A hand from Washington will be stretched out and placed upon every man's business; the eye of the Federal inspector will be in every man's counting house. The law will of necessity have inquisitorial features, it will provide penalties. It will create a complicated machinery. Under it businessmen will be hauled into courts distant from their homes. Heavy fines imposed by distant and unfamiliar tribunals will constantly menace the taxpayer. An army of Federal inspectors, spies and detectives will descend upon the state. They will compel men of business to show their books and disclose the secrets of their affairs. They will dictate forms of bookkeeping. They will require statements and affidavits. On the one hand the inspector can blackmail the taxpayer and on the other, he can profit by selling his secret to his competitor.

THE NATURAL RIGHTS PHILOSOPHY

The secret of happiness is freedom; the secret of freedom is courage.
—Thucydides

THE MOST IMPORTANT idea of the Framers and Founders. Wait, I need to explain these terms that I have thrown at you a few times and will much more. Founders include all those British citizens that began the nation, including the soldiers, writers, boycotters, thinkers that make up the foundations of our experiment. The Framers are all Founders, but they are the writers of the Constitution, *The Federalist*, Anti-Federalist essays, ratifiers at the state conventions, and ratifiers and writer of the Bill of Rights. Keep in mind James Madison's most famous quote when trying to digest the underlying ideas of the founding of the experiment. He and they understood that without a government, man may have problems.

> What is government itself but the greatest of all reflections on human nature? If men were angels, no government would be necessary. If angels were to govern men, neither external nor internal controls on government would be necessary (*Federalist 51*).

> We hold these Truths to be self-evident, that all Men are created equal, that they are endowed by their Creator with certain unalienable Rights, that among these are Life, Liberty, and the Pursuit of Happiness-That to secure these Rights, Governments are instituted among Men, deriving their just Powers from the Consent of the Governed, that whenever any Form of Government becomes destructive of these Ends, it is the Right of the People to alter or to abolish

it, and to institute new Government . . . (Declaration of Independence 1776).

This excerpt from the Declaration of Independence includes some of the most important philosophical ideas underlying our form of government. They are ideas that had been accepted by almost everyone in the American colonies long before the Revolutionary War. They had been preached in churches, written in pamphlets, and debated in public and private. These basic ideas had been developed and refined by political philosophers such as the Englishman John Locke (1632–1704) and by many others in Europe and in the colonies. Of these philosophers, John Locke, was the most important influence on the thinking of the Founders at the time of the revolution. The political philosophy Locke wrote about is often called the natural rights philosophy.

Thinking about what you think

The natural rights philosophy is based on imagining what life would be like if there were no government. Locke and others called this imaginary situation a state of nature. Whether such a state ever existed, thinking about what life would be like if there were no government was very useful to philosophers such as Locke in answering the following questions.

John Locke's answers to these questions were the answers accepted by most of the Founders. They used these ideas to explain and justify their declaration of independence from Great Britain. They also used these ideas in writing the various state constitutions after the Revolutionary War and later in writing the Constitution of the United States and Bill of Rights.

To understand the natural rights philosophy, it is helpful to try to answer the many questions it deals with. We may not all agree on your answers to these questions. It is important to know that you are not alone. Since the ancients thought of their own existence, people have had very different views on these matters. *Genesis* chapter 6 relates the oldest story of the state of nature.

When human beings began to increase in number on
the earth and daughters were born to them, [2] the sons of

God saw that the daughters of humans were beautiful, and they married any of them they chose. ³ Then the Lord said, "My Spirit will not contend with[a] humans forever, for they are mortal; their days will be a hundred and twenty years."

⁴ The Nephilim were on the earth in those days—and also afterward—when the sons of God went to the daughters of humans and had children by them. They were the heroes of old, men of renown.

⁵ The Lord saw how great the wickedness of the human race had become on the earth, and that every inclination of the thoughts of the human heart was only evil all the time. ⁶ The Lord regretted that he had made human beings on the earth, and his heart was deeply troubled. ⁷ So the Lord said, "I will wipe from the face of the earth the human race I have created—and with them the animals, the birds and the creatures that move along the ground—for I regret that I have made them."

¹¹ Now the earth was corrupt in God's sight and was full of violence. ¹² God saw how corrupt the earth had become, for all the people on earth had corrupted their ways. ¹³ So God said to Noah, "I am going to put an end to all people, for the earth is filled with violence because of them. I am surely going to destroy both them and the earth.

Imagine that all of you neighbors were transported to a similar place where there were enough natural resources for you all to live on but where no one had lived before, say, a Garden of Eden. When you arrived, you had no means of communicating with people in other parts of the world. Based on this situation, answer the following questions, maybe discuss with others, and then compare your answers with those of John Locke that follow.

Would there be any government or laws to control how you lived, what rights or freedoms you exercised, or what property you had? Why?

Would anyone have the right to govern you?

Would you have the right to govern anyone else?

Why?

Would you have any rights? What would they be?
Would it make any difference if you were a man or a woman?
What might people who were stronger than others try
to do? Why?
What might the weaker people try to do? Why?
What might life be like for everyone?

Your answers to the above questions may be like the following answers developed by John Locke or they may differ. Here is a brief, OH SO BRIEF, focus on Locke's answers. These ideas were widely shared by Americans living during the 1700s and played a very important role in the development of our government.

Locke believed that there were laws in a state of nature. He said, "The state of nature has a law of nature to govern it which obliges everyone . . . no one ought to harm another in his life, health, liberty, or possessions . . ." These laws were "the Laws of Nature and of Nature's God," as Thomas Jefferson called them in the Declaration of Independence.

However, the problem in the state of nature would be that you and others would probably disagree on what the "laws of nature" are, and there would be no one with the right to help you settle your disagreements. This is because there would be no government to say what the law was or to enforce it. According to Locke, there wouldn't be any government because a government can't exist until it has been created. And a legitimate or just government cannot exist until the people have given their consent to be ruled by it. Thomas Jefferson included this idea in the Declaration when he wrote that governments are instituted among men, deriving their just powers from the consent of the governed.

No one would have the right to govern you, nor would you have the right to govern anyone else. Per Locke, the only way anyone gets the right to govern anyone is if the person to be governed gives his or her consent. If people haven't consented to the creation of a government, there is no government. You would have the right to life, liberty, and property. This means you would have the right to defend these rights if other people threatened to take them away. These were called natural rights. We now call them fundamental, basic, or even human rights.

Locke believed that people are basically reasonable and sociable but that they are also self-interested. Since the only security people would have for the protection of their natural rights would be their own strength or cunning, people who were stronger or more able would often try to take away the life, liberty, or property of the weak. Weaker people might try to protect themselves by joining against the strong. There would be no laws that everybody agreed upon and no government to enforce them; everybody's rights would be very insecure.

John Locke and most Americans in the eighteenth century thought that people are equal in their rights to life, liberty, and property. They have these natural rights just because they are human beings. This means that in a state of nature, no one would have the right to interfere with your life or property or your freedom to do as you wished. However, Locke also believed that in that kind of situation, because of human nature, there would always be people who would try to violate your rights. Since there would not be any government, you and others would have to defend your rights against those who might want to take them away. The result would be that in the state of nature, your rights would be insecure and you would be in constant danger of losing them. For Locke and those who shared his ideas, the great problem was to find a way to protect our natural rights so that we can live at peace with one another and enjoy them.

- State of nature is a hypothetical condition used to describe humanity before civilization and law.
- State of nature may also be considered anarchy, a condition without government or rule of law.
- State of nature has no protection of human rights, since it is up to individuals to regulate themselves.

Let's take a deeper look at the nature of man. Whether the proper study of mankind is man, it is the only study in which the knower and the known are one, in which the object of science *is* the nature of the scientist. Man is different than nature primarily in the fact that he is able to study himself.

COGITO ERGO SUM: KNOW THYSELF

Freedom is being you without anyone's permission.
—Anonymous

WHAT IS THE nature of man? Is man a rational animal, and if so, does that imply that only man has reason and not animals in general? Does man have free will and he alone? Does man differ from animals in essence or only in kind from animals; does man merely differ in degree in the properties from animals? Charles Darwin believed that man is simply a better animal, while John Milton felt man is obviously a different being. He believed man is reasonable and able to govern the rest of nature. In addition, man is self-knowing and "magnanimous to correspond to heaven."

John Locke, our main natural rights philosopher, thought man can think up ideas but has no free will. Jean Jacque Rousseau assumed man is simply an animal that can make free choices from alternatives presented, unlike Buridan's Ass, which cannot choose among equal alternatives. Thomas Hobbes wrote that man uses language, which describes abstracts, that alone makes a man unique. René Descartes felt man is different because he is both mind and body, while animals are merely body.

Yet before a human nature can be addressed, one needs to know where man fits into the story of life and history. All things can be classified by unique characteristics. Like John Milton, the Founders—as did most Americans before the Progressives—believed that man was unique or different from the rest of creation. So how does man classify within the known world?

First, let's learn the idea of classification. Remember, all higher classes of things have the characteristics of things lower; for example, a frog is an animal, it has all the characteristics of "animal" but more that distinguishes it from other animals. A rose is a plant that flowers of the plant family *Rosa*.

So let's start slow, pause, make notes, and ask yourself if you are sure. To start all things are either physical or ideas: apple, love. All things have quality, quantity, and definition. They are definable by adjectives, number (one, five, a lot, or few) and excellence (right or wrong, good or better). Yet all physical things also take up space and have weight; you can touch them. All living things, in addition, eat, grow, and reproduce. Plants are unique from animals and man and quite different than the other animals.

All things, physical and ideal, have two main traits: accidental and essential. Accidental traits are things such as gender, weight, race, hair, and eye color. These traits are quite unimportant in defining a thing. The accidental traits are merely adjectives of the essential elements of things. He is a redhead male human. Red hair and masculinity make him a unique human but not human. That needs closer, finer definition.

Essential traits are those traits that make it unique from other things; attributes, characteristics, the other classes of things do not have. If another class has the same trait, it clearly is not unique, thus not an essential trait. The deer have antlers; rodents do not, except maybe jackalopes.

Let's try and define the characteristics of man. Use the diagram below to follow this discussion. First man is physical, not an idea. Remember ideas (math, myth, angels, characters in a play, language, God) are "real" but not tangible (touchable) as are physical things. Also, ideas cannot have "place"; theories and ghosts cannot be "some" where. Within physical things are living and nonliving, tree versus log. Living things need nutrients to grow and sustain their individual lives and the life of their kind. Some may move, others not, but all grow, "eat," and make more of itself. Thus, the purpose of life is more life, and built into all living things is the urge to reproduce. (We will address purpose later.)

Nonliving things are what we would call elements in chemistry or physics and those things made from elements, such as oxygen, pencils, and a Dodge Dart. If we talk of indivisible parts, atoms (maybe all the way down to quarks!) are the elementary particle. When combined, say two parts hydrogen and a shot of oxygen, water. These are classified as composite. In the area of the living, though sometimes simple or complex, we call these plants or animals. Animals are essentially different from plants in movement; plants are stationary without assistance from wind, water, or animals.

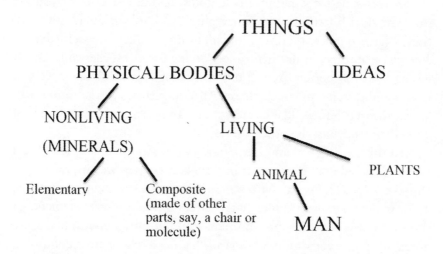

But other than the obvious upright appearance of man, what are our unique attributes? What separates man from other animals, other species, and other primates? The chart below lists the essential characteristics; though these fail to address the true essence of man, it's a good start to separate Bob from his cat Bubbles. The true man is one of purpose and dimension. Man is created, as Milton says, to "correspond to heaven," to speak with the Creator.

POLITICAL ANIMAL	PLAYS PHILOSOPHICAL GAMES	RATIONAL, THE ONLY ANIMAL THAT IS
FREE WILL (MORAL VIRTUE)	CAPACITY FOR VIRTUE	DESIRES TO BE VIRTUOUS
GOVERNS NATURE	NEARLY ALWAYS ACTS WITH AN END IN VIEW	KNOWS EGO
BOTH MIND AND BODY	THINKS IDEAS AND ABSTRACTS	DESIRES KNOWLEDGE

Man is most importantly a creation of three dimensions. All true men are first productive. They wish to be a maker of "beauty." The reason to create is to produce an item of beauty, perfection. Not that it is always possible, but the goal is "beauty" in all things made by man. Second, all men are practical. They are doers of "good." This would be ethics, the exercise of good choices, what is right and wrong actions to oneself, others or humankind. We will later deal with man's social contract and civic virtue, essential parts of a limited and sustainable community. Last, men are also speculative. They want to think about the "truth," not merely right and wrong, but now true and false.

As we move through our discussion of the experiment, these dimensions must always be front and center. When we do homework or examinations, when we clean the bathroom, when drinking a fine bourbon, when painting the shed, we should always make our best product, put in our best effort. Our actions in our family, school, job, and the world we live in must always be within a framework of ethics. Our purpose in any endeavor is foremost a search for truth:

> What is good government?
> What is a limited constitution?
> What are fundamental rights?
> What is the duty of government?
> When is rebellion our duty?
> When should we obey laws?
> What is the best economic system?

But as mentioned before, all things have a purpose. Plants are here for beauty, food, and oxygen production. Minerals are to be used by plants and animals for life. We know in other subjects, food webs, biodiversity, and sustainable agriculture are mentioned as to define the purpose of each species on the planet. But our concern in the purpose of man. Why are we here? What are we to do with our existence? Do I matter?

It's your turn to think about man's purpose

When one thinks of man's purpose generically, it is very difficult. So let's start simply. What are you here for? In French, it is *raison d'être*, "reason to be." Is it to realize one's potential and ideals, to achieve biological perfection, to seek wisdom and knowledge, to do good, to do the right thing, to love, to feel, to enjoy the act of living, to seek pleasure, to have power, or to be better? Or does life have no meaning? Or is it that one should not seek to know and understand the meaning of life. Is life itself bad?

What do you think? What are you here for? Just make some notes to yourself; we will be exploring this idea throughout this book. It really is the foundation of all social contracts; it helps answer other questions, such as the purpose of government and the best economic system.

We will begin with a discussion of an idea over two thousand years old. It is the cornerstone of everything that's ahead, a major building block in the experiment: happiness. Thomas Jefferson's famous essay, the Declaration of Independence, emphasizes the "pursuit of Happiness"; but what is it? Our discussion will be based on Aristotle's essay "On Happiness." Take good notes; read it a couple times and talk with others. That is the purpose of shared inquiry, LEARNING.

Some introduction is in order. Who was Aristotle? Aristotle was one of the three great Greek philosophers. Along with Socrates and Plato, he laid the foundation for the Western world. In science, history, logic, and education, Aristotle (384–322 BC), was the first philosopher to instruct how to think. Aristotle said that philosophy grew out of wonder:

> It is owing to their wonder that men both now begin and first began to philosophize. They wondered originally at the obvious difficulties, then advanced little by little and stated difficulties about the greater matters, e.g., about the phenomena of the moon and those of the sun and of the stars, and about the genesis of the universe. And a man who is puzzled and wonders thinks himself ignorant (whence even the lover of myth is in a sense a lover of Wisdom, for the myth is composed of wonders); therefore since they philosophized in order to escape from ignorance, evidently they were pursuing science in order to know, and not for any utilitarian end.

His own curiosity ranged wide. He wrote on the importance of experience in scientific investigation:

Lack of experience diminishes our power of taking a comprehensive view of the admitted facts. Hence those who dwell in intimate association with nature and its phenomena grow more and are more able to formulate, as the foundations of their theories, principals such as to admit of a wider and coherent development, while those whom devotion to abstract discussions has rendered unobservant of the facts are too ready to dogmatize on the basis of a few observations.

On the policy of tyrants:

Their first end and aim is to break the spirit of their subjects; they know that a poor-spirited man will never plot against anybody. Their second aim is to breed mutual distrust. Tyranny is never overthrown until men begin to trust one another, and this is the reason why tyrants are always at outs with the good. They feel that good men are doubly dangerous to their authority—dangerous, first, in thinking it shame to be governed as if they were slaves; dangerous, again, in their spirit of mutual and general loyalty and in their refusal to betray one another or anyone else. The third and last aim of tyrants is to make their subjects incapable of action.

Nobody attempts the impossible. Nobody, therefore, will attempt the overthrow of a tyranny when all are incapable of action.

On age and youth:

Elderly men . . . have lived many years; they have often been taken in and often made mistakes; and life on the whole is a bad business. The result is that they are sure about nothing and under-do everything. They "think," but they never "know"; and because of their hesitation they always add a "possibly" or a "perhaps," putting everything this way and nothing positively. They are cynical; that is, they tend to put the worse construction on everything. Further, their experience makes them distrustful and therefore suspicious of evil. Consequently, they neither love warmly nor hate bitterly, but . . . love as though they will someday hate and hate as though they will someday love.

Young men . . . would always rather do noble deeds than useful ones. Their lives are regulated more by moral feeling than by reasoning, and whereas reasoning leads us to choose what is useful, moral goodness leads us to choose what is noble. They are fonder of their friends, intimates, and companions than older men are because they like spending their days in the company of others and have not yet come to value either their friends or anything else by their usefulness to themselves. All their mistakes are in the direction of doing things excessively and vehemently . . . They think they know everything, and are always quite sure about it; this in fact, is why they overdo everything . . . They are fond of fun and therefore witty, wit being well-bred insolence.

In the following selections from *Rhetoric* and *Nicomachean Ethics*, Aristotle discusses happiness. Because he believes that every time we choose something, we do so because we think it will help make us happy, he considers happiness the highest good. It is, therefore, important to know what happiness is: as Aristotle asks in the *Ethics*, "Will not the knowledge of it have a great influence on our lives? Would we not, like archers who have a target to aim at, be more likely to hit the proper mark?"

On Happiness by Aristotle

It may be said that every individual man and all men in common aim at a certain end which determines what they choose and what they avoid. This end, to sum it up briefly, is happiness and its constituents. Let us, then, by way of illustration only, ascertain what the nature of happiness is in general, and what are the elements of its constituent parts. For all advice to do things or not to do them is concerned with happiness and with the things that make for or against it; whatever creates or increases happiness or some part of happiness, we ought to do; whatever destroys or hampers happiness, or gives rise to its opposite, we ought not to do.

We may define happiness as prosperity combined with virtue; or as independence of life; or as the secure enjoyment of the maximum of pleasure; or as a good condition of property and body, together with the power of guarding one's property and body and making use of them. That happiness is one or more of these things, pretty well everybody agrees.

From this definition of happiness, it follows that its constituent parts are: good birth, plenty of friends, good friends, wealth, good children, plenty of children, a happy old age, also such bodily excellences as health, beauty, strength, large stature, athletic powers, together with fame, honor, good luck, and virtue. A Man cannot fail to be completely independent if he possesses these internal and these external goods; for besides these there are no others to have. (Goods of the soul and of the body are internal. Good birth, friends, money, and honor are external.) Further, we think that he should possess resources and luck, to make his life really secure.

To call happiness the highest good is perhaps a little trite, and a clearer account of what it is is still required. Perhaps this is best done by first ascertaining the proper function of Man. For just as the goodness and performance of a flute player, a sculptor, or any kind of expert, and generally of anyone who fulfills some function or performs some action, are thought to reside in his proper function, so the goodness and performance of Man would seem to reside in whatever is his proper function. Is it then possible that while a carpenter and a shoemaker have their own proper functions and spheres of action, Man as Man has none, but was left by nature a good-for-nothing without a function? Should we not assume that just as the eye, the hand, the foot, and in general each part of the body clearly has its own proper function, so Man too has some function over and above the functions of his parts? What can this function possibly be? Simply living? He shares that even with plants, but we are now looking for something peculiar to Man. Accordingly, the life of nutrition and growth must be excluded. Next in line there is a life of sense perception.

But this, too, Man has in common with the horse, the ox, and every animal. There remains then an active life of the rational element. The rational element has two parts: one is rational in that it obeys the rule of reason, the other in that it possesses and conceives rational rules. Since the expression "life of the rational element" also can be used in two senses, we must make it clear that we mean a life determined by the activity, as opposed to the mere possession, of the rational element. For the activity, it seems, has a greater claim to be the function of Man.

The proper function of Man, then, consists in an activity of the soul in conformity with a rational principle or, at least, not without it. In speaking of the proper function of a given individual we mean that it is the same in kind as the function of an individual who sets high standards for himself: the proper function of a harpist, for example, is the same as the function of a harpist who has set high standards for himself. The same applies to any and every group of individuals: the full attainment of excellence must be added to the mere function. In other words, the function of the harpist is to play the harp; the function of the harpist who has high standards is to play it well. On these assumptions, if we take the proper function of Man to be a certain kind of life, and if this kind of life is an activity of the soul and consists in actions performed in conjunction with the rational element, and if a Man of high standards is he who performs these actions well and properly, and if a function is well performed when it is performed in accordance with the excellence appropriate to it; we reach the conclusion that the good of Man is an activity of the soul in conformity with excellence or virtue, and if there are several virtues, in conformity with the best and most complete.

But we must add "in a complete life." For one swallow does not make a spring, nor does one sunny day; similarly, one day or a short time does not make a man blessed and happy.

What then is this "HAPPINESS" Aristotle talks about? The simplest answer is the ultimate good or end in life, a good life well lived. One should always act with a purpose, act toward our desires, and be what one was created for. But how does one know? Some definitions need to be taken care of first.

"Wants versus needs" is one of history's essential questions. Many have debated wants versus needs morally, spiritually, and economically. But in truth, there are no true needs, only wants. Well, what about food, clothing, shelter, or even water? you may say. Are not these merely things to fulfill a want to live? All the things necessary to live are called goods, stuff, or wealth if you wish. But these are merely tools to the "GOOD." The good is happiness, a good life well lived. But how do goods lead to the "good"? How does one pursue this "happiness"?

First, one must be alive, thus "life, liberty, and pursuit of happiness." One must BE, interact with others, remember we are political animals, social creatures. One needs to learn, change; animals and plants also do these in general. Man must lead a good life, not just be alive but be alive well. Leading a purposeful life is not easy; only humans with good habits and good morals can lead the good life. So what is a good life?

First, a good life is an examined one. One needs to look at daily actions, goals/dreams, and the choices one makes to attain those dreams. We all need some real goods: bodily goods (health, strength, vigor, vitality, sight, and hearing). Some of these are external goods (wealth, food, clothing, sleep, leisure) and others goods of the soul (knowledge [skills, know-how, facts], association, love, the pleasure of art, making, acquiring knowledge, honor [if deserved], self-esteem, and friends). Some can only be achieved with association with others in cooperation, competition, and freedom; others are 100 percent in control of the individual.

Second, man must have moral virtue, the skill of making good choices. Moral virtue is the only one of the elements of happiness that is not someway external to man. In addition, one can never have too much virtue; too many bodily goods, too much wealth, even too many goods of the soul, friends maybe. Yet one can never be too moral, too correct in one's choice to lead a good life. There are trade-offs in all decisions, but the right choice is always there. Virtue can't be given or taken away, but can be practiced and modeled. The opposite of virtue is vice. A vicious person makes bad decisions, harming others or oneself, thus moving away from happiness.

Moral virtue is really divided into three areas, sometimes overlapping, often interacting. They are temperance, courage, and justice. "Temperance" is seeking only the amount of real goods needed to deal with wants. The opposite of temperance is greed or gluttony. One should resist the lure of pleasure, know limit of these goods. "Courage" is accepting the pain involved in doing what we ought to do for a good life. The opposite is cowardice or avoiding the "good" pain. This is when one does what feels good now and puts off till tomorrow what needs to be done today—for example, not reading the assignment because it is too hard or not as much fun as World of Warcraft* or FarmVille.* Then justice. "Justice" is doing what assists others to pursue their happiness. Don't initiate violence toward another or his property.

Like Jefferson, we have one more key element to being happy. That is "liberty." Without the freedom to choose, even if all wants are met, one cannot be human and pursue one's happiness. As Jefferson "stated":

> A government big enough to give you everything you need, is a government big enough to take away everything that you have . . .

And that is a crucial point: if there is no liberty, there is tyranny. Government must rest on justice, must serve the common good, but must never attempt to grant happiness, only man, individually can pursue his happiness. (See *Federalist 1*, below.)

Federalist No. 1 by Publius (Alexander Hamilton), October 27, 1787, General Introduction

After experiencing the ineffectiveness of the current federal government we are called upon to take part in a discussion about a new Constitution for the United States of America. The importance of this discussion is clear— nothing less than the Union itself, the safety and welfare of all of the states, and the fate of a nation, one which is in many ways the most interesting in the world, is at stake.

Many have observed that, because of their conduct and the example they've set, the People of this country have been put in the position of deciding a very important question: Are societies capable of freely choosing to establish good government for themselves, or will such things forever be determined by accident and force? If that observation is true, then we find ourselves at a time in history in which this question will be answered. If we are to falter now, it would be, in my opinion, to the detriment of all mankind.

To frame this debate another way, it is not simply about patriotism, it's also about philanthropy for the world. Given the stakes, we should all take this process very seriously. I will be happy if our decision is made through a sensible debate that ignores issues not having to do with the public good. That, however, is something more to be wished for than expected. Our undertaking, after all, affects so many people, so many local institutions, and so many varied interests, that it would be impossible for it not to be influenced by issues having little to do with the truth we are trying to discover. Among the greatest challenges the new Constitution will face will come from local politicians who fear that they might lose some of their current power, along with those who might seek to profit from the division of this nation into several confederacies, as opposed to its Union under a single government. It is not my intention to focus on such obstacles, since it really isn't fair to raise suspicions about a certain class of people simply because of the power they currently hold. An honest man can only acknowledge that such people can have good intentions and that opposition will no doubt come from good and honest people who have their own preconceived ideas and opinions. Since the motives behind each of the opinions surrounding this discussion are so strong, it is certain that wise and good people will be found on both sides of the issues. This fact should remind us all to remain modest in our opinion—no matter how right we might think we are. It should also be remembered that those on the side of the truth are not always led by more honest motives than those who oppose it. Ambition, greed, personal animosity, party opposition, and many other motives that are just as impure, are guaranteed to be at work on both sides of the debate. Even if these motives didn't exist, we must still remember that intolerance has always characterized political parties. In politics, just as in religion, it is absurd to try to win converts by fire and sword. Dissent, after all, can rarely be cured by persecution. And yet, despite the fact that honest men agree with all of these opinions, we have already seen indications that a torrent of angry and hateful rhetoric will be unleashed during this discussion—just as it has in every great national discussion of the past. Judging by their conduct so far, those who are opposed to this plan will attempt to grow their numbers and prove their point by being loud and bitter. Those who are enthusiastic about this plan will be stigmatized as lovers of despotic rule and haters of liberty. Those who fear for the rights of the People—a fear that most often comes from the head rather than the heart—will be exposed as being more interested in popularity than in the public good. On one hand, it will be forgotten that excessive jealousy for one's own rights is often the sister of violence, and that the enthusiastic desire for liberty is often infected with a spirit of distrust. On the other hand, it will also be forgotten that a strong government is essential to the security of liberty and that those two things can never be separated. Dangerous ambition often lurks more in those who have excessive enthusiasm for the rights of the People than those who believe in a firm and efficient government. History proves that the former more often leads to tyranny than the latter, and that the people who have trampled on the liberties of a republic often began their campaigns by being overly concerned with the rights of the People and helping to end tyranny. Fellow citizens, throughout these papers it is my intent to put you on guard against all those who might seek to influence your opinion on this important subject through arguments that have no basis in truth. You will find that I am convinced that this Constitution will protect your liberty, dignity, and happiness and, therefore, believe that it is in your interests to adopt it. I will not express any feelings to you other than my own, nor waste your time by debating what I have already decided for myself, since I will freely acknowledge my convictions and the reasoning behind them. I will be concise and to the point, and my motives are mine alone; my arguments will be available to all, may be judged by all, and will be nothing but truthful. The subjects I will discuss in these papers are: A. The extent to which the Union will promote your political prosperity; B. The inability of the current Confederation to preserve the Union; C. The necessity of a government that is at least as strong as the one proposed in the Constitution; D. The ways in which the Constitution conforms to the principles of a truly republican government; E. The Constitution's similarity to New York's state constitution; F. The additional security which the Constitution will provide not only to the republican form of government, but also to liberty and property.

Throughout this discussion, I will attempt to provide good answers to all of the objections that appear worthy of our attention. It may seem like a waste of time to justify the usefulness of the Union, since it is so obvious to so many, but, in private circles, it is already being argued against those who oppose the new Constitution that the Thirteen States are too large for any one General government, and must, therefore, remain separate confederacies. I have no doubt that this view will be expressed in the dark until it finds enough support to come into the light—meaning that either the new Constitution will be adopted, or the Union will be torn apart. Therefore, it's necessary to closely examine the advantages of the Union, as well as the evils and dangers that would result if it were to fall apart. And that is what we will now do (Publius).

Alexander Hamilton, a major Founder and a Framer, tried to convince, with James Madison and John Jay, the voters to accept the new constitution to be the Constitution, the law of the land. During 1787–1788, in *The Federalist*, Hamilton, mostly in a series of essays, laid down historical arguments why this new document was the best hope for mankind. It is ironic, some even say disingenuous, that his writings on the limits of power, the surety that no one need fear the "central" government, contradict his actions and later advocacy for a powerful central government, taxation, tariffs, mercantilism, weakening of the states. And opposition to a bill of rights. He even suggested a king during the Convention. Wait for that later!

He opens right away in his Hamiltonian style, brash, arrogant, and with little regard for the people. The American people, "after an unequivocal experience of the inefficacy of the subsisting Federal Government," were now being asked to consider an entirely new United States Constitution. Without this change, "nothing less than the existence of the UNION . . . the fate of an empire, in many respects, the most interesting in the world." Disagreeing with Hamilton would "deserve to be considered as the general misfortune of mankind."

Hamilton knew there were many opposed; we will look at them later, the Anti-Federalists; he grouped them into stereotypes. He used tactics still used today; remember the 2016 election hatred and hyperbole. Some were "conservatives," unable to accept any change under no circumstance or convincing. Others were just stirring the pot. Others self-interested opportunists hoping to keep their positions in the old system.

Yet even the many who were men with "upright intentions" were foolish, misinformed, followers of eighteenth-century "fake news." They were getting their opinions, not made by themselves but rather "from sources, blameless at least, if not respectable, the honest errors of minds led astray by preconceived jealousies and fears." They were "so numerous indeed and so powerful" others may be given a "false bias to the judgment." This could be disastrous, resulting in a "torrent of angry and malignant passions." The "wrong" decisions could be made, a la 2016. Anger, bitterness, actual hatred would blind them and lead them astray. The debates in the states needed to be free of politics, "nothing could be more ill-judged than that intolerant spirit, which has, at all times, characterized political parties."

However, it was Hamilton himself laying the groundwork for what his partner, James Madison, called "factions," calling his opponents "blameless at least, if not respectable," who could not discern because of "preconceived jealousies and fears," the truth from ignorance. His opposition, however, were many of the Founders, heroes from the war, even Framers: Thomas Jefferson, Patrick Henry, Richard Henry Lee, George Mason, Sam Adams, and Gov. George Clinton, Mercy Otis Warren, Roger Sherman, Oliver Ellsworth, Abraham Yates, Melancton Smith, Samuel Bryant, John Winthrop, Elbridge Gerry, Luther Martin, John Lansing, Robert Yates, John Mercer, to name a few. Hamilton demeaned them as ignorant, self-seeking, or just stupid. He asked for "moderation," yet he disdained their opposition. We will address his opposition later, and a great analysis of Hamilton can be found in Tom DiLorenzo's *Hamilton's Curse*. He attitude was not one of compromise or understanding; he frankly wanted not to hear from them; they were an unworthy, unqualified, ignorant opposition. See the musical *Hamilton* to see a good representation.

THE NEED FOR LAW

Freedom suggests responsibility. That's why many people are afraid of it.
—George Bernard Shaw

T HE SOCIAL CONTRACT stems directly from the natural rights philosophy. It is the theory based on the impossibility of a state of nature. Many philosophers have addressed the problems of a state of nature and how to deal with them. Two of the major issues dealing with the study of government are that (1) in a state of nature there are differing opinions on the natural rights, thus conflict, and (2) the uncertainty of the world we live in is ever present without some type of order and laws. Social contract theories attempt to explain the ways in which people create states to govern and maintain social order. A social contract is an agreement between the government and the governed regarding the limits of power on both parties. Implicit in a social contract is the notion that people are able and willing to surrender certain liberties and freedoms for the protection of other rights to establish a peaceful society. Without a social contract, human beings would be forced to live in a "state of nature," without the rule of law, a survival-of-the-fittest, brutish existence. This will be later restated by one of the great Founders of America, Benjamin Rush. In a letter to his friend in 1788, David Ramsay, Rush emphasizes the need for law.

> [W]here there is no law, there is no liberty; and nothing deserves the name of law but that which is certain and universal in its operation upon all the members of the community.

The *Crito* of Plato

Socrates, in Plato's *Crito,* deals with the essential nature of the "contract," even when faulty, something our modern-day losers of elections ought to understand. I have tried to modernize the language. Any commentary is bracketed. The setting of the *Crito* is Socrates in jail and his students trying to convince him to escape; they've bribed the jailor, all they need is their teacher's assent.

SOCRATES. Why are you here Crito? It's awfully early.

[Crito was a close friend of Socrates. Socrates trusted him, being neighbors, and entrusted Crito to invest Socrates's funds. He appears in Plato's *Euthydemus, Apology, Phaedo*; in the *Crito*, he is the main character.]

CRITO. It certainly is, it's about dawn.

SOCRATES. I am surprised that the guard let you in so early.

CRITO. He is used to me by now, Socrates, coming so often; and besides I've done something good for him.

SOCRATES. And have you just got her, or been here a while?

CRITO. I've been here a while.

SOCRATES. Why did you not wake me then, instead of just sitting by quietly?

CRITO. By Zeus, No way! Socrates, I only wish could sleep so sound and peacefully. I've been amazed at how pleasantly you sleep; and I didn't want to disturb your sleep. You've always had a happy disposition, even now in this situation, you bear it so easily and calmly.

SOCRATES. At my age, Crito, it would be a mistake to be resentful of dying.

CRITO. Well, I've seen others at your age is less serious situations, resenting their fate.

SOCRATES. Maybe, but you haven't answered my question, why did you come so early?

CRITO. I was selected to bring you a message from your students and friends. It appears we may be taking your situation harder than you, me maybe the worst.

SOCRATES. What is it? Has the ship come from Delos; it is time I must die?

CRITO. No yet, maybe today from reports of travelers from Sunium. So, they are sure it will be here today. And your life must end tomorrow.

SOCRATES. Crito, that's probably for the best. If it's the will of the gods, let it be. But, I doubt it'll be here today.

CRITO. Why not?

SOCRATES. I had a dream of a beautiful and good-looking woman dressed all in white. She came to me, called me and said, "Socrates, In three days you will come to fertile Phthia."

CRITO. Your dream aside, it is still possible to persuade you to save yourself. My dear friend, if you die, it isn't a single bad event. Apart from me losing someone I could never meet again, it will seem to many here, that I could have saved you, but I refused to try. What reputation could be worse? I kept my riches and let a friend perish. Most won't believe we tried to help you escape, but you yourself won't allow it.

SOCRATES. Dear friend, what do you care what the "many" think? For the reasonable ones, the only ones that matter, will agree with how things have happened.

[Socrates was not the kind of person that would say what is needed rather than the truth. He was called a gadfly for a reason, an irritating pain in the side of the populace. You would think that someone just convicted by a democratic vote, his derision for "the many" would be tempered. Democracy is government by "the many," mob rule. Socrates's point here is that Crito should make up his own mind, using his reason as best he could, about how to live, and not let others do his thinking for him. Each man is independent in his own morality.]

CRITO. But you see that it is necessary, Socrates, to care about popular opinion. Today's circumstances, what they've done to you especially, make it clear that the mob can do not only the smallest of evils but also nearly the greatest, if they are prejudiced against someone.

[Crito says right it out loud that "the many" can make life miserable for independent thinkers. Here we see Plato's antidemocratic views coming out. Take a look at today's polarized Facebook posts.]

SOCRATES. Crito, it would be probably good if they were able to do the greatest evil, so that they would also be able to do the greatest good, and that would be fabulous. But, they can't do either. They can't make you wise or stupid. It's at best haphazard what they do.

[The only real good that can be done to anyone is to make one wise, but that you do yourself. The only true harm is to make one stupid, but that also is self-inflicted. The idea that nothing external to one can be harmful, that what is good for one is solely a matter of the state of one's character, is typically Greek. We see it today in posters that your attitude decides the situation. Well, we saw it modified by Aristotle that external circumstances can have some effect on one's happiness, reputation, external goods in trade, or one's government.]

CRITO. Okay, maybe. But are you thinking about me and the others? It's true that if you get away, we may be caught, lose all our property or much money or even prison ourselves. If this is what you're worried about, don't. It was our decision to risk what we're risking. But listen to me, and follow my advice.

SOCRATES. I did consider that, yes Crito, and many other things.

CRITO. Then don't worry, it's not that much money that could save you and get out of here. My money is yours, and if you can't take mine, I have many connections ready to spend their money. A friend, Simmias the Theban has set aside even more if necessary; and so is Cebes and many others.

Putting all those objections aside, do not hesitate to save yourself. Don't bring up what you said in the court either. About that if you left Athens, you wouldn't know what to do with yourself. There are many places that would give you sanctuary and love to have you as a citizen. How about Thessaly, I have many friends there, they would love to have you there; no one there will bother you.

I can't see how you wouldn't save yourself when you're able. Won't this just prove your enemies correct? What about your children, whose raising and education you won't be there for? You will leave them as orphans, left to the community for raising. I'm sorry, but if that's your opinion, you shouldn't have had children. You seem to me to choose the laziest man's way;

[Is Socrates stuck between a rock and a hard place? His moral decision is "harming" another, his children. His standing on moral principle will leave his children orphans. Is it morally acceptable to risk danger or harm to his children to do the right thing? Is it morally acceptable to violate his integrity to protect his children? Socrates didn't accept Crito's self-interest argument; what about his family, his own children?]

But, you have your whole life taught virtue, yet you choose to harm. I am ashamed for you, and us for following you. You're taking the coward's way out. In court, you purposefully taunted the jury to be convicted, on appeal you irritated them more. Now with time running out, the decision is one, Socrates, obey me and don't do anything else at all.

SOCRATES. Oh Crito, your persuasion is great. If I should do this or not; must be based on logic. I have my whole life used reason as it appears to me best. And just because I'm in a situation that has major consequences, I cannot reject my own principles.

[Socrates is determined to make decisions based on reason and logic, not on fears or desires. Many of us may have been on the last train to Clarksville, but he will do so only if a rational argument can be made unless he can convince himself by rational arguments that it is the right thing to do. In the same situation, should not the same moral rules to everyone the same? Socrates had spoken many times that the law must be obeyed. No one is above the law.]

SOCRATES. Well, let's look at public opinions first. Should not the good opinions be honored, and the bad ones ignored?

CRITO. Yes.

SOCRATES. And are not the good ones from the wise, and the bad those from the stupid?

CRITO. Of course.

SOCRATES. Well then, how do we know? Does an athlete training for an event pay attention to the praise and blame and opinion of every fan or to his doctor or trainer?

CRITO. Only the one.

SOCRATES. Then one shouldn't disregard the criticism, and accept the praise of that one, but not that of the many.

CRITO. Clearly.

SOCRATES. So, practicing, training, eating and drinking based on the knowledge and understanding of the expert is better than that of everyone else.

CRITO. If he wants to win, yes.

SOCRATES. Well then, if the athlete disobeying the one and dishonoring his opinion and praises, while honoring the arguments of the many who have no understanding, will he suffer harm?

CRITO. Of course.

SOCRATES. And what is the extent of this harm to the athlete?

CRITO. Clearly into the body. For it ruins it.

SOCRATES. Good Crito, you point is well taken. Let's expand to bigger questions. We don't need to go into them all too deeply. When it comes to justice and injustice, or shame and honor, or good and evil, which we are now talking about, should we obey the opinion of the many and be worried about popularity, or listen to the one, if he is someone of understanding, who should be respected and feared more than all the others? If we do not follow that one, we will injure and ruin justice, and reward injustice. Or am I wrong?

CRITO. I believe it, I think you're right Socrates.

SOCRATES. So, with a healthy life we become improved, and by disease we are ruined is it not logical to listen to the opinion of those that know?

CRITO. Yes.

SOCRATES. Are we able to live well after the body is bad and ruined?

CRITO. Certainly not.

SOCRATES. What of wrong or justice, is this less important than the body?

CRITO. Certainly not.

SOCRATES. So more important?

CRITO. Much more.

SOCRATES. So, for wrong or justice, we should not bother with what the many will say to us, but what the aware, the one, will say, Truth itself. When you first entered this morning, you proposed to me incorrectly, introducing the opinion of the many as necessary for us to consider concerning justice and beauty and goodness and their opposites. But really, some might say, the many can kill us.

CRITO. That is ultimately clear here!

SOCRATES. You're correct. But, it seems we have said this before, see if it still holds for us or not, that it is not living that is best, but living well.

[Socrates, well, Plato, is laying the foundation of Aristotle's "Happiness," a good life well lived.]

CRITO. Yes, it holds.

SOCRATES. And that this well and beautifully and justly are the same thing holds or does it not hold?

CRITO. It holds.

SOCRATES. Then out of this agreement we must look at whether it is right for me to try to escape from here without permission of the Athenians, or whether it is not right. If it appears to be right, let us go. If not, let us dismiss all this talk of money, and bribes, and fleeing. The question is simple, whether we are acting justly in paying money to escape, or in truth are we wrong in doing this; and if we appear wrong in this action, it may be necessary to expand this idea to the ideal that whether to suffer anything whatsoever before doing harm.

CRITO. Exactly, Socrates; but what should we do?

SOCRATES. Let's look together, and if you can contradict anything I am saying, contradict it, and I will obey you; but if not, stop already, great friend, saying often to me the same argument, that I should escape from here without permission of the Athenians; since I value doing these things with your approval, but not unwillingly. Now, please be careful and follow our talk, try to answer the questions to the best of your belief.

CRITO. I will try.

SOCRATES. Are we saying that in no way are we to wrong intentionally, or is it okay to wrong in some situations, but not in others? Or is it never good nor beautiful nor just to wrong, as we have agreed often before this day? Should we throw out all those arguments, because "this is different"? Or above all is it as we have said, regardless of what the many say so or not, and whether we are suffering or not, that never is injustice neither good nor honorable to the wrong-doer in no circumstances? Did we say this or not?

CRITO. We said it.

SOCRATES. Then we must never wrong.

CRITO. Of course not!

SOCRATES. Nor retaliate against wrong, as the many think, since we must never wrong.

CRITO. Apparently not.

SOCRATES. You hesitate. Must one do evil or not?

CRITO. Doubtless one must not, Socrates, no.

SOCRATES. But what? Doing evil actions against the evil, as the many say, is just or not just?

CRITO. Never.

SOCRATES. For doing evil to people is no different than wronging.

CRITO. You say the truth.

SOCRATES. Then one must not retaliate nor do evil to any person, no matter what one may have suffered from them. Be careful, Crito, that in agreeing with these questions, you do not agree to something you don't believe in. For I know what I am saying, the many do not believe. Thus, some believe this and others do not, and there is little common ground. Much force by one side against the other is common.

Therefore, think carefully whether you agree with this opinion that it is never correct to wrong or retaliate or suffering evil to avenge by returning evil; or do you stand against me here from the beginning? For it seems to me thus both before and still now; but if to you it seems anything else, say it and teach. But if you still agree, let's take the next step.

CRITO. But I am holding to it and agree with you; go on.

SOCRATES. Then the next question is, should someone do what he has agreed is just or deceive?

CRITO. He should do it.

SOCRATES. So, consider what comes out of this. By our escaping from here, not obeying the state, are we doing evil to anyone, and to those whom we must least of all or not? And are we holding to what we agreed was just or not?

CRITO. I don't know, Socrates, I don't understand your question.

[Here Plato puts Socrates into a "debate" with the law. Socrates is confronted by the "laws" of Athens. These are the laws he lived under for most of his life and the same ones that just convicted him. He must answer similar questions as did the many protesters in 2016–17. After Donald Trump's election, the losers proclaimed, "He's not my president!" One living under the social contract must accept the system even when not the rulers. Football is still football when your team watches the Super Bowl.]

SOCRATES. Look at it from another direction. If we were about to run away from here, or whatever one should name this, the Laws and the community might come and ask: "Tell me, Socrates, what are you doing? Is this some other ploy to destroy our laws and the entire state as far as you're concerned? Or does it seem to you that the state may exist and not be overturned, in which court rulings have no strength, but private people can do whatever they wish, even if it makes the laws ineffective and ruined?"

What should I answer them, Crito? For one might have much to say, especially an orator, on behalf of this destroyed law, which directs that court judgments be effective. Or do we say to the Laws, "The state wronged us and did not judge us correctly"? Do we say these things or not?

CRITO. These things by Zeus, Socrates.

SOCRATES. What then, if the Laws add, "Socrates, and was this agreed to by you and us, or was it to abide by the verdicts which the state judges?" So, if I were surprised by what they were saying, perhaps they might say, "Socrates, don't be surprised by what you just heard, but answer, since also you are in the habit of using questioning and answering. Come on, what fault do you find with us and the state that you are attempting to destroy us? First did we not give you birth and was it not through our protection your mother and father conceived you? So, come on, tell us, the laws concerning marriage, are you complaining about them as well?"

"I do not complain," I would say.

"But what about those concerning nurturing and education, in which you also were educated? Or was it not well directed by us, the appointed laws, instructing your father to educate you in music and gymnastics?"

"Well," I would say. "Fine. And when born and raised and educated, can you deny you are our child and slave, like your ancestors before you? And if this is so, do you think justice is equal for you and for us, and whatever we want to do to you, do you think it is just for you to do dishonor us by escaping? Would you have the right to do what you want to your father and toward your master, if you had one? Do you feel you have the right to hearing bad things to talk back, or being struck to strike back, or many other such things? What about toward your country and the laws, will it be so for you, so that if we decide to destroy you thinking it is just, you also have the right to destroy us Laws and the country as much as possible, and then tell all what you did was just, you who claim truth and justice?

"Or is your wisdom such that you do not see that the state and the Laws are more honorable, holier, to be more revered, to be held in greater esteem than mother and father and all other ancestors, the gods, humans who have intelligence. She must be revered and more obeyed when angry than when the father is, and either persuaded in court to change her mind, or do what she has ordered, and suffer whatever she directs be suffered, keeping quiet, and if beaten or imprisoned or brought to war to be wounded or killed, these are to be done, and justice is like this, and not yielding nor retreating nor leaving one's post, not only in war and in court but everywhere one must do what the state and we, the Laws may order, or persuade her what is natural justice, but to be violent is neither holy to mother nor father, and even much less to one's country?"

Well then, Crito, are the Laws telling the truth or not?

CRITO. I think so.

SOCRATES. "Look now, Socrates," perhaps the Laws would say, "if what we say is true, what you are now attempting to do to us is not just. For we gave you birth, nurtured, educated you, gave you a share of everything which is beautiful to you and all the other citizens, and we gave to you the right upon maturity to leave if we do not please, you can take your stuff and go away wherever you wish. And none of our laws stand in the way nor forbid it, if any of you wishes to go into a colony, if we and the state do not please you, or move your home elsewhere, whoever wishes may go to those places keeping his things.

"But if you remain, having seen the way we judge cases and administer other things of the state, then we say have you agree with us in action to what we order them to do, and the one not obeying we say wrongs in three ways, because of not obeying us who gave birth, and because of those who nurtured, and because of having agreed with us to obey one neither obeyed nor persuaded us, if we were not doing what is beautiful or just,—also we are not proposing harsh commands to do what we order, but while we are offering two alternatives, either persuade us or do it, one does neither of these.

"We say that you, Socrates, will be liable for these responsibilities, if you do what you have in mind, and you not least of the Athenians, but are particularly responsible."

Then if I should say, "Why so?" Perhaps they might justly confront me with my own words of approval of the agreement [social contract?].

The Laws would say, "Socrates, we have lots of evidence, your own words, that we and the state pleased you; for more than any other Athenian you stayed at home, other than war, you have not left her for a festival, games, or travel. We and our state were adequate for you; so strongly did you prefer us and agree with our politics that you even raised your own children here, so pleased were you with the state.

"Further, in the trial you had the choice to leave Athens never to return, and now you are attempting to leave against the state's will. You were proud of not fearing death, but preferred, as you said, death before exile; and now aren't you ashamed of those false words, nor do you respect us Laws, attempting our ruin, you are acting as a fraud, attempting to run away contrary to contracts and agreements, which you yourself agreed to as a citizen.

"Are we lying or telling the truth that you agreed to be a citizen according to the Law, not by your word alone, but your actions?"

What do we answer to this, Crito? Do we agree?

CRITO. Absolutely, Socrates.

SOCRATES. "Are you not then," they would continue, "breaking your contracts and agreements with us, not agreed to by necessity nor deception nor forced to decide in a short time, but over seventy years, in any of those years you could have left if we did not please you and the agreements did not appear just? But you preferred to stay here rather than travel to Lacedaemon or Crete, which you say have good laws. Nor were other Greek states nor foreign nations your desire. You left Athens less than the lame and blind and other handicapped. You, more than many other Athenians, were pleased with the state and us the Laws. And now are you asking to be released from the agreements? If you are persuaded by us, Socrates; don't go abroad and look like a fool.

"This escape you're contemplating, what good will it do you, or your accomplices? They will risk both exile, loss of citizenship or property. In your case, say you make it to Thebes or Megara,—for both have good laws,—you will enter those states as a rabble rouser, an enemy of the state. Their citizens will see you as a corrupter of the laws. The judges that convicted you here will be confirmed in their judgment, a corrupter of the laws, might seriously be thought to be a corrupter of the young and thoughtless people.

"So you'll avoid the good states with good laws, the civilized nations. Will your life then be worthwhile? What will you discuss with them, these lawless ones? Virtue and justice? Institutions and laws? Would you succeed there in your business?

"However, you will leave these places, and go into Thessaly along with Crito's friends. There disorder and licentiousness are without limit. Maybe they would like to hear your stories of running away from prison, dressed in some disguise, or wearing a skin, altering your appearance. They will laugh at the crazy old man with a short time left in life who dared to live shamelessly. Perhaps, if you keep them entertained, they will tolerate you; if not, how will you live? You will hear many things about yourself, as they talk about you the beggar, maybe a slave. What will you have to do to feast in Thessaly? Where are those fancy arguments concerning justice and the other virtues?

"However you may wish to live for the sake of the children, so that you may raise and educate them? But what? Bringing them into Thessaly will you raise and educate them, forsaking their Athenian citizenship? Who would better care for them? We, the Laws, your companions here in Athens? If you go to Thessaly will they take care of them after you pass onto Hades?

"But, Socrates, listen to us who raised you, do not make your children more important nor your life nor anything greater than justice, so that in judgment in Hades you may have all these to argue in your defense; by listening to Crito all you have taught is for nothing.

Now depart in innocence, a sufferer and not a doer of evil; a victim, not of the laws, but of men. But if you go forth, returning evil for evil, and injury for injury, breaking the covenants and agreements which you have made with us, and harming those whom you ought least to wrong, yourself, your friends, your country, and we, the Laws, we will be angry with you while you live, and the Laws in the world below, will receive you as their enemy; for they will know that you have done your best to destroy us. Listen, then, to us and not to Crito."

My dear friend Crito, know well that this is what I hear. In my mind the sound of these arguments is clear, and it makes it impossible to hear any others. But, please speak if your mind has arguments to present.

CRITO. But, Socrates, I have nothing to say.

SOCRATES. Let it go then, Crito, and let us act the just way, God's will be done.

Time to think about why Plato's *Crito* is included in this text. It seems to be more pro-state than pro-liberty. Why does Socrates think breaking the laws is worse than having them unfairly applied to him? What is the source of the laws? Why are the state and the laws "more honorable, holier, to be more revered, to be held in greater esteem than mother and father and all other ancestors, the gods, humans who have intelligence"? In the *Apology*, Socrates was adamant that if the Athenian court forbade him to practice philosophy from then on, he would refuse to obey. Here in *Crito,* he seems to say that one must always obey the legal authorities, even when they command what is unjust. Is there a way to reconcile what he says in these two works? Can you think of a way to make his statements consistent with one another?

THE LONG AND WINDING ROAD
TO THE EXPERIMENT

Liberty is the possibility of doubting, the possibility of making
a mistake, the possibility of searching and experimenting, the
possibility of saying no to any authority—literary, artistic,
philosophic, religious, social and even political.
—Ignazio Silone

WHAT IS HUMAN nature—that is, what traits of personality and character, if any, do all people have in common? For example, are all people basically selfish, or do they tend to care for the welfare of others? This leads to our other big questions. What should be the purpose of government? How do the people running a government get the power to govern? How should a government be organized? What kinds of governments should be respected and supported? What kinds of governments should be resisted and fought?

Government, that "great reflection" of man, is the spontaneous development of individual men and women to solve the problems of life in a state of nature. As we will continue to emphasize throughout the text, all governments that are just should lead to happiness. But it should also be appropriate to the nature of humankind. Government that fails to see man's faults and true nature is destined to fail. If government is a contract; it must be legitimate to that contract: obey all "clauses" and not breach its faithfulness. And, last, government must promote the prosperity of its citizens, not selected groups. It may not itself violate the laws of nature.

The Ancients

From early times, debate has been over the purpose of man. The Judeo-Christian heritage of the West along with the Greeks and Romans set the foundations of all that follows. The Jewish and the Christian philosophies are interwoven in everything that one would consider Western thought, thus America's great experiment began with the elements of biblical truths. The Bible is clear in that all humans are unique and important. We all must serve mankind, not only ourselves. We are individually responsible for what we become or what we don't become. Providence has chosen us to be servants and stewards. Private morality is more important than civic virtue (public morality); but public morality is only an earthly justice based on the laws. These laws cannot violate the laws of God. Though God is a judging monarch, He is as well a loving and forgiving God.

The Greeks best deal with the ideal of happiness and recall Aristotle's essay "Happiness." Socrates (c. 469–399 BC), Plato's' teacher, died for his principles. He felt for every question, there was but one true answer; we are destined as men to search. There is no such thing as both sides have a point. In the *Republic*, Plato lays down his ideal of the perfect leader, a Philosopher king who would lead us all to the truth. However, this will of a master, though maybe benevolent, has led throughout history to millions of deaths and great losses of freedom. Plato (428–348 BC) felt this *Kallipolis* (ruled by the best) would lead to the good life: jobs, goods, marriage, children, education . . . everything!

Aristotle (384–322 BC), Plato's student, agreed with both his teacher and Socrates in the truth, but also that socially, as individuals, we could discover it. Debate is essential to truth. Because man is a political animal, it is natural and normal for us to argue and strive, thus iron does sharpen iron. But slamming swords into each other dull both edges.

Roman ideals were to serve the common good in a partnership of citizens and government. This was to be done by citizens having and using civic virtue. Citizens must be honest, love their country, be hardworking, and live a modest lifestyle. We will look again at the Roman Republic and civic virtue. But the Roman State was to provide moral education in small localized communities. It was felt that government that serves special interests, be it the poor, rich, oil producers, officeholders, rather than the common welfare, was corrupt.

Middle Ages

Following from Plato's *Republic*, let's move quickly to the end of the medieval period. A most famous and misunderstood philosopher is Niccolò Machiavelli (1469–1527). Writing to impress an Italian prince, and thus get a job, Machiavelli's *The Prince* has been considered the blueprint of oppressive governments since. His advice to his prince was straightforward and concise. To be a good prince and rule long and well, one should be feared rather than loved, but not hated, which usually leads to revolt. One needs the support of the people because without the people supporting one's decisions, no actions are possible. Leaders should always use their own arms, never relying on allies and/ or mercenaries. Intelligence is essential as a leader; being well-read and asking for advice and coherent decisions are the signs of leadership. And, last, five virtues must be exhibited to the outside, even if insincere: mercy, honesty, humaneness, uprightness, and religiousness. One recent leader who truly exhibited these qualities is Ronald Reagan.

The next major philosopher is Thomas Hobbes. Hobbes was a contemporary of John Locke and a follower of the social contract theory; however, his foundation varied greatly with Locke's approach. Hobbes' *Leviathan* was written forty years before Locke's most famous works, yet their "debate" is the main debate of the purpose of government. Hobbes generally felt, as did Plato and Machiavelli, that man was incapable of self-rule. His contract was to submit to the central authority for our own good. He felt that all men were created equal; but as rivals for the necessities of life, we fear each other. We are "solitary, poor, nasty, brutish, and short." We could not exist except by the power of the state. Again, to escape this miserable existence, man created the state for protection and peace. Alexander Hamilton?

This contract derives from common sense; look at kids at recess. Hobbes felt man wanted a peaceful life, and peace should be sought, and when it cannot be obtained, war ensues because of the shortages of life. To have peace, we must give up certain rights, mainly the right to do whatever we can. We need to agree with others how to interact, again recess. (Unfortunately, recess has gone the way or the 3 Rs.) This interaction is usually in the form of contracts: handshakes, words of promises, and acceptance to do A for B. Contracts made must be kept; Hobbes believed that the power to enforce must be given to a person or assembly to ensure that the laws are maintained. The social contract tells the ruler that we give up the right to self-government in exchange for requiring others to maintain their contracts. If government is to be appropriate to human nature, Hobbesians believe that government must be unlimited. The state, a monarchy or modern dictatorships, must have absolute control.

Scottish Enlightenment

But if government is to be legitimate, it must be free. Free to enter, free to dissent, free to leave. These ideas are the result of classical liberalism. Classical liberalism is the philosophy of the Scottish Enlightenment of the seventeenth and eighteenth centuries. The ideals of freedom, dignity, and equality in both economics and politics find their roots in these Scotsmen's ideas. The major thinkers of this period for our concerns are John Locke and Adam Smith, though there are many others that have contributed to the Framers' and Founders' ideals.

James Harrington (1611–1677) in his *Common-wealth of Oceana* (1656) stated that government is and must be separated into three bodies with different roles:

- proposing
- resolving and debating
- executing

Writing at the time of Glorious Revolution in England, he proposed several bodies chosen by the people, including a Senate and a body of the people to make the laws, and magistracy to execute the laws. *Oceana* was seized during printing but eventually released and published. It was clearly an attack on Cromwell; he was arrested, held without charge, and died insane from scurvy. His ideas will influence a later Frenchman named Montesquieu in his development of separation of powers, checks and balances, and a mixed balanced government.

Another Scotsman was Samuel Rutherford (1600–1661), a Scottish Presbyterian minister and part of the Scottish Enlightenment. Contrary to British law, he wrote his own catechism and organized seasons of fasting and prayer in response to the corruption of the church. In 1636, he was stripped of his ministry, forbidden to preach or even leave town. Yet he continued to write many letters to his parishioners. For example,

> Give Christ your virgin love; you cannot put your love and heart into better hand. Oh! If ye knew Him, and saw His beauty, your love, your liking, your heart, your desires would close with Him and cleave to Him.

> I never knew, by mine nine years' preaching, so much of Christ's love, as He has taught me in Aberdeen. Sweet, sweet have His comforts been to my soul; my pen, tongue, and heart have no words to express the kindness, love and mercy of my Well-beloved to me, in this house of my pilgrimage.

In 1638, the English Revolution between Parliament and King Charles and the religious "civil war" in Scotland between Presbyterians and Episcopacy of the Church of England drew in Rutherford. Presbyterianism won the day, and he was appointed professor of theology at St. Mary's College, St. Andrews. He only accepted with the promise to preach again. He preached before the Long Parliament in London 1640–45.

He wrote *Lex, Rex*, literally "the law [is] king" in 1644. He attacked the doctrine of "Rex Lex," meaning "the king is the law." Rutherford made a biblical argument against the absolute rule of monarchs based on the book of Deuteronomy, chapter 17, saying that men should be governed by law, not by the will of men. Its main thesis deals with his arguments against divine right of kings. The crown is bestowed by the voluntary consent of the people; therefore, the people are at liberty to resist a tyrant. Copies of *Lex, Rex* were burned after the English Restoration. Rutherford was accused of high treason but died of natural causes before he could be tried.

> The king receiveth royal power with the states to make good laws, and power by his royalty to execute those laws, and this power the community hath devolved in the hands of the

king and states of parliament; but the community keepeth
to themselves a power to resist tyranny . . .

John Locke's (1632–1704) ideas are known to have directly
influenced French, American, and Latin American Revolutions.
His ideas can be found in the Declaration of Independence and the
Constitution of the United States. If the Founders and Framers had
themselves a founder, Locke would be the founders' founder. Not only
was Locke a political philosopher, but also he wrote on a myriad of
topics: education, economics, religion, even psychology. His greatest
philosophical contribution is the use of empiricism by using experience
to find truth. Having already addressed Locke's philosophy, let's move
on to some others.

John Milton (1608–1674) was an English poet best known for his
epic poem *Paradise Lost*, written in 1667. Like Hobbes, in *Paradise Lost*,
Milton believed once humanity had "fallen" from the Garden of Eden,
it was condemned to a servitude to desire and a need for government.

> Since thy original lapse, true Liberty
> Is lost, which always with right Reason dwells
> Twinn'd, and from her hath no individual being;
> Reason in man obscur'd, or not obey'd,
> Immediately inordinate desires
> And upstart Passions catch the Government
> From Reason, and to servitude reduce
> Man till then free.

Yet, when younger, Milton in *Tenure of Kings and Magistrates*, 1649,
defended the right of people to execute a guilty sovereign.

The Whig theory of government was developed out of Scotland
but was essentially put into practice in England by Parliament in its
fight against the kings' idea of divine rights of kings. Algernon Sydney
(1623–1683) will be executed by King Charles II of England not only for
his beliefs but also for attempting to organize an assassination attempt
against a king he felt violated the laws of nature. His philosophies will
be a culmination of the Scottish Enlightenment and the catalyst for
later revolt, including the American Revolution. The Whig philosophy

states all men were by nature free and equal, that consensually men form a social contract to form a government should be constitutionally limited to protecting fundamental rights, which are life, liberty, and property. David Hume took Sydney's ideas further and stated that the nature of man was evil, or corrupt, that government by the many with negotiation and compromise promoting a union, a balance of interests, factions (Madison) would best be solved by establishing a republic.

The key element of the Whig theory of government is the protection of property. Having to live in a world where government controlled all, even economics, the importance of property could never be separated from liberty. As William Blackstone (1723–1780) stated:

> The third absolute right, inherent in every Englishman, is that of . . . the sacred and inviolable rights of private property.

Adam Smith (1723–1790) is called the "father of economics." His great book, *Wealth of Nations* (1776), was the beginning of the "economic" case for classical liberalism. His theory is simply that private property, free markets, and free trade are the only source of wealth and prosperity. He asked what institutions allow people to flourish and prosper. Private property and free trade lead to "justice." Government's only job should be to get out of the way so individuals' lives, property, and contracts are protected.

Richard Rumbold (1622?–1685) had served in Oliver Cromwell's army, had watched, been a guard at Charles I's beheading, and with John Locke had been a member of the Rye House Conspiracy to assassinate Charles II and James II. He fled to Scotland and was captured and executed on June 26, 1685. On the scaffold, his speech resonates with all free men wanting to be who they wanted without government interference or sanction. He echoes Jefferson's next-century essay,

> Tho I am sure there was no man born marked of God above another, for none comes into the world with a saddle on his back, neither any booted and spurred to ride him. Not but that I am well satisfied that God hath wisely ordered different stations for men in the world, as I have already said; kings having as much power as to make them great and the

people as much property as to make them happy. And to conclude, I shall only add my wishes for the salvation of all men who were created for that end.

The French Guys

Last, there are three Frenchmen who helped clarify the Scottish ideas and helped transfer them to the European continent. In addition, many of the ideas of the Scottish Enlightenment passed to Americans in French as being able to read French was the sign of a civilized and educated gentleman. The three are Montesquieu, Voltaire, and Rousseau.

Charles de Montesquieu (1689–1755) expanded on Locke. Using the British system as his example, he believed there were three forms of government: (1) republican, in an aristocracy or a democracy, (2) monarchy, and (3) despotic. In a republic, education is an absolute necessity because it is based on virtue, making good choices. Because democracy is based on equality, democracies are corrupted and devolve to despotism or at best a monarchy, at worse dictatorship based on fear. (Montesquieu was lucky to have died before they developed.) To protect minorities from the tyranny of democratic majorities, a fair and objective judiciary was essential to the health of democracy. His text *The Spirit of Laws* (1748) was on all the shelves of the American thinkers. He felt that liberty was the ultimate purpose of government, rights, and property mere tools. The best government then had to represent all segments (factions) of society. It had to be a mix of monarchy: king→president, aristocracy: nobles→Supreme Court, Senate, and democracy: legislature with two houses→Congress. These divisions of powers and checks and balances were to become the foundations of everything America was to be.

François-Marie Arouet (1694–1778), better known by his pen name Voltaire, was a writer, historian, and philosopher most famous for his support of civil liberties, including freedom of religion, freedom of expression, free trade, and separation of church and state. He wrote more than twenty thousand letters and more than two thousand books and pamphlets. Using Hume's and Montesquieu "factions," he believed that aggressive powers need to be checked by aggressive powers of others. His idea was that a republic was based on the "ambition of every citizen, which checks the ambition of others; on pride restraining pride and on the desire of ruling, which will not suffer another to rule. Hence it is a society where the guests eat at the same table with equal appetite." Our very Constitution was designed to be used as such: each branch, filled with ambitious men, would never allow to others to gain more power than allowed in the document. Or so the Framers thought.

And the last Frenchman, the most controversial and probably the least moral, is Jean-Jacques Rousseau (1712–1778). Rousseau's influence can be felt today in many of the "reforms" of the world. He felt man was malleable and could be created into something greater than what God could. His arrogance has led to violent revolutions and probably billions of lives lost or oppressed in the last two centuries. *The Social Contract* and his education book *Emile,* both published in 1762, are the foundations for every form of ism since: Fascism, Socialism, Progressivism, Communism, as well as the resulting casualties.

Rousseau felt that in a state of nature, there were no laws; but once together, man follows the laws that restrict people's natural freedom. Since once man joins society, he is corrupted. Thus, like Plato before, a select group needs to make man free again. Rousseau believed that direct democracy, where people voted direct without representation, was the best form of government. But citizens should submit to a government supported based on the general will. Locke believed that an individual's natural rights could not be abandoned, as they are "inalienable." Rousseau believed that the primary role of government is to enforce the will. This will was not merely a majority; he believed the majority of people could not know what was best for them; it is the social contract, an agreement of individuals to subordinate their judgments, rights, and powers to the needs and judgment of the community as a whole. It is a kind of ideal representing what was best for the whole state, "a will *for* the general good." If man does not follow the general will, the just must submit him. One enters this contract implicitly by accepting the protection of the communal laws. The general will, expressed in law, is sacred. Men are born essentially good, and thus the general will, which grows out of their social contract, could be trusted to protect the insecure rights within a state of nature. A man is never a master of himself. Why? He matters not except as a member of the contract; only if he turns strength into right and obedience into duty, to serve the general will. Clearly the general will is always right. The state's chief task was to shape society—control of education, common core, control of the economy, central banking, and regulation of behaviors through a police state. If someone were to disagree with it, then he must be wrong and, for his own sake, ought to be made to agree.

> He who would dare to undertake the political creation of a people ought to believe that he can, in a manner of speaking, transform human nature; transform each individual— who, by himself, is a solitary and perfect whole—into a mere part of a greater whole from which the individual will henceforth receive his life and being. Thus the person who would undertake the political creation of a people should believe in his ability to alter man's constitution; to strengthen it; to substitute for the physical and independent existence received from nature, an existence which is partial and moral. In short, the would-be creator of political man must remove man's own forces and endow him with others that are naturally alien to him.

Where does that leave freedom? Where does that leave human dignity? He felt that liberty was a social relationship. And, indeed, freedom from what must always be asked. Freedom from violence by our fellow men: theft, murder, and enslavement are all caused by one man oppressing another. Theft takes another's property, murder another's life, and enslavement another's liberty. Rousseau believed that we could trust government to regulate our social relations. It wasn't just Rousseau, the French Revolution under Robespierre (1758–1794), that put into practice the violence that the deep state can use if necessary. "The function of government is to direct the physical and moral powers of the nation toward the end for which the commonwealth has come into being." The bureaucrats, later Progressives call them experts, PhDs, technocrats, being themselves somehow immune to the foibles of weak, illiterate, and fallen man, would direct us to do what we ought.

Here are some of the Progressive thinkers of the late eighteenth century. Sound familiar to today's "experts." Louis Antoine Léon de Saint-Just (1767–1794) was a military and political leader during the French Revolution. The youngest of the deputies elected to the National Convention in 1792, Saint-Just rose quickly in their ranks and became a major leader of the government of the Reign of Terror. He was the "prosecutor" of King Louis XVI, standing by in all glory and excitement at the execution of the king. He later drafted the radical French Constitution of 1793. "The legislator commands the future. It is for him to *will* the good of mankind. It is for him to make men what *he wills* them to be." Jacques Nicolas Billaud-Varenne (1756–1819), architect of the Reign of Terror, was considered the most radical member of the Committee of Public Safety. He was a close friend and confidante of Robespierre. "A people who are to be returned to liberty must be formed anew. A strong force and vigorous action are necessary to destroy old prejudices, to change old customs, to correct depraved affections, to restrict superfluous wants, and to destroy ingrained vices . . . This parallel embraces the whole science of government." Like today's politically correct educational system, citizens were to have no beliefs, wants, or values not approved of by the government. He was seconded by Louis-Michel le Peletier (1760–1793), a member of the Committee of Public Safety and "educational" reformer; "considering the extent of human degradation, I am convinced that it is necessary to effect a total regeneration and, if I may so express myself, of creating a new people."

There were three basic liberties in social relations: natural, civil, and moral.

What is natural liberty? This is absolute right to take anything that tempts him, no limits but the strengths of the man, independence. This is what man loses in the social contract. Man is born good, but he has instincts (survive and reproduce) that must be controlled to make society possible. The next is civil liberty, the legal right of property in what he possesses; a man can be both ruled and free, if he rules himself, limited by the general will. And the one that men struggle with the most is moral liberty. This is living in accordance with one's conscience. Rousseau would probably not add a conscience that is virtuous.

Like Rousseau and his French co-do-gooders, Progressive romantics, using science to "fix" the world, Hamilton felt the general will may need force, violence, to force man to be free, make him do what was best for himself—compulsory education, licensing of all occupations tariffs to buy the right goods, regulation of food, births, wages, taxes, even death—a regime of perfection.

The American

Thomas Paine (1736–1809) was English-born American political activist, political theorist, and theologian. He was the author of two short pamphlets at the beginning of the American Revolution. These short "books" will set the foundations for the revolution and give motivations to continue. His ideas reflected Enlightenment rhetoric of transnational human rights. Paine came to America in 1774, arriving sick from typhoid fever and barely alive, taking six weeks to recover. He becomes a Pennsylvania citizen, editor, and later famous architect. He will save the American Revolution and spark the French. His principal contributions were the powerful, widely read pamphlet *Common Sense* (1776), the all-time best-selling American book that advocated colonial America's independence from the Kingdom of Great Britain, and *The American Crisis* (1776–83), a pro-revolutionary pamphlet series. *Common Sense* was so influential that John Adams said, "Without the pen of the author of *Common Sense*, the sword of Washington would have been raised in vain." He will later write the *Rights of Man* (1791), in part a defense of the French Revolution against its critics. He became even more controversial after his *The Age of Reason* (1793–94). This book supports deism over religions, promotes reason and freethinking, and argues against institutionalized religion in general and Christian doctrine in particular.

Like the others, he wrote that all men are born and remain always free and equal in their rights, and political associations are created solely to preserve these rights. The nation can only have powers granted to it by the people, thus governments are formed two ways: reason and ignorance, chosen freely or imposed forcefully. When reason triumphs over ignorance, the best form of government, a republic, emerges. Ignorance allows monarchy (despots) to survive. He rejects a mixed government as being driven by corruption. Look around today.

HOW DOES GOVERNMENT PROTECT
OUR NATURAL RIGHTS?

When the people fear their government, there is tyranny;
when the government fears the people, there is liberty.
—Thomas Jefferson

B UT HOW DO these philosophies work in practice? The
Framers used all the previous ideas from the Greeks to Locke
in creating the kind of government they thought would not only best
protect the natural rights of each individual and promote the good of
all but also be in conformity with human nature. They understood
the issues between limited and unlimited government, the difference
between written and unwritten constitutions, and how future Americans
have used the term constitutional government.

Examining government protection of
the basic rights of the people

How does one escape from the fear of living in a state of nature? You
and your fellow "citizens," maybe just you and your extended family,
agree to work together in agreement, voluntarily, or a "social contract"
to create a group, a "government" to protect your natural rights. What
kind of government would be best for your group? How do you establish
it? Hobbes and Locke, Aristotle and Plato, and Jefferson and Hamilton
debated this since time immemorial; history has seen this as a difficult
task. Governments have deprived, and still take away, property and
rights more often than not. The problem man has struggled with is
to create and sustain a government that will do what man has wanted
it to do—not only protect his natural rights but also to protect the

rights of all, not a select group or sector of the society, that created the government.

Man in this philosophical state of nature has agreed to live under a government. Locke and Hobbes, and Jefferson and Hamilton had to decide what kind of government was amenable to not only do its purpose and protect rights but also be commensurate with human nature. Before you read on, answers these questions as the Founders did.

1. According to what you've read so far, what do you think is the main purpose of government?
2. How does any government get its right (authority) to make laws for people to do or not do?
3. What can the people do if its government does not serve the purpose (s) for which it was established? Why does a people have this right?

Where does the "state" come from?

Many have argued throughout the centuries where government came from, how we fallible humans got the ideas that social cooperation and divisions of labor, power, and order would create a better life than living alone in a state of nature. The major theories are simple but often overlap. To understand the rising of the state, some definitions are in order first. The state as an organization has four characteristics: population, territory, sovereignty, and then government. A state must have people, the number of which does not directly relate to its existence. A state must be comprised of land—territory with known and recognized boundaries. Every state is sovereign. It has supreme and absolute power within its own territory and decides its own foreign and domestic policies. Every state has a government—that is, it is politically organized.

States came into existence by people, individuals, deciding their lives, liberties, and properties would be better protected cooperatively. Regardless if you are a Hobbesian and believe that man is ruthless, or a Lockean and believe in the uncertainty of the state of nature, man is better off socially and politically together. Many historians and philosophers have surmised on how this happened.

- The force theory: The force theory states that one person or a small group took control of an area and forced all within it to submit to that person's or group's rule.
- The evolutionary theory: The evolutionary theory argues that the state evolved naturally out of the early family.
- The divine right theory: The theory of divine right holds that God created the state and that God gives those of royal birth a "divine right" to rule.
- The social contract theory: The social contract theory argues that the state arose out of a voluntary act of free people.

The force theory seems to apologize for one group's historical creation as a way to legitimize oppression over another group. This allows racism, genocide, war, and even religious fanaticisms to rule the day. After John Locke, few still believe that God's choice is predominant in man's electoral decisions. But if one looks closely, as did Aristotle himself, the evolution of man from family to clan to village to city-state confederations to empires has been a continuous thread throughout time. But why and how did a family decide to join with others to form a clan, etc.? The social contract theory completes the argument; all these arrangements were voluntary. Decisions made by free individuals created the best world man can do on earth, free markets, free governments.

How do Locke's answers compare with yours?

Locke and his fellow natural rights philosophers down through Jefferson, John Calhoun, and Grover Cleveland believed the purpose of government has been to "secure" natural rights. We see it in the Declaration, the Gettysburg Address, and the speeches of Andrew Jackson. The protection of man's rights is the purpose of government.

Stemming from this is where and how does government get its authority to govern? From the consent of the people! Power is inherent in the people; their powers are delegated to government by, and only by, the owners of that authority. People can give that consent in a number of ways, explicitly or implicitly. People give explicit consent by agreeing to the contract that establishes the society whose members then establish the government and choose its officers or joining a society that already is established, as in new citizens swearing to defend and uphold the Constitution. Those individuals who ratified our Constitution in 1787 gave explicit consent to their new government. As do the many immigrants who come to America to seek a better life,

> I hereby declare, on oath, that I absolutely and entirely renounce and abjure all allegiance and fidelity to any foreign prince, potentate, state, or sovereignty, of whom or which I have heretofore been a subject or citizen; that I will support and defend the Constitution and laws of the United States of America against all enemies, foreign and domestic; that I will bear true faith and allegiance to the same; that I will bear arms on behalf of the United States when required by the law; that I will perform noncombatant service in the Armed Forces of the United States when required by the law; that I will perform work of national importance under civilian direction when required by the law; and that I take this obligation freely, without any mental reservation or purpose of evasion; so help me God.

Most people give implicit consent, also called tacit consent, by accepting the laws and services of the government and nation of their birth. Those born here have implied their consent by remaining in this country and living under its laws. Every native-born American, as he or she grows up, has the choice of seeking the citizenship of another country. By remaining in this country, accepting its laws, and enjoying its benefits, they imply consent to be governed by the national, state, and local governments. Many state consent every time the Pledge of Allegiance is recited, one votes in an election, or one engages in other civic actions.

But Locke firmly felt, since a people gives the power to the government, it can, and has the right to, even a moral obligation to, take that consent back if government is not fulfilling well the purpose for which it was established, protecting rights of the individual. Locke argued and the Founders agreed that if a government fails to protect the people's rights, the people have a right of revolution but, because of the insecurity of the state of nature, must establish a new one in its place.

Who is to judge if a government has failed? Locke and the Founders were firm that only the people has this right to decide: "Whenever any form of government becomes destructive of these ends, it is the right of the people to alter or abolish it, and to institute new government . . ."

Revolution is an extreme way to deal with bad government. Government should be designed or organized to limit its powers to protect individual rights and thus reduce the need for such extreme measures. But that option can never be taken off the table.

What is constitutional government?

A government without limits is illegitimate, immoral, and not God-endorsed. Only government with respected restraints on its powers, such as laws, bills of rights, and free and periodic elections, is legitimate. Unfortunately, most of the world's historical and present governments are unlimited governments. These governments are in the hands of those who govern, free to use power as the elites choose, unrestrained by laws, elections, or any bill of rights. Tyranny, autocracy, dictatorship, and totalitarianism are other words to describe these unlimited governments.

What government was best suited to prevent the abuse of power in the newly independent states of America? From the Framers' study of history and the belief in natural rights, they believed that any government that served its proper ends must be a limited, a constitutional government. In a constitutional government, the powers of the person or group controlling the government are limited by a set of laws, customs, or a constitution.

A constitution is defined as "a set of customs, traditions, rules, and laws that set forth the basic way a government is organized and operated." Many constitutions are in writing, some are partly written and partly unwritten, and some are not written at all. But written or not, the constitution of a people is a rule book of what is allowed and what is NOT allowed.

Thus, every nation has a constitution. Good governments and bad governments have constitutions. Some of the worst governments have constitutions that include lists of the basic rights of their citizens. The former Soviet Union had one of the longest and most elaborate constitutions in history, but in reality, its citizens enjoyed few, if any, rights "guaranteed" by it.

Are all governments with written constitutions constitutional governments? If you look at a nation's constitution, you should be able to answer the following questions about the relationship between the government and its citizens:

- What are the purposes of government?
- How is this government organized?
- How does the government do its job?
- Who is a citizen?
- How do citizens control their government?
- What rights and responsibilities, if any, do citizens have?

Unfortunately, a constitution does not guarantee constitutional government. If a constitution provides for the unlimited exercise of political power—by one, few, or even many, say, president for life—that is not a constitutional government. If a constitution provides that the government's power is to be limited, but it does not include ways to enforce those limitations, it is not a constitutional government. A constitutional government with a constitution—higher or fundamental law—is a government that obeys as does its citizens, including those in power, its constitution; the elites, deep state, an aristocracy, no one is not exempt.

The United States Constitution is considered the "supreme law of the land." But, of course, there are other laws too—those passed by Congress, by state legislatures, and by city councils, for example. These are called statutory laws. Statutory laws are passed every day so government can function, but these laws are not supposed to violate the Constitution. The Constitution is considered the fundamental law. It is the general rule book for all other actions in the government. Any law in conflict with fundamental law is not a law; it is "null and void." A null and void law must not be obeyed; to obey an unconstitutional law would be in essence treason. You would be violating the supreme law of the land by obeying an unconstitutional law.

Although the United States is a relatively young country, its Constitution is the oldest functioning written constitution in the world. Constitutionalism, though—the belief that governments should be based on a constitution—is an old concept. In the fourth Century BC, the Greek philosopher Aristotle described several kinds of possible constitutions for the Greek city-state, of which he believed the best would be a "monarchy." By this he meant rule by a good and honorable king. Many Greek city-states had clear procedures for the enactment of laws and the conduct of government. In the sixth century AD, the Roman emperor Justinian I collected and published not only a new law code but also his subjects' rights as established through custom.

As Western nations developed, kings became the sovereigns of nations, and nobles sought to protect their rights. In England, that struggle produced the Magna Carta of 1215. We will look more closely at the Magna Carta later, but it is remembered as first documents in the West to establish certain rights, thereby limiting the king's power. But the English Constitution is not the Magna Carta or any written documents like the United States' it is "unwritten." It is the accumulation of all legal actions over the centuries, traditions, and law court cases, beginning with the Magna Carta.

Ron Paul in his recent manifesto of liberty, *The Revolution at Ten Years,* says something amazing happens after thousands of years of oppression, subsistence lifestyles, and short and brutish lives.

> While the concept of liberty remained in its infancy for thousands of years, something amazing happened in the 18th century. The importance of the individual and his inherent liberty was recognized and defined. This occurred most notably in America and in other Western countries. This recognition led to the explosion of human progress from which we continue to benefit to this very day. It proved to be the most important development for all of mankind.
>
> The preparation of a habitable place for the human race thrive took billions of years. The amazing progress of mankind in comparison has been accomplished in a flash of time.
>
> The authority of one person to control others with force became an important issue for all societies. Development of a full understanding of the morality of liberty has been slow, but the benefits provided in the last 250 years have been remarkable. Considering the actual time involved, it amounts to a very small drop, not in the bucket, but in the ocean!

Ludwig Mises, in *Omnipotent Government*, saw the late eighteenth century as the beginning of a movement "toward freedom, the rights of man, and self-determination . . . This individualism resulted in the fall of autocratic government, the establishment of democracy, the evolution of capitalism, technical improvements, and an unprecedented rise in standards of living. It substituted enlightenment for old superstitions, scientific methods of research for inveterate prejudices. It was an epoch of great artistic and literary achievements, the age of immortal musicians, painters, writers, and philosophers."

But Jefferson, to his friend Adams, warned that liberty and the release of innovation were always under threat from "ignorance and barbarism." That ignorance can be labeled Marxism, Fascism, Socialism, Communism, and Progressivism. The barbarism would be 262 million killed to coerce a "new Socialist man."

By the eighteenth century, most of Europe had written complex arrangements of law and custom, written and unwritten. The Framers of the American Constitution looked at many of these and ancient systems of government when establishing our nation. What they created demonstrated many precedents, but many new ideas we'll see later: ideals of individual rights, separation of powers, checks and balances, and republican government, and consent of the people.

To the Founders, especially the Framers in 1787, a constitution was the fundamental law, or what they called the higher law. They felt, with history and experience behind them, that the higher law must have the following characteristics:

- It should guarantee basic rights of citizens to life, liberty, and property.
- Government's main responsibility was to protect those rights.
- There was to be private domain—areas of citizens' lives that are no business of the government and in which the government cannot interfere.
- There needed to be clear limits on government powers in areas of
  o   citizens' rights and responsibilities,
  o   the distribution of resources, and
  o   the control of conflict.
- It could only be changed by citizens who understood their history, the law, and the philosophy of limited government.

These citizens, according Jefferson, needed to be well educated, thus his concern for a publicly supported education system; he made sure it was included in his Northwest Ordinance of the summer of 1787. Higher law is clearly distinct from the ordinary laws governments regularly create and enforce.

One of the purposes of the limitations imposed by constitutional government is to check tyranny of the majority. How is a system supposedly "democratic" block a majority decision? What advantages does a limited government have? What are some disadvantages? Are there advantages to unlimited government? Issues such as these continue to be serious with the growth of an imperial presidency, first studied by Arthur Schlesinger Jr. The executive branch and its unelected bureaucracy are making more and more of our laws rather than Congress. Executive orders often do what many think is right, or good for the country, but these orders or actions are not permissible, not constitutional, under our system.

If government is to protect life, liberty, and property, how does a constitutional government protect these natural rights? Constitutional government was created to secure the rights of its citizens. A constitution does this in two major ways:

- It limits on powers of government to prevent it from abusing, violating natural rights.
- It states how government is to be organized and how its powers are distributed among the separate bodies of the government. Tyranny is all powers in the hands of one or a few, or an abusive majority. This division of powers and checks and balances was felt to be the best way that those limitations would work.

The first was merely a legal protection of rights and freedom. The second was an organizational protection; the Framers hoped it would prevent the abuses they had previous studied and lived through. Powers need to be distributed and shared among the separate branches of government. It is hoped that this distribution and sharing of power would make tyranny less likely. It is also less likely that any group, or as Madison called these groups "factions," will gain so much power that it can ignore the limitations placed on it by a constitution and use government for their own interests instead of the common good.

Our government was designed to prevent abuse of its powers; the Framers provided for distribution and sharing of powers between three branches of national government. Each branch has a primary responsibility to do certain functions, but each branch also shares these functions and powers with the other branches. For example,

- Congress passes laws, but the president can veto them.
- The president nominates his bureaucracy and other government officials, but the Senate can approve or reject them.
- Congress passes laws, but the Supreme Court could declare them unconstitutional, thus invalidate them.
- Only Congress has the power to declare and pay the costs of war, and the president's power and duty to set strategy and tactics.

This system of distributed, shared powers, and checks and balances is the foundation of limited but sufficient government. The complicated ways constitutional governments are organized and function mean that it takes them a long time to get things done. It may seem strange, but this "inefficiency" was seen by the Framers as an advantage. They thought that these difficulties would help to prevent the abuse of powers they had seen in history. The slow process, slowing the passion of majorities, makes it more likely that political decisions are for the general welfare.

Why did the Framers fear government?

Based on their knowledge of history and experiences with the British government, it is not surprising that they were afraid of abuse of government. Government cannot be left to itself; it is inevitable that the holders of office would abuse powers. Power corrupts!

> Give all power to the many, they will oppress the few. Give all power to the few, they will oppress the many (Alexander Hamilton, 1787).
>
> There are two passions which have a powerful influence on the affairs of men. These are ambition and avarice; the

love of power and the love of money (Benjamin Franklin, 1787).

From the nature of man, we may be sure that those who have power in their hands . . . will always, when they can . . . increase it (George Mason, 1787).

The Framers knew that a constitutional government could take many forms. Some have one ruler (monarchy), have a group of rulers (aristocracy), or are ruled by the people as a whole (republic). As long as those in power obey the limitations placed on them by the "higher law" of their constitution, these would be limited government. In history, there are examples of constitutional governments of all types—monarchies, republics, and democracies.

History has shown problems always emerge even in a constitutional government ruled by one person or a small group of people, say, one political party. All power in the hands of a few, especially an "enlightened" few, leads the limitations placed on them by a constitution to be ignored for our own good. Those in charge take it upon themselves to control the armed forces, local law forces, and tie local officials to the elites with hopes of joining the top echelon, or large funding to keep the locals under control. How can we citizens force them to obey the constitution?

The Framers had few options. They knew of the "democracies" of ancient Greece and cantons of Switzerland and the republics of Rome and Italian city-states of the Renaissance. They had lived under monarchy—rule by a king or queen—the most common form of government of their time. They wanted a government more representative of the diverse interests of the whole society. They felt the most obvious alternative and opposite to monarchy was a republic. However, there was great debate as to what exactly was "republican government." They knew from idealized versions of Roman history that it was government devoted to promoting the public good, common good, general welfare, the *res publicae*, Latin for "thing of the people." Power had to be shared by all or most of the citizens rather than held by a hereditary king or queen; power was to be exercised through the citizens' chosen representatives.

Today, many mistakenly use the terms "republican" and "democratic" government; we believe our government is both a republic and a democracy. The Framers knew better; they drew a sharp distinction between the two forms of government. Democracy is a form of government in which ultimate authority is based on the will of most voters/decision-makers. This majority usually consists of those in the community that have the greatest number of people—the Greek *demos*, meaning "people"—the poorer people. In its ideal form, democracy is government where members participate directly in their own lawmaking and usually very open transparent discussions.

Both Jefferson and Madison knew the dangers of democracy and "tyranny of the majority." Jefferson feared that promises of benefits would lead to demagogues that could buy elections. In his *Notes on the State of Virginia*, he felt "an elective despotism was not the government we fought for." Madison in *Federalist 10* was clear that history has shown that democracies have the symptoms of "instability, injustice, and confusion introduced into the public councils, have, in truth, been the mortal diseases under which popular governments have everywhere perished."

The Framers had lived nearly two hundred years under local democracies. During the time of England's distractions in Europe, local governments in the colonies tended to be democratic in nature; today's New England "town meetings" are the best example. Based on their reading of history and their own experience, many of the Framers (e.g., Hamilton) had seen democracy as the worst of governments but acceptable for the purpose of getting the masses to put the right people in office. We cannot understand the complete confusion of the use of the terms "democracy" and "republic" unless you see that these are mere tools, not ideals of the deep state. I quote from Bastiat's *Law* the only clear explication of today's deep state democracy.

> The strange phenomenon of our times [and ours]—one which will probably astound our descendants [exactly, why?]—is the doctrine based on this triple hypothesis: the total inertness of mankind, the omnipotence of the law, and the infallibility of the legislator. These three ideas form the sacred symbol of those who proclaim themselves totally democratic.
>
> The advocates of this doctrine also profess to be *social*. So far as they are democratic, they place unlimited faith in mankind. But so far as they are social, they regard mankind

as little better than mud. Let us examine this contrast in greater detail.

What is the attitude of the democrat when political rights are under discussion? How does he regard the people when a legislator is to be chosen? Ah, then it is claimed that the people have an instinctive wisdom [unless you vote the wrong way, deplorables]; they are gifted with the finest perception; their will is always right; the general will cannot err; voting cannot be too universal.

When it is time to vote, apparently the voter is not to be asked for any guarantee of his wisdom [nor an ID]. His will and capacity to choose wisely are taken for granted. Can the people be mistaken? Are we not living in an age of enlightenment? What! are the people always to be kept on leashes? Have they not won their rights by great effort and sacrifice? Have they not given ample proof of their intelligence and wisdom? Are they not adults? Are they not capable of judging for themselves? Do they not know what is best for themselves? Is there a class or a man who would be so bold as to set himself above the people, and judge and act for them? No, no, the people are and should be *free*. They desire to manage their own affairs, and they shall do so.

But when the legislator is finally elected—ah! then indeed does the tone of his speech undergo a radical change. The people are returned to passiveness, inertness, and unconsciousness; the legislator enters into omnipotence. Now it is for him to initiate, to direct, to propel, and to organize. Mankind has only to submit; the hour of despotism has struck. We now observe this fatal idea: The people who, during the election, were so wise, so moral, and so perfect, now have no tendencies whatever; or if they have any, they are tendencies that lead downward into degradation.

Why are we Republicans?

The Framers had been schooled and frankly idolized ancient Rome, the Roman Republic (509 BC to 27 BC). Many philosophers and historians believed the Roman Republic had provided Roman citizens with the most liberty under a government that the world had ever known. That might have been essentially true, relatively, since the rest of history showed them empires, theocracies, and slave societies. The "history" was that the Roman Republic promoted the common good—that is, what was best for the entire society. The Framers believed this type of government—classical republicanism—was best suited for a new people, with a new experiment of self-rule. Classical republicans believe the best kind of society is one that promotes the common good instead of the interests of only one class of citizens, special interests, the deep state, factions. In a classical republic, citizens and their government work cooperatively to achieve the common good rather than personal or selfish interests. The Roman Republic, short-lived and idyllic, was thought to be the best example of a republic.

The moral ideal of civic virtue and the nature of man were much debated before and during the Convention, as well as after and still today. Was man good and should be left alone, or bad and needed direction? Could we rely on man to act on his own for the common good or forced to do so? The difficulties they struggled with in attempting to apply those idealized principles to a new and changing American nation are the struggles we seem to be abrogating to professional rulers. Americans of the eighteenth century shared this view that citizens should work to promote the common good. They fought the revolution to bring this type of government and society into existence. The course of American history, as Lincoln stated in the Gettysburg Address, was to bring this to fruition.

The common good was only possible if the society and its citizens shared the following characteristics:

- civic virtue, restraint of self-interests
- moral education, civics
- small homogeneous communities

The classical republics demanded that their citizens have a high degree of civic virtue. A person with civic virtue was one who set aside personal interests to promote the common good, or general welfare as stated in the Preamble. Today we might describe this as "public spiritedness," patriotism. Citizens were expected to participate fully in their government to promote the common good—obey the law, vote, pay taxes, or hold office. They were not to be left free to devote themselves only to their personal interests, even to the point of spending less time doing such things as making money or caring for their families.

Classical republicanism differed from the natural rights philosophy in two key points, the nature of man and importance of individual rights. Classical republican idea of civic virtue conflicted with the Locke's natural rights philosophy and with Hobbes's understanding of human nature, both of which the Founders and Framers held, no matter how contradictory. The natural rights philosophy considered the rights of the individual to be primary in importance. The state existed to serve the interests (property) of the individual, instead of the other way around. In classical republicanism, the rights of the community as a whole, *res publica*, came first. In many cases, classical republics often drastically limited individuals' rights. There was little in the way of protection of an individual's privacy, freedom of conscience or religion, or nonpolitical speech or expression.

People who believe in classical republicanism are convinced that civic virtue is not something that comes automatically to people; citizens must be taught to be virtuous by moral education based on a civic religion consisting of gods, goddesses, and their rituals. Young citizens must be raised in a manner that develops the right habits. They should learn to admire the people with civic virtue described in literature, poetry, and music. The Framers themselves admired such heroes of antiquity as the Roman patriot and orator Cato and the citizen farmer/soldier Cincinnatus. The Founders believed they were examples of civic virtue whom Americans should emulate.

His fellow Americans admired George Washington as a modern-day Cincinnatus because he sacrificed his private pursuits to lead the nation in war and peace. George Washington was often called "our Cincinnatus" because his fellow citizens believed he was an example of the civic virtue that all citizens should possess.

Children should be encouraged—partly by the belief in a watchful God or gods—to practice virtues such as generosity, courage, self-control, and fairness. They should learn the importance of taking part in political debate and military service. The whole community must closely supervise the upbringing of the next generation of citizens and be attentive to how individuals behave in their daily lives.

One major issue that is boiling to the surface today is that maybe the United Sates has become too large. It is believed that republican government can only work in small communities where people know and care for each other and their local common good. People must be very much alike; a great degree of diversity should not be tolerated. People should be very different in their wealth, religious or moral beliefs, or ways of life.

Classical republicans believed that if people differed greatly, they would divide into factions or interest groups rather than work together for the common good. To prevent this, citizens should be encouraged, by education and example, to avoid the development of great differences in their ownership of property, religion, and way of life. To prevent diversity in religious beliefs and lifestyles, they believed the community should have an official, state-supported religion and one set of family and moral standards to which all must conform.

Great inequalities of wealth led inevitably to corruption as well as to factions or interest groups. Individuals would be more concerned with their own interest rather than the interest of the community. Fear of great economic inequality and the corrupting effect of luxury led many classical republicans to be wary of money-making and economic growth. Such economic growth, they thought, gave rise to the great economic inequality, which was inconsistent with the goals of republicanism. Madison felt factions, later even political parties, emerged from difference in property.

In addition to the example of the ancient Roman Republic, the Founders also learned about republican government from writers of their own time. One of the most important of these was the Baron de Montesquieu (1689–1755), the French writer who was widely admired by Americans.

Montesquieu, as you recall, advocated a system that divided and balanced the power of government among the classes. This, he believed, was the best way to ensure that the government would not be dominated by a single social class and would be able to enhance the common good.

He admired the Roman Republic as a representative government that combined elements of three basic types of government: monarchy, aristocracy, and democracy. Since all classes shared power, this type of government seemed best for serving the common good. Even though Britain was a monarchy, Montesquieu admired the British constitution.

He believed it embodied the idea of a mixed government in which power was divided among different classes in British society. He also believed that the best societies were those of common descent; today that would be called segregation.

In some respects, the Framers were too uncritical of the Roman Republic. They were tended to overstate how Rome truly represented the interests of the community rather than just the interests of the rulers. They overlooked slavery upon which the ancient republics depended. Women had little authority, and war was the major product of the state. Yet most were well aware of the difficulty in grafting ideals of government to the reality of newly independent American states. They debated the degree to which these ideals could be adopted. Jefferson felt it would work in small, uniform agricultural communities. Hamilton believed Jefferson's was a pipe dream of an idealist.

Some of the more pressing adaptations of classical republicanism in the "modern" world of this new American experiment:

- caring for each other and the common good in small communities (civic virtue)
- believing that people must be very much alike (immigration, how much)
- supervising citizens to avoid the development of great differences among them in their ownership of property, religion, and way of life (role of public education)
- believing that great economic inequality is destructive of the common good (class development and inequality)
- having one official "established" religion and one set of family and moral standards that everyone would follow (diversity and assimilation)

Today the lack of character has diminished and on the way to destroying the American dream, the idea that man can rule himself prosperously, peacefully, and noncoercively. Lawrence Reed, president of the Foundation of Economic Education and author of numerous books and countless articles, writes that "bad character leads to bad economics, which is bad for liberty."

Even among the most ardent supporters of free-market causes are people who "leak" when it comes to their own bottom lines. A recent example was the corn farmer who berated me for opposing ethanol subsidies. Does he not understand basic economics? I've known him for years, and I believe he does. But that understanding melted away with the corrupting lure of a handout. His extensive economics knowledge was not enough to keep him from the public trough. We are losing the sense of shame that once accompanied the act of theft, private or public.

The missing ingredient here is character. In America's first century, we possessed it in abundance and even though there were no think tanks, very little economic education, and even less policy research, it kept our liberties substantially intact. People generally opposed the expansion of government power not because they read policy studies or earned degrees in economics, but because they placed a high priority on character. Using government to get something at somebody else's expense, or mortgaging the future for near-term gain, seemed dishonest and cynical to them, if not downright sinful and immoral.

Within government, character is what differentiates a politician from a statesman. Statesmen don't seek public office for personal gain or attention. They often are people who take time out from productive careers to temporarily serve the public. They don't have to work for government because that's all they know how to do. They stand for a principled vision, not for what they think citizens will fall for. When a statesman gets elected, he doesn't forget the public-spirited citizens who sent him to office, becoming a mouthpiece for the permanent bureaucracy or some special interest that greased his campaign.

Because they seek the truth, statesmen are more likely to do what's right than what may be politically popular at the moment. You know where they stand because they say what they mean and they mean what they say. They do not engage in class warfare, race-baiting, or other divisive or partisan tactics that pull people apart. They do not buy votes with tax dollars. They don't make promises they can't keep or intend to break. They take responsibility for their actions. A statesman doesn't try to pull himself up by dragging somebody else down, and he doesn't try to convince people they're victims just so he can posture as their savior.

When it comes to managing public finances, statesmen prioritize. They don't behave as though government deserves an endlessly larger share of other people's money. They exhibit the courage to cut less important expenses to make way for more pressing ones. They don't try to build empires. Instead, they keep government within its proper bounds and trust in what free and enterprising people can accomplish. Politicians think that they're smart enough to plan other people's lives; statesmen are wise enough to understand what utter folly such arrogant attitudes really are. Statesmen, in other words, possess a level of character that an ordinary politician does not.

By almost any measure, the standards we as citizens keep and expect of those we elect have slipped badly in recent years. Though everybody complains about politicians who pander, perhaps they do it because we are increasingly a panderable people. Too many are willing to look the other way when politicians misbehave, as long as they are of the right party or deliver the goods we personally want.

Our celebrity-drenched culture focuses incessantly on the vapid and the irresponsible. Our role models would make our grandparents cringe. To many, insisting on sterling character seems too straight-laced and old-fashioned. We cut corners and sacrifice character all the time for power, money, attention, or other ephemeral gratifications.

Yet character is ultimately more important than all the college degrees, public offices, or even all the knowledge that one might accumulate in a lifetime. It puts both a concrete floor under one's future and an iron ceiling over it. Who in their right mind would want to live in a world without it?

Chief among the elements that define strong character are these: honesty, humility, responsibility, self-discipline, self-reliance, optimism, a long-term focus, and a lust for learning. A free society is impossible without them. For example: dishonest people will lie and cheat and become even bigger liars and cheaters in elected office; people who lack humility become arrogant, condescending, know-it-all central-planner-types; irresponsible citizens blame others for the consequences of their own poor judgment; people who will not discipline themselves invite the intrusive control of others; those who eschew self-reliance are easily manipulated by those on whom they are dependent; pessimists dismiss what individuals can accomplish when given the freedom to try; myopic citizens will mortgage their future for the sake of a short-term "solution"; and closed-minded, politically correct or head-in-the-sand types will never learn from the lessons of history and human action.

How was a political ideal based on small, tightly knit communities to be applied to a new country as large as the young United States, which represented people of different ethnic cultural backgrounds, economic conditions, and religious beliefs? Americans of the founding era seemed more representative of human nature as described by the natural rights philosophers than the ideal expected by the civic virtue of the classical republicanism. They and their ancestors had come to the new land to take advantage of the opportunities it offered. Such restless, diverse, and ambitious people were ill suited for the ideals of self-sacrifice and conformity of a classical republic.

James Madison was one of the most important Framers, sometimes called "the father of the Constitution," though what will come out of the Convention was not a nationalist constitution but rather exactly the opposite of what he wanted, a Federalist one. (He will, after listening to the Virginia ratification debates, and fellow Virginians Henry and Jefferson, come to support it, even against an attempt by Adams and the Federalists to move it closer to a nationalist document.) He was very influential in translating the ideals of classical republicanism to the new American Republic. Madison knew democracy was impractical to civil society and a republic was impractical to the new experiment if too large: In a democracy, people administer the government themselves. These "direct democracies" may be effective for small communities like the ancient city-states of Greece, or for small decisions like allowing chickens to be raised in town. In a republic, the people's wishes are administered and addressed by elected representatives. This could work for a larger area.

Madison not only believed America must have a republican form of government but also had faith man was capable of having one. Laws would be made and enforced by representatives elected by the people democratically. He wanted members of government elected by a large number of the people rather than by a small number or a specially favored group not controlled by a select few. Such a form of government was a "democracy" in the sense that it derived its authority—its right to govern—from We, the People. Madison's new republican government, therefore, also could be defined as a representative democracy. In this way, the two classical ideas of republic and democracy were adapted to the new form of government created by the Framers.

Like Jefferson, Madison knew this type of government would be a failure unless an informed and public-spirited citizenry selected their representatives. He had to modify the classic definition of civic virtue to make it practical in the very different conditions in various parts of America. He accepted the natural rights philosophers' view of human nature—people were motivated primarily by self-interest. He also believed that the pursuit of self-interest could, if done ethically, promote the common good. For example, a statesman's desire for fame and admiration from others would lead him to practice civic virtue. The common good could be served by each individual pursuing his or her economic self-interest. Each would contribute to the general prosperity, very similar to the "invisible hand" of Adam Smith.

Madison also realized that as people pursue their own interests, they sometimes act against the interests of others and against the common good. Any sound government had to make allowances for this, courts that protected contracts and punished fraud. As we saw before, Madison knew if all people were angels, there would be no need for government. He argued for a government that would encourage people to act as good republican citizens possessing the quality of civic virtue; he, like Jefferson, believed that was the purpose of public education. At the same time, this government would guard against the consequences if they did not. This is why Madison favored a constitution that limited government by separation of powers, checks and balances, and Federalism.

The American adaptation of the principles of classical republicanism was, then, a sort of compromise. The Founders created a form of government they called republican, even though it was different from the models of republicanism in the ancient world. They believed that it was important for citizens to possess civic virtue; however, civic virtue could not always be relied upon. Therefore, the proper structure provided by a system of representation with separation of powers and checks and balances also was necessary to protect the common good.

Under a republican form of government, if elected officials hold views of the common good contrary to those of their constituents, what do you think the officials should do? Why? Should a member of Congress vote against antismoking legislation intended to protect the health of the general population if it would hurt the economy of his or her state and put people out of work in that state? Isn't that a decision for the owners and her customers? To what extent do you think the common good in today's American society depends on the classical republican ideal of civic virtue, and to what extent on the natural rights philosophy idea of everyone pursuing his or her own self-interest?

What is the common welfare?

Republican government promotes the common welfare. But what is the common welfare? This is not always an easy question to answer. Different people have had and will continue to have very different ideas about what the common welfare is. The Founders, however, believed that a government that promotes the common welfare is one that protects each individual's natural rights. As we saw with Monsieur Rousseau, the common welfare, he called the general will, is what is best for the whole of society. His general will actually exists, and all must submit to it. Since there is a general will, there is no place for differences of opinion, desires, pursuits of happiness, "only one supreme good and a single overriding goal toward which a community must aim. The general will is always a force of the good and the just. It is independent, totally sovereign, infallible, and inviolable."

In politics, this means all powers, persons, and their rights are under control and wishes of the community; no one can do anything without the consent of all; all are completely dependent on everybody for all aspects of their lives. This monolithic dependency eliminates the possibility of independent individual achievement and inequality of property and wealth. In addition, when the individual joins society to escape death or starvation, he can be a sacrificial victim ready to give up his life for others. Life, liberty, and even individual happiness are all gifts of the state.

In 1962, the SDS (Students for a Democratic Society) under the influence of Marxist Herbert Marcuse (1898–1979) called this Rousseauian power grab "participatory democracy." All power is exercised by an omnipotent, omniscient central authority or sovereign that is the total community. Major decisions are made by a vote by all in "plebiscites," an annual town or school board meeting, yet no debate is allowed. Lawmakers, the legislative branch, may propose laws but decide on them. They are "an intellectual elite" body that works out carefully worded alternatives, brings people together, and has people vote with the results binding on all. The authority of these lawmakers is their superior insight, charisma, virtue, and mysticism. The legislator words the propositions of the plebiscite so that the "right" decision will result. The right decisions are those that change human nature, the new Socialist man. That's why Emile, his book on educational indoctrination, is still so popular today in training teachers. Education, as Marx, Lenin, Mussolini, Stalin all agreed, is the major institution, not the family, in socializing the members of the general will. All unlimited power of the state is legitimized by "consent" of the majority.

> The education of all children, from the moment that they can get along without a mother's care, shall be in state institutions at state expense (Karl Marx, *The Communist Manifesto*).

Give me four years to teach the children and the seed I have sown will never be uprooted (Vladimir Lenin).

Education is a weapon, whose effect depends on who holds it in his hands and at whom it is aimed (Josef Stalin).

It is the State which educates its citizens in civic virtue, gives them a consciousness of their mission, and welds them into unity (Benito Mussolini).

THE MARKET ECONOMY VERSUS
A PLANNED ECONOMY

Beware the greedy hand of government thrusting itself
into every corner and crevice of industry.
—Thomas Paine

WHY IS A chapter on economics stuck in the middle of a book on government? Well, in a "state of nature," man lives without government supposedly, but he cannot live without economics. Bastiat, writing these words shortly before his death on Christmas Eve, 1850, felt the instruments of freedom, life, liberty, property, being all economic, preceded the establishment of government, thus we should begin there. Economic liberty preceded political liberty, and I always started my lectures with the Nelson Mandela quote, "There is no such thing as part freedom."

A science of economics must be developed before a science of politics can be logically formulated. Essentially, economics is the science of determining whether the interests of human beings are harmonious or antagonistic. This must be known before a science of politics can be formulated to determine the proper functions of government.

Immediately following the development of a science of economics, and at the very beginning of the formulation of a science of politics, this all-important question must be answered: What is law? What ought it to be? What is its scope; its limits? Logically, at what point do the just powers of the legislator stop?

I do not hesitate to answer: *Law is the common force organized to act as an obstacle of injustice.* In short, *law is justice.*

Rousseau observed that although life was peaceful in the state of nature, people were unfulfilled. Like Aristotle, they need others to find that fulfillment. But once with others, kind of like Adam and Eve (Garden of Eden, the ultimate state of nature), their eyes are opened, and evil, greed, and the self emerge; people "become" bad. The worst part of this selfishness is private property, which encourages even more greed and self-interest. As all central planners, he saw private property as destructive, impulsive (Keynesian "animal spirits"?), and egotistical, rewarding greed and luck. Society was born. People began fencing off their property, "homesteading," claiming a piece of nature as theirs, finding other people who agreed.

Yet, as all know, talents are evenly or equally possessed. Life is one of inequality. The more talented, able, and intelligent people brought about advances in science, technology, commerce, and so on. However, people are born with certain natural endowments: no one can benefit or not from talents or lack of them. He recognized that talent leads to further achievement, leading to more inequality as the more talented produced more, better, and cheaper, and earned more. His Socialism failed to see the "invisible hand" of incentives, profit, and loss, the imagination of the bourgeoisie ethic to benefit others to make more.

Ludwig von Mises (1881–1973), the well-known economist, wrote prolifically and with great clarity about the advantages of a market economy over an economy with state allocation of resources. Indeed, in 1922, he demonstrated that Socialism of any kind cannot survive as an economic system. This became clear to the world with the fall of the Iron Curtain in 1989, exposing an economic system that had been unable to provide a decent standard of living for people and left the environment in shambles. Closer to home, the Housing Bubble Crash of 2008 and continuing as of this writing the Great Recession showed that any governmental interference in the economy causes many unintended consequences, leading to further and further interventions by planners.

Mises had been correct. Free markets allocate resources efficiently, sending things because of prices to those who most value them. This demand for things is unlimited, but we live in a limited world. What should be made? How? Who gets it? It is consumers like you and me and the billions across the globe that determine prices of goods and services, thus setting wages and costs and answering these questions. Rousseau's inequality is true. It does come from inequality of talents, motivations, and entrepreneurship. And the distribution of income is generally fair in a market economy. And in a republican government of political liberty, the free market, capitalism if you like, is the only method of organizing society to allocate resources consistent with the laws of nature and individual liberty.

Capitalism

The free market is defined as private or corporate ownership of capital goods and monies used and determined by private decision makers, not some central "general will." Sometimes called by the French term *laissez-faire*, it is a theory whereby government plays the role of referee, very limited and hands-off; its proper role of government in economics is limited to promoting and protecting, a la Locke private property by ensuring no fraud, contract violation, or cronyism. What are the key elements of this system sometimes called "classical liberalism"?

Individual initiative. As all men are born free politically, all are free to work, start and run their own businesses, and consume what they want.

Private ownership. Part and parcel of individual freedom and initiative is the right to own the resources to produce goods or services and to dispose of these goods as one wishes to whomever one wishes. These resources, inputs, or factors of production are the basic resources used to make all goods and services. One factor of production is land, which in economic terms includes all natural resources, stuff made by God. Labor is the work done by individuals to produce goods and services and earn incomes (wages) to purchase the things they desire. Capital includes all the human-made resources; these are created by some combination of labor, land, and maybe other capital goods. Someone who owns capital and puts it to productive use is called a capitalist, a derogatory term of Marx. I prefer bourgeois or innovator. An entrepreneur, "undertaker," is an individual with the drive and ambition to combine land, labor, and capital resources to produce goods or offer services that people want. If he satisfies others' desires, he gains profits. If not, he "gains losses." Mises will say that the general welfare rests on private property, nothing else.

Profit. The "profit motive" is the desire to gain from business dealings. Profit is the amounts of money you earn from the business once costs incurred running the business have been subtracted, if successful in providing others with what they wish. Profits and losses come to you if you are doing the right things or the wrong things, respectively. Resources are efficiently used for what people most desire. All are better off. Losses and eventually bankruptcy reallocate mistakes of the poor capitalists to those more successful. This success saves resources, allocates to those that want, motivates, or incentivizes; for my economist readers, innovation, higher standards for all, and a better world.

Competition. Competition has Progressives tied in apoplectic knots. Unlike Rousseau, social arrangements require cooperation. I plant corn, Susan collects water, and Jami builds decks. By cooperating, we all trade and get richer! This situation works; it's what makes the state of nature slip away to social, political, economic organization. Competition is when men are free to create better, cheaper, or both goods and services to gain the profit of another. Oh! Someone is losing! I guess I must concede; not all get better off. Deidre McCloskey called it "Win, win, win, win, win, lose!" But society is better off; time and resources are being wasted with the capitalist that was wrong; she didn't get it. She tried to do the "follow your passion" plan of action. No one agreed, or at least not enough that her efforts were not rewarded. She is wasting paint on posters that others are willing to pay for to paint their sheds.

Mises sums up the both profits, I mean losses, and competition and the benefit bestowed on all, rich and poor alike.

> The direction of all economic affairs is in the market society a task of the entrepreneurs. Theirs is the control of production. They are at the helm and steer the ship. A superficial observer would believe that they are supreme. But they are not. They are bound to obey unconditionally the captain's orders. The captain is the consumer. Neither the entrepreneurs nor the farmers nor the capitalists determine

what has to be produced. The consumers do that. If a businessman does not strictly obey the orders of the public as they are conveyed by structure of market prices, he suffers losses, he goes bankrupt, and is thus removed from his eminent position at the helm. Other men who did better in satisfying the demand of the consumers replace him.

Command economies

Any economy that is not free is "hampered." It wastes resources; without prices, there can be no way to know if we are producing the right thing the right way. Economies that are not free are all forms of Socialism. They go by different names based on techniques of implementation, but the goals are the same: centralized control, the general will, hampers individuals' ability to choose. Economics is not a machine to be tweaked; like politics, society, language, it emerges from human actions, though NOT human design. Hayek called it spontaneous order.

Socialism, Communism, Fascism, Progressivism all are command economies; someone else decides your well-being. All place enterprises under government control, often by taking over privately owned industries, is called nationalization. Socialists aim to guarantee the public welfare by providing for the equal distribution of necessities and services. Because social welfare services are quite expensive, taxes in Socialist countries tend to be high and "progressive"; the rich pay higher percentages, not just higher amounts. In a centrally planned economy, government officials, bureaucrats, technocrats today, plan how an economy will develop over a period of years.

A Democratic Socialist, an oxymoron, may or may not endorse strict central planning, but still chains down the individual with the regulatory state. Regulations today cost $2 trillion annually, or $15,785 extra for each American; that's the US SBA's (Small Business Administration) numbers. Add $16,000 to your pension, paycheck, Social Security payments. Some economists call this a "mixed" economy; many call the US economy mixed. Yet there is no such thing as part free. Deidre McCloskey in her trilogy's third volume, *Bourgeois Equality*, lays open the dissection of both sides of equality—equal opportunity, equal results.

The ideas of equality led to other social and political movements not uniformly adorable. Hannah Arendt remarked in 1951 that "equality of condition . . . is . . . among the greatest and most uncertain ventures of modern mankind." Alexis de Tocqueville had said much the same a century earlier. And Scottish equality has a harsh, even tragic, side. It entails equal reward for equal merit in a marketplace in which others, by freedom of contract, can also compete. As John Stuart Mill put it in *On Liberty*, "society admits no right, either legal or moral, in the disappointed competitors to immunity from . . . suffering [from successful competition]; and feels called on to interfere only when means of success have been employed which it is contrary to the general interest to permit—namely, fraud or treachery, and force." An ill-advised and undercapitalized pet store, into which the owner pours his soul, goes under. In the same neighborhood a little independent office for immediate health care opens half a block from a branch of the largest hospital chain in Chicago, and seems doomed to fail the test of voluntary trade. Although the testing of business ideas in voluntary trade is obviously necessary for betterment in the economy (as it is too by non-monetary tests for betterment in art and science and scholarship), such failures are deeply sad, if you have the slightest sympathy for human projects, or for humans. But at least the pet store, the health-treatment office, the Edsel, Woolworth's, Polaroid, and Pan American Airlines face the same democratic test by trade: Do the customers keep coming forward voluntarily?

We could all by state compulsion backed by the monopoly of violence remain in the same jobs as our ancestors, perpetually "protected" at $3 a day. Or, with taxes taken by additional state compulsion, we could subsidize new activities without regard to a test by voluntary trade, "creating jobs" as the anti-economic rhetoric has it. Aside even from their immediate effect of lowering national income, such ever-popular plans—never mind, too, the objectionable character of the state's compulsion they require—seldom work in the long run for the welfare of the poor, or the rest of us. In view of the way a government of imperfect people actually behaves in practice, the job "protection" and job "creation" often fail to achieve their gentle, generous purpose. The protections and creations get diverted to favorites. In a society of lords or clan members or Communist Party officials or even voters restricted by inconvenient voting times and picture IDs the unequal and involuntary rewards generated by sidestepping the test of trade are seized by the privileged. The privileged are good at that.

The double ideas of liberty and dignity, summarized as Scottish equality, or political liberalism in a mid-nineteenth-century definition, mattered as causes of the Great Enrichment more than any fresh material incentives, real or fancied—they mattered more than wars or trade or empire or financial markets or accumulation or high wages or high science. The Bourgeois Revaluation led to a Bourgeois Deal. "Let me creatively destroy the old and bad ways of doing things, the scythes, ox carts, oil lamps, propeller planes, film cameras, and factories lacking high-tech robots, and I will make you rich."

Myths of Socialism

Maybe the caption should read "Lies of Socialism." These are the things children, your children are being taught. Some are lies about capitalism; others are the lies of false dreams of Socialism. But all have led generations from freedom toward Friedrich Hayek's road to serfdom. Our children's and grandchildren's futures cannot be a lie; one hundred million humans have perished under the glories of Socialism. As we've seen recently, Communism is thriving on America's college campuses; yet without the freedom of the market, Socialism wouldn't be possible. As Margaret Thatcher, former prime minister of Great Britain, said, "Socialist governments traditionally do make a financial mess. They always run out of other people's money."[1]

But it doesn't stop there; as many as 94 percent of college professors are useful dupes for Communism. Grover Furr, a professor of Medieval English at Montclair State University, New Jersey, denied Stalin was responsible for the murder of millions, saying he has "yet to find one crime—one crime that Stalin committed . . . I know they say he killed 20, 30, 40 million people, but it's bullshit." Your taxes created the next generation of Socialist apologists.

Most students are in college on someone else's dime. State universities are funded by taxpayers. In-state tuition is subsidized by money confiscated by property owners in the form of property taxes, sales taxes, and state income taxes.

Most young people grow up under Socialism. Everything is paid for them—food, clothing, shelter—by someone else—namely, their parents. They expect their parents to pay for their college education as well, and when they can't afford it, it's off to government-backed loans and grants and subsidized tuition.

Remember the quotes before of Mussolini, Stalin, and Lenin about education? They, like today's Progressives, are reading right out of the *Communist Manifesto*. In addition to "a heavy progressive or graduated income tax" is "free education for all children in public schools." "Free education comes with a price—bondage to the state.

Income equality. Capitalism leads to inequality and a downtrodden class. Socialism believes everyone contributes an equal amount and equally shares the rewards. But what we've seen under the regimes of Hitler, Stalin China, North Korea, and Cuba is that everyone is equally poor. Some people work harder than others. Some are willing to let others do work for them. Not recognizing this aspect of human nature and rewarding everyone equally regardless of merit breed resentment, envy, and laziness. The result is no innovation and little economic growth.

Capitalism is evil. As above, capitalism is the cause of the ills of today's societies—inequality, poverty, discrimination, unemployment, and rising prices. So let the state provide and take care of you by setting "living wages" and forcing companies to charge "reasonable prices" for necessities of life. Prices are a measure of perceived value at a moment in time. When government steps in and lowers (or increases) prices to "make goods more available," it limits the ability of entrepreneurs to know what customers actually need. Prices are information of what people need more (or less) of; Socialism gives bread lines, soup kitchens, and misery.

"Democratic" Socialism. An oxymoron that promises to make our economy grow. Venezuela had an eighteen-year experiment with democratic Socialism; one of the richest countries in the world with oil, its people now struggle to find food, medicines, even toilet paper. Inflation has skyrocketed to 720 percent; its currency has lost 93 percent of its value in the past two years. Its supermarkets are without adequate food, and they now must import oil, incapable of producing anything from their own reserves.

Equality for all in a class-free society. We all were born with different DNA, talents, motivations, and dreams. It is impossible for a few elites or bureaucrats to know the individual needs, wants, dream, and desires of millions of people. Their one-size-fits-all plans conflict with people's personal goals. Inevitably, it requires forced compliance and restrictions on freedom to execute "the plan." "You will be forced to be free . . . resistance is futile."

Free college education, free health care. These are considered rights, not in the form of opportunities but as unalienable as life, liberty, and property. And all will pay their fair share. Everyone benefits! Nothing of value can be free; everything has a cost, trade-off. Using the power of the state to confiscate wealth from one person to give to another does not make a good or service free. It distorts the market's ability through prices to assign realistic values. Providing tuition or health care for free causes too much demand for those services. This creates shortages, meaning those who really need them are less likely to get them, as "consumers" are chosen by political connections rather than true demand.

End boom-and-bust cycles. Socialism claims to end the economic downturns and disruptions common to market economies. The business cycle occurs because of government interference in the market—printing money, monetary and fiscal policies, deficits, and debts. Socialism kills economic growth by penalizing success and rewarding failure. Wealth tends to accumulate in politically connected hands in Socialist economies. As more and more are identified as "in need" of other people's money, the more the successful are penalized. That means fewer jobs and even greater need. As in Greece, and now in Venezuela, this vicious cycle continues until the economy is so weak it can't produce enough to function.

Everyone is entitled to material goods. The state will ensure all people get them. If the state is in the business of picking winners and losers, we end up with a favored elite with access to special privileges denied to the masses. When some benefit off of others, that's not capitalism; that's *crapitalism*, crony capitalism.

Workers are liberated. Instead of having the excess of workers' production going to a capitalist, boss, everyone will cheerfully work for the good of society. Well, workers are subject to the orders of the state, and their earnings are redistributed by the state for any purpose the state wishes; they now do what they're told rather than for their wages. They can no longer bargain with their employer because the employer is subjected to the requests of the state for the good of the majority/ collective.

Socialism works in Sweden. Democratic Socialism has created a workers' paradise in Sweden, making it the envy of the Western world, or is it Denmark or Cuba? Reality is that today, Sweden has a long way to go on the road to economic freedom but is overcoming the damage done by a decade of Socialism through an agenda of deregulation, free trade, a national school voucher system, partially privatized pensions, elimination of property and inheritance taxes, and reduction of corporate taxes. Quality medical care in Cuba is a favorite Socialist myth. In fact, only government officials and foreign visitors, useful idiots, have access to the kind of medical care Americans take for granted. Socialism in the end is failure to the common good.

How does the free market interact with the free republic? Did the rhetoric of bourgeois—innovation, profit creates wealth for all, that freedom does not come out of a barrel of a gun, rather a basket of goods—cause the political revolution? Or did the political upheaval break ground for freedom of the market and the liberation of the poor? We know the "industrial revolution," though not recognized by even economists at the time, first began in Britain and spread to the rest of northern Europe and most amazingly in North America.

We now know that it wasn't just the gift of natural resources, land, because land has become irrelevant in the explosion of wealth—in 1776, the average wage was three dollars per day; today nearly $140. It is the mind, imagination, of man that is the one important factor of production. The environmentalists are wrong! Even Thomas Malthus, the doomsayer of mankind, the environmentalists' source along with

Rachel Carson, changed his mind in his second edition of his *An Essay of the Principle of Population* (1803). It was not inevitable that man was doomed. His imagination knows no bounds, if unhampered, unfettered. It was not man that was his own worst enemy but tyranny. His student in 1843 extended this most succinctly.

> The only persons by whom any other opinion seemed to be entertained, were those that prophesized advancements in physical knowledge and mechanical art [man's ingenuity], sufficient to alter the fundamental conditions of man's existence on earth [three dollars to over one hundred dollars]; or who professed the doctrine, that poverty is a factitious [caused by man, not an ordained] thing, produced by the tyranny and rapacity of governments and of the rich.

That John Stuart Mill was not one of optimism for the first, ingenuity, but knew the second, the end of tyranny of the mind, would be the liberator of the poor. It began in England and Scotland and then spread west. Let's go west!

But today, polls show that over half of college students prefer Socialism to capitalism, or at least what they've been told by leftist universities. Students are told that capitalism is out-of-date, that "government can make our society, and us, better." It's not true from any statistical, observational, or historical perspective. Government, since the rise of Progressivism in the late nineteenth and early twentieth centuries, has stolen from one group of citizenship to redistribute, through democracy, by regulation, taxation, and inflation.

HISTORY BEHIND THE EXPERIMENT

To know nothing of what happened before you
were born, is to forever remain a child.
—Cicero

MANY OF THE ideas of our great experiment in freedom
are really reactions to historical experience. The thought
of man being free, natural rights, and self-government as we have
already seen are not recent ideas. From Socrates through the Romans,
into the Enlightenment of France and Scotland, men were developing
foundations and rationales to build that great house we will call Western
society. America took those ideals and in a land where freedom cannot
help to grow, a New Jerusalem some called it, and built man's first
attempt to live free or die.

In England, the struggles between divine right and natural rights,
between Puritans and Catholics, between kings and Parliament, sowed
the seeds in man of a New World. With the addition of the Indian
cultures in America, something will germinate, something great. Man's
thirst to be what he was meant to be.

Many of these ideals will emerge edited in Jefferson's Declaration
of why government exists and why it was necessary to tell the world
we were creating an experiment of man living free to pursue what God
placed him here.

The beginnings of English government

For the first thousand or so years after the birth of Christ, England
was divided into warring tribes, each ruled by its own leader or king.
Many invasions kept the island unstable economically and politically.
The early kings were selected by councils of advisers because they were

the strongest and most powerful members of the tribes. Eventually, these tribes were conquered and became subject to one king. Many know the story of St. Patrick converting the Irish Celts to Christianity; these now Irish Catholics spread to England, and England became a Christian country. The kings claimed that the source of their authority was the will of God, *Deus Vult*. This is the "divine right of kings." The people were subject to the king's rule—thus his subjects. The king exercised absolute control with the help of a council of trusted advisers. These councillors were often placed in charge of large sections of England to manage the people. Like they will later in their North American colonies, the monarchs allowed these landlords to control their own local areas based on the customs that had developed over the years. Local control of what mattered most to the inhabitants was done locally.

Feudal government

In the summer of 1066, the king of "Angleland," or England, died. He had three relatives next in line for the throne. On October 14, 1066, William the Conqueror, the leader of the Normans (Vikings), invaded England from Normandy and defeated his cousin King Harold at the Battle of Hastings. He brings with him a system from the end of the Roman Empire to rule his large and diverse area, to settle down the land, and to hear local disputes. His first order of business to accomplish this was for him and his knights to count the people and record the lands—for taxation and control. These records were written down in the *Domesday Book* (pronounced "Doomsday"); his continental land order we call feudalism.

The feudal system had the following characteristics:

- The people of the nation were classified as belonging to one of three groups, called orders. These were (a) royalty, which included the king and queen and their family; (b) the nobility, which included the lords and ladies who were the major followers of the king or queen and who held titles such as earl or baron, and thus were granted land and the people living there; and (c) the commons or common people, made up of such different groups as knights, merchants, and peasants. At that time, the peasants or serfs were not free socially, economically, politically, or familiarly, and were forced to work on the land.

- All the territory of England was considered to belong to the king or queen. Everyone living in the kingdom was subject to the monarch's rule.
- Because there was so much territory to control, the king or queen gave some of the responsibility for governing the kingdom to the nobility. The nobles could control parts of the royal territory and the common people who lived upon it in exchange for military service. This convenient sharing of power by royalty with the nobility eventually led to the development of a different kind of government as you will soon learn.
- Common law codes developed with judges deciding cases based on experience or precedent. This differed from civil law codes on the continent developed from Roman law, which was written law. The written law could change when new councils met, but precedent was based on local traditions, which tend to be more stubbornly held to.

The Magna Carta

One of the most important changes in the government of England took place in 1215. This date is important in the development of constitutional government in England because in that year, the power of the king became limited by a written document called the Magna Carta.

By this time, it had become traditional for the kings and queens of England to share some of their powers with the nobility. This had been given by Henry I in 1100 in the Charter of Liberties. It consented to bind the monarch to specific laws about the treatment of clergy and nobles. It will set a precedent for laws limiting the authority of English kings, and our presidents.

Yet in 1215, King John tried to take back some of the rights and powers the nobles had grown accustomed to having. The result was a war between the nobles and their king, a war between divine rights and a social contract, a war that the nobles won. It was actually a peace treaty, an agreement, a contract between the monarch and his nobles.

The nobles then forced King John to sign the Magna Carta. It listed traditional rights of the nobles that the king could not take from them; many of these rights went back ages before William, before Harold, before the Roman invasions to the Druids, the builders of Stonehenge. Some of the rights guaranteed included (a) the freedom of the church from the control of the king; (b) the independence of the courts of England, justice was not for sale, see Article 40 of the *Great Charter* in reference section; (c) the right of people who owned land to pass it on to their oldest son; (d) the right of people who owned land to a fair trial; (e) the right to travel; and (f) the freedom from unnecessary searches of their homes. This is in no way the beginning of a republic or democracy that we see later in England; the nobles sought only specific remedies for specific abuses and not the abuses they were imposing on the commons.

Government should be based on the rule of law, due process; rights may not be denied by a king. The most essential of these rights was the right of habeas corpus, written into Chapter 39 of the Charter. Anyone taken into custody can ask a judge for a writ of habeas corpus. It is a summons by a court to the custodian or jailor of a defendant to bring the defendant before the court to determine if the defendant is being legally detained. The purpose of habeas corpus is to prevent illegal detention and allow the due process of law to determine innocence, guilt, and punishment. *Habeas corpus* is Latin for "You (shall) have the body."

This version of the Magna Carta never took full effect. A new war between John and the nobles. By September 1215, the barons had garrisoned Rochester Castle in opposition to the king, while John had successfully petitioned the Vatican to have the Magna Carta annulled and all the rebels excommunicated. In 1225, the new king, nine-year-old Henry III, reissued an abridged version of the Magna Carta as his own coronation charter, sixty-nine clauses reduced to twenty-seven. However, by the mid-twentieth century, only three clauses remained: freedom to the Church of England, guarantee the customs and liberties of the city of London, and the important habeas corpus. While we may worship it as the step of many steps in our political history, it is an amusement in British law.

Though early English customs and traditions and the Magna Carta protected certain basic rights, it is important to know that these rights did not apply to all of the people of England. Men who owned property were given far more rights than were women or children or others without property. This was because of the idea that they paid the taxes, thus their rights were valid in relation to the Crown. No taxation without representation? No representation without having paid your taxes. See the Twenty-Fourth Amendment. Today in America, the Magna Carta is often used as the starting point in the race for liberty; yet today, it no longer pertains to the "king or his advisors."

Conflicts between the kings and their nobles continued after the signing of the Magna Carta. The Magna Carta showed how a written document or constitution could be used to place limits on governmental power. The next great change in the English government resulted in the separation of its powers.

In 1258, King Henry III and the nobles agreed to create a new council, called Parliament (from the French "to speak to the mountain") to advise the king. During the next thirty years, Parliament became the branch of government that represented the most powerful orders or groups in the kingdom. In 1295, Edward I, "Long Shanks," the king that will fight the great Scotsman William Wallace, called it the Model Parliament. This Parliament was made up of two houses: House of Lords, which represented the interests of the nobility; and House of Commons, which represented the common people. However, remember at this time the common people were mainly people who owned large amounts of land or businesses but were not members of the nobility. His reason for calling it the Model Parliament was to raise taxes and for men to continue his wars against the French and the Scots.

> What touches all, should be approved of all, and it is also clear that common dangers should be met by measures agreed upon in common . . .

King James Bible

The religious struggle for the control of man's heart, or the money of the church for you cynics, culminated in the separation under Henry VIII. Based on Henry VIII's desire for an annulment of his marriage, the English Reformation was at the outset more a political affair than a theological dispute. The reality of political differences between Rome and England allowed growing theological disputes to come to the fore.

Immediately before the break with Rome, it was the pope and general councils of the church that decided doctrine. Church law was governed by the code of Canon Law developed under Roman emperor Justinian with final jurisdiction in Rome. Church taxes were paid straight to Rome, and it was the pope who had the final say over the appointment of bishops. The split from Rome made the English monarch the Supreme Governor of the English church by "Royal Supremacy," thereby making the Church of England the established church of the nation. Doctrinal and legal disputes now rested with the monarch, and the papacy was deprived of revenue and the final say on the appointment of bishops.

The structure and theology of the church were a matter of fierce dispute for generations and still is in what's left of Christian England. These disputes were finally ended by a coup d'état (the "Glorious Revolution") in 1688 from which emerged a church polity with an established church and a number of nonconformist churches whose members at first suffered various civil disabilities, which were only removed over time, as did the substantial minority who remained Roman Catholic in England, whose church organization remained illegal until the nineteenth century.

The greatest event from this struggle and what concerns our story is the King James Bible in 1611. The king brought together many scholars and original Greek and Hebrew texts to create a readable and listenable masterpiece. But by publishing it in English, it now became an individual faith; no priesthood, no national church was necessary. It made Christ sovereign over man, not kings *or* Parliament. This will lead to the great Puritan struggle of Cromwell. It will cause many to leave England for safer, more tolerant lands. It gave sanction and allowed men to be self-governing under the sovereignty of God, not men. "[W]here the Spirit of the Lord is, there is Liberty."

For hundreds of years, royalty, nobility, and commoners struggled against each other for power. But no one group could control all of the power for very long. This struggle for the control of the government had a dramatic history. There will be peasants' revolts, religious struggles, even war between branches of the royal tree, but the most contentious is the power to rule. Who is the enforcer of the social contract, the king or Parliament? Consider, for example, the following events during the important years between 1621 and 1689—the time of the early settlement of the English colonies in America.

- 1621. Members of the House of Commons insisted on having the right to take part in making governmental decisions. King James I responded by disbanding Parliament the following year. "No taxation without representation."
- 1628. Members of Parliament forced the king to sign the Petition of Right. The petition included the liberties Englishmen had won in the past and the customs they lived by and supported. Now the customs, traditions, and liberties of Englishmen were clearly set forth in an official written document agreed upon by Parliament and signed by the king. Sir Edward Coke (pronounced "Cook") listed among the grievances taxation and quartering of troops, both violations of "fundamental rights." The king could not imprison critics without a jury trial, declare martial law in peacetime, and billet troops in private homes without consent.

Upon this dispute not alone our lands and goods are engaged, but all that we call ours. These rights, these privileges, which made our fathers freemen, are in question (Sir John Eliot, March 1628).

- 1640. Triennial Act, limiting the duration of every parliament to three years, unless sooner dissolved, adding,
- 1641. Parliament was powerful enough to pass a law denying the king the right to disband it without its consent. See Article I, Section 5 US Constitution.
- 1649. During the English Civil War, Parliament was powerful enough to put King Charles I on trial for treason and to have him executed!
- 1653-1658. Oliver Cromwell, an English general, took power and completely abolished the title and positions of the king and the House of Lords.
- 1660. The monarchy was restored, and Charles II became king.
- 1679. Habeas Corpus Act
- 1688. King James II was forced to flee England because of his arbitrary methods of government. This ended the doctrine of the divine right of kings; Parliament now decides the monarch. This

Glorious Revolution of Christmas brought James's daughter and her husband to the throne, William III and Mary II.

- 1689. Toleration Act increased the religious freedom of most people in England by allowing members of a variety of religious groups to practice their beliefs.
- 1689. Parliament created a Bill of Rights.

English Bill of Rights

The English Bill of Rights of 1689 restored the balance of power between the king and Parliament that had been upset by King James II. Kings and queens were not allowed to (a) collect taxes without the consent of the Parliament, (b) interfere with the right to free speech and debate that went on in Parliament, (c) maintain an army in times of peace (since it might be used to take over the government), (d) require excessive bail or administer cruel punishment for those accused or convicted of crimes, or (e) declare that laws made by Parliament should not be obeyed, as King James had done, and recently Barack Obama did with his own Obamacare and not enforcing Congress's immigration laws.

The Bill of Rights also included the principles that (a) everyone must obey the law, even the king and Parliament; (b) elections must be free; (c) the people have the right to keep and carry weapons; (d) the people have the right to petition the king; (e) the people have the right to legal due process and trials with juries; and (f) the people have the right to privacy and security in one's home.

You can see how during this relatively short period the balance of power in the English government shifted from the king to the Parliament. The basic idea of representative government had become firmly established. However, only men with property had the right to vote and to be members of the House of Commons. Most people today would consider the government corrupt because these men, the seventeenth-century 1 percent, often served their own interests at the expense of the common welfare.

In 1707, England and Scotland (which until then had its own parliament) agreed to join along with Wales to create the kingdom of Great Britain. Therefore, in this book, England is referred to as Great Britain for events occurring after that date.

In addition, something in the mind of man was changing. The eighteenth century brought new ideas of the nature of man, of liberty and government.

> We cannot be certain to what height the human species may aspire in their advances toward perfection; but it may safely be assumed that no people, unless the face of nature is changed, will relapse into their original barbarism . . . We may therefore acquiesce in the pleasing conclusion that every age of the world has increased, and still increases, the real wealth, the happiness, the knowledge, and perhaps the virtue of the human race (Edward Gibbon, 1776).

> It is impossible to imagine the Height to which may be carried, in a thousand years, the Power of Man over Matter (Benjamin Franklin, 1780).

And men will rise from what they are;

> Sublimer and superior, far,
> Than Solon guessed, or Plato saw;
> All will be just, all will be good—
> That harmony, not understood,
> Will reign the general law (Philip Freneau, 1797).

> Men will make their situation in this world abundantly more easy and comfortable; they will probably prolong their existence in it, and will daily grow more happy, each in himself and more able (and, I believe, more disposed) to communicate happiness to others. Thus, whatever was the beginning of this world, the end will be glorious and paradisiacal, beyond what our imaginations can now conceive (Joseph Priestley 1764).

Colonial governments

Because of the new rhetoric—ideas—the British government was becoming increasingly limited in what it could do by a constitution, which included the following:

- a set of documents and customs, including the Magna Carta, the Petition of Right, and the English Bill of Rights, which set limits on the powers of the government and spelled out the rights of English freemen;
- a system of responsible government in which ministers appointed by the king were directly responsible to Parliament;
- a system in which the executive, legislative, and judicial powers were separated among the monarchy, Parliament, and the courts.

This is the balanced constitution of the British government that was greatly admired in other nations. The French political philosopher Montesquieu called the British government the "beautiful system" because he felt that it was perfectly balanced and, therefore, the only one in the world in which the constitution guaranteed political liberty. These ideas, I prefer ideals, emigrated with the colonials.

> The ... law of England is the ... law of the [colonies] ...
> Let an Englishman go where he will, he carries as much of
> law and liberty with him, as the nature of things will bear
> (Opinion of the counsel to the Board of Trade in London,
> 1720).

The English colonials who came to the New World considered themselves loyal subjects of England. They brought with them English customs, English laws, and English ideas about good government. For more than 150 years, the colonies were ruled by the government of England. They needed to have their own local governments as well with a great deal of freedom to govern themselves as they wished. This freedom was a result of their great distance from England. In addition, England was often at war with other European countries and did not have time to supervise the colonies. Because of this *Salutary Neglect*, the colonists became used to the idea of having a large voice in their own government. Edmund Burke said it was because of this neglect that the colonials under "a generous nature has been suffered to take her own way to perfection."

Since these thirteen colonial governments were ultimately under the control of the English government, their powers were limited, and they could not violate the English constitution, laws, traditions, or government policies.

Those who left Great Britain came to this New World expecting many things. Some came for wealth (Jamestown), some for religious freedom (Puritans and pilgrims), and some a new start far away from home (many of the indentured servants and debtors). It was at best a risky, at worst, a dangerous venture. This ideal of individuals struggling in the "wild" began to create a new type of man. These colonists will divide themselves into thirteen different colonies. Each one was unique. Some were merchants, some small farmers, and some large plantation owners.

There were three ways colonies were formed: private owners, corporations, or king's lands. In royal colonies, the king was the owner. Power came from king through appointed governors. The governor was the agent of the king and responsible only to him. Judges were appointed by the governors. Legislatures were in two houses (bicameral) with the upper house advisors to the governor and selected by him. The lower house usually elected by property holders still held power by approving taxes; this was in addition to all who paid rent to the king for land use. This power of the purse will be a determining factor in the revolution to come. Georgia, New Hampshire, New York, New Jersey, North and South Carolinas, Virginia, and Massachusetts after 1691 were the royal colonies.

In proprietary colonies, the colony was property of individual landlords. Some received the land from kings as payment for services rendered, gambling debts, or as refuges from problems in England. Governors were agents of owners and responsible to them only. Judges and legislatures were like royal colonies, excepting Pennsylvania, which all Quakers met in a unicameral house, one chamber. The proprietary colonies were Pennsylvania, Delaware, and Maryland.

Charter colonies were freely formed corporations that held a corporation charter issued by the king. Control was by the colonials, the signers of the charter. The governors were elected by the lower house (elected by colonials); he was responsible to the lower house of legislature. The governor selected the upper house as a "cabinet," but judges were selected by the lower legislatures. Connecticut, Rhode Island, Massachusetts before 1691 were the charter colonies.

Economies of the colonies

Maybe to overgeneralize, the colonies could also be divided into types of economies. Some of this is due to where the colonials came from, but much was based on the lands they settled on. New England colonies along the coast and with many forests tended to develop fisheries and a rum trade. They used their own family labor but also indentured servants who gave seven years usually for the payment from Europe. The mid-Atlantic colonies, sometimes called the bread basket colonies, developed after fur trade the large grain farms that later will fill the Midwest of the United States. Hired labor or family labor will do the work on these larger farms. The South was a unique land. In the Virginia Colony and North Carolina, tobacco was king, even used as money throughout this period. Slavery had been introduced into the colonies in Virginia by Dutch slave traders in 1619 after Indians proved too hard to enslave. This form of labor, a peculiar institution in a land founded on a variety of freedoms, was used more so in the deeper South. South Carolina, and later Georgia, grew indigo, rice, and some tobacco as well but on large plantations.

By the time of the Constitutional Convention in 1787, slavery in the United States was a grim reality. In the census of 1790, there were slaves counted in nearly every state, with only Massachusetts and the "districts" of Vermont and Maine being the only exceptions. In the entire country, 3.8 million people were counted, seven hundred thousand of them, or 18 percent, were slaves. In South Carolina, 43 percent of the population was slave. In Maryland, 32 percent, and in North Carolina slaves represented 26 percent. Virginia, with the largest slave population of almost three hundred thousand, had 39 percent of its population made up of slaves. However, as you should have learned in history classes, slavery was about to be inefficient—that was until the cotton gin made cotton king. With the new crop now easier to process, the "industrial"-like plantation system needed cheap labor; black humans fit the bill.

Yet regardless of labor, free or slave, commerce or agriculture, breadbasket or shipwrights, the basic ideals of the colonies held on to the English traditions, common law, acts of Parliament, and political customs and a constitution, though not in a single written document. The following basic ideas of English constitutional government were embodied in the governments of the English colonies.

Natural rights

The laws of the colonial governments were, even before Locke, founded on the idea that the purpose of government was to protect the people's natural rights to life, liberty, and property. These rights were traditionally included in English common law including the Magna Carta and were enforced by local and royal courts.

It is important in reading the history of this period to remember that rights—for example, the right to vote—usually meant the rights of white men who owned a certain amount of property. At the time of the American Revolution, only about 10 percent of the men in Great Britain had the right to vote. People who did not have such rights were (a) women, (b) free white men who did not own property, (c) white men who were indentured servants, (d) free black men, (e) slaves, and (f) Indians. For example, women not only did not have the right to vote, but also under English law, the husband and wife were one person, "the very being or legal existence of the woman is suspended during the marriage."

Higher law

This idea was the center of all the colonial charters. Most of these charters explicitly stated that members of colonial government could not make any laws or do anything that violated English law. English law was superior to any laws the colonial governments might make.

Separation of powers

As in England, to protect the people from the abuse of power, the governmental powers in the colonies were separated into three competing branches of government: a legislative branch for lawmaking in the colonies, an executive branch for carrying out and enforcing these laws, and a judicial branch for resolving conflicts between colonial law and the colonists. Even though at the Revolution, most governors were chosen either by the king or the proprietors, Connecticut and Rhode Island were electing theirs by those men who could vote. All the colonies had legislatures with the power to make local colonial laws; especially during that time when left alone in the pre-William-and-Mary era. Each was a variation of British Parliament with an upper house like the House of Lords and a lower house like the House of Commons. Members of the upper houses were either appointed by the governor or elected by the wealthiest property owners of the colony. The lower house was elected by all the men in the colony who owned enough property. Pennsylvania was the exception; it had a unicameral, had one house, legislature, as does Nebraska today. The judiciary was made up of judges called magistrates, usually appointed by the governor. Their chief responsibility was to handle conflicts over the laws (judicial review, responsible for making sure the colonies were being governed consistent with English law and tradition) and to decide trials of those accused of breaking the law.

Checks and balances

Powers were separated and in some cases shared so that the use of power by one branch of government could be checked by that of another. The powers of the governors were checked by the following: (a) their inability to collect taxes without the consent of the legislatures, (b) they could not violate habeas corpus without a trial by a magistrate, and (c) their salaries and colonial budgets—power of the purse—were decided upon by the legislatures. The legislative powers were held in check by the following: (a) having to rely on the governor to (faithfully) enforce the laws passed, and (b) just like the governors' use of power, the judiciary was to make sure these laws did not violate English law those of England. In some of the colonies, governors had the veto power. The powers of the magistrates were checked by the following: (a) not only being appointed by the governor, but also the power of the governors or legislatures to remove them if their decisions were "inappropriate"; (b) the courts, as today, relied on the governors to enforce the decisions; (c) the basic right of Englishman to a trial by a jury of his peers from the community; and (d) like the governors, legislatures set the judges' salaries.

Representative government and the right to vote

Representative government began soon after the first colonies were established. The first representative assembly was held in Virginia as early as 1619. As you have learned, the English Bill of Rights of 1689 gave Englishmen who owned a certain amount of property the right to elect representatives to serve their interests in the House of Commons.

Soon after passing the Bill of Rights, the English Parliament insisted upon applying the idea of representative government in the colonies. At least one house in each colony's legislature was required to be elected by eligible voters.

The right of citizens to elect representatives was a way to (a) reduce the possibility that members of government would violate the people's rights and (b) make sure that at least a part of the government could be counted on to respond to the needs and interests of the people, or at least of those people who had the right to vote.

These ideals are best illustrated in the first charter in the New World, the Mayflower Compact (1620). In November 1620, a group of religious separatists known as the Pilgrims landed off Cape Cod, what would later be called Massachusetts. The group had been awarded a right to establish a plantation from the Virginia Company. Their ship had landed much further north, and some members of the group convinced the others that the Virginia Company had no authority to govern them. They would have to establish their own government.

To begin some form of government, the settlers agreed to cooperate under the conditions of a compact, or agreement. The Mayflower Compact was not a constitution. The Compact was less than two hundred words long. It stated a theory of government, not a system of government. It stated a revolutionary new theory about the way that people should be governed. It contained the idea that a government should be formed by the consent of the people and that the government should work for the common good of the people. It embodied the principle that the government obtained its authority to rule from the people. It was a covenant, a contract, whereby the settlers would subordinate their rights to follow laws passed by *their* government to ensure protection and survival. This was decades before the social contract theory of Hobbes and Locke.

The original version of the Mayflower Compact has spelling and punctuation that make it difficult to read for us "modern" readers, and it's in cursive a lost and forgotten art today; this version makes the document easier to read.

> In the name of God, Amen. We, whose names are signed to this document are the loyal subjects of our great leader, Lord King James.
>
> Our great king rules Great Britain, France, and Ireland. Our king rules by the grace of God, and he is the defender of the Christian faith and all things honorable.
>
> We have undertaken a voyage on the ship *Mayflower* to plant the first colony in the Northern parts of Virginia. We have undertaken this voyage for the glory of God, the advancement of the Christian faith, and the honor of our king and country.
>
> At this time, in the presence of God and one another, we do solemnly and mutually pledge and combine ourselves together into a single united community. We form this compact for our better ordering and preservation, and the advancement of the goals we all believe in. And in order to accomplish our ends, we will from time to time enact, make up, and frame, such just and equal laws, ordinances, acts, constitutions, and offices as shall be thought most important and convenient for the general good of the colony. In addition, we promise all due submission and obedience to the colony and its leaders.
>
> In witness to our pledge, we have written our names on this document at Cape Cod on November 11, 1620, in the year of the rule of our leader, Lord King James of England, France, Ireland, and Scotland.

New World rejects the old

For much of that time, the colonists had few problems with the British government; eventually, however, the situation became so unsatisfactory that the colonists decided to fight for their independence from the mother country. When the colonials (I thought they were colonists? Well, England called them colonials; the colonials called themselves colonists! If I say colonial or colonist, it's like England or, Britain, or Great Britain or United Kingdom, depends if it's sunny or not) felt the corruption of their memories of the Mother Country, they felt betrayed as English subjects. Many people in Europe and the colonies believed that the great strength of the English government was that its powers were separated among different branches that represented different classes of people. They thought that the separation and balance of powers among the different branches would prevent the king, the nobles, or the people themselves from abusing the power of government. However, during the colonial period, a number of events led some people to think the British system of government was no longer working properly.

I apologize for this long blah, blah, blah on the history of the colonies and the revolution in the minds of men. I am assuming many attended public schools, for them and because of modern educators, humor me. As John Adams stated, colonial history built the American revolutionary, "acquired from their infancy the habit of discussing, of deliberating, and of judging of public affairs."

In the late 1600s, England was becoming a powerful nation. It had an army and navy that could exert its power all over the world. It had many colonies that provided it with great wealth and other resources. The larger and more complicated the nation became, the more need there was for an efficient and effective national government, or frankly, an imperial order. To improve their ability to govern the nation, Parliament and the king agreed to establish ministries, or departments of government, bureaucracies. These were headed by ministers. The ministers' responsibility was to help the king develop new policies and to administer the laws that were passed by Parliament. But as today, the ministers owed their loyalty to the king, not to the Parliament or the colonists. As today's Congress passes laws and leaves it to the bureaucrats to interpret and enforce, many times the intent of the legislature and the executives gets muddled.

By the early 1720s, there were some people in Great Britain who believed that the executive branch was becoming more powerful than the other branches of government. They were worried that this loss of a proper balance of power among the different branches of government would enable the king and his ministers to gain so much power that they could (a) ignore the limitations placed upon them by the English constitution, (b) violate the rights of the people, and (c) favor their own interests at the expense of the common welfare.

Cato's Letters were essays by British writers John Trenchard and Thomas Gordon, first published from 1720 to 1723 under the pseudonym of Cato. (Roman orator, 95–46 BC, the uncompromising foe of Julius Caesar and a famously stubborn champion of republican principles.)

The Letters are considered a seminal work in the tradition of the Commonwealth men. The 144 essays were published originally in the *London Journal,* later in the *British Journal.* These newspaper essays condemning tyranny and advancing principles of freedom of conscience and freedom of speech were a main vehicle for spreading the concepts that had been developed by John Locke.

The Letters were collected and printed as *Essays on Liberty, Civil and Religious.* A measure of their influence is attested by six editions printed by 1755. A generation later, their arguments immensely influenced the ideals of the American Revolution; it is estimated that half the private libraries in the American colonies held bound volumes of *Cato's Letters* on their shelves.

- All men are born free; liberty is a gift which they receive from God himself . . .
- . . . the nature of government does not alter the natural right of men to liberty, which is in all political societies their due.
- By liberty, I understand the power which every man has over his own actions, and his right to enjoy the fruits of his labor, art and industry, as far as by it he hurts not the society, or any members of it, by taking from any member, or hindering him from enjoying what he himself enjoys. The fruits of a man's honest industry are the just rewards of it, ascertained to him

by natural and eternal equity, as is his title to use them in the manner which he thinks fit: And thus, with the above limitations, every man is sole lord and arbiter of his own private actions and property . . . no man living can divest him but by usurpation, or by his own consent.

- True and impartial liberty is therefore the right of every man to pursue the natural, reasonable, and religious dictates of his own mind; to think what he will, to act as he thinks, provided he acts not to the prejudice of another; to spend his own money himself, and lay out the produce of his labor his own way; and to labor for his own pleasure and profits, and not for others who are idle, and would live . . . by pillaging and oppressing him, and those that are like him . . .

- Free government is the protecting of the people in their liberties by stated rules: Tyranny is a brutish struggle for unlimited liberty to one or a few, who would rob all the others of their liberty, and act by no rule but lawless lust.

Because of this increase in the power of the executive branch, many critics in Great Britain claimed that the British government was becoming corrupt. It was common for the king to bribe members of Parliament to get them to do what he wanted. He did this by giving them money or by appointing them as ministers or to other positions in the government. The critics pointed to the increases in taxes requested by the ministers and the king and to the large army that the king began to keep. They were concerned that many ministers and the king seemed to be cooperating closely with bankers and businessmen to favor their own selfish interests at the expense of the common welfare. This is exactly what political philosophers meant by corrupt government.

The colonists were aware of these criticisms of the British government. However, since that government had left them alone for the most part, they were not, at first, seriously concerned about the warnings of the critics. But ideas once released are seldom contained. In the colonies, a religious revival was brewing called the Great Awakening (1730s–1743); its leading speaker was George Whitefield. He preached a commonality to all men, different races, classes, and regions together, an equality of man, spiritual equality for all. The Scottish Enlightenment with reason and logic stated man could improve society. The social contract between governments and the people no longer was a whisper in illegally published documents. There were some who even in the wilderness were aware. One of them was a reverend in Massachusetts. Jonathan Mayhew (1720–1766) was a noted colonial minister at Old West Church, Boston, Massachusetts. He is credited with coining the phrase "no taxation without representation."

The extent of his political feeling can be seen in his *Discourse Concerning Unlimited Submission*, a sermon delivered on the one hundredth anniversary of the execution of Charles I (January 30, 1649/50). Taking vigorous issue with recent efforts to portray Charles as a martyred monarch, Mayhew began with observations on the antiquity of English liberties. The English constitution, he asserted, "is originally and essentially free." Roman sources, such as the reliable Tacitus, made it clear that "the ancient Britons . . . were extremely jealous of their liberties." England's monarchs originally held their throne "solely by grant of parliament," so the ancient English kings ruled "by the voluntary consent of the people." After forty pages of such historical discourse, Mayhew reached his major point: the essential rightness of the execution of an English king when he too greatly infringed upon British liberties.

The vigor of Mayhew's sermon established his reputation. It was published not only in Boston but also in London in 1752 and again in 1767. In Boston, John Adams remembered long afterward that Mayhew's sermon "was read by everybody." Some would say later that this sermon was the first volley of the American Revolution, setting forth the intellectual and scriptural justification for rebellion against the Crown.

> While Britain claim'd by laws our rights to lead,
> And faith was fetter'd by a bigot's creed.
> Then mental freedom first her power display'd
> and call'd a MAYHEW to religion's aid.
> For this great truth, he boldly led the van,
> That private judgment was the right of man.

Britain tries to reign the colonies back in

The *American* (it's time for the new adjective!) colonists did become alarmed when the British government began to develop an increased interest in tightening its control over them. This interest was at least partially because the colonists had been able to get away with not obeying laws made by Parliament that they didn't like, such as the Navigation Acts, which controlled their trade. Also, Great Britain had been at war with France. During this French and Indian War, the French had used American Indians to help them fight against the British forts and the colonists' settlements in the west. No longer concerned with the French, she now turned to the colonies. Although Great Britain had won the war, the cost of keeping their troops in America to protect the colonists was high.

As early as 1753, disagreements began about the relationship between king, Parliament, and the colonies. Richard Bland, older cousin and mentor to a young Thomas Jefferson, wrote in *An Inquiry into the Rights of the British Colonies* (1753) that the colonies were a new people starting again in an uncivilized state of nature, and because of the "Law of Nature, that they have a Right to a civil independent Establishment of their own, and that *Great Britain* has no *Right* to interfere in it." Having emigrated, a natural right according to Bland, the colonials had left behind citizenship and any relationship that may have existed between them and Great Britain. They had accepted the king as their king voluntarily, but not Parliament.

Others could not go that far, especially this early. Most will follow the lead of Patrick Henry and Jefferson that the laws of Parliament, especially since the Glorious Revolution, were violating the constitution of English law; that the rights of Englishmen back to the days of the Saxons and Britons were from time immemorial to time not yet to come; that taxation, rather any law, could not be placed on them without representation elected by them. A decade later, Parliament will seemingly put to rest Bland's propositions in the Declaratory Act.

Even after the war, there was still trouble on the frontier because the colonists were moving westward and taking the Indians' lands. To reduce this problem, the British government ordered the colonists to move back from the frontier. With the Proclamation Line of 1763, colonials were forbidden to move onto Indian lands to the west. Parliament increased the colonists' taxes to help pay for the costs of keeping British troops in the colonies to protect them from the Indians. And the British government also tightened its control over the colonists' trade.

George Grenville (1712–1770) was chosen to produce these taxes and control trade. As prime minister, he was now ruling a vast worldwide empire. Empires are not easily amenable to freedom. He strengthened Customs officials who used writs of assistance (blanket search warrants), British warships, and troops to find contraband and hidden taxable. The accused would be tried away in admiralty courts in Nova Scotia with little due process.

Although some colonists accepted these acts of Parliament, a number resisted them. This resistance was, in part, because of new taxes and trade laws, which meant that some colonists were going to lose money. But perhaps a more important reason was that over the years, the colonists had become more firmly attached to their idea of representative government at the local level.

The colonists were convinced that representative government was the best way to be sure that their government would respect their rights and interests. Since the colonists did not have the right to vote for representatives to serve their interests in the British Parliament, some of them argued that Parliament did not have the right to pass laws taxing them. They thought that tax laws should only be made by their own colonial legislatures where they had the right to vote for representatives to protect their interests. Again, colonists demand that there be no taxation without representation. The fears of some of the leading colonists were increased when the British government continued to tax the colonists and to increase its control over their trade. It passed acts that placed additional import duties and burdens on the colonies.

Sugar Act. In 1764, Parliament reduced the tax on imported foreign molasses by half, unlike its predecessor, the Molasses Act, the Sugar Act was strictly enforced. Colonists responded with written protests, occasional boycotts, and cries of "No taxation without representation." The Declaration will later state: "Cutting off trade with all parts of the world. Imposing taxes without our Consent."

Currency Act. Originally the taxes in the colonies were for regulation; now Grenville needed more money. The Currency Act of 1764 was no longer taxing for regulation but for revenue. It made specie money the only legal tender; this is hard money, gold and silver. Yet this was scarce in colonies. This move bankrupted many colonial merchants and radicalized professions and the middle class.

Quartering Act. Next was the Quartering Act requiring the colonists to allow British soldiers to live in their homes. This action increased the colonists' fears of having a large army in the colonies that was controlled by the British government. Most colonial legislatures refused to pay supplies as required by the Quartering Act. Again, in the Declaration: "Kept among us in time of peace, Standing Armies, without the Consent of our legislature. Rendering the Military independent of and superior to the Civil power. Quartering large bodies of armed troops among us." Standing armies have always been a threat to freedoms as recognized in the English Bill of Rights.

Stamp Act. The 1765 Stamp Act was the first direct taxation of colonists. It taxed legal and commercial documents and printed matter such as newspapers. Even with a written freedom of the press, control of the paper eliminates any real freedoms. The colonial response was violent. Sons of Liberty began to appear, breaking windows of tax collectors; tarring and feathering was frequent. Ten colonies met in the Stamp Act Congress and began a boycott of British goods. The Congress sent a Declaration of Rights and Grievances to the king. William Pitt became the new prime minister, and with businesses in England repealed, Pitt did not repeal the right to tax. In repealing the Stamp Act because of colonial protest and British business losses, Parliament passed the Declaratory Act, which was a statement of England's right to rule the colonies in any way it saw fit. Though a seeming victory for both sides, Jefferson stated, Pitt was "abolishing the free System of English Laws in a neighboring Province, establishing therein and Arbitrary government . . . absolute rule into these Colonies. Taking away Charters, abolishing our most valuable Laws and altering fundamentally the Forms of our Governments." But Locke himself had declared legislative supremacy was to protect the rights of man. One thing to think about is that in England itself, nine out of ten could not vote; were they represented? What about juveniles today?

Townshend Acts. In response, the following year, Britain passed a series of taxes and regulations called the Townshend Acts. These included import taxes on lead, paper, tea, paint, and glass collected at the ports where the goods came in. Revenues were used to support British troops, royal governors, and royal judges, taking the power away from colonial assemblies. Also they created a customs commission and suspended the New York assembly for failing to comply with the act. A widely read series of letters protesting the act, "Letters from a Farmer in Pennsylvania," were published in colonial newspapers. Colonists resumed boycotting British goods. Jefferson will later refer to these events: "Dissolved Representative Houses, made Judges dependent on his Will, erected New Offices, kept Standing Armies without Consent of our legislature, Quartering large bodies of armed troops, imposing Taxes without our Consent." But as Jefferson will say later, ideas, minds, need to be changed. It is a message we need to remember today.

> If at length it becomes undoubted that an inveterate resolution is formed to annihilate the liberties of the governed, the English history affords frequent examples of resistance by force. What particular circumstances will in any future case justify such resistance can never be ascertained till they happen. Perhaps it may be allowable to say generally, that it never can be justifiable until the people are fully convinced that any further submission will be destructive to their happiness. —Letter III

Resistance is organized

Critics in Great Britain had warned about the growing power of the king and his ministers and of the threat that their control of the army and navy was to the rights of the people. The colonists became more and more alarmed. Their concern over the corruption of the British government was growing stronger, as was their opposition to that government.

On February 5, 1765, James Otis, having spoken the words many felt in 1761 in his attack against arbitrary writs of assistance, "Taxation without representation is tyranny," walked into a Loyalist hall, the Boston British Coffee House. He has declared those words in the Massachusetts Superior Court of Judicature; but he had only begun. He swore,

> I will to my dying day . . . oppose all such instruments of slavery on the one hand or villany on the other as this writ

of assistance is . . . No acts of parliament can establish such a writ; tho it would be in the very words of the petition 'twould be void. An act against the constitution is void.

And then in advocating open rebellion,

[I]f the King of Great Britain in person were encamped on Boston Common, at the head of twenty thousand men, with all his navy on the coast, he would not be able to execute these laws.

It was these words that led to his beating by royalists, not unlike the one in 1856 of Charles Sumner on the Senate floor by Preston Brooks that led to the Civil War. Both, nearly one hundred years apart, were so badly beaten that recovery was minimal. Otis lasted in and out of lucidity until stuck by lighting in his own doorway in 1783. James Otis, called the father of the Fourth Amendment, became the first casualty of the revolution.

May 17, 1769, Virginia defied the king and reconvened the disbanded House of Burgesses at the local Raleigh Tavern—similar to the beginnings of the French Revolution when the National Assembly reconvened the Etats-General on the nearby Tennis Courts—and under the direction of George Mason, future writer of Virginia's Declaration of Rights, its constitution, and delegate to the Philadelphia Convention of 1787, they decided to act against the myriad of taxes and regulations by the Crown on colonial commerce. Their Non-Importation Agreement was to boycott any goods coming from England that were taxed, thus not paying taxes. Also present were Patrick Henry, George Washington, Thomas Jefferson and Edmund Randolph under Mason's mentoring. Britain fearful of losing too much revenue blinked and repealed all taxes except the notorious tea tax.

The Boston "Massacre" of 1770 was another event that convinced some of the Americans that the British government was a threat to their rights, if not their lives. A mob of citizens that had attacked a sentry at the Customs House in Boston was fired on by British troops. Seven people were killed. Later, the British soldiers who had been charged with murder were found innocent of the charges, defended by John Adams. Taxes and duties may have been a subtle sign of tyranny, but killing citizens was not. The Boston Massacre made the colonists more resistant to British efforts to control them. Many Committees of Correspondence sprung up in various colonies spreading the stories and much propaganda throughout the New World.

The Tea Act of 1773, which lowered the tax on tea imported to the colonies but reasserted the right of Parliament to tax the colonists, was resisted everywhere. It was an example for later policies of corrupt business and government scheming to hurt the consumers. It was created to benefit the East India Company. It allowed the company to sell surplus tea in the colonies. It retained the tax on tea, the only tax remaining from the Townshend Acts.

The most dramatic resistance was the Boston Tea Party, a raid by colonists masquerading as Indians who boarded British ships in Boston Harbor and threw the tea overboard. The British government responded angrily with the Coercive Acts, called by the Americans the Intolerable Acts, which closed Boston harbor to all trade.

Great Britain also weakened representative government in Massachusetts by giving more power to the royal governor, severely limiting town meetings, weakening the court system, and planning for a massive occupation of the colony by British troops.

One of the first responses was Paul Revere calling the Intolerable Acts "unconstitutional" and calling for a boycott of British goods. In his Suffolk Resolves, he called on Massachusetts to form a new government, free of Britain authority. And he adamantly called for colonials to prepare for war.

In the fall of 1774, twelve of the thirteen colonies sent representatives to a meeting in Philadelphia to decide on the best response to the actions of the British government. This meeting was the First Continental Congress. Its members agreed to impose their own ban on trade with Great Britain in an attempt to force the government to change its policies toward the colonies. Also, a written petition was sent; the Olive Branch Petition asked the king to support repeal of the taxes. The British government, however, considered this on an act of irresponsible defiance of authority and ordered its troops to arrest some leading colonists in Massachusetts.

By this time, many of the more-radical colonists, especially in New England, were beginning to prepare for war against Great Britain. They believed it was the right of the people to overthrow any government that no longer protected their rights. The colonists formed civilian armies made up of Minutemen, so called because of their pride in how quickly they could be ready to fight off the British attack that everyone expected. British confiscations of guns and powder (Powder Alarm) had "patriots" to began hiding weapons and gunpowder throughout the countryside.

On April 19, 1775, British troops tried to march to Concord, Massachusetts, where they had heard that the Minutemen had hidden arms and ammunition, and in hopes of capturing John Hancock and Sam Adams, financier, and orator of the revolution, respectively. But the colonists learned what was happening. Paul Revere, William Dawes, and Samuel Prescott rode through the countryside warning the people that the British were about to attack. On that day, at the towns of Lexington and Concord, war broke out between the colonies and Great Britain—the shot heard 'round the world had been fired. By May 10, Fort Ticonderoga fell in upstate New York.

Representatives from the colonies met in Philadelphia for a Second Continental Congress to hear the king's answer. His answer was clear; more troops were sent. This Congress decided to resist the British. On June 15, 1775, George Washington was chosen to be commander in chief of the colonial "army." A year later, the Congress asked a committee to draft a document that would explain to the world why these colonials, colonists, Americans felt that it was necessary to revolt and free themselves from the government that had established the colonies. Thomas Jefferson drafted this document with the assistance of the other members of the committee. It has become known as the Declaration of Independence. Women took an active role in the revolutionary struggle, forming anti-tea leagues and nonimportation groups to see that colonists did not buy British goods during the boycott, even fighting side by side with their men.

> Let the Daughters of Liberty, nobly arise,
> And tho's we've no Voice, but a negative here,
> The use of the Taxables, let us forbear.

The Declaration of Independence contains the basic ideas about government upon which our nation was founded. Take note of the importance of the second and last paragraphs of the Declaration as statements of the foundations of good government. Dissent had already begun to be loud and active. In the *Farmer Refuted* (1775), Alexander Hamilton quotes William Blackstone:

> The Sacred Rights of Mankind are not to be rummaged for,
> among old parchments, or musty records. They are written,
> as with a sun beam, in the whole volume of human nature,
> by the Hand of the Divinity itself; and can never be erased
> or obscured by mortal power.

Thomas Jefferson was a statesman, a diplomat, an author, an architect, and a scientist. Born in Virginia, Jefferson was a quiet member of the Continental Congress during the early period of the Revolutionary War. He was not known as a great speaker before large groups, but he had a reputation for working well in small committees and was admired for his excellent writing style. Because of his talent for writing, he was chosen to draft the Declaration of Independence. He was helped by John Adams, Roger Sherman, Roger Livingston, and the always present Ben Franklin.

Jefferson had in his possession a small pamphlet he had read in the spring, *Common Sense* by Thomas Paine. Published anonymously on January 10, 1776, it had immediate success, being sold throughout the colonies and in Europe. In the pamphlet, Paine explains his idea of society, government, and the tyranny of the English system of government. Paine describes the monarchy as a "tyranny in the person of the King" and the aristocracy as a "tyranny in the persons of the Peers."

> Society is produced by our wants, and government by our
> wickedness; the former promotes our happiness positively
> by uniting our affections, the latter negatively by restraining
> our vices.

> In order to gain a clear and just idea of the design and end
> of government, let us suppose a small number of persons
> settled in some sequestered part of the earth, unconnected
> with the rest; they will then represent the first peopling of
> any country, or of the world. In this state of natural liberty,
> society will be their first thought.

Paine felt that it was absurd for an island to rule a continent. America was not a "British nation"; rather, it was from influences and peoples from all of Europe. The "Mother country"? No mother would harm her children so brutally. His greatest fear was that Great Britain would drag America into the many unnecessary European wars, a concern of George Washington and, later, Ron Paul.

Another inspiration for Jefferson was the Virginia Declaration of Rights. It stated that men have natural rights. It was drafted by George Mason with help from James Madison and later amended by Thomas Ludwell Lee to include the right to equal treatment under the law.

> Article I: That all men are by nature equally free and independent, and have certain inherent rights, of which, when they enter into a state of society, they cannot, by any compact, deprive or divest their posterity; namely, the enjoyment of life and liberty, with the means of acquiring and possessing property, and pursuing and obtaining happiness and safety.

> Article II: That all power is vested in, and consequently derived from, the people; that magistrates are their trustees and servants, and at all times amenable to them.

> Article III: That government is, or ought to be, instituted for the common benefit, protection, and security of the people, nation or community; of all the various modes and forms of government that is best, which is capable of producing the greatest degree of happiness and safety . . .

The Declaration of Independence, adopted by the Continental Congress on July 4, 1776, is the best summary available of the colonists' basic ideas about government and their complaints about British rule that led the Americans to begin the revolution.

Most of the early complaints were directed against the British Parliament. However, in the Declaration of Independence, the Americans accused the king; the least of his crimes was not protecting his subjects from an oppressive Parliament. This was the first time the colonists had attacked the British king and the idea of monarchies in general.

The British response was to up the ante. In 1777, Colonial Undersecretary William Knox's "What is Fit to Be Done with America?" intended to prevent any further rebellions in America. His plan was to establish the Church of England as the official religion, to institute an hereditary aristocracy even to include many of the landed members of the colonies, and to bring in a permanent standing army.

> The Militia Laws should be repealed and none suffered to be re-enacted, [and] the Arms of all the People should be taken away . . . nor should any Foundery or Manufactuary of Arms, Gunpowder, or Warlike Stores, be ever suffered in America, nor should any Gunpowder, Lead, Arms or Ordnance be imported into it without Licence . . .

The Declaration of Independence was also an important turning point in the development of constitutional government in America. As mentioned before, the second paragraph and the final section are essential reading; they pledge to achieve not easily attained goals, as Lincoln states in the Gettysburg Address on "unfinished work." The ideals within are the seeds of the future Constitution, the great experiment of self-government. It sets the foundation of our constitutional republic. No one can truly understand the Constitution without an understanding of its foundation. Much of the history of the United States has been an effort to make these ideals a reality for everyone, blacks, other minorities, and women.

What are the basic ideas of the Declaration of Independence?

To begin, let's go deep and then take a breath. There are certain propositions that are true everywhere, always to all reasonable men; only fools or contrarians would state opposite propositions. One idea is self-evident (*a priori* doesn't need to be taught, all know it; it's part of the uniqueness of man) that all humans are by nature equal. We discussed this before. Jefferson added all men have certain inalienable rights. That means these *rights should not be transgressed or abrogated*. The rights of the people are based on natural law, which is a higher law than laws made by men. Neither constitutions nor governments can violate the higher law. If a government violates this law and deprives the people of their rights, they have the right to change or abolish it and form a new government. He lists three primary rights: life, liberty, and pursuit of happiness. Happiness is primary, life and liberty are means, and happiness is an end; it is also a moral obligation.

From Locke, Hobbes, Mayflower Compact, we see there was a contract or an agreement existed between the colonists and the king. By the terms of this compact, the colonists consented to be governed by the king so long as he protected their rights to life, liberty, and property. Since there was no compact between the colonists and Parliament that gave Parliament the right to participate in their governments, Parliament had no right to tax the colonies. This was especially true, argued the Americans, since they did not have the right to send representatives to Parliament.

If government is instituted to secure (protect) these rights, what does one do when that contract is violated? Unjust government is to be altered; if unalterable and despotic, it must be overthrown. Rebellion is not to be taken lightly, but it is a law of nature. Duty requires a new government that does secure their rights because of the uncertainty of a state of nature. The king had violated the compact by repeatedly acting with Parliament to deprive the colonists of the rights he was supposed to protect. Therefore, the colonists had the right and responsibility to withdraw their consent to be governed by him and to establish their own government.

What were the ideas of the Declaration that Jefferson used to build this philosophy that continues to inspire others to believe in the Experiment? Equality, God-given inalienable rights, happiness, consent, and dissent.

Equality

One hears the word "equality" often, but what is it? Equality is defined as neither more nor less. How does that apply to humans? All people are human, *Homo sapiens;* this distinguishes us from other species as a different kind of creation. But that is called personal equality; we are all persons, humans. Humans do have a "nature," potentialities or capacities for development. All men are morally accountable, contemplate right from wrong, and have a capacity for liberty. Each man is his own natural ruler; we all have the capacity to govern ourselves.

Yet regardless of Socialists, Progressives, today's Liberals, humans can still be unequal in having more or less of an attribute, degree, or individual differences. Many differences occur in amounts, as well as nurturing, both pre and post. Imaginations, deliberations, judgments, and choices we make are all based on our differences. This is circumstantial equality: equality of conditions or results, equality of opportunity, and equality of treatment. We are not equal in kind. Every physical being, every physical capacity, and every intellectual aptitude is different in each of us. We are unique; inequality is inevitable.

> [N]o two are perfectly equal in person, property, understanding, activity, and virtue, or ever can be made so by any power less than that which created them (John Adams).

Inalienable rights

All humans are equal in nature. If certain rights are natural rights, then all humans have these rights. Inalienable rights can be transgressed, like life and liberty. That is an injustice. Civil rights are different: they can be given or taken away; they are alienable. They are the rights we use to guarantee our natural/inalienable rights. What about criminals in jail or death penalty? Jail is a restriction because of antisocial behavior, yet the right is still there. If life is an inalienable right, how can it be taken away (unjust), yet the general welfare is not being served (a greater injustice)?

Be careful about to split hairs. Natural rights are not the same as civil rights. Life and liberty are natural rights used to achieve our individual purpose/happiness. Civil rights are used to secure human rights. Civil rights are instrumental in implementing natural rights, but they come from just governments. Our Bill of Rights is not a grant of rights from government; governments weren't yet. Man has to create it to protect these rights, thus our rights must have existed before. The bill prevents the national government from abridging the rights of the citizens of states.

- First Amendment
  - o Speech, press, assembly, petition—exercise of political liberty and freedom of action
- Second and Third Amendments
  - o Experience from previous injustices under Crown
- Fourth Amendment
  - o Liberty from oppressive government
- Fifth and Sixth Amendments
  - o Due process, life, liberty, and property
- Seventh Amendment
  - o Common law, not especially important as a right
- Eighth Amendment
  - o Freedom from excessive force
- Ninth to Tenth Amendment
  - o Rights than mentioned
- First to Tenth Amendments
  - o Life and liberty amendments

The true right that Locke declared and Jefferson restated as happiness is property. A man's right to use and hold property separates us from savages. John Adams believed this as essential to a free community. In 1787, writing in support of the newly drafted Constitution, he believes property is sacred.

> The moment the idea is admitted into society that property is not as sacred as the laws of God, and that there is not a force of law and public justice to protect it, anarchy and tyranny commence. If "Thou shalt not covet" and "Thou shalt not steal" were not commandments of Heaven, they must be made inviolable precepts in every society before it can be civilized or made free.

At the Convention, James Wilson stated:

> By exclusive property, the productions of the earth and the means of subsistence are secured and preserved, as well as multiplied. What belongs to no one is wasted by everyone.

What belongs to one man in particular is the object of his economy and care.

Happiness

Human rights are needed to lead a decent life (happiness). Happiness is a whole life well-lived with all the goods that a morally virtuous human ought to desire. One needs a will to act through virtue; this is moral virtue. Wants can be bad. Moral virtue needs to be practiced. We can want too much, never need too much! We don't have a right to wants, but we do to needs to make good lives. Since happiness must be pursued by all humans: it is natural—thus not exactly a right—moral obligation to try to achieve. Life and liberty are dependent on external society. Our free will (choices) cannot be given, either one has it or not; moral freedom is the freedom to choose right from wrong. Speech, arms, privacy, habeas corpus, due process, and rights are property; like grace, God gave man them freely. Even the denial of a single one denies freedom to be, um, human.

Consent

Jefferson was very straightforward: all powers of government derive from the consent of the governed. Man makes the contract; it might be natural to live under a social contract, but its existence is man-made. Constitutions delegate man's powers to offices, not officeholders. Political liberty necessitates this consent. Consent is when citizens rule and are ruled; subjects are only ruled. The idea of consent is that people, never governments are sovereign. Lincoln called it "government of the people, by the people, for the people." Now people are not the same as the general population. Only those able to consent can do so; only citizens can play this game, others cannot be abused, but they have NO say in the game. Government derives its just powers from the consent of all those who are politically able to give their consent. They must be able to knowingly give up some of their rights to a delegated authority. The key problem in the "failing" of the experiment is the ignorance of those playing. Civics is no longer a key subject for American students. It, like economics, if taught at all, is merely rote memory of terms of office, how things are done, say the Electoral College, never an understanding of why it is done. Why are we a republic, yet everyone thinks democracy? Why did the states want the Tenth Amendment? Why is a Bill of Rights a condition of ratification by many of the state ratifying conventions? Why are consensual governments the only legitimate ones in the eyes of God?

Man is free; made that way to love God. Though many use the term "unconditionally," God doesn't love you unconditionally; there is a condition, actually conditions. The key one is choice; you must choose to love Him too. With joining the social contract, Man can do it explicitly by ratifying a government, say when a new state is formed. Mainly it is given implicitly by accepting and/or participating in government. Accepting benefits with apathy is still consent. Just because one does not vote, speak up, or hold office but accepts the power or benefits of the state, one is still a consenting member. Those elected are your government; he is your president!

Dissent

So, then, what is dissent? Though dissent is neither a civil nor a natural right, it stems from liberty. If I can freely associate with others to form a state, I must be able to break that association. But what is dissent? Jefferson said when government is destructive; one can alter or abolish it. Altering is not dissent. It is consenting even in civil disobedience if punishment is accepted. Rioting and destruction are neither consent nor dissent; it is criminal. There are only two ways to dissent, both forms of abolishing the state. One is rebellion, force, violence, but revolt can only be done toward despotic governments, not against fellow citizens, and never done lightly; "long train of abuses." The other is to sever the connection, to leave. Dissent is a moral duty because despotism is an obstacle to happiness, a sin against God. A new just government is required; anarchy cannot exist. A state of nature precludes a pursuit of happiness for all; man cannot be secure except within a just government.

Throughout history, the Declaration has been an inspiration to many people looking for the freedoms God has given to all but often kept from them. The French Revolution was inspired to write its own Declaration of the Rights of Man and Citizen (1789). Others based on Jefferson's words include the Venezuelan Declaration of Independence (1811), the Liberian Declaration of Independence (1847), the declarations of secession by the Confederate States of America (1860–61), and the Vietnam Declaration of Independence (1945), Tiananmen Square (1989).

Lincoln considered the Declaration the foundation of this nation. Many times, he referred to it. Speaking in opposition to the spread of slavery with the passage of the Kansas-Nebraska Act in 1854, he called for a reissuing of it.

> Nearly eighty years ago we began by declaring that all men are created equal; but now from that beginning we have run down to the other declaration, that for some men to enslave others is a "sacred right of self-government" . . . Our republican robe is soiled and trailed in the dust. Let us repurify it . . . Let us re-adopt the Declaration of Independence, and with it, the practices, and policy, which harmonize with it . . . If we do this, we shall not only have saved the Union: but we shall have saved it, as to make, and keep it, forever worthy of the saving.

Again, while running for the Senate against Stephen Douglass, he stated in a letter to Henry L. Pierce and others (April 6, 1859):

> [T]he man who, in the concrete pressure of a struggle for national independence by a single people, had the coolness, forecast, and capacity to introduce into a merely revolutionary document, an abstract truth, applicable to all men and all times, and so to embalm it there, that to-day, and in all coming days, it shall be a rebuke and a stumbling-block to the very harbingers of reappearing tyranny and oppression.

The most famous was his Gettysburg Address, where he simply states that we must complete the work of this experiment begun with Jefferson.

> Four score and seven years ago our fathers brought forth on this continent a new nation, conceived in liberty, and dedicated to the proposition that all men are created equal.

It is rather for us to be here dedicated to the great task remaining before us . . . that this nation, under God, shall have a new birth of freedom—and that government of the people, by the people, for the people, shall not perish from the earth.

Woodrow Wilson believed the Declaration was a springboard for all future actions of a government. Each generation, as Lincoln said, must have a new birth of freedom.

We think of it as a highly theoretical document, but except for its assertion that all men are equal it is not. It is intensely practical, even upon the question of liberty It names as among the "inalienable rights" of man the right to life, liberty, and the pursuit of happiness, as does the Virginia constitution and many another document of the time; but it expressly leaves to each generation of men the determination of what they will do with their lives, what they will prefer as the form and object of their liberty, in what they will seek their happiness. Its chief justification of the right of the colonists to break with the mother country is the assertion that men have always the right to determine for themselves by their own preferences and their own circumstances whether the government they live under is based upon such principles or administered according to such forms as are likely to effect their safety and happiness. In brief, political liberty is the right of those who are governed to adjust government to their own needs and interests.

ESTABLISHING NEW GOVERNMENT

Without a struggle, there can be no progress.
—Frederick Douglass

S OON AFTER THE Revolutionary War started in 1775, the new states began to develop their own written constitutions. Never had so many new governments been created using the basic ideas of the natural rights philosophy, republicanism, representative government, and constitutional government. These new nations, not yet a nation, contained in their constitutions various attempts to protect the rights of their citizens and promote the common welfare. One experiment in Massachusetts was designed to protect rights much differently from the way the constitutions of the other states were designed. Let's see how this document written by none other than John Adams changed the world.

Six basic ideas again

As with the Declaration before and the Constitution that follows, the states, based on the individual desires and problems of each region, drew up plans to secure rights but to limit power as much as possible. The experiences of the Founders with their state accomplishments and shortcomings under new constitutions greatly influenced the way they wrote the Constitution of the United States.

1. Higher law and natural rights

Every state constitution was considered a higher law that must be obeyed by the citizens and those in government.

Each contained a statement of purpose to preserve and protect citizens' natural rights to life, liberty, and property.

2. Social contract

Each colonial constitution was written with the idea that government was formed because of a social contract—an agreement among its people to create this government to protect their natural rights. The Massachusetts Constitution of 1780,

Article I. All men are born free and equal, and have certain natural, essential, and unalienable rights; among which may be reckoned the right of enjoying and defending their lives and liberties; that of acquiring, possessing, and protecting property; in fine, that of seeking and obtaining their safety and happiness. (This article was later amended to substitute the word "people" for the word "men.")

3. Popular sovereignty

All contained the idea of popular sovereignty—people are the source of the power of government; see right to vote below.

4. Representation and the right to vote

Each state constitution placed representation of the people foremost in their governments. All legislatures were composed of elected representatives of the people.

In most states, the right to vote for representatives was limited to white males who owned a specified amount of property. However, because it was relatively easy to acquire property in the colonies, this limit on who could vote did not eliminate as many people as it did in Great Britain. In the United States during the period of the American Revolution, about 70 percent of the white males owned enough property to make them eligible to vote. While in England, it was only about 10 percent with suffrage.

In seven, free blacks and Indians could vote if they met the property requirements. And in New Jersey, the vote was given to all of full age who were worth fifty pounds and who met a twelve-month residency requirement. Under these rules, both women and free blacks could vote until 1807 when the law in New Jersey was rewritten to exclude women. Twelve states specifically denied women the right to vote by inserting the word male into their constitutions.

5. Legislative supremacy

While all included checks and balances and the separation of powers, most of them relied on a strong legislature and majority rule (democracy!) to protect the rights of the citizens. Legislative supremacy means a government in which most of the power is given to the legislature; fear of a resurgence of a king or an American Cromwell never was placed on the backburner. Some of the problems raised by legislative supremacy will be discussed later. The reasons for the belief in legislative supremacy were as follows.

- The legislative branch of government, composed of representatives elected by the voters who can also be removed by the voters, is the most democratic branch of government. Therefore, it is considered the safest branch in which to place the most power and the most likely to protect the rights of citizens and to promote their welfare.
- The executive branch should not be trusted with too much power because it is not easily controlled by the people. You may remember that the colonists' greatest problems with the British government had been with its executive branch—the king and his ministers—as well as with the royal governors in the colonies.
- The colonists had also had some difficulty with the judicial branch, the king's magistrates, who tried colonists for

breaking British law. However, the power of this branch had been limited by the colonists' right to a trial by a jury of other colonists. These juries often refused to find them guilty of breaking a law with which the colonists did not agree.

- Executive branches were made dependent on the legislatures. For example, legislatures were given the power to select the governor or to control his salary, power of the purse—he who owns the gold makes the rules.

- Governors could stay in office for only one year. This limit was an attempt to be sure that the governor would not have time to gain much power while in office.

- Appointments made by a governor had to be approved by the legislature.

- Governors were almost totally excluded from the process of lawmaking, which the legislatures kept to themselves. Governors had no power to veto legislation to which they objected.

6. Checks and balances

Although the powers in the state governments were unevenly balanced in favor of strong legislatures, there were some checks in their constitutions. However, most of these checks existed within the legislatures themselves. For example, in every state except Pennsylvania and Georgia, the legislature was divided into two houses, just as in the British Parliament. Since most important decisions had to be made by both houses, each had a way to check the power of the other house. However, unlike Parliament, and unlike the colonial governments, both houses of state legislatures were made up of representatives elected by the people. The voters could check their power by electing new representatives to both houses if they did not like the way the government worked.

You may remember that in Parliament, the House of Lords, and the House of Commons were designed to represent different classes of people in the British society. This gave each class a way to check the power of the other, if necessary, to protect its interests. Some states tried to organize their legislatures in the same way. Only people with a great deal of property could elect representatives to the upper house, while people with less property were allowed to elect representatives to the lower house.

Massachusetts Constitution

In 1780, Massachusetts became the last state to ratify its constitution. Written principally by John Adams, help from Sam Adams and James Bowdoin, the Massachusetts Constitution was different from those of the other states. It relied not only upon representation as a means of preventing the abuse of power but also on the traditional methods of separation of powers and checks and balances. It gave the other branches of government more-effective checks on the powers of the state legislature than did the other state constitutions. It contained more similarities to the British government than did the constitutions of the other states.

Perhaps one of the most important reasons the Massachusetts Constitution was different was that during the time that it was being developed, problems were arising in the other states because of instances of tyranny of the majority in legislatures with too much power. Since the Massachusetts Constitution is more like the present Constitution of the United States than are the other state constitutions. Let's look more closely.

Under the Massachusetts Constitution, the governor was elected by the people. Adams believed if elected by the people, it would be safe to trust him with greater power so that he would be able to protect their rights and welfare. For the governor to be more independent of the legislature and to allow him to check the legislature's use of power, his salary was fixed and could not be changed by the legislature. He had the power to veto laws made by the legislature, though his veto could only be overridden by a two-thirds vote of the legislature. He could appoint officials to work in the executive branch and judges to the judicial branch with little interference from the legislature.

Remember that in English government, the powers were separated among different groups of British society: royalty, nobility, and commons. A basic reason for separating powers among these groups was to prevent one group from completely dominating the others. In the United States, there was no royalty or nobility for a monarch or a House of Lords. The Massachusetts Constitution divided the people of the state into groups based upon their wealth and the amount of taxes paid. Taxation also brings representation. Only people with a large amount of property could vote to elect the governor. People with slightly less property could vote to elect members of the upper house of the state legislature. People with the minimum amount of property that enabled them to vote could vote for members of the lower house.

The Massachusetts Constitution provided for a more even balance among the powers of the different branches of government. It did not make the legislature the most powerful branch as it was in the other states. In some ways, this difference reveals different beliefs about the best ways to prevent the abuse of power by members of government. The constitutions of the other states were based on the idea that representation of the people in a strong state legislature was the best way to protect their rights, legislative supremacy, and majority rule. The Massachusetts Constitution was based on the idea that representation, separation of powers, and checks and balances were all essential for the protection of the rights of the people.

> We, therefore, the people of Massachusetts, acknowledging, with grateful hearts, the goodness of the Great Legislator of the Universe, in affording us, in the course of His Providence, an opportunity, deliberately and peaceably, without fraud, violence or surprise, on entering into an Original, explicit, and Solemn Compact with each other; and of forming a new Constitution of Civil Government, for Ourselves and Posterity, and devoutly imploring His direction in so interesting a design, Do agree upon, ordain and establish, the following Declaration of Rights, and Frame of Government, as the Constitution of the Commonwealth of Massachusetts.

Never before was man's hope for a better world more enthusiastic. Both in Europe, including Britain and in the experimentation in the New American States, the ideals of freedom, prosperity, man no longer chained by his past, her church, my family could prevent man from the pursuit of happiness. The New Jerusalem was emerging from the mind of man.

It deserves to be remarked, perhaps, that it is in the progressive state, while the society is advancing to the further acquisition, rather than when it has acquired its full complement of riches, that the condition of the laboring poor, of the great body of people, seems to be the happiest and the most comfortable. It is hard in the stationary, and miserable in the declining state. The progressive state is in reality the cheerful and the hearty stats to all different orders of society (Adam Smith, *The Wealth of Nations* 1776).

. . . The great and leading object of his (Adam Smith's) speculations is to illustrate the provisions made by nature in the principles of the human mind, and in the circumstances of man'3 external situation, for a gradual and progressive augmentation in the means of national wealth; and to demonstrate that the most effectual plan for advancing a people to greatness, is to maintain that order of things which nature has pointed out; by allowing every man, as long as he observes the rule of justice, to pursue his own interest in his own way, and to bring both his industry and his capital into freest competition with those of his fellow citizens (Dugald Stewart c.1780).

The arts and sciences, in general, during the three or four last centuries, have had a regular course of progressive improvement. The inventions in mechanic arts, the discoveries in natural philosophy, navigation, and commerce, and the advancement of civilization and humanity, have occasioned changes in the condition of the world, and the human character, which would have astonished the most refined, nations of antiquity (John Adams c.1793).

Articles of Confederation

In 1776, the Second Continental Congress voted to declare the colonies independent of the British government. The thirteen colonies were now independent nations, states. But the states needed to cooperate to fight the war against the powerful British army and navy, the most powerful empire on earth. It was the empire in all excepting the Death Star. On the same day the Congress created a committee to write the Declaration, it established a committee to write a new charter for a general government; a national government was necessary to perform all the activities of government: control trade among the states and between the states and foreign nations, and manage conflicts among the states over such issues as where their borders were to be.

The first government created by the Founders did not work well despite all their knowledge of political philosophy, history, and government. Knowledge of the shortcomings of that government is important in understanding that unless a government is organized properly, it may not work very well. It also helps in understanding why our government is organized as it is.

In 1776, a committee appointed by the Congress and led by John Dickinson of Pennsylvania wrote a draft of a constitution for the first national government. It was called the Articles of Confederation. It was approved by the Second Continental Congress on November 15, 1777, and sent to the states to approve/ratify. But the Americans quickly realized that agreeing on what kind of national government to create would not be easy. Members of the Congress argued on and off for more than a year before they came up with a constitution they could agree to present to the states for approval. Then the states argued about the constitution for four more years before all of them approved it.

Two major contradictory fears made it difficult for the Founders to agree upon the Articles of Confederation—fear of creating a national government that was too strong and that some states would have more power than others in the national government.

Once the war against Great Britain had started, each state was as a separate nation with its own constitution and government. To the people, their state was their "country" and all eligible voters should have a voice in government to elect members of their communities to represent their interests in their state legislatures. These governments were close enough to most citizens so they could even participate in some of its activities.

The Founders agreed they needed a national government. But they were afraid of making one that was too strong. They believed that most of the powers of government should be kept by the states because citizens could control state governments more easily than they could control a national government.

Meanwhile, the states were cooperating in the fight to free themselves from the control of a distant government in Great Britain. The Founders believed that the British government had deprived citizens of their rights, including their right to representation in the affairs of government. Many were afraid that if they agreed to create a strong national government, it could dominate the state governments and might become as dangerous to the rights of citizens as the British government had proved to be and would replace a tyrant three thousand miles away for one three hundred.

The Founders finally arrived at a solution to this problem: they created a weak national government under the Articles of Confederation with just a national legislature, the Continental Congress. There was no executive or judicial branch. While Congress was permitted to establish courts for certain limited purposes, most legal disputes were handled in state courts.

The Articles of Confederation left most of the powers of government with the states; the national government had little power over the states and their citizens. The Continental Congress did not have the power to control any person within a state. Only state governments had power over its people. It did not have the power to collect taxes from the states or from the people directly. It could only request money from the state governments, which were supposed to raise the money from their citizens. And no important decision could be made by the Continental Congress unless at least nine of thirteen states approved. This limitation on the powers of Congress applied, for example, to its ability to declare and conduct war, enter into treaties or alliances with other nations, and coin or borrow money.

The leaders in each state wanted to make sure that the new national government would be organized in a way that would not threaten their state's or its citizens' interests. Thus, the most important disagreement was over how states would vote in Congress. Would each state have an equal vote, or would states with greater population or wealth be given more votes than others? Decisions in the Congress would be made by majority vote, as are all republics. Some leaders were afraid that the majority would use their power for their own interest at the expense of those who were in the minority. The solution adopted was to give each state one vote in the Continental Congress regardless of its population.

On March 1, 1781, after four years of discussion, all the state governments agreed to accept the Articles of Confederation as the constitution for the national government of the United States. For the first time since the term was used in the Declaration of Independence, the former colonies became officially known as the United States of America. The first president was Samuel Huntington of Connecticut. This "second government" was under the Congress of the Confederation, though some have said it is the "first governing constitution."

The Articles of Confederation provided the framework for the first government of the United States. The guiding principle of this government was to spread power among the states. The powers of the national government were severely limited. Altogether there were thirteen articles. Here are excerpts from nine of them.

- Art. I. The name of this confederacy shall be The United States of America. [Note the capital *S*.]
- Art. 11. Each state retains its sovereignty, freedom, and independence, and every power, jurisdiction, and right, which is not by this confederation expressly delegated to the united states, in Congress assembled.
- Art. 111. The said states hereby enter into a firm league of friendship with each other, binding themselves to assist each other against all attacks made upon them. [This be more of an alliance than a constitution.]
- Art. V. For the more convenient management of the general interests of the united states, delegates shall be annually appointed by their states to meet in Congress on the first Monday in November in every year.
- In determining questions in the united states in Congress assembled, each state shall have one vote.

- Art. VI. No state, without the consent of the united states in Congress assembled, shall enter into any agreement, alliance, or treaty with any king, prince, or state.
  - o Every state shall always keep up a well-regulated and disciplined militia, sufficiently armed.
  - o No state shall engage in any war without the consent of the united states in Congress assembled.
- Art. VIII. All expenses incurred for the common defense shall be paid for out of a common treasury, which shall be supplied by the states, in proportion to the value of all land within each state. The taxes for paying that proportion shall be laid and levied by the authority and direction of the legislatures of the states.
- Art. IX. The united states in Congress assembled shall have the sole and exclusive right and power of determining on peace and war, of sending and receiving ambassadors, and of entering into treaties and alliances. [Though the states were required to fight these wars.]
- The united states in Congress assembled shall also be the last resort on appeal in all disputes and differences between two or more states.
- The united states in Congress assembled shall also have the sole and exclusive right and power of regulating the value of coin struck by their own authority or by that of the states, fixing the standard of weights and measures, regulating the trade and managing all affairs with the Indians, establishing and regulating post offices, and appointing all officers of the land and naval forces.
- The united states in Congress assembled shall have the authority to appoint a committee to manage the general affairs of the united states and to appoint one of their number to preside, provided that no person be allowed to serve in the office of president more than one year.
- The united states in Congress assembled shall never engage in a war, nor enter into any treaties or alliances, nor coin money, nor regulate the value thereof, nor borrow money on the credit of the united states, nor appropriate money, nor appoint a commander in chief of the army or navy, unless nine states agree.

- Art. XI. Canada agreeing to this confederation, and joining in the laws of the united states, shall be admitted into this union. No other colony shall be admitted unless nine states agree.
- Art. XIII. The Articles of this confederation shall not be altered unless such alteration be agreed to in a Congress of the united states, and be afterward confirmed by the legislatures of every state.

Problems?

You have seen how the people of the states solved the problem of their fear of a strong national government: they created a government that had very limited power. Because the states were afraid that the Continental Congress might be able to control them, they made sure that they controlled it. Every action taken by the Continental Congress had to be with the consent, approval, and cooperation of most of the states. As a result, the nation began with a very weak national government.

Many of the difficulties that arose under the Articles of Confederation led to the decision to develop our present Constitution. The Confederation Congress had no money and no power to get it; Congress had to rely upon voluntary contributions from the state governments to pay for the costs of the national government. It had no power to force the states to live up to their promises to make the contributions. This system did not work. The states had promised to give the national government $10 million to pay for the costs of fighting the Revolutionary War. They only paid $1.5 million. Congress had borrowed most of the money it needed to pay for the war by selling revenue bonds (or paid soldiers in future redeemable pieces of paper) to Americans and foreigners, and it had no way to pay its debts. The state governments and many of the people living in the states were also deeply in debt after the war.

Congress did not have the power to make laws regulating the behavior of citizens or the states or to force state governments or their citizens to do anything. The citizens could be governed only by their own state governments. This meant that if members of a state government or citizens within a state disobeyed a resolution, recommendation, or request made by the national government, there was no way the national government could make them obey. The Articles clearly stated that each state kept its "sovereignty, freedom, and independence." The national government's inability to make state governments and their citizens live up to treaties it had made led to a serious situation. Not all of the colonists had been in favor of the Revolutionary War; some had remained loyal to Great Britain. Thousands of these people, called Loyalists, still lived in the United States. When the war was over, the national government signed a peace treaty with Great Britain called the Treaty of Paris, which was intended in part to protect Loyalists' rights and ensure that they were treated fairly. Some of these Loyalists owned property in the states, and some had loaned money to other citizens. Some state governments refused to respect this treaty. They often made it difficult for Loyalists to collect the money owed to them by other citizens. Sometimes the states had confiscated the Loyalists' property during the war. The national government had no power to force the state governments to respect the property rights of the Loyalists or to force individual citizens to pay back money owed to the Loyalists. Thus, the national government was powerless to live up to its promise to the British government to protect the rights of these citizens.

Although Congress had the power to make agreements with foreign nations, it did not have the power to make state governments live up to these agreements. This raised another difficulty. Some citizens imported goods from other nations and then refused to pay for them. Not surprisingly, people in foreign countries became reluctant to trade with people in the United States. In addition, when Great Britain recognized how weak Congress was in controlling foreign trade, it closed the West Indies to American commerce. As a result, many Americans lost money because they were unable to sell their goods to people in other nations. Others were not able to buy goods from abroad. Congress had no power to make laws controlling business or trade among the states. Thus, people in some states, often with the help of their state governments, tried to take advantage of people in other states. For example, to benefit local businesses, some state governments passed laws forbidding the sale of goods from other states. Such activities prevented efficient and productive trade among the states and caused serious economic problems for the country. Businesses failed, and many people became poverty stricken and unable to repay money they had borrowed from other citizens. This created another serious situation.

Many people believed that one of the most serious problems in the United States during the 1780s was the failure of the state governments to protect their citizens' property rights. As you have learned, in most states, the government was controlled by the legislative branch, composed of representatives elected by a majority of the people. A faction is a group of people that seeks to promote its own interests. During this period, a number of factions developed that often captured majorities in the state legislatures. These majorities were accused of making laws that benefited themselves at the expense of the minority and of the common welfare. For example, they passed laws that canceled debts, confiscated the property of Loyalists, and created paper money resulting in inflation, which benefited the debtors at the expense of those to whom they owed money. People who were being hurt by such laws argued that their property was not being protected by their state governments. They claimed that the state governments were being used by one class of people to deny the rights of others and that they were not acting for the common good. Some people argued that there was too much democracy in the state governments. They claimed that representative government with majority rule did not adequately protect the natural rights of individual citizens or the common welfare. They argued that majority rule, when the majority pursued its own selfish interests at the expense of the rights of others, was just another form of tyranny, every bit as dangerous as that of an uncontrolled king.

The Treaty of Paris that ended the American Revolution established American sovereignty over the land between the Appalachians and the Mississippi; the job of determining how that land should be governed and how the conflicting claims to it by several of the states should be resolved were one of the first major tasks facing the new nation. There were two potential problems of these claims. The first was clear: many claims had more than one state laying claim, but clearly only one would be ultimately recognized as the owner. The other conflict also threatened the peace of the new Union. Only seven of the thirteen states had western land claims, and the other "landless" states were fearful of being overwhelmed by states that controlled vast stretches of the new frontier. Virginia in particular, which already encompassed one in five inhabitants of the new nation, laid claim to modern-day Kentucky, Indiana, and Illinois, and the smaller states feared that it would come to completely dominate the Union. In the end, most of the trans-Appalachian land claims were ceded to the national government between 1781 and 1787; New York, New Hampshire, and the area later to be Vermont resolved their squabbles by 1791, and Kentucky was separated from Virginia and made into a new state in 1792. The cessions were not entirely selfless—in some cases, the cessions were made in exchange for national assumption of the states' Revolutionary War debts—but the states' reasonably graceful cessions of their often-conflicting claims prevented early, perhaps catastrophic, rifts among the states of the young Republic and eased the fears of the "landless" states enough to convince them to ratify the new United States Constitution. The cessions also set the stage for the settlement of the Upper Midwest and the expansion of the United States into the center of the North American continent, and established the pattern by which land newly acquired by the United States would be organized into new states rather than attached to old ones. Georgia held on to its claims for another decade, but this claim was complicated by the fact that much of the land was also disputed between the United States and Spain. When Georgia finally sold the land west of its current boundaries to the United States for cash in 1802, the last phase of western cessions was complete.

Shays' Rebellion and the seeds of change

A dramatic event that finally convinced many people of the need for a stronger national government was Shays' Rebellion. Farmers in Massachusetts had serious economic problems. When they could not pay their debts, many of them lost their homes and their farms. Some were even put into prison. Popular discontent rose, and angry crowds prevented the courts from punishing people or selling the property of those who could not pay their debts.

Yet this was not the first or the last "rebellion of the lower classes versus the corruption of debts, war, and consolidated central government. There have been many such battles. Two that preceded Shays' were the Regulation in North Carolina and the fight in Vermont over land grants.

The War of Regulation (1764–1771) began shortly after the French and Indian War. North Carolina farmers were being forced to pay the bills for the war but because of the war were much in debt. Colonial lawyers and colonial officials had padded tax bills and now charged exorbitant legal fees for remortgages and bankruptcies. In addition, it was more than a city versus country conflict. There were English in the eastern coastal towns and Scotch Irish and Germans in the western hinterlands, a prelude of future Eastern intellectuals and working-class common man (Hamiltonians versus Jeffersonians). The farmers were called the Regulators—meaning they were merely checking up, keeping honest the politicians and tax collectors. The movement never really had a leader as such. James Hunter, "command" of the Regulators, emphatically said, "We are all free men, and every man must command himself."

The struggle came to an end most ingloriously for Governor Tryon at the Battle of Alamance on May 16, 1771. The governor, outnumbered, ordered artillery to fire on the farmers. Governor Tryon lost nine men, with sixty-one wounded; the Regulators lost twenty, killed, and about one hundred were wounded. The governor, contrary to history, declared "a signal and glorious victory was obtained over the obstinate and infatuated rebels." Twelve Regulators were tried for treason, and all were convicted. Six were hanged, and the rest were pardoned by the governor. James Pugh, with a rope around his neck, cited a list of charges against government abuse; the governor "kicked the barrel out from under Pugh's feet in midsentence."

The second prelude to Shays' Rebellion took place in disputed lands in what is today Vermont. Starting before the French and Indian War, New Hampshire had granted lands in payment to a number of families. As early as the 1740s, these families talked of a new charter for a new colony. When New Yorkers petitioned the king over the lands, he sided with New York. New York began issuing titles to the land, and now each piece had two titleholders.

New York claimed right to sell land to "gentlemen of weight and consideration." The small holders could rent their land from the rich "land-owners." The Granters (Vermonters) put surveyors on trial, drove out the Yorker militias, and burned the homes of justices of the peace that recognized NY grants.

When one hundred unarmed farmers occupying the county courthouse at Westminster refused to leave, a Yorker sheriff ordered his men to shoot them. Panic ensued, and forty men, including the wounded, were herded like animals into the courthouse jail and left to die.

William French, twenty-two years old, died from a gunshot to the head. Massachusetts and New Hampshire militia did come to the farmers' aid the next day and arrested the sheriff. The Westminster Massacre of March 13, 1775, is viewed by some as the first battle of the American Revolution.

The Westminster confrontation was a continuation of the Grants versus Yorkers dispute. The farmers needed to put off their creditors until the fall harvest when they would have money to pay off their debts. They resented the New York land speculators they owed and feared being jailed or losing their land.

Up until this time, most Grants settlers on the east side of the Green Mountains had peacefully negotiated disputes with New York. They had not been enthusiastic supporters of the Green Mountain Boys. The New York sheriff's actions changed their minds, and they were happy when Ethan Allen's men rode into town the next day. He called the fight "a violent struggle . . . that pitted a small cadre of wealthy gentlemen against an entire community of settled and industrious yeomen and their families."

Following the same pattern, in November 1786, a group of several hundred frustrated farmers gathered under the leadership of Daniel Shays. While several states managed to pay off their debts (namely, Virginia and New York), others like Massachusetts (who had invented the idea of fiat [fake] paper money to pay bills) experienced open rebellion. Soldiers and hungry patriots had sold their war bonds to speculators at pennies on the dollar, later redeemed to speculators under Treasury Secretary Alexander Hamilton at 100 percent. The Massachusetts legislature in cahoots with the now "creditors" now promised to pay holders at full value. To raise the funds, the Massachusetts government drastically raised property taxes by as much as 60 percent. Citizens in western Massachusetts lost farms in foreclosure. These farmers, most whom were Revolutionary War veterans, faced high taxes and an economic recession after the war, making it difficult to pay their mortgages. Debtors' courts siding with the banks confiscated property and sent debtors to prison. Farmers demanded stable paper currency and tax relief. The wealthy class, concerned with getting bonds redeemed by the government, wanted more taxes. Revolutionary War soldier Daniel

Shays petitioned the state for help and being denied first shut down the county court house and then threatened to march on the capital.

Because they needed weapons to use to protect their properties against the state government, they tried to capture the arsenal at Springfield, where arms were kept for the state militia. Although Shays' men were defeated, their rebellion frightened many property owners who feared similar problems might arise in their states. Yet the "insurrection" had few real debtors; most were productive and hardworking people led by the most prominent members of the western lands. Shay's farmers never called themselves rebels; they used the term "political regulators." They were trying to "chasten the governing elite to restore order." This excerpt from *The Winter Soldier*, a novel of Shays' Rebellion by James Lincoln Collier and Christopher Collier (1978), shows utter disregard for the complaints of the commoners vis-à-vis those at the reigns of power.

> The sheriff stopped tying the rope and stared at Peter. "Look," he said, "I don't like this either. It's the law. You borrowed money from Mattoon and you didn't pay him. He's got a legal right to take the oxen."
>
> "As the law he signs the order; as my creditor he takes my oxen," Peter shouted. "How can I pay anybody anything when every time I turn around Mattoon and his kind in the General Court have plastered on another tax?" [...]
>
> "You're not the only one," Sheriff Porter said. "Yesterday I took a horse and a plow from James Bacon and the day before, a hundred weight of flax from Hezakiah White. And last week we had to foreclose on a farm down in Amherst. I didn't like any of it, either, Peter, but that's the law."
>
> "Mattoon's law," Peter shouted. "How come the high and mighty have got the laws on their side and the plain man hasn't got any on his? Who makes the laws?"
>
> "The General Court—"

The fears raised by such conflicts as Shays' Rebellion, combined with the difficulties in raising taxes and regulating foreign trade, convinced a growing number of people of the need to strengthen the national government. George Washington was one of these people. He wrote to James Madison, "We are either a united people or we are not. If the former, let us act as a nation. If we are not, let us no longer act a farce by pretending to it." Samuel Adams: "Rebellion against a king may be pardoned, or lightly punished, but the man who dares to rebel against the laws of a republic ought to suffer death." Thomas Jefferson: "A little rebellion now and then is a good thing. It is a medicine necessary for the sound health of government. God forbid that we should ever be twenty years without such a rebellion."

Many have listed the weaknesses of the Articles of Confederation but too little on the strengths and accomplishments. It was under the Articles that hostilities eased and peace was signed. On January 20, 1783, "Suspension of Arms and Cessation of Hostilities" was agreed to between England and the United States; on September 3, 1783, Treaty of Paris officially ended the Revolutionary War. Though Shays' makes it sound as no troops were paid, the Confederation Congress paid most troops with western lands after removing foreign troops and flags. British troops stayed in many parts of the Ohio Valley waiting for payments of losses to Loyalist colonials. The Great Seal of the United States and the American flag were designed under the Articles. The future structure of departments of government was begun with the Departments of Treasury, War, and Foreign Affairs. The first Thanksgiving, the fourth Thursday in November, was established as a day of prayer for the war effort. Two important laws that will later develop the progress of the new nation, the Land Ordinance of 1785 and the Northwest Ordinance of 1787, both laid out the design and rules of new states (to be equal members to the original thirteen) and banned slavery in the new Northwest Territories. In addition, it was the freest national government at the time, maybe ever.

THE GREAT EXPERIMENT: UNITED
STATES CONSTITUTION

We the people are the rightful masters of both Congress
and the courts, not to overthrow the Constitution but to
overthrow the men who pervert the Constitution.
—Abraham Lincoln

THE GREAT EXPERIMENT, the world's first federal system, the first presidency, the first system of self-government, the first Enlightenment government, was about to move from the mind of man to expression in the actions of a people. The Convention of demigods understood and was adamant that this great experiment was fragile. It required a citizenry that was educated and modest and had civic virtue. If it worked, it would be a miracle. As Katie Drinker Bowen in her classic, *Miracle at Philadelphia*, wrote, it was as if the stars danced in the sky when the document was approved. It was not an easy task; compromise was the norm. The debates at the Convention continued in the ratification conventions in all the states. That debate continued through the first presidencies with Federalists (not actually Federalists) that argued for a strong consolidated government that would direct the nation to a worldwide empire in constant warfare and welfare, while the Anti-Federalists (true believers in Federalism and republicanism) will seem to fade after the Civil War, whispered during the Progressive Age of the early twentieth century and appear dead when today's Republicans and Democrats are both Hamilton's vision holders. But with the rise of the Tea Parties, Occupy Wall Street, Austrian free market explanations of the continual crashes of big governments manipulating the markets, Ron Paul's push among the young, freedom, republicanism, and capitalism are again on the rise. The failure of men to stay within the bounds of the Constitution, as well as disillusionment with the experiment because of the disendoctrination of the West, the Enlightenment and the value of man, and the control of education by the national government, had made it seem as though man's experiment was a doomed failure of naïve history.

Philadelphia Convention

The Constitution was written at a convention held in Philadelphia in 1787. Many leaders of the revolution were afraid that the Articles relied too heavily on civic virtue. The state governments fearful of a strong centralized central government had weakened their governors and placed most powers in the hands of elected legislatures. They believed the electorate would select governments filled with officeholders with the interests of the rights of man foremost in decision-making. One serious mistake underlies all the issues of the Articles: man is greedy and self-interested in general. Civic virtue requires putting that aside one's own self-interest. But how? That is the great question in the great experiment. That is the question the Framers will ask and attempt to solve with the Constitution. But what were they attempting to fix?

The Articles did have problems: economic, political, fiscal, and military. Economically, states began to set up barriers, tariffs, with each other, charging taxes to cross state borders; some to raise money, some to "protect" merchants of their own state. Ironic as it seems, what they had fought against, regulation of free trade, the states now did to each other. Some of these trade "wars" will become near or actual shooting wars. Many states will refuse to enforce contracts and debts between their citizens and those of other states. Some even were attempting to cancel debts or restitution owed Loyalists for damages and/or confiscations from the war.

But the most crucial of these economic concerns was inflation (paper money). This rotten economic idea went all the way to the Confederation Congress. Prices were soaring for common everyday goods. Farmers who had borrowed at stronger dollars could pay back in cheaper dollars, harming creditors and banks. Many state legislatures attempted to require hard money only for repayment. With a shortage of gold and silver, real money, debts went unpaid, mortgages foreclosed upon, and many farmers, many veterans of the war lost everything (leading to many of the rebellions seen in the time, Shays' only the most famous). When rebellion did result, the central government could not help the states restore order, and societies spiraled further down.

Militarily, the British were still located in the Northwest Territories encouraging Indians to harass the western edges of the new states, supplying weapons and promises of returning the land. The British will later encourage Tecumseh and others up through the War of 1812. The central government with no standing army of its own asked state militias for help; but with no money and the issues not relevant to each state's militia, little could be done. In addition, Spain, an ally during the war, controlled the Mississippi by holding the Yazoo Territory (see map). This small strip of land controlled the trade south to New Orleans from an extensive area to later include the Midwest and the Southeast. (A side note: One of Lincoln's chief objectives in the Civil War was to control this area as well. See Vicksburg in the center? Grant took Vicksburg, while Lee was losing Gettysburg.)

In that area and in the Ohio Valley, Indians were still very powerful, probably stronger than the new nation. The Northwest Indian War (1785–1795), also known as Little Turtle's War and by other names, was a war between the United States and a confederation of numerous Indian tribes for control of the Northwest Territory.

Later, Pres. George Washington ordered the US Army to halt the hostilities between the Indians and settlers and enforce US sovereignty over the territory. The US Army, consisting of mostly untrained recruits supported by equally untrained militiamen, suffered a series of major defeats, including the Harmar Campaign (1790) and St. Clair's Defeat (1791), major Indian victories. About one thousand army regulars and militiamen were killed, and the United States forces suffered many more casualties than their opponents.

After the St. Clair's disaster, Washington ordered Gen. "Mad" Anthony Wayne to organize and train a proper fighting force. Wayne took command of the new Legion of the United States late in 1793. He led his men to a decisive victory at the Battle of Fallen Timbers in 1794. This finally brought the conflict to an end. The defeated Indian tribes were forced to cede extensive territory, including much of present-day Ohio, in the Treaty of Greenville in 1795.

Another issue not settled until under Thomas Jefferson was Moroccan pirates. They had a policy of kidnapping anyone travelling in the Atlantic or Mediterranean of any nation not paying the bribes requested. With no central navy, the Articles could not protect its own citizens, and ransom and bribes will be the procedure until the Marines storm the "Shores of Tripoli" in 1804.

Power and politics will bring all this to a head in the years 1783–1787. Meetings and letters among later Framers highlight many weaknesses in the power of the Articles. But Congress had no power to tax, having to borrow from the states for operating costs. Seldom was there even a quorum to discuss and pass laws. Rebellious rumblings began almost immediately after the Treaty of Paris.

Even while the war was raging, with few supplies and a ragtag army behind him, Washington dealt with a near rebellion of his own army. One of his officers, Lewis Nicola, suggested that the army disregard the civil authority and make Washington a king; Washington was filled with anger. But he exercised great restraint over his own temper. He wrote a letter—reasoned and even-handed, the Newburgh Letter— rebuking Nicola.

Also at Newburgh, New York, Washington's headquarters, there was more unrest, this time among his officers. The Newburgh Conspiracy was due to unrest in 1783 for pay that many of the officers and men of the American Continental Army had not received pay for many years. The officers had been promised a lifetime pension of half pay; instead, Congress gave them five years' full pay. Congress had no money because the states refused to send the money they had promised. The content of this Newburgh Letter reveals the frustration of the army. It states that they would refuse to disband if they were not paid, and they would refuse to fight to protect the Congress if it were attacked.

Washington, in response to a letter from Alexander Hamilton, said that while he sympathized both with the plight of his officers and men and with those in Congress, he would not use the army to threaten the civil government: a course, which Washington believed, would violate the principles of republicanism for which they had all been fighting. A small group of officers, led probably by Maj. John Armstrong Jr., an aide to Maj. Gen. Horatio Gates, attempted to forestall Washington's intervention, viewing him as too moderate; they would have forcibly installed Gates in his place as commander in chief. They published placards, the "Newburgh Addresses," calling for a meeting on March 12. They warned that come peace Congress would ignore them, as they "grow old in poverty, wretchedness and contempt."

Washington canceled the March 12 meeting and called his own meeting of officers on March 15. After Gates opened the meeting, Washington entered the building to everyone's surprise. He asked to speak to the officers, and the stunned Gates relinquished the floor. Washington could tell by the faces of his officers, who had not been paid for quite some time, that they were quite angry and did not show the respect or deference as they had toward Washington in the past. He gave a short but impassioned speech, the Newburgh Address, counseling patience. His message was that they should oppose anyone "who wickedly attempts to open the floodgates of civil discord and deluge our rising empire in blood." He then took a letter from his pocket from a member of Congress to read to the officers. He gazed upon it and fumbled with it without speaking. He then took a pair of reading glasses from his pocket, which were new and few of the men had seen him wear them. He then said, "Gentlemen, you will permit me to put on my spectacles, for I have not only grown gray but almost blind in the service of my country." This caused the men to realize that Washington had sacrificed a great deal for the revolution, just as much as any of them. These, of course, were his fellow officers, most having worked closely with him for several years. Many present, including Washington, were moved to tears, and with this act, the conspiracy collapsed as he read the letter. He then left the room, and Gen. Henry Knox and others offered resolutions reaffirming their loyalty, which were accepted by the group. Congress finally resolved the crisis by giving a sum equal to five years' pay to each officer entitled to half pay for life. They received government bonds, which at the time were highly speculative but were in fact redeemed one hundred cents on the dollar by the new government in 1790.

In response to the officers' frustrations, the Society of Cincinnati was established. It was begun as the brainchild of Maj. Gen. Henry Knox. Supported by George Washington, Knox initiated the society and helped draft the institution upon which it is based. The basis for the creation of the Society of the Cincinnati was to provide a means of ongoing fellowship for the officers of the Continental Army and to develop charitable funds to assist the families of original members. The society also acted on behalf of the army's officers to secure military pensions for surviving Revolutionary War veterans.

Later that summer, riots by unpaid Pennsylvania veterans, in June 1783, again showed the weakness of the Congress to pay its bills or have the states assume the war debts.

Because of the problems experienced under the Articles of Confederation, a number of prominent leaders suggested holding a meeting of representatives of all of the states. Virginia and Maryland sent delegates to resolve issues of commerce, fishing, and navigation on the Potomac River. George Washington invited them to convene at his home in Mount Vernon in March 1785. The two states discussed adjustments to improve commerce. George Washington admonished them: "We are either a united people or we are not. If the former, let us act as a nation. If not, let us no longer act a farce by pretending to it." Under George Mason's help, the two states solved their problems without the need for a central government, something he will remember in Philadelphia. The success of the meeting led James Madison of Virginia to call for another meeting, this time in Maryland.

In the spring of 1781, Robert Morris, a wealthy Philadelphia merchant and member of the Articles of Confederation Congress, pushed through a British-style national central bank. Having made millions in war contract corruption, he and his followers (nationalists, later deceptively called Federalists) wanted to establish a localized British system, mercantilism, and big government. According to Murray Rothbard in his *Mystery of Banking*, Morris wanted "to have a strong central government, particularly a strong president or king as chief executive, built up by high taxes and heavy public debt. The strong central government was to impose high tariffs to subsidize domestic manufacturers, develop a big navy to open up and subsidize foreign markets for American exports, and launch a massive system of internal public works. In short, the United States was to have a British system without Great Britain."

His first attempt, the Bank of North America failed when, as history says, its currency was not worth a Continental, the public rejected the useless inflated money, and within a year, the bank failed. Instead of blaming the failed policies of cheap money and massive revolutionary spending and printing, Morris blamed the Articles.

That summer, things turned from bad to worse. New York's delegation vetoed Morris's twenty-five-year plan to raise revenue. The following spring, his 1786 impost requested $3.8 million, and the

Congress gave him all it had; he received only $663. The British, and now the French, were blockading our shores to confiscate ships to pay debts owed. In May 1786, Charles Pinckney of South Carolina suggested granting Congress power over foreign and domestic commerce, and more controversially, providing means for Congress to collect money from state treasuries. And in August, Shays' "Rebellion" shocked Massachusetts and the "nation."

In September 1786, all thirteen states were invited to send representatives to a meeting in Annapolis, Maryland. Virginia and Maryland's agreement at Mount Vernon was technically a violation of Article VI of the Articles; states could not sign treaties, only Congress. Only five states sent representatives: Alexander Hamilton, James Madison, Abraham Clark, Edmund Randolph, and John Dickinson. Disappointed at the turnout at the meeting, Madison and the others decided not to discuss the Articles of Confederation. Instead, they wrote a report, which they sent to Congress and every state legislature. The report asked each state to send representatives to a meeting that was to be held in Philadelphia in 1787. The purpose of the Philadelphia meeting was to change the Articles of Confederation to strengthen the national government. The Virginia General Assembly now requested a meeting of all thirteen states.

At first, Congress ignored the report. Then in February 1787, Congress voted to support the meeting of the state representatives. However, it only gave them the authority to develop a plan to improve the Articles of Confederation. This plan was then to be sent to Congress for it to use as it wished. As far as Congress was concerned, the men who met in Philadelphia were just advisers to Congress.

Fifty-five delegates attended the meeting, which later became known as the Philadelphia Convention. It was a remarkable group of men that we now call the Framers of the Constitution. Most of them were fairly young. About three-fourths of the Framers had served in Congress. Most had been prominent in their states, where many had held political positions. Most had played important parts in the revolution. Some were rich, but most were not. A French diplomat in America at the time said that the Framers "without being rich are all in easy circumstances."

There was a wide range of high and middle-status occupations, but mainly younger and less senior in their professions. There were thirty-five lawyers, thirteen merchants, six land speculators, eleven speculated in securities on a large scale, twelve owned or managed slave-operated plantations or large farms, two small farmers, nine public officers. three retired, two scientists, three physicians, a college president, and a Protestant minister.

Another French diplomat stationed in America observed: "If all of the delegates named for the Philadelphia Convention are present, one will never have seen, even in Europe, an assembly more respectable for talents, knowledge, disinterestedness, and patriotism than those who will compose it." From Paris, Thomas Jefferson wrote to John Adams in London that the Convention "really is an assembly of demigods."

We should remember, however, that some of the Framers were men of modest abilities and questionable motives. Probably the most balanced view of the men at Philadelphia has been given by Max Farrand, a historian, who wrote: "Great men there were, it is true, but the Convention as a whole was composed of men such as would be appointed to a similar gathering at the present time: professional men, businessmen, and gentlemen of leisure; patriotic statesmen and clever, scheming politicians; some trained by experience and study for the task before them; and others utterly unfit. It was essentially a representative body."

Most of the 1787 delegates were natives of the thirteen colonies; only eight were born elsewhere. Several others had studied or traveled abroad. Most were married and raised children. Sherman fathered the largest family, fifteen children by two wives. The average age was forty-two, most in late thirties and early forties; the oldest was Benjamin Franklin at eighty-one; the youngest, Charles Pinckney, twenty-seven? twenty-nine? twenty-four?

Most of the stories of the Framers are worth telling in detail. But we will limit ourselves to introducing you to some of the most important. We will also mention some of the leaders who did not attend but who played a part in the establishment of our constitutional government.

George Washington

George Washington, the most respected and honored man in the country, had left his farm and family at Mount Vernon, Virginia, to lead the American "army" in our victory over the British. When the war was over and there was no longer a need for a large army,

Washington returned to private life on his plantation. He was one of the leading citizens who was convinced that a stronger national government was necessary, mostly under the influence of his war aide-de-camp Alexander Hamilton. He had been writing numerous leaders in the last years of his opinion. After meetings at Mount Vernon with some of these gentlemen, George Washington, having first refused to attend a convention, agreed to represent Virginia. His change of mind came because he feared that if he did not attend, people might think that he had lost faith in republican government. Washington was not active in the debates, but his presence and his support of the Constitution were essential to its ratification later by the states. He supposedly spoke only once to berate someone who had dropped notes of the day's debate in a nearby inn. When the time came to select a president for the new government, there was no doubt Americans would unite behind the American Cincinnatus who, time and time again, exercised civic virtue, setting aside his own interests and devoting himself to the common welfare of a new nation.

James Madison

James Madison, of all the Framers, probably influenced the new government created at the Convention. Born in 1751, Madison was one of the youngest of the revolutionary leaders. He became active in Virginia politics in the 1780s and was one of the most influential leaders in favor of a stronger national government, though later will be considered a foe of Hamilton's nationalism and become a leader of the opposition under the Republicans of Jefferson. His influence at the Convention was largely because he brought with him a plan that he and others had already developed, the Virginia Plan. After some debate over alternatives, this plan was used as the basis for debates on how to improve the government.

Had it not been for Madison, we probably would not know much about what happened during the Convention. The Framers had decided to keep the discussions of the meetings secret, but they trusted Madison to take notes during the proceedings. Most of what we know today about what happened is based on those notes.

After the Convention, Madison's convincing arguments about the best way to organize the new government led him to be one of three men asked to write a defense of the newly written Constitution. This defense was a series of articles written for newspapers in New York. It is now called *The Federalist*. It was used to convince the citizens of New York to vote for delegates to the state ratifying convention who were favorable to the Constitution. It is the most important work written by Americans on the basic principles and ideas underlying our constitutional government. Madison later became the fourth president of the United States.

In addition to Washington and Madison, the delegates included many other prominent men. Benjamin Franklin was in poor health—he was eighty-one at the time—but because he was so well respected, his participation at crucial moments contributed a great deal to the success of the Convention. Alexander Hamilton, while one of the greatest supporters of a strong national government, left in frustration before the Convention was half over, returning for a few days to help finalize and sign the completed document. However, as you will learn, he was one of the authors of *The Federalist* and played a major role in the struggle over the ratification of the Constitution. George Mason, the author of the Virginia Bill of Rights, was a great champion of the rights of the people and of the states. He believed the national government created by the Constitution threatened those rights. He was one of the three delegates who later refused to sign the Constitution at the close of the Convention.

There were also some important political leaders who did not attend the Convention. Thomas Jefferson had drafted the Declaration of Independence, served as governor of Virginia, and was a member of Congress under the Articles of Confederation. At the time of the Convention, he was ambassador to France and was unable to attend. Thomas Paine, the author of *Common Sense* and *The Rights of Man,* was with Jefferson in France. John Adams, one of America's most important political thinkers and the second president of the United States, was on a diplomatic mission to England.

> Though written constitutions may be violated in moments
> of passion or delusion, yet they furnish a text to which those
> who are watchful may again rally and recall the people; they
> fix too for the people the principles of their political creed
> (Thomas Jefferson, letter to Joseph Priestly, July 19, 1802).

Patrick Henry, the great revolutionary orator, refused to attend because he was against the development of a strong national government. He suspected what might happen at there and said that he "smelled a rat." Henry will be one of the leaders who campaigned against adoption of the Constitution. Samuel Adams and John Hancock were not selected by their state; they were too radical.

The central question the delegates had to address is the balance between the common good and individual rights. You have already seen the failure of the first American document of government, the Articles of Confederation. The Articles had created a central government so ineffective that it had little or no control over the nation as a whole.

> A Constitution is framed for ages to come, and is designed to approach immortality as nearly as human institutions can approach it (John Marshall, *Cohens v. Virginia,* 1821).

The Convention begins

By May 25, 1787, delegates from all states but Rhode Island were present in Philadelphia. Rhode Island had a history of individualism, self-reliance, and dissent. It had a largely rural population, and the people feared high national land taxes. Later, its state legislature was Anti-Federalist. George Washington was unanimously elected to be the presiding officer.

Almost immediately the Framers agreed on two things:

- They decided to ignore the instructions they had received from Congress to limit their work to improving the Articles of Confederation. Instead, they began to work on the development of a new constitution. They were convinced that the defects of the Articles were so serious that it would be better not to use them as the basis for their discussion.
- They decided to keep the record of what they said at the Convention a secret for thirty years.

There were two reasons for this.

- They wanted to develop the best constitution they could. This required a free exchange of ideas. They were afraid that if their debates were made public, many of the delegates would not feel free to express their opinions.
- They thought that the constitution they developed would have a greater chance of being accepted if people did not know about the arguments that went on while it was being created.

They also agreed that although the delegations from each state varied in size, each state would have one vote at the Convention.

They were committed to the development of a stronger national government; at what level was still a debate, from Hamilton's near monarchy to Mason's tweaks of the Articles of Confederation. During the Convention, there was a great deal of agreement on fundamental principles and most of the basic issues. Thus, they were able, in less than four months, to create a constitution that has lasted for over two hundred years, electing forty-five presidents. This remarkable achievement began with a first session at which only seven of the thirteen states had delegates present. By the end of the Convention, every state except Rhode Island was represented.

More than one plan

Both the Virginia and the New Jersey delegates to the Philadelphia Convention submitted plans to organize the new national government for the attendees' consideration. After considerable debate, the Virginia Plan was used as the basis for the new Constitution. Not all the recommendations in the plan were accepted. An understanding of it and the other plans and the debates over them should increase your understanding of the Constitution and the continuing debates over how our government is organized. The majority of the Constitution is, however, the Virginia Plan of James Madison.

Many delegates came to Philadelphia convinced that the defects of the Articles were so serious it would be better not to use them as a starting point. One of these was James Madison. Before the Convention, he already had drafted a plan for a new national government, which came to be called the Virginia Plan. While they waited for the other state delegations to arrive, the Virginia delegates had agreed to put Madison's plan forward as a basis for the Convention's discussions.

The most important thing to know about the Virginia Plan is that it proposed a strong national government. Under the Articles of Confederation, the national government could act only on the states, not on the people directly. For example, the national government could request money, but only the states had the authority to raise that money through taxes.

Under the Virginia Plan, the national government would have the power to make and enforce its own laws and to collect its own taxes. Each citizen would be governed under the authority of two governments, the national government, and a state government. Both governments would get their authority from the people. The existence of two governments, national and state, each given a certain amount of authority, is what we now call a federal system. In addition, the Virginia Plan recommended the following:

- Three branches—legislative, executive, and judicial—would compose the national government. The legislative branch would be more powerful than the other branches because, among other things, it would have the power to select people to serve in the executive and judicial branches.
- The national legislature, Congress, was to have two houses. A House of Representatives would be elected directly by the people of each state. A Senate would be elected by the members of the House of Representatives from lists of persons nominated by the legislature of each state.
- The number of representatives from each state in both the House and the Senate would be based on the size of its population or the amount of its contribution to the national treasury. This system of proportional representation meant that states with larger populations would have more representatives in the legislature than states with smaller populations.
- The Virginia Plan gave the legislative branch of the national government the following powers:
  o to make all laws that individual states were not able to make, such as laws regulating trade between two or more states;

o   to strike down state laws that it considered to be in violation of the national constitution or the national interest;

o   to call forth the armed forces of the nation against a state, if necessary, to enforce the laws passed by Congress; and

o   to elect people to serve in the executive and judicial branches of government.

What do you think?

1. What are some advantages and disadvantages of having two houses of a Congress?
2. Why do you think the Virginia Plan gave Congress the power to strike down state laws? What arguments could you make for or against giving a national Congress this power?
3. How did the Virginia Plan correct what the Framers saw as weaknesses in the Articles of Confederation?

There was considerable debate among them over the Virginia Plan. In the early weeks of the Convention, as specific features of the plan were discussed, a major disagreement over representation became apparent.

- The larger states wanted both houses of the national legislature to be based on proportional representation. They argued that a government that both acted on and represented the people should give equal voting power to equal numbers of people.
- The smaller states wanted equal representation—equal voting power for each state. Their position was based on their fear that unless they had an equal voice, as they did under the Articles of Confederation, the larger states would dominate them.

By mid-June, this disagreement had created a crisis for the Convention. The delegates from the small states, led by William Paterson of New Jersey, asked for time to come up with an alternative to the Virginia Plan.

New Jersey Plan

On June 15, William Paterson presented the small states' plan, which has become known as the New Jersey Plan. The small states did not wish to create a national government in which they had little power. They argued that the best and safest thing to do would be to keep the framework of the Articles of Confederation, as they had been asked to do. The following are some of the main parts of the plan.

1. Legislative branch. Congress would have only one house, as in the Confederation, and it would be given the following increased powers:

   - Taxes. The national government would be given the power to levy import duties and a stamp tax to raise money for its operations, together with the power to collect money from the states if they refused to pay.
   - Trade. Congress would be given the power to regulate trade among the states and with other nations.
   - Control over the states. The laws and treaties made by Congress would be considered the supreme law of the land. No state could make laws that were contrary to them.

2. Executive branch. This branch would be made up of several persons appointed by Congress. They would have the power to administer national laws, appoint other executive officials, and direct all military operations.

3. Judicial branch. A supreme court would be appointed by the officials of the executive branch. It would have the power to decide cases involving treaties, trade among the states or with other nations, and the collection of taxes.

A quick summary is presented in the chart below. The key differences are listed and are quite significant.

Virginia Plan	New Jersey Plan
Popular representation, proportional	Equal votes from each state
Bicameral legislature	Unicameral legislature
Power to levy and collect taxes, regulate commerce	Some power to levy taxes, regulate commerce
Executive (including cabinet) size undetermined, elected and removed by Congress	Executive – more than one, elected by legislature, removed by state majority of governors
Judicial – life tenure, can override state laws, elected by legislature	National judiciary appointed by the president
Judicial – life tenure, can override state laws, elected by legislature	No power over states
Ratification by citizens	Ratification by the states

Charles Pinckney of South Carolina believed the Confederation was a treaty among the thirteen states but could be adapted to deal with the current problems. He suggested a two-house, bicameral legislature: a Senate and a House of Delegates. There would be one member for every one thousand inhabitants in the House. It would elect senators who would serve by rotation for four years and represent one of four regions. Congress would meet in a joint session to elect a president and would also appoint members of a cabinet, a group of advisors for the president. Congress, in joint session, would serve as the court of appeal of last resort in disputes between states. The Pinckney Plan was not debated, but it may have been referred to by the Committee of Detail, using some of his language and terms.

Alexander Hamilton wanted a British-type strong national government. Thus, he thought the president and Senate would be elected but serve for life on "good behavior." The House of Representatives directly elected for three-year terms. Hamilton was not really a "monarchist," but to the delegates, this plan smelled like a European monarchy. They could not accept it at all; Hamilton left the Convention in humiliation. However, not liking how the final document was developing, he returned to help draft the wording in the Committee of Style. He made sure that in disputes over "progress" imminent domain—power of a state or a national government to take private property for public use—was in the hands of the national government. And, of course, the "necessary and proper" clause was inserted into the powers of Congress. Later his interpretation when advising Washington will create the "monarchy" he wanted by strengthening the executive branch and the central government in general.

John Dickinson, the writer of the original Articles, also suggested a "plan." He fell ill during the Convention, so he did not press his issues. He believed representation upon financial contribution. Those who paid more taxes should have more representation. No representation without taxes. He also felt that those states without ports would have no source of revenue (customs and tariffs), therefore would be taken over in the government by wealthier states. He will sign the final while suffering from "severe headaches."

The New Jersey Plan continued the system of government existing under the Articles of Confederation. In this system, the national government represented and acted upon the states rather than directly representing and acting upon the people. The New Jersey Plan did contain useful suggestions to solve some weaknesses of the Articles of Confederation. By the time the New Jersey Plan was presented, after two weeks of debate on the Virginia Plan, many delegates had become convinced that the national government needed new powers and a new organization for exercising those powers.

When the vote was taken on June 19, the New Jersey Plan was supported by the delegations from New Jersey and Delaware, by a majority of the New York delegation, since Hamilton was always outvoted by his two colleagues and by half the Maryland delegation. So the Virginia Plan continued to be the basis for the Convention's discussion.

Several major issues had not been resolved, however. Among them were two potentially explosive ones.

- How should the number of representatives from each state be determined? Based on population? Many delegates still argued that each state should have an equal vote no matter how large or small its population.
- What powers should the national government have?

There were serious disagreements among the delegates. These disagreements were so intense that the Convention nearly failed.

Congress

Let's take the legislative branch first, Locke's favorite. The Framers also believed that the most important role would be held by the legislative branch. That is why Article I of the Constitution deals with the legislative branch. The first debates, therefore, were about the duties and powers that should be given to Congress and how it should be organized. They encountered problems in developing Article I that are still being debated today.

Continuing the British and colonial practice of two-house legislatures, every state except Pennsylvania had a legislative branch with two houses. There also was a widespread belief that a two-house legislature would be less likely to violate the people's rights. Each house could serve as a check on the other.

The Virginia Plan's proposal to create a two-house Congress was not controversial. What was controversial in the plan was the principle of proportional representation. James Madison, James Wilson, Rufus King, and others who represented states with large populations thought that the number of members in both houses should be based on the number of people they would represent. They argued that because the new government would operate directly on the people, it was only fair that a state with a larger number of people should have a greater voice—that is, more votes in the national government.

The delegates from states with smaller populations were afraid that proportional representation would result in a national government dominated by the more-populated states. They argued that each state should have the same number of representatives in Congress—equal representation. These delegates also were convinced that the people of their states would never approve the Constitution if it did not preserve equality among the states.

On July 2, they voted on whether there should be equal representation in the upper house of Congress. The result was a tie, five states to five, with Georgia divided. Neither side seemed willing to compromise; delegates began to fear that the Convention would end in disagreement and failure.

Then a special committee composed of one delegate from each state, headed by Elbridge Gerry, was formed. This committee was responsible for developing a plan to save the situation. Some supporters of the Virginia Plan, including James Madison and James Wilson, were against giving this responsibility to a committee. Most of the delegates disagreed with them, however, and the committee went to work. Gerry was selected because he had not yet picked a side in the Virginia/New Jersey struggle and was adamant that compromise was needed. "If we do not come to some agreement among ourselves, some foreign sword will probably do the work for us."

The result of the special committee's work is known as the Connecticut Compromise or the Great Compromise. The committee adopted a proposal previously suggested by Connecticut delegates Roger Sherman and Oliver Ellsworth. The Great Compromise, a.k.a. Connecticut Compromise, the Sherman, not Gerry, Compromise, contained the following ideas:

- The House of Representatives would be elected by the people on the basis of proportional representation—larger states having more votes.
- There would be equal representation of each state in the Senate. The legislature of each state would select two senators.
- The House of Representatives would be given the power to develop all bills for taxing and government spending. "Direct" taxes would be assigned and divided—apportioned—among the states by population. The Senate was limited to either accepting or rejecting these bills, but it could not change them. This provision was later changed to permit the Senate to amend tax bills developed in the House and to develop appropriation bills itself.

As in most compromises, each side gained a little and lost a little. The small states received the equal representation in the Senate that their delegates wanted to protect their interests. Many delegates also believed that a constitution without equal representation of states in at least one house of Congress would not be approved by the smaller states. The large states gave up control of the Senate but kept their control of the House of Representatives. The House was also given important powers regarding taxation and government spending, the power of the purse.

The result was that the more-populous states would have more influence over laws to tax the people and over how the money would be spent; the larger states were paying the larger share of any direct taxes imposed by Congress. The decisions of the House of Representatives, however, always would be subject to the check of the Senate, in which the small states had equal representation.

When the committee presented this compromise to the Convention, it was bitterly fought by some members from the larger states, including Madison, Wilson, and Gouverneur Morris. They viewed the idea of state equality in the Senate as a step away from a national government, back toward the system under the Articles of Confederation. Delegates from the small states remained suspicious as well. Two delegates from New York who had consistently voted with the smaller states left the Convention and did not return. The crisis was over when the compromise passed by one vote.

Under Article I of the Constitution of the United States, all legislative powers of the country are vested in Congress. The primary function of Congress is to enact legislation that is conveyed to the president for approval or veto. The Constitution establishes the organizational structure of Congress. The US Congress is what is known as a bicameral legislature. Bicameral means that the Congress is composed of two legislative bodies; these are the House of Representatives and the Senate. Legislation passed by one of the houses must be approved by the other chamber before being sent along to the president.

The Senate is composed of one hundred members. The vice president of the United States is president of the Senate, the only example of a US governmental official serving in two branches of government. The vice president's leadership role in the Senate largely is ceremonial. The vice president, in his role as Senate president, votes only in the event of a tie. The president pro tempore of the Senate is the ceremonial head of the Senate in the absence of the vice president. The functional or actual leader of the body is the Senate majority leader, selected by the political party with a majority of members. The Senate minority leader is the official who heads up the minority party.

The House is made up of 435 voting members and six nonvoting members. The Speaker of the House is the leader of the House of Representatives, elected by the majority party. The House majority leader is the second in command of the House, also selected by the majority party. The House minority leader is head of the minority party in the House of Representatives.

The organizational structure of both houses of Congress results in different voting rules in each body. In the House, legislation passes upon a majority vote of members present. The Senate, being a smaller body, requires what is known as a supermajority to end debate and move legislation to a vote. A supermajority to terminate debate requires a vote of at least sixty members.

A great deal of the work of both the Senate and the House of Representatives is done through committees and subcommittees. Through committees and subcommittees, proposed legislation initially is considered, including hearings on bills. If a piece of legislation is approved by a committee, the bill heads to the full House or Senate for consideration and an ultimate vote.

According to Article I, Section 2 of the Constitution, a candidate for the House must be

- twenty-five years of age (when seated, not when elected),
- a citizen of the United States for at least seven years, and
- an inhabitant of the state from which he or she is elected, not the district.

According to Article I, Section 3 of the Constitution, a candidate for the Senate must be

- thirty years of age (when seated, not when elected),
- a citizen of the United States for at least nine years, and
- an inhabitant of the state from which he or she is elected.

The Senate leadership includes the

- president of the Senate (the vice president of the United States);
- president pro tempore (usually the most senior member of the Senate majority party);
- majority leader;
- majority whip, or assistant majority leader;
- minority leader; and
- minority whip, or assistant minority leader.

The representatives are generally less independent of party leaders than senators and usually vote as the leadership directs. Incentives to cooperate include the leadership's power to select committee chairs, determine committee assignments, and provide reelection support in the primary and general elections. Thus, the leadership plays a much greater role in the House than in the Senate, an example of why the atmosphere of the House is regarded by many as more partisan.

The House leadership includes the

- Speaker of the House (elected by the House members),
- majority leader, and
- minority leader.

The Framers intended the new government to be a government of enumerated—specifically listed—powers. They thought it was important to list the powers of each branch of government so that there would not be any confusion about what they could and could not do.

Most of the powers of Congress are listed in Article I, Section 8 of the Constitution. It includes such important matters as the power

- to lay and collect taxes,
- to pay the debts and provide for the common defense and general welfare of the United States,
- to regulate commerce with foreign nations, and among the several states,
- to declare war,
- to raise an army and navy, and
- to coin money.

They also intended the new system to be a government of separated powers, or, as political scientist Richard Neustadt has called it, "a government of separated institutions sharing powers."

As each branch of the government is given powers that enable it to check the use of power by the others, in Article I, Congress was given the power to impeach the president, other executive branch officials, or members of the national judiciary and remove them from office.

The executive and judicial branches in their respective article also have checks, or controls, on Congress. Yet one of Hamilton's "edits" has become a major obstacle to the experiment. They specifically gave Congress the power to make all other laws that are "necessary and proper" for carrying out the enumerated powers—the necessary and proper clause.

We will address the reach of this clause when discussing the judiciary, but there are really two camps on this clause, Jefferson's and Hamilton's. Jefferson, or the strict constructionists, believed Congress should only be able to exercise actual enumerated or expressed powers and any implied powers (not stated in the Constitution) absolutely necessary to carry out those expressed powers; this is the position of Ron Paul. Hamilton's reason is only conjecture, but Liberal Constructionists, broad interpretation of the powers given to Congress, felt, or Progressives still do today, any power not specifically denied Congress is OK. If it doesn't say "No!" it's OK!

Some examples may help understand Hamilton's approach. The biggest one most will remember is the US Bank set up under Hamilton to store money of the Treasury. The expressed power in to borrow money; this implies, according to Hamiltonians, the power to establish a central bank, like the Federal Reserve. The power to lay and collect taxes allows the Congress to arrest and punish tax evaders, to stop smokers and drinkers with excise taxes, to make the states do what they are told, mandated, and to receive those taxes as funds. To establish naturalization laws, Congress has taken to regulate or limit immigration. This has occurred numerous times since the Alien and Sedition Acts of the 1790s to the Chinese Exclusion Act of the 1890s to Carter banning Iranians, to Obama banning Iraqis, to Trump delaying visas to citizens of "terrorist" nations.

But the most egregious expansion of powers by the national government has been under the commerce clause, which merely says to regulate commerce between the states (interstate) and with Indian tribes. With Indians, it means only Congress can deal with the tribes. More detail on that later. But in essence, states cannot deal with Indian issues unless Congress lets them. Yet the clause has allowed things no one at that Convention, even Hamilton, could have imagined. Congress has used this power to set minimum wages, regulate banking (and causing the Great Recession by requiring banks to create more homeowners to diminish discrimination), ban discrimination in public facilities, order bathrooms in schools to be nongendered, impose same-sex marriages, even prohibit a simple gardener from eating his own food from his own yard.

This is not to say some of these are not great ideas, but—and this is a HUGE but—it is not Congress's power to do them. If I believe that Christmas is a great holiday, it does not give me the right to steal from my neighbor on the right to buy a tree for my neighbor on the left. It was supposed to be a limited government—well, supposed to be.

One reason the Framers agreed to meet in Philadelphia was their concern about some things that state governments were doing. They believed that some states were undermining Congress's efforts to conduct foreign relations, and they feared that, in others, individual rights might be threatened by the state governments. They also knew that the national government had no power to enforce its decisions. They all agreed they had to create a national government with more power than the government had under the Articles of Confederation. They did not agree, however, about how much power the new national government should have over citizens and the state governments.

They resolved their disagreements by establishing a national government with authority to act directly on the people in certain specific areas. The national government no longer would be dependent on the states for income or for law enforcement. The state governments, however, would keep many of the more-important powers over people's daily lives. The states would keep their powers over education, family law, property regulations, and most aspects of everyday life. The people would not feel they had surrendered too much power to a distant government. Or so they thought. Today states are at best an administrator of DC laws.

They included a number of phrases in the Constitution that set forth the powers of the national government. They also included phrases that limited the power of both the national government and state governments. Some of the more important of these are listed below.

1. Some powers of the national government.

    - The supremacy clause, Article VI, says that the Constitution and all laws and treaties approved by Congress in exercising its enumerated powers are the supreme law of the land. It also says that judges in state courts must follow the Constitution, or national laws and treaties, if there is a conflict with state law.
    - Article I, Section 8 gives Congress power to organize the militia of the states and to set a procedure for calling the militia into national service when needed.
    - Article IV, Section 3 gives Congress the power to create new states.
    - Article IV, Section 4 gives the national government the authority to guarantee to each state a republican form of government.
    - Article IV, Section 4 also requires the national government to protect the states from invasion or domestic violence.

2. Limits on power of the national government. The Constitution includes several limitations on the power of the national government.

    - Article I, Section 9 prohibits the national government from banning the slave trade before 1808; suspending the privilege of the writ of habeas corpus except in emergencies; passing any ex post facto laws, laws that make an act a crime even though it was legal at the time it was committed; passing any bills of attainder, laws that declare a person guilty of a crime and decrees a punishment without a judicial trial; taxing anything exported from a state; taking money from the treasury without an appropriation law; and granting titles of nobility.

- Article III defines the crime of treason and prohibits Congress from punishing the descendants of a person convicted of treason.
- Article VI prohibits the national government from requiring public officials to hold any particular religious beliefs.

3. Limits on powers of state governments

- Article I prohibits state governments from creating their own money; passing laws that enable people to violate contracts, such as those between creditors and debtors; making ex post facto laws or bills of attainder; entering into treaties with foreign nations or declaring war; and granting titles of nobility.
- Article IV prohibits states from unfairly discriminating against citizens of other states and refusing to return fugitives from justice to the states from which they have fled.

The Great Compromise had settled the disagreement between large and small states over how they would be represented in Congress. Many other issues still had to be resolved. Two of the most critical disagreements were those between the southern and northern states on the issues of slavery and regulation of commerce. Gerry had hoped slavery would be eliminated by the Convention, but as George Mason predicted, it would take a war to cleanse the nation of so vile an institution.

Slavery had been practiced for almost as long as there had been colonies in America. Many Framers were opposed to slavery, and some northern states had begun to take steps toward abolishing it. Still, in the South, slave labor was widely used in producing crops. Slaveholders considered their slaves to be personal property and wanted to continue using them.

Delegates from the southern states told their fellow delegates that their states would not ratify a constitution that denied citizens the right to import and keep slaves. If the Constitution interfered with slavery, North Carolina, South Carolina, and Georgia made it clear that they would not become part of the new nation. Some delegates from the New England states, whose shipping interests profited from the slave trade, were sympathetic to the southern position. Benjamin Harrison of Virginia proposed slaves to be counted at one-half a person. Other representatives from northern states suggested three-fourths.

After considerable debate, the Framers agreed on a way to satisfy both northern and southern delegates. This agreement gave Congress the power to regulate commerce between the states, which the northern states wanted. The delegates defeated a southern attempt to require a two-thirds vote of both houses to pass laws regulating commerce. To satisfy the southern states, the Constitution provided that the national government would not be able to tax export (primarily tobacco, later cotton) and could not interfere with the slave trade earlier than 1808.

James Wilson, who would become a Supreme Court Justice, proposed the Three-Fifths Compromise at the Constitutional Convention. Here they agreed that each slave would be counted as three-fifths of a person when determining how many representatives a state could send to the House of Representatives. Each slave also would be counted as three-fifths of a person when computing direct taxes. The fugitive slave clause of Article IV was another concession to the southern states. It provided that slaves who escaped to other states must be returned to their owners.

The capital would also be located in the South, well below the Mason-Dixon Line in a Federal District between Maryland and Virginia.

Northern and Southern Positions on Slavery

The words "slave" and "slavery" are never used in the Constitution. Although the delegates voted to give constitutional protection to slavery, many of them were not proud of having done so. They considered it to be a necessary evil, at best, and many hoped it would go away by itself, if left alone. As we now know, this protection of slavery almost destroyed the United States.

1. Why do you think the Framers decided to include the value of property, including enslaved Africans, in calculating the number of representatives a state should have? Should slaves have been treated differently from other forms of property?
2. Should the settling of fundamental problems, say, to allow slavery, have been left up to each state?

3. What problems, if any, today that are hampered by positions took in 1787?

Executive power

The Articles of Confederation did not provide for an executive branch, but the Confederation Congress had found it necessary to create executive officials for specific purposes. The Framers wanted to give the executive branch of the new government enough power and independence to fulfill its responsibilities. They did not, however, want to give the executive any power or independence that could be abused. Americans and Englishmen believed that the king, using bribes and special favors, had been able to control elections and exercise too much influence over Parliament. The British constitution permitted members of Parliament to hold other offices at the same time, and even today members of the executive branch, such as the prime minister, are also members of Parliament. In the eighteenth century, the Crown used its exclusive power to appoint people to office to reward friendly members of Parliament.

They thought these actions upset the proper balance of power between the monarch and Parliament. It was the destruction of this balance that Americans referred to when they spoke of the corruption of Parliament by the Crown. They also believed that royal governors had tried to corrupt colonial legislatures in the same way.

This destruction of the proper balance of power among different branches of government, many Americans thought, led to tyranny. Consequently, it is not surprising that, after their experience with the king and his royal governors, the Americans provided for very weak executive branches in most of the state constitutions. This, however, created other difficulties. The weak executives were unable to check the powers of the state legislatures. These legislatures passed laws that, in the opinion of many, violated basic rights, such as the right to property.

The problem that faced the Framers then was how to create a system of government with balanced powers. They wanted to strengthen the executive branch without making it so strong that it could destroy the balance of power among the branches and thus endanger the rights of the people. They had to resolve several basic questions in organizing the executive branch. Each question concerned the best way to establish an executive branch strong enough to balance the power of the legislature but not so powerful it would endanger democratic government.

Should there be more than one chief executive? They agreed that there should be a single executive to avoid the possible problem of conflict between two or more leaders of equal power. Some delegates also argued that it would be easier for Congress to keep a watchful eye on a single executive. On the other hand, those who argued for a plural executive claimed that such an executive would be less likely to become tyrannical.

How long should the chief executive remain in his position? They considered a seven-year term for the president, but many delegates thought seven years is too long. The final decision was to set the term of office at four years.

Should the executive be eligible for reelection? Under the original proposal for a seven-year term of office, the president would not have been eligible for reelection. When the term was reduced to four years, they decided to allow the president to run again. The Constitution originally set no limit on the number of times a president could be reelected. The Twenty-Second Amendment, passed in 1951, however, sets the limit at two terms.

The most important question they faced was what the powers of the executive branch would be. The executive powers are stated in three clauses: the commander in chief clause, Art. II, Sec. 2, Cl. 1, "The President shall be Commander in Chief of the Army and Navy of the United States"; the take care clause, Art. II, Sec. 3, Cl. 5, "he shall take Care that the Laws be faithfully executed"; and the vesting clause, Art. II, Sec. 1, Cl. 1, "The executive Power shall be vested in a President of the United States." These powers include the responsibilities for carrying out and enforcing laws made by Congress as Congress wrote and interpreted them, nominating people for national offices, negotiating treaties with other nations and conducting wars, pardoning people convicted of crimes, and sending and receiving ambassadors to and from other countries. These were primarily powers to run the national government in dealing with other national governments.

Although they thought the executive branch should have enough power to fulfill its responsibilities, they also wanted to be sure it did not have too much power. They limited the powers of both the executive branch as well as the legislative by making them share many of their powers. This was intended to keep the powers balanced and to provide each branch with a way to check the use of power by the other branch. This sharing of powers was accomplished in the following ways:

- **Veto.** The president shares in the legislative power through the veto. Although the president can veto a bill passed by Congress, the bill can still become a law if two-thirds of both houses of Congress vote to override the veto.
- **Appointments.** The power to appoint executive branch officials and national judges is shared with Congress. The president has the power to nominate persons to fill those positions, but the Senate has the right to approve or disapprove of the persons nominated. To prevent corruption of Congress, members of Congress are not allowed to hold another national office.
- **Treaties.** The power to make treaties also is shared. The president has the power to negotiate a treaty with another nation, but the treaty must be approved by a two-thirds vote of the Senate.
- **War.** Although the president is commander in chief, only Congress has the power to declare war. Congress also controls the money necessary to wage a war. Therefore, the power to declare and wage war also is shared.

Although it includes several important powers, Article II seems short and vague when compared with Article I. It speaks of "executive power" but does not define it. Executive departments are mentioned, but there are no provisions for creating them, deciding how many there should be, or how they should operate.

By comparison, Article I included a specific list of "legislative powers" granted by the Constitution. The veto power appears in Article I, Section 7, although the term is not used. Article II, Section 3 states that the president has the ability to suggest legislation. These are examples of the executive sharing the legislative power.

The Constitution also gives Congress the power to impeach the president, members of the executive branch, and national judges. Only the House of Representatives can bring the charges. The Senate holds a trial to determine the official's guilt or innocence. If found guilty by two-thirds of the Senate, the official will be removed from office.

The Framers had some experience with elected executives in the states, yet they could not be sure exactly what the presidency of the United States should be like. Many decisions were left to Congress. They also trusted George Washington, who was almost universally expected to become the first president. They thought that he could be counted on to fill in the Constitution's gaps and set wise examples that would be followed by later presidents.

But even Thomas Jefferson abused his power. Once elected, he was determined to clean house of Federalist judges. We will look closely at the famous case of *Marbury v. Madison* under the topic of judicial review, but there were others. As soon as he took office—itself not certain, having tied his vice president Aaron Burr, who was actively seeking to "take" the presidency from Jefferson in backdoor deals—President Jefferson used all his influence and more power than the Framers forethought to remove judicial opposition. First, John Pickering was impeached and removed—though being insane according to his own counsel made that case easy. Then the ruthless case against Samuel Chase. Here Jefferson tried to use his lame-duck vice president Aaron Burr to remove Chase. Burr had been dumped in 1804 election, yet Jefferson thought he could get Burr to do his dirty deed by breaking another tie, this time in the Senate; there is good evidence Jefferson promised Burr and many of his relatives positions in new Louisiana Territory Jefferson had "extra-constitutionally" purchased from France. As vice president is the president of the Senate, he votes in cases of ties. Burr has often historically been portrayed as an opportunist at its worst.

Burr had no intention of dishonoring either the Senate or himself. He called the Senate "a citadel of las, or order, of liberty." His vote in favor of Chase marked him as an enemy of Jefferson, who will later attempt to rig charges against Burr as a traitor to the Republic. Today's senators could take advice from Burr:

> [H]ere, if anywhere, will resistance be made to the storms of political frenzy and the silent arts of corruption; and if the Constitution be destined ever to perish by the sacrilegious hands of demagogue or usurper, which God avert, its expiring agonies will be witnesses on this floor.

The Electoral College

The main alternatives debated by the Framers were to have the president selected indirectly or directly by a majority vote of the people. Among the indirect methods they considered was selection by Congress, leaving it to state legislatures or governors, or a temporary independent group elected solely for that purpose. They knew that the group with the power to select the president would have great power over the person who held the office. They were concerned that this power might be used to benefit some people at the expense of others. It might also make it difficult for the president to function properly.

If Congress were given the power to choose the president, then limiting the term of office to a single long term would be a way to protect the president from being manipulated by Congress to get reelected. Therefore, they also decided that Congress could neither increase nor decrease the president's salary once in office. If a president were not chosen by Congress, then providing for a shorter term of office would make the president more accountable to the people. Reelection then would be the will of the people, and the president could run for reelection many times.

The problem was given to a committee to develop a plan that a majority would support. The committee's plan was a clever compromise. It did not give any existing group the power to select the president. The plan shows that the Framers did not trust any group—the people, the state legislatures, or Congress—to make the selection. In such a large country, the people could not be personally familiar with the candidates and their qualifications, in the Framers' judgment. The state legislatures and Congress, they thought, might use their power to upset the balance of power between the national and state governments, or between the executive and legislative branches.

Instead, the committee proposed what we now call the Electoral College, which would have the responsibility of electing the president. The Electoral College would be organized once every four years to select a president. After the election, the college would be dissolved. Each state would select members of the Electoral College, called electors. Each state would have the same number of electors as it had senators and representatives in Congress. The method for choosing electors would be decided on by the state legislature. Each elector would vote for two people, one of whom had to be a resident of another state. This forced the elector to vote for at least one person who might not represent her particular state's interests. The person who received the highest number of votes, if it were a majority of the electors, would become president, 270 out of 538 now. The person who received the next largest number of votes would become vice president. If no one received a majority vote, then the House of Representatives would select the president by a majority vote, with each state having only one vote. In the case of a vice-presidential tie, the Senate would select the vice president. This happened in 1800, 1824, and 1876. Since the mid-nineteenth century, all electors have been popularly chosen in open elections; the Electoral College also has selected the candidate who received the most popular votes, except in four elections: 1876, 1888, 2000, and 2016.

This compromise was eventually approved, but only after much debate and revision. Although quite complicated and unusual, it seemed to be the best solution to their problem. There was little doubt in their minds that George Washington would easily be elected the first president. There was great doubt among them, however, that anyone after Washington could ever get a majority vote in the Electoral College. They believed that in almost all future elections, the final selection of the president would be made by the House of Representatives.

There have been some slight variations in the selection and powers of the presidency. The first occurred in 1804 to fix the problem of ties and the development of political parties. Both Jefferson and his VP Aaron Burr received the same votes in 1800. Per the Constitution, the top vote-getter was president and the second vice president. But with the development of parties, electors voted twice for their party candidates, thus the tie between Burr and Jefferson. In the House, Jefferson won, but only after a struggle behind the scenes with Hamilton hating Burr more than Jefferson and moving his Federalist Party votes to Jefferson. The Twelfth Amendment fine-tuned the voting. Each elector received two votes, now, though, one was for president, the other for vice president. The Twentieth Amendment shortened the wait for inauguration from March to January. The Twenty-Second limited all future presidents to two terms, after FDR broke the tradition of George Washington, serving four terms in the 1930s and 1940s. The Twenty-Third added the District of Columbia, not a state, to those that could vote for electors. And, finally, not only to put into writing a tradition that the vice president was next in line but also to allow a majority of the cabinet to assure the president was always capable of being president because of disabilities or illness. The Twenty-Fifth Amendment also created the line of succession for other members of the executive if the top was eliminated.

Advice and consent

In the United States, "advice and consent" is a power of the United States Senate as the "upper house," to be consulted on and approve treaties signed and appointments made by the president of the United States to public positions, including cabinet secretaries, national judges, and ambassadors. This power is also held by several state Senates, which are consulted on to approve various appointments made by the state's chief executive, such as some statewide officials, state departmental heads in the governor's cabinet, and state judges (in some states).

Article II, Section 2, paragraph 2 of the United States Constitution states:

> [The President] shall have Power, by and with the Advice and Consent of the Senate, to make Treaties, provided two thirds of the Senators present concur; and he shall nominate, and by and with the Advice and Consent of the Senate, shall appoint Ambassadors, other public Ministers and Consuls, Judges of the Supreme Court, and all other Officers of the United States, whose Appointments are not herein otherwise provided for, and which shall be established by Law: but the Congress may by Law vest the Appointment of such inferior Officers, as they think proper, in the President alone, in the Courts of Law, or in the Heads of Departments.

The term "advice and consent" first appears in the United States Constitution in Article II, Section 2, Clause 2, referring to the Senate's role in the signing and ratification of treaties. This term is then used again to describe the Senate's role in the appointment of public officials, immediately after describing the president's duty to nominate officials.

The Framers included the language as part of a delicate compromise concerning the balance of power in the national government. Many delegates preferred to develop a strong executive control vested in the president, while others, worried about authoritarian control, preferred to strengthen the Congress. Requiring the president to gain the advice and consent of the Senate achieved both goals without hindering the business of government. But they also understood that the office of the president would not be filled with omniscient (all-knowing) men, thus many, knowing Washington would be the first office holder, believed that advisors would assist the president with advice in their specialties. This will later be called the cabinet. Today there are sixteen such departments, each with a head and many bureaucrats running the system behind the scenes.

Recently, "treaties," "appointments," and even "laws" have been "executed" by presidents in absolute violation of the Constitution. The Iranian "nuclear treaty" was signed without Senate advice and against its consent. Under 2012 Presidential Appointment Efficiency and Streamlining Act, 321 presidential appointments no longer need Senate's OK. Presidents have gone to war without congressional declarations in violation of the Constitution and Congress's War Powers Act. And under a massive bureaucracy and executive orders, regulations (laws) burden citizens, business, and freedom. Good research and primary documents of the Convention discussion of the control of war powers can be found at TomWoods.com/Levin.

What are the limits of the presidents' powers to send thousands to die killing millions of unknown people, spending billions subverting others' governments, economies, and societies? Some have said none, quoting Hamilton in *Federalist 74*, as having more power than the very King George from whom Americans had just separated.

> Of all the cares or concerns of government, the direction of war most peculiarly demands those qualities which distinguish the exercise of power by a single hand. The direction of war implies the direction of the common strength; and the power of directing and employing the common strength, forms a usual and essential part in the definition of the executive authority.

Sounds pretty sound for one man to direct a massive military with unlimited power, discretion, and blood of young men to "protect" the homeland but, taking one sentence, even from Hamilton, the cheerleader of active executive power, gives a very hawkish, neoconservative, and poor interpretation of what the Framers wanted. Here in his earlier essay, *Federalist 69*, Hamilton is clear, no emperor controlling the world's superpower is within the Constitution, oh well!

> The President will have only the occasional command of such part of the militia of the nation as by legislative provision may be called into the actual service of the Union. The king of Great Britain . . . at all times the entire command of all the militia . . . the power of the President would be inferior to that of . . . the monarch . . . The President is to be commander-in-chief of the army and navy of the United States. In this respect his authority would be nominally the same with that of the king of Great Britain, but in substance much inferior to it. It would amount to nothing more than the supreme command and direction of the military and naval forces, as first General and admiral of the Confederacy; while that of the British king extends to the *declaring* of war and to the *raising* and *regulating* of fleets and armies—all which, by the Constitution under consideration, would appertain to the legislature.

In the early part of his term, President Trump cancelled the Paris Agreement on Climate Change. Regardless of the merit of the agreement, or if climate change is an issue, Trump's withdrawal from the agreement illustrates the failure of the Senate to do its job, to "advise and consent." Former president Obama, with his accomplice, the Senate, never submitted this treaty, and it was the very definition of a treaty, to the Senate for approval. Obama has the power to negotiate, sign, and enforce this or any treaty, but—and this is a big one—no president can implement a treaty until approved by the Senate.

The Framers were very aware of this; that's why they put more power with the Senate, less with the president. The Senate is the upper house, lasts forever, new senators come and old senators go, but the Senate never goes. It is the wisest house of the wisest branch, at least in theory. Even foreign affairs, in the Paris Agreement especially, the legislative branch should have the greatest power. War, only Congress was to start one. Why? If citizens must pay the bills in blood and gold, they must have a say; that's the legislature. In a treaty, like the Paris one, that have monies attached—in this case, the United Sates was to pay $1 billion!—we must have a say, taxation without representation, remember?

Why was the Paris Agreement, an Obama executive order, never submitted to the Senate? That's easy. Obama knew there were no two-thirds of the votes there! Why would the Senate not complain? That's easier. The Senate has abdicated its job to prevent the hard issues; in this case, voting yes was wrong, voting no was wrong. Voting yes would have made American taxpayers pay for European and Asian pollution, transferring billions. Voting no would have been seen by the environmental activists as voting against Mother Nature. Opponents running against voting senators could have used either yeses or nos against in the elections. The one clear thing President Trump must do is say he cancelled our participation because it wasn't a treaty; this will make the next president unable to do another Obama executive order to reinstate it; and it will force the Senate to do its job, oversee foreign affairs as a representative body of the people.

Executive privilege

Related to advice and consent of the Senate is the development of the cabinet form of government where the president looks for advice from a wide range of "experts." To get honest and sometimes contradictory opinions from others, the idea emerged that what was said in the president's presence was similar to client-lawyer and minister-parishioner. Executive privilege is the power claimed by presidents and other members of the executive branch to resist certain subpoenas and other interventions by the legislative and judicial branches of government. The concept of executive privilege is not mentioned explicitly in the United States Constitution, but the Supreme Court of the United States ruled it to be an element of the separation of powers doctrine, and/or derived from the supremacy of executive branch in its own area of Constitutional activity.

The Supreme Court confirmed the legitimacy of this doctrine in *United States v. Nixon* but only to the extent of confirming that there is a qualified privilege. Once invoked, a presumption of privilege is established, requiring the prosecutor to make a "sufficient showing" that the "Presidential material" is "essential to the justice of the case." Chief Justice Warren Burger stated that executive privilege would most effectively apply when the oversight of the executive would impair that branch's national security concerns. Historically, the uses of executive privilege underscore the untested nature of the doctrine, since presidents have generally sidestepped open confrontations with the United States Congress and the courts over the issue by first asserting the privilege and then producing some of the documents requested on a "voluntary" basis.

The authors of the Constitution believed that military defense was crucial to the survival of their new country. At the same time, they worried about the potential danger of a strong military establishment. The military is highly organized, heavily armed, and very powerful. Standing armies are a major threat to any free people. Both the limitations on the military and the Second Amendment emphasize this point. Therefore, they wrote into the Constitution many provisions to make sure that the military would stay under the control of *civilian* authorities.

In a very important provision, the Constitution makes the president—who must be a civilian—the commander in chief of the nation's armed forces. Presidents usually delegate much authority to military subordinates, but ultimate authority and responsibility remain in the president's hands. His war powers are shared with Congress to declare war; to grant letters of marque and reprisal; and to make rules concerning captures on land and water, to raise and support armies, to provide and maintain a navy, to make laws governing land and naval forces, to provide for calling forth the militia to execute national laws, suppress insurrections, and repel invasions, and to provide for organizing, arming, and disciplining the militia and for its governing when in the service of the nation.

The president is aided in being the commander in chief by the Department of Defense, which was created in 1947 (though maybe should revert to its original "War" designation. Don't we have Homeland Security to protect us at home now?). This executive department is headed by a secretary of defense who, like the president, must be a civilian. Furthermore, the secretary of defense cannot have served on active duty in die armed forces for at least ten years unless specifically OK'd by Congress. Under the secretary of defense are numerous civilians who hold important positions in the Department of Defense. All are appointed by the president and approved by the Senate. Each of the three military departments within the Department of Defense (the army, the navy, and the air force) is headed by a civilian secretary. Like the president, these civilian secretaries often delegate authority to military subordinates, but ultimate authority and responsibility again remain in civilian hands.

The secretary of defense also sits on the president's National Security Council (NSC), which was created in 1947 to provide the president with information, including military information. Other officials who meet with the NSC are the vice president, the secretary of state, the secretary of the treasury, the director of the Central Intelligence Agency (CIA), and the chairman of the Joint Chiefs of Staff (the Joint Chiefs of Staff comprise the highest-ranking uniformed officers of each branch of the armed forces). Of all members of the NSC just mentioned, only the chairman of the Joint Chiefs of Staff is a military officer, although the NSC does use military personnel on its staff.

As an expansion of civilian control of the military and as a check on the potential military power of the executive branch, the Constitution also gives considerable military powers to Congress. Only Congress can declare war. Only Congress can raise money to finance the military. In fact, of the seventeen specific constitutional grants of power to Congress, at least six deal with regulating the military. The balance of power between civilians and the military continues to be an issue of concern. In 1961, President Eisenhower, himself an ex-general, warned against the danger of excessive military influence.

Even today the question remains: How can we balance the need for an adequate national defense with concern over a too-powerful military? There has been constant war since WW II, all unconstitutional, all undeclared, resulting in trillions of wasted American productivity, standards of living, and thousands of lost children and their futures.

I think maybe we should stop and think about what makes a president a good one? There have been over the years rankings of the presidents. George Washington, Abraham Lincoln, FDR, Teddy Roosevelt, and Woodrow Wilson tend to rise to the top. All are war presidents; all believed in an expansion of the presidency.

What do you think?

What are the characteristics of a good president? Leadership, ethics, morality, administrative organization, popularity? Should he be great at solving the problems domestically? Foreign? Jot down some key things you look for in a president.

In 2014, the *Washington Post* surveyed 162 members of the American Political Science Association's Presidents & Executive Politics section and asked them to rate the US presidents. Here is what they found. The most highly ranked presidents contained many of the usual suspects. Abraham Lincoln was rated the greatest president, with an average score of 95 out of 100, followed by George Washington and Franklin D. Roosevelt. The rest in the top ten were Teddy Roosevelt, Thomas Jefferson, Harry S. Truman, Dwight D. Eisenhower, Bill Clinton, Andrew Jackson, and Woodrow Wilson. Arthur Schlesinger's list, first started in 1946, places Lincoln, Washington, and FDR 1,2, 3 as well; he labels them "great." Jefferson, Jackson, Teddy Roosevelt, Wilson, Truman, and Polk are his "near greats." The rest are "average" at best.

The bottom in Schlesinger's eyes from best to worst are Coolidge, Fillmore, Tyler, Pierce, Grant, Hoover, Nixon, Andrew Johnson, Buchanan, and Harding. Most textbooks and teachers in public schools would tend to agree. *WaPo* does! Its list agrees except it includes all to Obama; Art's only goes to 1996 and Clinton. The bottom feeders are Nixon, Grant, William Henry Harrison, Pierce, Andrew Johnson, Harding, and, last and least, James Buchanan.

As you would suspect, I disagree with both lists. There is only one thing that makes a good president: did he do what he was supposed to do under the Constitution, and, second, did he keep his promises (though some may violate the first requirement)? The best rankings and qualities for a great president I've taken lock, stock, and barrel from Brion McClanahan in his 2016 *9 Presidents Who Screwed Up America: And Four Who Tried to Save Her.* When the Framers sent the Constitution to be ratified by the states, Hamilton—yes, Hamilton again—in *Federalist 69*, was adamant no occupier of the presidency could abuse power because the power in the Constitution was limited, checked, and specific. Alex stated clearly, though again disingenuously, no one sitting in the later Oval Office would have power to make "rules concerning the commerce or currency of the nation." His coauthor,

Madison, said no president had any power to "execute such other powers 'not legislative nor judiciary in their nature' as may from time to time be delegated by the national legislature." Regardless of Woody Wilson's progressive "research," the president is not the "chief legislator"; nor can he "create" jobs; nor can he "solve" America's problems. He can only make them oh so much worse. Today's imperial presidency may be exactly what Hamilton wanted in Philadelphia in '87, but I would suspect he'd even pause at what has occurred the last twenty or so years.

First, the person taking office as the president must take the Oath of Office as written, word for word, "to preserve, protect, and defend the Constitution of the United States." This means he is not a king; all powers are limited and circumscribed by the Constitution; he is obliged by his own oath to execute the laws of Congress, not initiate legislation, not to circumvent legislation, not its intent by Congress. Did he do only what is allowed and do it well?

These are the worst thirteen, (though his book gives nine, he combined some together in certain chapters): George Washington, Andy Jackson, Abraham Lincoln, Teddy Roosevelt, Franklin Roosevelt (gotta keep it in the family), Harry Truman, Lyndon Johnson, Richard Nixon, Jimmy Carter, George H. W. Bush, Bill Clinton, George W. Bush, Obama.

I know you've been waiting, the best! Now don't get all sappy here; they aren't perfect. Even Jefferson in his second term went a little off the tracks, though he wouldn't have known it yet; tracks weren't invented. No significance to the order, just the best ten: Jefferson, Madison, Monroe, Tyler, Martin van Buren, Zachary Taylor, Pierce, Andrew Johnson (hey, wait, wasn't he on the bottom in both *WaPo*'s and Art's lists?), Coolidge, and, number one, Grover Cleveland. Quite a different list! You must read Brion's book for his rankings and justifications; but simply, this list is based on the only measurement, the Constitution. If so many have not measured up to or followed it, has the experiment been a failure? Does man need a Hobbesian, Machiavellian iron fist? Was Franklin wrong in his comments to that lady when asked what he and the others were doing in there, building "a Republic, if you can keep it." He added later,

> only a virtuous people are capable of freedom. As nations
> become corrupt and vicious, they have more need of masters.

He echoed Sir Edmund Burke, a friend and supporter of the revolutionaries in America, though turned off greatly by the French revolutionaries' violence. Man, when freed from a fallen dictator—Libya, Iran, Iraq—have a feeding frenzy, even to the point of cannibalistic self-destruction. If man cannot control his appetite, is the great experiment a failure? Was Hamilton right?

> Men are qualified for civil liberty in exact proportion to their disposition to put moral chains upon their own appetites . . . Society cannot exist unless a controlling power upon will and appetite be placed somewhere, and the less of it there is within, the more there must be without. It is ordained in the eternal constitution of things, that men of intemperate minds cannot be free. Their passions forge their fetters.

Judicial branch

The Framers thought that they needed to add a central judicial branch. A national government, with power to act directly on citizens, needed a system for deciding cases involving its laws. This function could be left to state courts, but then the national laws might be enforced differently from state to state. They realized that some kind of national courts would be needed, at least to resolve disputes involving national laws. A judicial branch also would complete the system of separation of powers. They had fewer problems agreeing on how to organize the judiciary than they had with the other two branches. Many of the Framers were lawyers, and so most of them already agreed about how courts should be organized and what responsibilities and powers they should be given. They also agreed that all criminal trials should be trials by jury. This was a very important check, in their minds, on the power of the government.

They created a Supreme Court as the head of the judiciary and gave Congress the power to create lower national courts as they felt were needed. Judges should be independent of politics so that they can use their best judgment to decide cases and not be influenced by political pressures. The best way to make sure that judges would not be influenced by politics was to have them nominated by the president. The president's nomination would need to be ratified by the Senate.

Appointing judges by this method rather than electing them would remove them from the pressures of political influence. In addition, the judges would keep their positions "during good behavior." This meant that they could not be removed from their positions unless they were impeached and convicted of "treason, bribery, or other high crimes and misdemeanors."

There was also a good deal of agreement about the kinds of powers that the judicial branch should have. The judiciary was given the power to decide conflicts between state governments, decide conflicts that involved the national government. The Supreme Court was given authority in only two types of cases. These are cases in which the Supreme Court has original jurisdiction. These are cases that the Constitution says are not to be tried first in a lower court but are to go directly to the Supreme Court. Such cases involve a state government, a dispute between state governments, and cases involving ambassadors and cases that have first been heard in lower courts and are appealed to the Supreme Court. These are cases over which the Supreme Court has appellate jurisdiction.

Break time: What do you think?

1. What are the advantages and disadvantages of having national judges appointed rather than being elected to serve "during good behavior"? What is "good behavior"?
2. Wouldn't it be better if the Supreme Court was more reflective of changing political, economic, racial, ethnic, and gender diversity of our citizenry? Why or why not?
3. Should public opinion play a role in the Supreme Court deciding a controversial case?
4. Many feel the Supreme Court is the least democratic branch of our government. What do you think?

The current court system was organized by the 1891 Judiciary Act. There are ninety-four district courts, at least one in each state; some large states have four. These are the original jurisdictional courts with jury trials, usually one judge for civil and criminal cases. At times, there will be bench trials (no jury). Each district court has US Attorney appointed by the president, approved by the Senate. These courts hear two hundred thousand cases per year, 90 percent of national caseload. For instance, in my state of Wisconsin, there are three district courts: Northeast (Green Bay), West (Madison), and Southeast (Milwaukee).

The appellate or circuit courts hear appeals on issues of law, not guilt or innocence. There are thirteen, twelve circuits and the DC Circuit Court. The Seventh Circuit was formed in 1911 in Chicago. It hears cases from Wisconsin, Illinois, and Indiana. No trials but rather hearings by a three-judge panel. There are twenty-eight judges that hear twenty-eight thousand to thirty thousand decisions a year (25 percent of total cases). The Thirteenth Circuit is located in Washington DC. It handles specific cases of appeals (claims, customs, patents, veterans, international trade). Many of the current Supreme Court justices have come through this circuit. The Supreme Court sits in Washington DC. It contains a chief justice, eight associate justices. Along with the Court of International Trade, all these judges serve for life.

Other Congressionally-created courts are the US Tax Court, the Court of Military Appeals, the US Court of Claims, and the US Court of Appeals for Veterans' Claims. These judges serve a variety of terms, depending on how their courts were setup.

Just to be sure on this, each branch is limited in its authority. The three branches have specific powers. First, the legislative branch makes the law. Second, the executive branch executes or enforces the law. Last, the judicial branch interprets the law. Each branch has an effect on the other. Each branch was to use its powers as fully as possible. The Framers understood human nature well. They believed that power was very addictive ambrosia, and if all drank equally, each man within each office would guarantee no power was abused, thus stepping on the powers of other offices. They knew that ambitious men would seek office and attempt to use their powers fully. If all men used them, this would be the surest check on exceeding the powers given. Each branch was given powers to check the other two. The legislative branch, in addition, had other checks for each House to watch the other.

See charts that follow. These were "horizontal checks." In addition, a system of "vertical checks" was the whole idea of Federalism and delegated powers. Limits to prevent tyranny. A cage for the tiger of government. A necessary institution but dangerous if not watched and controlled. For the first century of operation, a few glitches here and there, it worked pretty well.

Legislative Checks			
Checks on the Executive	Checks on the Courts	House Checks on Senate	Senate Checks on the House
Impeachment power (House) Trial of impeachments (Senate)	Senate approves national judges	Impeachment power	Trial of impeachments (Senate)
Selection of the president (House) and vice president (Senate) in the case of no majority of electoral votes	Impeachment power (House) Trial of impeachments (Senate)	Selection of the president in the case of no majority of electoral votes	Selection of vice president in the case of no majority of electoral votes
May override presidential vetoes	Power to initiate constitutional amendments	Bills must be passed by both houses of Congress.	
Senate approves departmental appointments	Power to set courts inferior to the Supreme Court	House must originate revenue bills.	
Senate approves treaties and ambassadors	Power to set jurisdiction of courts	Neither house may adjourn for more than three days without the consent of the other house.	
Approval of replacement vice president	Power to alter the size of the Supreme Court	All journals are to be published.	
Power to declare war			
Power to enact taxes and allocate funds			
President must, from time to time, deliver a State of the Union address.			

Executive Checks	
Checks on the Legislature	Checks on the Courts
Veto	Power to appoint judges
Vice president is president of the Senate	Pardon power
Commander in chief of the military	President still must enforce decisions.
Recess appointments	
Emergency calling into session of one or both houses of Congress	
May force adjournment when both houses cannot agree on adjournment	
Compensation cannot be diminished	
Internal check: Vice president and cabinet can vote that the president is unable to discharge his duties.	

Judicial Checks	
Checks on the Legislature	Checks on Executive
Judicial review	Judicial review
Seats are held on good behavior.	Chief justice sits as president of the Senate during presidential impeachment.
Compensation cannot be diminished.	

THE PREAMBLE

It's really a wonder that I haven't dropped all my ideals, because they seem so absurd and impossible to carry out. Yet I keep them, because in spite of everything I still believe that people are really good at heart.
—Anne Frank

THE UNITED STATES Constitution is the guidebook, the rule book, for our nation. It is not a checklist or a discussion. It is not only the limited, delegated powers of offices but also a written document of the mind of this nation. All power resides in individuals. They agree for their common benefit to form a social contract, to cooperate, to divide the labors of that society based on the skills and aptitudes of each. The resulting contract is what they are willing to place in the hands of offices, not the officeholders, who are merely selected for a period, to do what the society has asked of them. The United States Constitution is our social contract. The Preamble of that contract specifically addresses why we have the contract, what purposes are to be served, and how those purposes are to be done. The Constitution does not grant to our officeholders the powers to do what is right or good, only those powers given. There are six goals for which the Framers met: establish justice, ensure domestic tranquility, provide for the common defense, promote the common welfare and the blessings of liberty, and, most importantly, create a "more perfect" contract. Though the Preamble was penned after the document was completed, these ideals were in the minds of the newly freed Americans.

The writer of the Preamble, Gouverneur Morris, had in mind hundreds of years of philosophy. The contract was clear to both the Framers and the ratifiers; it was a compact between the people and their government. The states were here before the Constitution; the Declaration states clearly they were "free and independent" with "full power to levy war, conclude peace, contract alliances, establish commerce, and to do all other acts and things which independent states may of right do." The British accepted this as well, signing a treaty with a group of states. As we saw in the Articles of Confederation, all retained "their sovereignty, freedom, and independence." They could only "retain" something they already had. There were ratifications by each individual state, each one by its citizens assembled in separate conventions. These citizens of each separate state were, and are, sovereigns giving away their powers to their state governments or to the national government.

This does not mean sovereignty is given away, only powers they want exercised by a government for them. And if a power is exercised that was not expressly given, it is the people who are to judge. Tom Woods gives the example of an agent being asked what powers he has; he has only those powers given; anything else done is fraud, breach of contract. The people, the sovereign, retains all power to limit their agent. Madison, in 1800, explaining his Virginia Resolution of 1798,

> The resolution of the General Assembly relates to those great and extraordinary cases, in which all the forms of the Constitution may prove ineffectual against infractions dangerous to the essential right of the parties to it. The resolution supposes that dangerous powers not delegated, may not only be usurped and executed by the other departments, but that the Judicial Department [Supreme Court's legislating from the bench, see *McCulloch, Brown*] also may exercise or sanction dangerous powers beyond the grant of the Constitution; and consequently that the ultimate right of the parties to the Constitution, to judge whether the compact has been dangerously violated, must extend to violations by one delegated authority, as well as by another, by the judiciary, as well as by the executive, or the legislature.

We the People

Who were "we the people"? Both Thomas Paine and Thomas Jefferson believed America had been a people since before the war of these united States. The new lands of America brought the battles of the Enlightenment: Puritan versus Cavalier, Parliament versus divine right, and free markets versus mercantilism. Those battles took on new meaning in the New World. The ideals of freedom were not born in the colonies, but oh how they flourished and grew. When the Framers were in Philadelphia in the summer of '87, there were 3.89 million Americans. This number did not include women, children, slaves, non-property owners. It included both those in favor of ratification and those not. Remember some were even Loyalists. Of those then that created this "more perfect union" may have consisted of only 10 percent of the population. Yet only men with property, usually white over the age of twenty-one, could vote.

Does that make the contract less valid? No. Today all are required to obey the law, many pay taxes, and not all who comply are enfranchised (have the right to vote). They are implicitly accepting the contract or may leave when capable. Consent of the governed is only consent of the enfranchised, not the consent of the population.

The Framers were to be the representatives of thirteen individually created states. Rhode Island did not attend, as you recall. Some delegates left early, some returned. Some even refused to agree to the final document. Yet the document begins with "We the People" (in common) "do ordain and establish" a new social contract, one better than the Articles of Confederation. All legitimate governments are made by the consent of the governed. But consent of the governed is really only consent of the enfranchised, not the consent of the population. The consenting creates (ordains) a legal government with not only the monopoly to use force but also the authority, the right to use that power. Force is the power to rule. All governments have force; without the ability to enforce the laws and keep order, government would not be a government. Even tyranny has force.

A legitimate social contract is a constitutional government. It is limited with delegated powers and the necessary means to serve the common good. It has the authority, the consensual right to rule. It is based on the current rules of the game, de jure (by law) not by the random will of a few, de facto ("in practice or actuality, but not officially established"). It is thus a system of law and right, not based on men and their charisma, popularity, or what they feel is good or bad. The office has the power, and the occupant may use it to its fullest limits to do the will of the majority, if that majority is correct. Even the voters, the consenting, cannot violate the common good.

Constitutional	Despotic
Authority and force	Force
Republic	Dictatorship
Limited	Unlimited
De jure	De facto
Right	Might
Law	Men
Offices	Officeholders

A constitution is a definition of governmental powers delegated to it by the people who are sovereign (We the People). It is not only an arrangement of offices of magistracies, together with a statement of the powers vested in each (Aristotle), but also a statement of powers not granted.

Establish justice

In the living of life, we all are self-interested; both Hobbes and Locke began with that assumption. The Framers knew that well. They had tried to overcome, maybe naïvely ignored, human nature. In the Convention, they had to develop a system that acknowledged man's self-interest while finding a way to serve the common good. That concept is called justice. To establish justice is to realize that justice is always a relationship within society. There are six types of justice. The first two were set forward by Enlightenment thinking in the Declaration. Jefferson stated just government must be primarily to secure human rights. Second, it must be derived from the consent of the governed. Even if government does what is best and good for the people, without their permission, it is unjust. It is a contractual agreement.

Yet there are more justices. If all humans are equal, all equals have a right to be treated equally. Yet unequals should be treated unequally in proportion to their inequality. To do otherwise would be unjust. Number three is fairness. Liberty and equality are of times used together and interchangeably. Liberty and equality are not the same; they are contradictory.

Equality is not in the Constitution but is part and parcel of a legitimate system. This equality is equality before the law. It can never be equal treatment or condition. To assist those with need or to take unfairly from A to feed B is an injustice. The easiest formula would be to give to those in need what they need, nothing more, nothing less. To give more would be a waste and unjust. To give less would be selfish. As you recall, Aristotle said all men should achieve their fullest potential. He never said all men were equal. The best in today's language might be equality of opportunity, the right to be what you can be. The third justice is fairness, nothing more, nothing less. Justice is as much liberty as is fair and as much equality as is necessary.

The next three are the specific details of fairness. There are distributive justice, commutative justice, and contributive justice. Distributive is the relationship of government with the governed. Equal and unequal treatment should be based on equality and inequality of the citizens' behavior. Commutative justice is between an individual and another. This is civil law and/or natural rights. Contributive justice is the individual serving to the common good. As Jack Kennedy so famously declared, "Ask not what your country can do for you . . ." This is civic virtue tempered by moral virtue. The law is organized justice. The law's job is to protect all members from harm, plunder, theft from each other, without the law itself causing harm. Bastiat is clear: law is force, man is no angel, a nudge to stay on the straight and narrow is often needed, but,

> now this must be said: When justice is organized by law— that is, by force—this excludes the idea of using law (force) to organize any human activity whatever, whether it be labor, charity, agriculture, commerce, industry, education, art, or religion. The organizing by law of any one of these would inevitably destroy the essential organization—justice. For truly, how can we imagine force being used against the liberty of citizens without it also being used against justice, and thus acting against its proper purpose?

Why is justice *so* important? It is the most important of the goals in the Preamble. Justice relates closely to all the other goals, except common defense; sometimes these two conflict. All the goals, even defense, must always be considered in relation to what is fair to the citizens. Can you think of conflict of the Preamble's other goals with that of justice? Bastiat again,

> [But,] this negative concept of law is so true that the statement, *the purpose of the law is to cause justice to reign*, is not a rigorously accurate statement. It ought to be stated that *the purpose of the law is to prevent injustice from reigning*. In fact, it is *injustice*, instead of justice, that has an existence of its own. Justice is achieved only when injustice is absent.

> But when the law, by means of its necessary agent, force, imposes upon men a regulation of labor, a method or a subject of education, a religious faith or creed—then the law is no longer negative; it acts positively upon people. It substitutes the will of the legislator for their own wills; the initiative of the legislator for their own initiatives. When this happens, the people no longer need to discuss, to compare, to plan ahead; the law does all this for them. Intelligence becomes a useless prop for the people; they cease to be men; they lose their personality, their liberty, their property.
> Try to imagine a regulation of labor imposed by force that is not a violation of liberty; a transfer of wealth imposed by force that is not a violation of property. If you cannot reconcile these contradictions, then you must conclude that the law cannot organize labor and industry without organizing injustice.

To ensure domestic tranquility

The civil peace is essential for all individuals striving for personal success and happiness. Civil peace is an indispensable component of the common good; it is a positive condition in contrast to international peace (see later).

Many social interactions of man, nuisance, contracts, domestic relations are deeply personal. When one or a group or very likely government itself violate the tranquility of life, one's opportunities and goals are stepped upon. This could be slander, libel, or other torts (damages). Those responsible are liable or negligent (careless). Criminals disrupt the civil peace; they have used unauthorized force. The goals of all groups are to resolve all conflicts without resort to violence. This, unfortunately, is done through the adequate machinery of the state. Civil peace is not the absence of problems—that's impossible—but rather the resolution without violence.

Police use authorized delegated force. Sometimes it appears liberty is suppressed in maintaining the peace. We have given the state police power to settle individual disputes, promote health and safety, protect the general welfare, and prevent harm. Today it is not a question of power but rather, "How far?" With today's government growing beyond our ability to control it and our fear of dangers, has homeland security gone too far?

Provide for the common defense

All the other elements of the Preamble are positives; we want more. More liberty, more justice, more peace. Yet history teaches us that international peace is a negative condition; in other words, war is natural between nations because there are conflicts and no way to settle them if the parties refuse to talk; there is no sovereign power over nations other than God. And until man becomes less man, defense is necessary for common good. Nonetheless, people are better able to pursue happiness during peacetime. Resources that could be used to serve the common good (better) are wasted in war. No one denies that. Defense is like car insurance—hopefully, we never use it, but without it, all could be lost. The Founders and Framers understood this; we seem not to. Washington, Jefferson, and John Quincy Adams consistently reiterated the need to keep us out of other nations' business. Wars cause debts, corruption, and waste, all elements that prohibit a free nation. The Framers had experience of standing armies, having fought a great superpower and won. Well-trained militias and people fighting for home have won time and again in history. From General Giap in

Vietnam to Francis Marion in the American Revolution, free men have fought valiantly and successfully.

Many at the Convention, like Hamilton, wanted standing armies to build empires, thus a well-trained militia was replaced by a national army. It was used sparingly in the early Republic but now is the established way to invade others, to maintain fear in the world, and maybe to suppress free peoples there and here. It is a national or central concern, common to all; it was no longer in the hands of the states (Art. I, Sec. 10). But only defense is constitutional; peace equals defense.

John Quincy Adams, as secretary of state, addressed Congress in 1821, that the Republic does not go "abroad in search of monsters to destroy"; yet US troops are now stationed in 70 percent of the world's nations. Monsters galore.

Less than a century later, the "great" Teddy Roosevelt, hoping for a war in 1917, stated every Progressives' dream that war is honorable and peace is a farce. His big stick sounds like Hamilton yelling from the grave, "We should regard with contempt and loathing the Americans . . . crying on behalf of peace, peace, when there ought not to be peace."

Though Hamilton received his imperial forces, the Republicans hoped it would be controlled (or so they thought). There are major conflicts between defense and other five Preamble goals, so there are lots of safeguards. There is to be a small standing army under civilian control; president is commander in chief (Art. II, Sec. 2). All military appropriations must come through Congress and can last no more than two years (Art. I, Sec. 8, Cl. 9). All officers are picked by the president and approved by Senate (Art. II, Sec. 2). And essentially, only Congress can declare war (Art. I, Sec. 8). It is a necessary evil to prevent worse evils.

Common welfare

Let's preface this discussion with John Adams's statement in 1780 while preparing the Massachusetts Constitution,

> Government is instituted for the common good; for the protection, safety, prosperity and happiness of the people; and not for the profit, honor, or private interest of any one man, family, or class of men: Therefore the people alone

have an incontestable, unalienable, and indefeasible right to institute government; and to reform, alter, or totally change the same, when their protection, safety, prosperity and happiness require it.

To serve the common good, man must put aside his self-interest. Nothing government does can benefit one citizen over another, one class over another; self-interest or, today, special interests cannot play a role in republican government. This is a very difficult task for man; the Framers knew this. Franz Oppenheimer (1864–1943), German-Jewish sociologist and political economist, in his classic *The State*, said there are two ways to get rich, two ways to succeed—the political means and the economic means. The economic means is to produce something of value people are willing to pay you for—iPhones, new Eric Clapton album, a better haircut. That takes skill, knowledge, and time. The easier way, and man will always take the easier route, is the political means, using the state to legally plunder others instead of serving others. Frédéric Bastiat called it legal plunder, the law not serving the common good but rather a segment of a society. There are three types of plunder:

1. The few plunder the many.
2. Everybody plunders everybody.
3. Nobody plunders anybody.

Special interests, factions, cronyism, all corrupt the common good, the general welfare, the law. The ideal would be if nobody harmed anybody, a Libertarian dream. Socialist economies, totalitarian states, everybody plunders everyone. This would destroy man as a man; republicanism is an attempt to match government with the failed society of man. Taxation, regulation, military service, all are forms of plunder. Bastiat's explanation,

> Now, legal plunder can be committed in an infinite number of ways. Thus we have an infinite number of plans for organizing it: tariffs, protection, benefits, subsidies, encouragements, progressive taxation, public schools, guaranteed jobs, guaranteed profits, minimum wages, a right to relief, a right to the tools of labor, free credit, and

so on, and so on. All these plans as a whole—with their common aim of legal plunder—constitute socialism.

If kept to the common good, within the limits of the granted powers, the chains of the Constitution Jefferson hoped, legal plunder is the cost of living under government. But what is it that constitutes, who defines, and what are the limits of the serving of the common welfare?

The common good is stated twice in the Constitution: Preamble and Article I, Sec. 8. What is the common good? General welfare, common good, or common welfare is a means of serving the pursuit of happiness. The ultimate end to be achieved by a just and benevolent government is to construct a world where all can achieve their own greatness. But what is it? Let's take it apart first.

What is common? It could be a good shared by all (public good). Or it might be a good that is the same for all who enjoy it (personal good): happiness. If general welfare is number one, it is redundant; if it is number two, it is impossible because no government can give happiness.

It isn't either but leads to these two. Let's see what the Framers thought. Madison felt the two clauses were just for style, had no meaning; to him, it was just an introduction to what followed; otherwise, it and the "necessary and proper" clause would make Congress unlimited: "Government that governs least governs best"; only the enumerated powers mattered.

Hamilton: "Government that governs most governs best." Congress is limited, but it is up to the discretion of Congress to decide its own powers. The central government should "triumph altogether over the state governments and reduce them into an entire subordination." John Marshall in *McCulloch v. Maryland* (1819) wrote that necessary and proper were now "convenient." Madison was aghast at this decision saying the court had gutted the intent of enumerated powers, with Marshall's opinion; Madison Congress was given power "to which no practical limit can be assigned." He had said in his Virginia Resolution of 1798 that the court was not the final say on the Constitution; at the Virginia Ratifying Convention, Madison had promised Henry that if the Congress oversteps its powers, Virginia was "exonerated" from obeying it.

But a government that governs most justly and most benevolently is best. National spending should not be rent-seeking. Rent-seeking is when one goes to the government to gain something she can't gain on her own; laws that benefit one segment of society at the expense of another. National spending should be restricted to only those purposes whose benefits are national in scope rather than purely local or confined to a single interest group. In referring to Marshall's decision in *McCulloch v. Maryland*, Spencer Roane said the phrase "necessary and proper" was to allow carrying out of enumerated powers, not new powers. So what are the limits? Abraham Lincoln believed that "government should do for the people whatever people cannot do for themselves, either individually or collectively." Are these economic rights?

Hamilton felt economic prosperity is the goal of all; this was his plan all along government and business working together. FDR felt the state should provide any necessity needed by its citizens; there should be no forgotten man. Karl Marx's ideology, to each and all according to their common human needs with constitutional support, seems the norm of both political parties today. Today's Progressives believe economic rights are implicit in Declaration; among these inalienable rights are life, liberty, and whatever else one needs to pursue happiness and the Constitution permits it.

If acquiring wealth is a necessary element of happiness, today's Progressives feel it is not wholly within the individual's domain. All humans have a right to a decent livelihood. Welfare is no longer seen as antiliberty and a burden, or as communistic, or even totalitarian, a threat to those that favor no special privilege over individual equality; individuals can't be free if insecure. Compassion by a government comes with compulsion. Whether American government and American individuals are compassionate are two distinct questions. McCloskey is adamant that governments cannot be compassionate. "It is also bourgeois love to care for employees and partners and colleagues and customers and fellow citizens, to wish all of humankind well, to seek God, finding human and transcendent connection in the marketplace . . ." The richer man becomes, the better the environment, conditions for workers, and education, and the more the charity. Americans in 2015 gave $373 billion; that's more than the GDPs of the Socialist compassionate countries.

Life is more than security of life and limb and not merely subsisting, but to live well in human terms. This then includes everything needed to a successful pursuit of happiness, or what we could call economic rights:

decent supply of the means of subsistence
living and working conditions conducive to health
medical care
pleasures of senses, play, and aesthetics
education in youth and adult life
free time to take advantages of and participate in all aspects of society

What is a decent life? Equality? Political equality is citizenship and suffrage, equality under laws as stated in the Fourteenth Amendment. Economic equality is not equal wealth, merely enough wealth for all. More wealth is OK if one's contribution to production of wealth justifies more. Maybe only so much economic equality as justice would allow is legitimate. What do you think? "Since the things man needs for survival have to be produced, and nature does not guarantee the success of any human endeavor, there is not and cannot be any such thing as a guaranteed economic security." Ayn Rand believed government's job was to play referee, to make sure competition is rivalrous yet fair. Low restrictions, property and contract protection, markets free of regulations, stable currency, thus stable prices, along with no debt and low taxes would guarantee small government and freed citizens.

The blessings of liberty

To truly understand liberty, we need to begin with the idea that it is a gift; the only form of freedom that is a blessing is free will, the power of free choice. It is not given by a government, it is natural, one either has it or not; it is a gift from God. Natural liberty flows into political liberty; this is what is meant by the last phrase in the Preamble. Then the question quickly emerges: do laws restrict freedom?

Doing what one pleases to do in violation of just laws is not liberty but rather license or immorality. People who act this way are restrained from bad decisions by coercive force if necessary, for their own good and/or the common good. A morally virtuous person with a proper understanding of what are just and unjust acts lawfully by free choice needs no law and hence loses no liberty; he/she chooses to restrict him/

herself. Freedom should be limited only by just laws (which are only a limit on the unjust!).

Just laws are regulations of our conduct for the sole purpose of preventing us from injuring others or the common good. There can be no crime where there is no victim, where no individual is injured or society adversely affected; restricting sins is not a just law. To obey an unjust law, a null and void law, and unconstitutional law is sin, violating the law. To disobey a just law is to throw the law to the wind. Remember Rosa Parks? Had she not violated the law or paid the fine required by the law, she would have been a bad person, a sinner, a criminal in the eyes of God.

Today, many believe to change a law, to fix an opinion they disagree with, or do not like, that violence is the solution until the system gives in, as in a child squirming and screaming until ice cream is delivered. But Bastiat, 150 years ago, said freedom was the solution to all problems; like Jefferson, he was willing to risk too much freedom rather than limit freedom.

> It seems to me that this is theoretically right, for whatever the question under discussion—whether religious, philosophical, political, or economic; whether it concerns prosperity, morality, equality, right, justice, progress, responsibility, cooperation, property, labor, trade, capital, wages, taxes, population, finance, or government—at whatever point on the scientific horizon I begin my researches, I invariably reach this one conclusion: The solution to the problems of human relationships is to be found in liberty.

THE FINAL DOCUMENT

This Magistrate is not the King. The People are the King.
—Gouverneur Morris

TO BRING TOGETHER all the debates and final decision, the Convention selected a Committee of Style and Arrangement. It was headed by Gouverneur Morris, chief draftsman and whose words are the Preamble. It also included Alexander Hamilton, William Samuel Johnson, Rufus King, and, of course, James Madison. It was his notes they used to format the final draft. Jacob Shallus, the assistant clerk of the Pennsylvania State Assembly, engrossed the Constitution. It was signed on September 17, 1787. It was then rushed to the states to be approved in conventions of individual state citizens.

Most of the delegates argued for the adoption of the Constitution, although many had reservations about all or parts of it. The reservations of three were so serious that they refused to sign the document. The position of one of these, George Mason, is important enough to take an in-depth look over.

The following remarks are representative of two opinions of the new plan; these two will soon be the beginning of Madison's "factions," today's political parties. One of them signed the Constitution; the other did not. What do the following comments tell you about the differences of opinion among the Framers concerning the Constitution they had developed? What were some problems they thought might arise in getting it approved? The first is Alexander Hamilton; the second, Elbridge Gerry.

> . . . Every member [of the Convention] should sign. A few characters of consequence, by opposing or even refusing to sign the Constitution, might do infinite mischief . . . No

> man's ideas were more remote from the plan than [mine are] known to be; but is it possible to deliberate between anarchy . . . on one side, and the chance of good to be expected from the plan on the other?

> . . . A Civil war may result from the present crisis . . . In Massachusetts . . . there are two parties, one devoted to Democracy, the worst . . . of all political evils, the other as violent in the opposite extreme . . . for this and other reasons . . . the plan should have been proposed in a more mediating shape.

The Constitution has been described as "a bundle of compromises." As you have seen, such prominent features of the Constitution as the different plans for representation in the House and the Senate and the method of selecting the president were settled by compromise, slavery. Compromise, however, means that everyone gets less than they want. There were enough compromises in the completed Constitution that nearly every delegate could find something he did not like. During the four months the delegates had spent putting the Constitution together, there were some strong disagreements. Some had walked out of the Convention. Three refused to sign the finished document.

Benjamin Franklin argued in support of the Constitution. George Mason argued against it. Mason was one of the three delegates remaining until the end of the Convention who refused to sign the document. He roared defiantly he would "sooner chop off his right hand than put it to the Constitution as it now stands."

On the last day of the Convention, September 17, 1787, Benjamin Franklin prepared a speech intended to persuade all the delegates to sign the completed Constitution. The speech was read by James Wilson, because Franklin's age and illness made him too weak to deliver it himself.

> I confess that there are several parts of this Constitution which I do not at present approve . . . [But] the older I grow, the more apt I am to doubt my own judgment, and to pay more respect to the judgment of others . . . In these

sentiments . . . I agree with this Constitution with all its faults, if they are such; because I think a general Government necessary for us . . . [and] I doubt . . . whether any other Convention we can obtain, may be able to make a better Constitution. For when you assemble a number of men to have the advantage of their joint wisdom, you inevitably assemble with those men all their prejudices, their passions, their errors of opinion, their local interests, and their selfish views. From such an assembly can a perfect production be expected? It therefore astonishes me . . . to find this system approaching so near to perfection as it does . . . Thus I, consent . . . to this Constitution because I expect no better, and because I am not sure, that it is not the best . . .

If every one of us in returning to our Constituents were to report the objections he has had to it . . . we might prevent its being generally received, and thereby lose all the salutary effects and great advantages resulting naturally in our favor among foreign Nations as well as among ourselves, from a real or apparent unanimity . . . On the whole . . . I cannot help expressing a wish that every member of the Convention who may still have objections to it, would with me on this occasion doubt a little of his own infallibility, and to make manifest our unanimity put his name to this instrument.

In the last couple days of the Convention, George Mason from Virginia and writer of the first bill of rights in the new America wrote a list of objections on his copy of the draft of the Constitution. The list was later printed as a pamphlet during the ratification debate.

1. The Constitution does not contain a Bill of Rights.
2. Because members of the Senate are selected by state legislatures, it means that they are not representatives of the people or answerable to them. They have great powers, such as the right to approve the appointment of ambassadors and treaties recommended by the president. They also have the power to try the president and other members of the government in cases of impeachment. These powers place the senators in such close connection with the president that together they will destroy

any balance in the government and do whatever they please with the rights and liberties of the people.

3. The national courts have been given so much power that they can destroy the judicial branches of the state governments by overruling them. If this were to happen and the only courts available were these courts, most people would not be able to afford to have their cases heard in these courts because they would need to travel a great distance. Rich people would have an advantage that would enable them to oppress and ruin the poor.

4. The Constitution does not provide for a council to serve as advisers to the president. Any safe and regular government has always included such a council. Such a council would take the place of the Senate in advising the president on appointments and treaties, and the head of the council would take the place of the vice president. Without it, the president will not get proper advice and will usually be advised by flattering and obedient favorites; or he will become a tool of the Senate.

5. The president of the United States has the unlimited power to grant pardons for crimes, including treason. He may sometimes use this power to protect people whom he has secretly encouraged to commit crimes and keep them from being punished. In this way, he can prevent the discovery of his own guilt.

6. The Constitution says that all treaties are the supreme law of the land. Since they can be made by the president with the approval of the Senate, together they have an exclusive legislative power in this area. This means they can act without the approval of the House of Representatives, the only branch of the legislature that is directly answerable to the people.

7. The Constitution only requires a majority vote in Congress, instead of a two-thirds vote, to make all commercial and navigation laws. The economic interests of the five southern states, however, are totally different from those of the eight northern states, which will have a majority in both houses of Congress. Requiring only a majority vote means that Congress may make laws favoring the merchants of the northern and eastern states at the expense of the agricultural interests of the southern states. This could ruin the southern states' economies.

8. Because the Constitution gives Congress the power to make any laws it thinks are "necessary and proper" to carry out its responsibilities, there is no adequate limitation on its powers. Congress could grant monopolies in trade and commerce, create new crimes, inflict severe or unusual punishments, and extend its powers as far as it wants. As a result, the powers of the state legislatures and the liberties of the people could be taken from them.

Mason also had made other criticisms of the Constitution during the Convention. Some were accepted by the Convention; others were incorporated in the Bill of Rights, which was added in 1791.

The final entry that James Madison made in his notes on the meetings describes the scene as the delegates were signing the document they hoped would become the Constitution of the United States.

As the last members were signing it, Benjamin Franklin looking toward the president's chair, a Masonic master's chair, at the back of which a rising sun was present, observed to a few members near him that it was hard to distinguish a rising from a setting sun. "I have," said he, "often in the course of the Session . . . looked at that [sun] behind the President without being able to tell whether it was rising or setting: But now at length I have the happiness to know that it is a rising and not a setting Sun." What optimism for something man was about to attempt, a great experiment, self-rule.

What do you think?

1. Why do you think Benjamin Franklin's attitude toward the Constitution was so optimistic?
2. Take an objection of George Mason; describe an event in American history or even a contemporary event that provides evidence in support of that objection.
3. What remedies has our Constitution provided for the problem he identified?

The Anti-Federalists

The people who opposed ratification of the Constitution, which created a "federal" government, were called Anti-Federalists. To understand their point of view, we will focus on a few of them, primarily the writings of Mercy Otis Warren, the author of many plays and political pamphlets. The Anti-Federalists' position was based mainly on the ideas that had been discussed for more than two thousand years about the kind of society that was necessary for a republic.

The name Anti-Federalists captures an attachment to certain political principles as well as stands in favor and against trends that were appearing in late eighteenth-century America. It will help in our understanding of who the Anti-Federalists were to know that in 1787, the word "federal" had two meanings: one was universal or based on principle, and the other was particular and specific to the American situation.

The first meaning of "federal" is a set of governing principles in opposition to a central, national, or consolidated system. That's why the Articles of Confederation was understood to be a federal arrangement: the Confederation Congress was limited to powers expressly granted, the States as states were represented equally regardless of the size of their population, and it took all members to change the arrangement; Jefferson and Madison will recall this in '98, a central or national government that diminished local or state powers all bound under a restrictive and binding document.

But in the second definition, "federal" had a more American character. It was a group that wanted a "firmer and more connected union"; these gentlemen were called, derisively, "federal men." They included many under the loose direction of George Washington, Gouverneur Morris, James Madison, Alexander Hamilton., and James Wilson.

As in the Bolsheviks in the Russian Revolution taking the name, majority, the opposition called the Mensheviks, in American politics, the name by which one is known, is often not of one's own doing. The Anti-Federalists would have preferred to be known as democratic republicans, a name they will take under Jefferson's rise to power, or federal Republicans, but they acquired the name antifederal, or Anti-Federal, or Antifederal because of events of American history. What they believed was a federal system; thus, the Anti-Federalists were the Federalist, the true Federalists.

Put differently, the actual name "Anti-Federalists" did not exist before 1782. As good propagandists, the pro-constitutional nationalists like Madison and Hamilton consciously "stole" the name Federalist to improve their chances of persuading the electorate and the delegates to the ratifying conventions to adopt the Constitution. Rhetoric both on behalf of and in restraint of, the role of the federal government is built into the very fabric of the American system. And the controversy over the name "Anti-Federalist" reflects that inherent quarrel.

Most Americans were, and are, very suspicious of government, but the Anti-Federalists were especially mistrustful of government in general and strong national government in particular. This mistrust was the basis of their opposition to the Constitution. They feared it had created a government the people could not control.

In general, the Anti-Federalists were older Americans who had grown up believing in the basic ideas of republicanism. These included the idea that in a republic, the greatest power should be placed in a legislature composed of representatives elected by the people of the community. It had always been thought that this kind of representative government would only work in a small community of citizens with similar interests and beliefs, because in such a community, it would be easier for people to agree on what was in their common interest.

In addition, it was widely believed that people living in small agrarian communities would be more likely to possess the civic virtue required of republican citizens. Living closely together, they would be more willing to set aside their own interests when necessary and work for the common good.

The Anti-Federalists understood that the Federalists were proposing a government that was the opposite of this type of republican government. It was large and powerful, it included numerous diverse communities, and its capital would be far away from most of the people it represented. The Anti-Federalists believed such a system would inevitably pose a threat to the rights of the people.

Many distinguished Americans were Anti-Federalists. Leaders included George Mason and Elbridge Gerry. Both had attended the Philadelphia Convention but had refused to sign the Constitution. Richard Henry Lee was a leading revolutionary and signer of the

Declaration of Independence but fought against the ratification of the Constitution. Patrick Henry had always opposed the idea of a strong national government; he became a leading Anti-Federalist. Mercy Otis Warren, a playwright, also opposed ratification. She, like the others, wrote pamphlets explaining why she did not support the Constitution. Other prominent Anti-Federalists included Robert Yates, George Clinton, Patrick Henry, Sam Adams, John Hancock, and, of course, Thomas Jefferson.

Many arguments were made both for and against the Constitution. Most of them had to do with three basic questions:

- Would the new Constitution maintain a republican form of government?
- Would the central government have too much power?
- Was a bill of rights needed in the Constitution?

Luther Martin was a key Anti-Federalist before the Convention itself. Good friends with Patrick Henry, he arrived late to the Convention but made up for his absence with many long and sometimes drink-enhanced speeches. He began by criticizing the secrecy of the meetings, feeling that things in the Convention were being decided that would be best kept from the public. He said that frankly the president as written in the document was "a king in everything but name." State sovereignty, or true Federalism, was all but gone. By the time he arrived, the Virginia Plan had been presented and used as the rough draft of a government with "principles which would be right and proper only on the supposition that there were no State governments at all" and that was an overt and, as we see today, a future threat to liberty. He reminded his fellow delegates that distant government was more prone to corruptions and abuses of power.

It wasn't as though Martin was an early conspiracy theorist; he knew Washington and Franklin and Madison were in support of big government without the nuisances of the states. In a letter to Washington before the Convention opened, Madison was adamant—it was in the original Virginia Plan—that the new government must "have a negative [a veto], in all cases whatsoever, on the Legislative acts of the States"; without this, "every positive power that can be given on paper [to the national government] will be evaded and defeated. The States will continue to invade the national jurisdiction, to violate treaties and the law of nations and to harass each other with rival and spiteful measures dictated be mistaken views of interest." Martin using Locke, and Thomas Jefferson himself, argued "that the States like individuals were in a State of nature equally sovereign and free" and that "happiness was preferable to the Splendors of a national Government."

His Anti-Federalism ends up in our Tenth Amendment, though the most important word "expressly" was deleted before being sent to the states, an issue that has led to abuse after abuse since.

> The powers not [expressly] delegated to the United States
> by the Constitution, nor prohibited by it to the States, are
> reserved to the States respectively, or to the people.

In *Federalist 62*, Madison tends to indirectly support Martin, and today's Tea Partiers. Like Obamacare's supporter, at the time speaker of the House Nancy Pelosi, stated, "But we have to pass the [health care] bill so that you can find out what's in it . . .," laws have become so oppressive in their complexity that many of you have probably broken dozens, maybe *Three Felonies a Day* by Harvey Silverglate.

> It will be of little avail to the people, that the laws are made
> by men of their own choice, if the laws be so voluminous
> that they cannot be read, or so incoherent that they cannot
> be understood; if they be repealed or revised before they are
> promulgated, or undergo such incessant changes that no
> man, who knows what the law is to-day, can guess what it
> will be to-morrow. Law is defined to be a rule of action; but
> how can that be a rule, which is little known, and less fixed?

Mercy Otis Warren is the best Anti-Federalist writer, bar none. She is noteworthy because of her unusual ability to enter the man's world of early American politics. Her main criticisms of the Constitution are a good example of the Anti-Federalist position, but also her complaints resonated in the election of 2016 when a nonpolitician, an outsider, wins the election. The Anti-Federalists argued that the Constitution had many flaws that needed fixing before they could accept it.

- It should have been developed in meetings whose proceedings were open to the public; why were as the meetings secret?
- It would undermine a republican form of government.
- It gave too much power to the national government at the expense of the powers of the state governments.
- It gave too much power to the executive branch of the national government at the expense of the other branches.
- It gave Congress too much power because of the "necessary and proper clause."
- It did not adequately separate the powers of the executive and legislative branches.
- It allowed the national government to keep an army during peacetime.
- It did not include a bill of rights.
- It favored the wealthy and powerful aristocracy, too elitist.
- Constitution was not legal; the delegates had no right to do what they did.

In her *Observations on the New Constitution, and the Federal and State Conventions*, not published until 1805, not attributed to her until WW I, she as "a Columbian Patriot" outlined the list above but her greatest concern was rule by an aristocracy. She notes that the first election drew only 43,782 votes out of over four million. Only five states allowed the people to select their electors—Delaware, New Hampshire, Pennsylvania, Maryland, and Virginia; and with eleven states (Rhode Island and North Carolina came in after the election) now with seventeen states, how was that a representation of the people? Was she asking for an end of the Electoral College? Was she warning us of the Leviathan to come? Warning us not to look to safety over liberty? She spared no one in her *Observations*. As she notes, many Loyalists and previous revolutionaries are part of the new cabal. Even her friend John Adams was not spared; she noted, "Mr. Adams's former opinions . . . were beclouded by partiality for monarchy," in her opposition to his Alien and Sedition Acts. Like Jefferson's conflict and falling out with John, she was reconciled before her death by John's wife, Abigail Adams.

> On these shores freedom has planted her standard, dipped
> in the purple tide that flowed from the veins of her martyred

heroes; and here every uncorrupted American yet hopes to see it supported by the vigor, the justice, the wisdom and unanimity of the people, in spite of the deep-laid plots the secret intrigues, or the bold effrontery of those interested and avaricious adventurers for place, who intoxicated with the ideas of distinction and preferment have prostrated every worthy principle beneath the shrine of ambition. Yet these are the men who tell us republicanism is dwindled into theory—that we are incapable of enjoying our liberties— and that we must have a master.—Let us retrospect the days of our adversity, and recollect who were then our friends; do we find them among the sticklers for aristocratic authority? No, they were generally the same men who now wish to save us from the distractions of anarchy on the one hand, and the jaws of tyranny on the other; where then were the class who now come forth importunately urging that our political salvation depends on the adoption of a system at which freedom spurns?—Were not some of them hidden in the corners of obscurity, and others wrapping themselves in the bosom of our enemies for safety? Some of them were in the arms of infancy; and others speculating for fortune, by sporting with public money; while a few, a very few of them were magnanimously defending their country, and raising a character, which I pray heaven may never be sullied by aiding measures derogatory to their former exertions. But the revolutions in principle which time produces among mankind, frequently exhibits the most mortifying instances of human weakness; and this alone can account for the extraordinary appearance of a few names, once distinguished in the honorable walks of patriotism, but now found in the list of the Massachusetts assent to the ratification of a Constitution, which, by the undefined meaning of some parts, and the ambiguities of expression in others, is dangerously adapted to the purposes of an immediate *aristocratic tyranny*; that from the difficulty, if not impracticability of its operation, must soon terminate in the most uncontrolled despotism.

Warren and the other Anti-Federalists feared that, because of these flaws in the Constitution, the new national government would be a threat to their natural rights. They also thought that the Constitution had been developed by an elite and privileged group to create a national government to serve its own selfish interests. See Donald Trump's inaugural address later. Warren and most of the Anti-Federalists thought that the only safe government was one that was local and closely linked with the will of the people, controlled by the people, by such means as yearly elections and replacing people in key positions often, not that she did not see flaws in the Articles but just that the Convention went too far.

> Our situation is truly delicate & critical. On the one hand we are in need of a strong federal government founded on principles that will support the prosperity & union of the colonies. On the other we have struggled for liberty & made costly sacrifices at her shrine and there are still many among us who revere her name to much to relinquish (beyond a certain medium) the rights of man for the dignity of government.

The Anti-Federalists often disagreed with each other about why they opposed the Constitution, and they were not a well-organized group. They were united, however, in their opposition to the new central government described in the Constitution. They soon realized that the best way to defeat the Constitution was to use the issue of a bill of rights.

There was a widespread fear of a strong and powerful national government combined with the belief that a bill of rights was necessary to protect people from government. If people needed to be protected from their relatively weak state governments, they certainly needed protection from the vastly more powerful national government. In addition, it was easier for the Anti-Federalists to dramatize the lack of a bill of rights than the issues of taxes or the powers of the state governments.

The lack of a bill of rights became the focus of the Anti-Federalist campaign. It was a highly emotional issue for the men and women who had just fought a revolution to secure their rights. In several states, the question of a bill of rights was used effectively to organize opposition to the ratification of the Constitution.

Many Anti-Federalist leaders, like Mason, Warren, and Martin, hoped to defeat the Constitution so that a second constitutional convention would be held. There, the Anti-Federalists hoped, they would have more influence in creating a new government.

The most frequent arguments they used were the following:

- The way the government is organized does not adequately protect rights. Only the House of Representatives is chosen directly by the people. The national government is too far removed from average citizens to care about their concerns. The national government's power could be used to violate citizens' rights.

- The national government's powers are so general and vague that they can be used to give the government almost unlimited power. It can make all laws that are "necessary and proper" to promote the "general welfare." The Constitution allows the central government to act directly on citizens. Therefore, its powers over citizens are almost unlimited.

- There is nothing in the Constitution to stop the new central government from violating all the rights that are not mentioned in it. Some rights are included and some are not. There is no mention, for example, of freedom of religion, speech, press, or assembly. Since they are omitted from the Constitution, the government is free to violate them.

- A bill of rights would quiet the fears of many people that a strong central government could violate their rights. After all, Americans recently fought a revolutionary war to secure their fundamental rights. They do not want a constitution that places those rights in jeopardy.

- A bill of rights is necessary to remind the people of the principles of our political system. As one Anti-Federalist put it, there is a necessity of "constantly keeping in view . . . the particular principles on which our freedom must always depend."

- Eventually, the Anti-Federalists argued, people would lose many of their freedoms. As one Anti-Federalist stated, "We know that private interest governs mankind generally. Power belongs originally to the people; but if rulers be not well guarded, that power may be usurped from them. People ought to be cautious in giving away power."

One of the most important persons who opposed the Constitution was Patrick Henry. Henry was not opposed to a union of the thirteen states. However, he was concerned that the proposed Constitution lacked enough protection for state and individual rights. Henry was not alone in his desire for the protection of rights. His fears were echoed by others, including Thomas Jefferson. James Madison listened to his friends Jefferson and Henry, and soon after the ratification of the Constitution, he introduced a series of amendments that created the Bill of Rights.

A general provision should be inserted in the new system, securing to the States and the people every right which was not conceded to the general government. I trust that gentlemen . . . will see the great objects of religion, liberty of the press, trial by jury, interdiction of cruel punishments, and every other sacred right, secured, before they agree to that [Constitution].

The necessity of a bill of rights appears . . . to be greater in this government than ever it was in any government before. All nations have adopted the construction, that all rights not expressly and [definitely] reserved to the people are [inevitably] relinquished to rulers . . . If you give up these powers, without a bill of rights, you will exhibit the most absurd thing to mankind that ever the world saw,—a government that has abandoned all its powers—the powers of direct taxation, the sword, and the purse. You have disposed of them to Congress, without a bill of rights, without check, limitation, or control.

Unfortunately, there were no three Anti-Federalists who got together in New York, or Richmond, and said, "Let's write 85 essays in which we argue that the Constitution should be either rejected or modified before adoption." Thus, in contrast to the pro-Constitution advocates, there is no one book—like *The Federalist*—to which the modern reader can turn to and say, "Here's *The Anti-Federalist Papers*." Their work is vast and varied and, for the most part, haphazard. Again, an attribute of Federalism, different opinions should be determined at a level closer to the people, local or state. It may be why there is a sense of awe toward the Constitution; most of our understanding of how it works, what it means is through the minds of the Hamiltonians, Progressives, big government nationalist. Yet what made this nation so great are the ideals of the Anti-Federalists, ideals deeply embodied in the Constitution and the American tradition. The Anti-Federalists are still very much alive and well in twenty-first-century America.

There are—yes, I use the present tense—three kinds of Anti-Federalists: politicians, outsiders, and conservatives.

The politicians are those who participated in the Convention, both from Connecticut, Rodger Sherman and Oliver Ellsworth. They came suspiciously to Philadelphia having already heard of the Virginia Plan to give broad powers to a new congress and an obvious placing in the backseat, the states. They had much success in modifying this national plan retaining federal principles. The powers of Congress are listed, each state is represented equally in the Senate and composed of senators elected by the state legislatures, the president is to be elected by a majority of the people plus a majority of the states, the Constitution was to be ratified by the people of nine states, and any changes needed plus three-fourths of the state legislatures to happen. They made sure the new Constitution was a federal constitution, at least partly national and partly federal.

The next group of Anti-Federalists was those not selected to the Convention. Their greatest fear is the potential for this Constitution for corruption in the powers in the new government. Many of them wrote under pseudonyms somewhat fearful of losing and the power in the hands of the enemy, the Federalists. We are talking about people such as Melancton Smith (Federal Farmer), Robert Yates (Brutus or Sydney), George Clinton (Cato) in New York, Samuel Bryant (Centinel) in Pennsylvania, and John Winthrop (Agrippa) in Massachusetts. They also warned that without including a bill of rights that stated clearly and in writing what the new government could and could not do, the presidency and the judiciary would dominate. They warned that the attempt by the first type of Anti-Federalists' tweaking of the document was not enough. Power corrupts, and there were still too many uncertain areas where a completely centralized system without specific limits on the national government would end any existence of Federalism. We can thank them for the Ninth and Tenth Amendments.

The third and final group was what we would conservatives; they wanted little change of the Articles of Confederation as possible. They saw the tweaks as even too far. They felt that any compromise was totally unsustainable. Like the second group, though more pessimistic, they saw it as inevitable that the very structure and powers would lead within a short time, would make the president a monarch, and would turn the states into mere administrators of national law, that the differences in states would evaporate into one large centralized empire. Ratifying delegates like Patrick Henry come to mind; he deliberately made a nuisance of himself at the Virginia Ratifying Convention disrupting the orderly process of debates at will. George Mason and Elbridge Gerry also come to mind. They started off as warm supporters of a stronger national government but within twelve months had become open opponents of even the friendly amendments proposed by the second type of Anti-Federalist. Within this third type of Anti-Federalist, we would also include Philadelphia delegates Luther Martin, John Lansing, Robert Yates, and John Mercer. Their legacy can best be found in later generations of secessionists, Libertarians, and free marketers John C. Calhoun, Ron Paul, and Donald Trump.

Though *The Federalist* may be the best reference to understanding the Constitution, many believe the writers of those eighty-five essays would not have done such an extraordinary job or written as many as they did or covered every clause of the document if it weren't for the brilliance of the Anti-Federalists of what a government ought to do, which government ought to do it, and the possibility of its overreach into the liberties of man.

The Federalists

The people who supported ratification of the Constitution, which created a new stronger national government, were called Federalists. It is important to understand the difference of opinion between the Federalists and the Anti-Federalists and the strategy and the arguments the Federalists used to get the Constitution ratified. These include the concepts of the social contract and consent. Even in the larger states, such as New York and Virginia, the debates about ratification were very close, and to get some Anti-Federalist support, the Federalists, primarily Edmund Randolph and James Madison, agreed that when the first Congress was held, it would draft a bill of rights to be added to the Constitution.

The Federalists knew that many members of Confederation Congress and the state governments were against the new Constitution largely because it reduced their powers. The Federalists decided not to ask the Congress or state to approve the Constitution, even though they were expected to do so under the original purpose of the Convention.

James Madison developed the plan presented by the Federalists. The plan was to go directly to the voters to get them to approve the Constitution. The Constitution would be presented to special ratifying conventions to be held in each state. The delegates would be elected by popular vote of the people for the sole purpose of approving the Constitution. Madison's plan was consistent with the idea in the Preamble to the Constitution that says, "We the People . . . do ordain and establish this Constitution . . ."

This plan relied on the social contract idea. The people who were to be governed by the new national government were asked to consent to its creation and obey its decisions. You may recognize this as the method for establishing a government set forth in the natural rights philosophy of John Locke and in the Declaration of Independence. In Jefferson's words, just governments "derive their just powers from the consent of the governed." Some people had argued, for example, that the Articles of Confederation were not valid or legitimate under the laws of nature because they had never been presented to the people for their consent. The Convention approved this method for ratifying the Constitution, and as soon as it was ratified by just nine of the thirteen state conventions, it would go into effect.

Once they had agreed on their strategy, the Federalists encouraged their associates in the states to organize the state conventions and elect delegates to them as quickly as possible. They knew the Anti-Federalists had not had enough time to organize their opposition. They had worked on the Constitution for almost four months and knew the arguments for and against it were building. They hoped if the conventions acted quickly, Anti-Federalists would have little time to organize their opposition to the Constitution's ratification.

Despite the advantages of the Federalists' position, the Anti-Federalists put up a strong fight. The debates in the states over ratification lasted ten months. It was an intense and sometimes bitter political struggle. One of the most difficult fights for ratification was in New York. To help the Federalist cause, three men—Alexander Hamilton, James Madison, and John Jay—wrote a series of essays published in three New York newspapers under the pseudonym *Publius*. Maybe the best source of Federalist opinion, these articles were not intended to present all sides. Their purpose was to convince people to support the ratification of the Constitution. They will later be assembled and are now called *The Federalist*, the most important work in defense of the new Constitution; though they were probably read by few if anyone outside of New York, especially since New York was the eleventh state to ratify.

In defending the new Constitution, the writers of *The Federalist* were very skilled at using basic ideas about government that most Americans understood and accepted. They presented the Constitution as a well-organized, agreed-on plan for national government. The conflicts and compromises that had taken place during its development were not stressed to present the Constitution as favorably as possible. Though probably very difficult to read, if even known, they were read by the average citizen and most of the delegates to New York and later conventions.

The Anti-Federalists had some traditional arguments about what made a good government on their side as well. The Federalists were better organized, however. The Federalists' arguments in support of the Constitution claimed that it provided a solution for the problem of creating a republican government in a large and diverse nation. They were able to convince a significant number of people to support their position by the following three arguments:

1. The civic virtue of the people cannot be relied on alone to protect basic rights.
2. The way the government is organized will protect basic rights.
3. The representation of different interests in the government will protect basic rights.

The civic virtue of the people could no longer be relied on as the sole support of a government that would protect the people's rights and promote their welfare. Throughout history, the Federalists argued, the greatest dangers in republics to the common good and the natural rights of citizens had been from the selfish pursuit of their interests by groups of citizens who ignored the common good. Therefore, for almost two thousand years, political philosophers had insisted that republican government was only safe if the citizens possessed civic virtue. By civic virtue, they meant that citizens had to be willing to set aside their interests if it was necessary to do so for the common good. In *Federalist 51*, James Madison felt man needed government.

If men were angels, no government would be necessary. If angels were to govern men, neither external nor internal controls on government would be necessary. In framing a government which is to be administered by men over men, the great difficulty lies in this: You must first enable the government to control the governed; and in the next place, oblige it to control itself.

Recent experiences with their States had led several people to doubt that they could rely on the virtue of citizens to promote the common good and protect the rights of individuals. Many of the state legislatures had passed laws that helped people in debt at the expense of those to whom they owed money. These laws were seen by many as an infringement on property rights that were, after all, one of the basic natural rights for which the Revolution had been fought in the first place. These "majorities" were being tyrannical, abusing minorities. As today, the majority of a national decision can be oppressively imposed on a minority of the states.

If the proper working of a republican form of government could not rely on the virtue of its citizens, what could it rely on? How could a government be organized so it would not be dominated by self-interested individuals or factions at the expense of others? Madison's *Federalist #14* attempts to explain why democracy cannot work.

We have seen the necessity of the Union as our [strength] against foreign danger, as the conservator of peace among ourselves, as the guardian of our commerce and other common interests, as the only substitute for those military establishments which have subverted the liberties of the old world . . .

In a democracy, the people meet and exercise the government in person; in a republic they assemble and administer it by their representatives and agents. A democracy consequently must be confined to a small spot. A republic may be extended over a large region.

The natural limit of a democracy is that distance from the central point, which will just permit the most remote citizens to assemble as often as their public functions demand, and will include no greater number than can join in those functions. The natural limit of a republic is that distance from the center which will barely allow the representatives of the people to meet as often as may be necessary for the administration of public affairs . . . It is to be remembered that the general government is not to be charged with the whole power of making and administering the laws. Its jurisdiction is limited to certain [specific issues], which concern all the members of the republic . . . The subordinate [states], which can extend their care to all those other objects which can be separately provided for, will retain their due authority and activity.

A second observation to be made is that the immediate object of the federal Constitution is to secure the union of the thirteen primitive States . . . and to add to them such other states, as may arise in their neighborhoods . . .

. . . In the third place, [the Constitution will see] that [movement] throughout the Union will be facilitated by new improvements [such as] roads . . . accommodations for travelers . . . interior navigation . . .

A fourth and still more important consideration is . . . in regard to the safety [of the individual States. Each State should] find an inducement to make some sacrifices for the sake of the general protection. The States which lie at the greatest distance from the heart of the union, and which of course may partake least of its benefits, will be at the same time near foreign nations. These States will consequently stand on particular occasions in greatest need of the entire nation's strength and resources. It may be inconvenient for [some States] to send their representatives to the seat of government, but they would find it more so to struggle along against an invading enemy, or even to support alone the whole expense of taking precautions which may be dictated by continual danger.

. . . Happily for America . . . [the revolutionary leaders] pursued a new and more noble course. They accomplished a revolution which has no parallel in the annals of human society . . . if they erred most in the structure of the Union, this was the work most difficult to be executed; this is the work which has been new modeled by the act of your convention, and it is that act on which you are now to deliberate and decide.

The way in which the Constitution organized the government, including the separation of powers and checks and balances, was the best way to promote the goals of republicanism. A major idea in *The Federalist* is that the national government set forth in the Constitution did not have to rely solely on the civic virtue of the people to protect citizens' rights and promote their welfare. The writers believed that it was unrealistic to expect people in a large and diverse nation, living hundreds of miles apart, to be willing to give up their own interests for the benefit of others.

They argued that the rights and welfare of all would be protected by the complicated system of representation, separation of powers, Federalism, and checks and balances provided by the Constitution. They also believed that the method of electing senators and presidents would increase the possibility that they would have the qualities required of good governing officials.

The Federalists took the position that the Constitution's strength was that it provided for different branches of government that would represent the different interests of the people. They also claimed that this complicated system would make it impossible for any individual or faction—or even a majority—to take complete control of the government to serve its own interests at the expense of the common good or the rights of individuals. Despite Hamilton's propaganda in the *Federalist*, he and his party, under Washington and Adams, began to emasculate the Constitution, something he felt was "a frail and worthless fabric." He had written to Washington that this nation needed "a government of more energy." He'd be very proud of his plan. George Will once wrote, "We honor Jefferson, but live in Hamilton's country."

The large size of the nation, they argued, would make it particularly difficult for any one faction to attain a majority. Since so many interests and factions would be represented in the national government, it would be less likely that any one of them would dominate.

Some would argue that the system was so complicated that it would be difficult to get anything done, especially if one or more interested and powerful groups objected to something that was being planned. Madison, in *The Federalist,* clearly did not see this as a disadvantage. One of his criticisms of the state legislatures had been that they passed too many laws in the first place. Most Framers believed that the best way to prevent a bad law from being passed was to prevent a law from being passed at all.

The representation of different interests in the government would protect basic rights. The branches of the national government, the power each had distributed to it by the Constitution, and the interests each was supposed to represent are as follows:

- Legislative branch. The House of Representatives would protect the people's local interests since representatives would be chosen from small congressional districts. The Senate would protect the states' interests, since it would be selected by state legislatures.
- Executive branch. The president would protect the people's national interests, since he would be elected by a method that required electors to select him from among leaders who had achieved national prominence.
- Judicial branch. The Supreme Court would protect the people's fundamental interests, since it was independent of political manipulation and therefore responsible only to the Constitution.

What do you think?

1. Are the arguments of the Federalists reflective of their point of view in regard to natural rights, republicanism, and constitutionalism?
2. Why did the Federalists think we cannot rely on civic virtue to make a republic work properly? Do you agree?
3. How have the changes in our size and population of the United States tempered or reinforced the positions of the Federalists?

The Federalists admitted that the new national government had much more power than the old national government. It had more control over the states, but it was a government limited to enumerated powers. The federal system and checks and balances ensured that those limits would not be violated. As a result, they claimed, the increased powers given to the government under the Constitution could only be used to protect, not violate, the rights of the people. Critics feared that giving so much power to a national government might be a serious threat to their rights and welfare.

The Federalists used several arguments to counter those demanding a bill of rights. The most important of these arguments follow:

- The complexity of the government and the diversity of the nation protect rights. A large republic makes it nearly impossible for a "majority faction" to have its way.
- The Constitution does protect several specific rights. These include the right to habeas corpus, prohibition of ex post facto laws and bills of attainder, protection against violations of contracts, guarantee in criminal cases of trial by jury in the state where the crime was committed, and protection against accusations of treason by its careful definition.
- A bill of rights is unnecessary in a nation with popular sovereignty. Previous bills of rights, such as the English Bill of Rights, protected people from a powerful monarch over whom they had no control. Under the Constitution, the people have the power to remove elected officials from office. The protections of such bills of rights are therefore unnecessary under the Constitution.

- The Constitution does not give the central government the power to deprive people of their rights. It gives government only limited powers to do specific things—enumerated powers. There is no need to list rights that the government has no power to violate.
- Declarations of rights are ineffective and dangerous. Most state constitutions are prefaced with bills of rights, but these bills did not stop state governments from violating citizens' rights. No state had a comprehensive list of rights—that is, a bill that listed all the rights that were protected. Apparently, some state governments felt free to violate important rights unlisted in their bills. Since it is impossible to list all rights, it is better to have no list at all. Government officials might feel free to violate unlisted rights.

The Federalists worked hard to overcome the objections of the Anti-Federalists. By June 1788, nine states had voted to ratify the Constitution. New Hampshire was the ninth and last state needed to make the Constitution the highest law of the land. The important states, New York and Virginia, had not yet approved the Constitution. The debates were very close in these states because of the fear of creating such a large and powerful national government.

Finally, a compromise was reached. To get Anti-Federalists to support the Constitution, the Federalists agreed that when the first Congress was held, it would draft a bill of rights to be added to the Constitution. The bill was to list the rights of citizens that were not to be violated by the federal government. The Federalists insisted that the bill of rights include a statement saying that the list of rights should not be interpreted to mean that they were the only rights the people had.

The Federalists' agreement to sponsor a bill of rights reduced much of the Anti-Federalists' support. It deprived the Anti-Federalists of their most powerful weapon. In some states—Massachusetts, for example—the agreement was enough to win a close ratification vote, 187 to 168. Then, at last, New York and Virginia also voted for ratification. The Anti-Federalists had lost their battle to reject or revise the Constitution, but they had won an agreement to add a bill of rights.

The Federalists deserve the credit for writing the Constitution, which created our present form of government. The debate resulting from the Anti-Federalists' objections to the Constitution resulted in the addition of the Bill of Rights. The Bill of Rights has proved to be vitally important to the protection of basic rights of the American people and an inspiration to many beyond America's shores.

What do you think?

1. Why did the Federalists believe the Constitution did not need a bill of rights? Do you agree with their position? Why or why not?
2. What rights did the Framers protect right in the body of the Constitution and not others?
3. Of the many reasons given by the Federalist to support the as-is Constitution of 1787, which were most important? Which do you think were the least important?

Delaware	December 7, 1787	30–0
Pennsylvania	December 12, 1787	46–23
New Jersey	December 19, 1787	38–0
Georgia	January 2, 1788	26–0
Connecticut	January 9, 1788	128–40
Massachusetts	February 6, 1788	187–168
Rhode Island	March 24, 1788	327–2708
	May 29, 1790	34–32
Maryland	April 28, 1788	63–11
South Carolina	May 23, 1788	149–73
#9 New Hampshire	June 21, 1788	57–46 (47)
Virginia	June 25, 1788	89–79
New York	July 26, 1788	30–27
North Carolina	August 2, 1788	84–185
	November 21, 1789	194–77

Article VII of the Constitution describes the process by which the entire document was to become effective. It required that conventions of nine of the thirteen original states ratify the Constitution. The citizens of Delaware were the first state to accept. Once word was received that the ninth state had ratified the constitution—New Hampshire, June 21, 1788—a timetable was set for the start of operations under the Constitution, and on March 4, 1789, the government under the Constitution began operations. Yet the real fight was in Virginia and New York. With the propaganda of *The Federalist* and assurances in the Virginia Ratification Convention, the last four states of the original thirteen colonies joined the Union.

The Virginia Ratifying Convention was a wonder of the Age of Enlightenment. Great speakers, great ideas were on both sides of the debate; Framers on one side, republicans on the other. The debate of what the great experiment meant was fought over a document on a table surrounding by some of the greatest minds to have ever lived. Leading the republicans and other Anti-Federalists was the eloquent speaker Patrick Henry. Leading the Federalists was the writer of the Virginia Plan and "Father of the Constitution," James Madison. Moderating the debate was another writer of the Virginia Plan, yet a nonsigner at the Convention, Edmund Randolph, governor of Virginia.

Patrick Henry had major concerns, but foremost were the "general welfare clause" and the "necessary and proper clause." Henry was concerned that these two clauses were to give the central government unlimited power. Madison, with the backing of Edmund Randolph, said the list is exhaustive in Article I, Section 8. Only those powers listed were Congress's. As to a bill of rights: "All rights are therein declared to be completely vested in the people, unless expressly given away." Henry persisted, asking Henry's warning about the subtle trap of "We the People" instead of "We the States," of the dangers of a strong executive and the unwarranted power of a national judiciary. In response, Madison added two comments. He would guarantee he would introduce personally to the new Congress a Bill of Rights.

Elbridge Gerry will be elected to that new Congress, serving two terms and then resigning. While in the House, he will work closely with James Madison on that bill of rights. There will be twelve sent, the states; ten will be approved, ratified. He added freedom of assembly to the First Amendment (third amendment on the list, first and second of the twelve were not approved in 1791, the second ratified in 1992 as the twenty-seventh). The words you read in the Second Amendment are his: "A well regulated Militia, being necessary to the security of a free state . . ." Like today's fearful patriots, Gerry believed, "When Governments mean to invade the rights and liberties of the people, they always attempt to destroy the militia, in order to raise an army upon their ruins." He introduced our Fourth Amendment in memory of his friend James Otis. John Adams will say of Gerry, "If every Man here was a Gerry, the Liberties of America would be safe against the Gates of Earth and Hell." Madison, though often frustrated with Gerry, agreed and later picked Gerry as his vice president.

Henry and the delegates were afraid that once agreeing to join, they may later be oppressed by a majority of states, offensive to the Constitution. The point was made numerous times, as it had been done in Pennsylvania that this was a voluntary compact. James Madison assured delegates that "if we be dissatisfied with the national government, if we choose to renounce it, this is an additional safeguard to our defence." Notice the word "additional." Madison is saying here that the right to secession is an additional part of his intricate system of checks and balances.

The president of the Virginia Convention, Judge Edmund Pendleton, asked what recourse they would have if it turned out the constitution they were debating did not live up to its promises. He answered his own question with the reassurance that it would not be necessary to resist through force of arms:

> No, we will assemble in Convention, wholly recall our delegated powers, or reform them to prevent such abuse . . . Virginia need not fear joining the Union, in other words, because it had the right to leave it or reform it.

Several states, following Virginia, issued formal statements of ratification that made a similar point, declaring that a government freely entered into by the people could be freely left. Alexander Hamilton and John Marshall conceded the right, not because they necessarily approved but because they wanted the Constitution ratified. They knew most states and delegates would not ratify without the right to leave the Union.

Differences on the Constitution have created political parties, many of the later debates on policies, and actions by the separate branches; even the Civil War all stem from a discussion of what the words meant and mean today. One way is to look at the philosophies of those who wrote it and those that opposed it. Below is a chart showing comparing the ideals of the eighteenth-century classical liberals, John Locke, Jefferson, and those that feared the experiment. Opposition on the Left, today's Progressives, Democrats, Socialists prefer to do what they want socially but ask for help economically; they want political freedom without economic freedom. While those on the Right want to impose on not just Americans but the world, a moral agenda with crony business connections.

Today's classical liberals, called Libertarians because of the "theft" of liberal by today's Socialists, share the best of both while opposing those principles that hamper man in any way. In the second diagram, the struggle of two different Americas through history illustrates the development of policies and politics.

Opposition on the Left	Classical Liberals Libertarians		Opposition on the Right
Centrally controlled economy	Personal freedom	Economic freedom	Government-regulated morality
UN led US military	Nonintervention	Strong military	Nation building
Flexible property rights (eminent domain)	Right to private personal decisions	Respect for others' property	War on drugs
Banning guns	Civil liberties and privacy	Individual right to bear arms	Patriot Act
Taxpayer funding versus charity	Separation of church and state	Giving generously to those in need	Taxpayer funding versus faith-based charity
Classes of people need special treatment	No corporate welfare	Individual inequality affects achievement	Classes of business need special treatment

The Split in American Politics

Party Labels	Jeffersonians, Democratic-Republicans, Democrats, Republicans	Federalists, Whigs, Republicans, Democrats, Progressives
Social Composition	Artisans, shopkeepers, frontier settlers, small farmers, small business, middle class	Slaveholders, merchants, bankers, professional, wealthy farmers and southern plantation owners
Where	South, West	New England, Atlantic seaboard, West Coast
Attitudes toward Government	• More democratic than that of England • Common people were capable of self-government • Small property owners' democracy • Lowering voting qualifications • Strict interpretation of the Constitution to limit the powers of the central government and conserve state rights • Reduce the number of national officeholders • Freedom of speech and press, essential • Local or state governments central • Liberty > Security	• Admired the English aristocracy and the English system of government and wished to see it used as a model • Considered the common people ignorant and incapable of self-government • Men of wealth and property to rule • High voting qualifications, claiming that unfettered democracy was anarchy • Broad interpretation of the Constitution to strengthen the central government at the expense of state rights • Large bureaucracy • Favored restrictions on speech and the press, for national security • Security > Liberty

Economic Concerns	• Preferred an agrarian society, but with some industry subordinate to agriculture. • Government should offer no special favors to business • No special favors should be given to manufacturers, such as tariffs • Opposed a central banking system and wanted to encourage state banks • National debt was harmful to the nation, that the debt should be paid as quickly as possible, and that the nation should remain out of debt	• Preferred an industrial society with a balanced economy • Government should foster business and contribute to the growth of capitalistic enterprise • Favored a protective tariff to aid manufacturers • Powerful national bank, modeled after the Bank of England • Considered the national debt a blessing to be used to advantage in the establishment of credit and a way to guarantee support from wealthy and banks (holders of the debt)
Foreign Policy	• Distrusted England and wanted a policy favorable to France • Believed in nonintervention in others' affairs	• Wanted the United States to establish break official bonds with France and tie itself closely to England • World cop
People	Thomas Jefferson, James Madison, Ronald Reagan, Grover Cleveland, Andrew Jackson, Martin Van Buren, Ron Paul	Alexander Hamilton, Henry Clay, Daniel Webster, Abraham Lincoln, Teddy Roosevelt, FDR, Herbert Hoover, George W. Bush, Barack Obama

I am not so naïve to assume all is well; that all politicians, or voters for that matter, are in tune with the "rule book," the Constitution. But I am idealistic enough, even now after six decades of watching, studying, teaching, cheering, complaining, rationalizing, and apologizing for to believe We the People still are in control if—BIG IF—we want to be. I'll come back to some solutions toward the end of this book; but before we look closer at individual rights, I want to give due weight to critics of what the experiment has become. Has it failed? It appears so. Lofgren, in *Deep State*, and someone who worked within the bowels of this system, gives a rather dire picture. Maybe Hamilton was right—a massive imperial state is what we need to be.

Anyone who has spent time on Capitol Hill will occasionally get the feeling when watching debates in the House or Senate chambers that he or she is seeing a kind of marionette theater, with members of Congress reading carefully vetted talking points about prefabricated issues. This impression was particularly strong both in the run-up to the Iraq War and later, during the mock deliberations over funding that ongoing debacle. While the public is now aware of the disproportionate influence of powerful corporations over Washington, best exemplified by the judicial travesty known as the *Citizens United* decision, few fully appreciate that the United States has in the last several decades gradually undergone a process first identified by Aristotle and later championed by Machiavelli that the journalist Edward Peter Garrett described in the 1930s as a "revolution within the form." Our venerable institutions of government have outwardly remained the same, but they have grown more and more resistant to the popular will as they have become hardwired into a corporate and private influence network with almost unlimited cash to enforce its will.

Even as commentators decry a broken government that cannot marshal the money, the will, or the competence to repair our roads and bridges, heal our war veterans, or even roll out a health care website, there is always enough money and will, and maybe just a bare minimum of competence, to overthrow foreign governments, fight the longest war in U.S. history, and conduct dragnet surveillance over the entire surface of the planet.

This paradox of penury and dysfunction on the one hand and unlimited wealth and seeming omnipotence on the other is replicated outside of government as well. By every international metric of health and living standards, the rural counties of southern West Virginia and eastern Kentucky qualify as third-world. So do large areas of Detroit, Cleveland, Camden, Gary, and many other American cities. At the same time, wealth beyond computation, almost beyond imagining, piles up in the money center of New York and the technology hub of Palo Alto. It piles up long enough to purchase a $95,000 truffle, a $38 million vintage Ferrari GTO, or a $179 million Picasso before the balance finds its way to an offshore hiding place.

These paradoxes, both within the government and within the ostensibly private economy, are related. They are symptoms of a shadow government ruling the United States that pays little heed to the plain words of the Constitution. Its governing philosophy profoundly influences foreign and national security policy and such domestic matters as spending priorities, trade, investment, income inequality, privatization of government services, media presentation of news, and the whole meaning and worth of citizens' participation in their government.

I have come to call this shadow government the Deep State. The term was actually coined in Turkey, and is said to be a system composed of high level elements within the intelligence services, military, security, judiciary, and organized crime. In John le Carré's recent novel *A Delicate Truth*, a character in the book describes the Deep State as "the ever-expanding circle of non-governmental insiders from banking, industry and commerce who were cleared for highly classified information denied to large swathes of Whitehall and Westminster." I use the term to mean a hybrid association of key elements of government and parts of top-level finance and industry that is effectively able to govern the United States with only limited reference to the consent of the governed as normally expressed through elections.

The Deep State is the big story of our time. It is the red thread that runs through the war on terrorism and the militarization of foreign policy, the financialization and deindustrialization of the American economy, the rise of a plutocratic social structure that has given us the most unequal society in almost a century, and the political dysfunction that has paralyzed day-to-day governance.

Edward Snowden's June 2013 exposure of the pervasiveness of the National Security Agency's surveillance has partially awakened a Congress that was asleep at the switch and has ignited a national debate about who is really in charge of our government. At the same time, a few politicians, most notably Elizabeth Warren of Massachusetts, are beginning to argue that the American economy is rigged. But these isolated cases have not provided a framework for understanding the extent of the shadow government, how it arose, the interactions of its various parts, and the extent to which it influences and controls the leaders whom we think we choose in elections this book, based in large part on my experiences and observations while in public service, aims to provide that framework.

My reflection on our shadow system of government has come only after my retirement in 2011 and my physical withdrawal from Washington, D.C., proper and the institutions located there. Unlike the vast majority of Capitol Hill strivers who leave the place for greener pastures, I had no desire to join a lobbying shop, trade association, think tank, or consultancy. But I did have a need to see in perspective the events I had witnessed, and I came to realize that the nation's capital, where I lived and worked for more than half my lifetime, has its own peculiar ecology.

To look upon Washington once again with fresh eyes, I sometimes feel as Darwin must have when he first set foot on the Galapagos Islands. From the Pentagon to K Street, and from the contractor cube farms in Crystal City to the public policy foundations along Massachusetts Avenue, the terrain and its people are exotic and well worth examining in a scientific manner. The official United States government has its capital there, and so does our state within a state. To describe them in the language of physics, they coexist in the same way it is possible for two subatomic particles to coexist in an entangled quantum state. The characteristics of each particle, or each governmental structure, cannot fully be described independently; instead, we must find a way to describe the system as a whole.

Lofgren's DC is not Madison's or Jefferson's Philadelphia; probably opportunist Hamilton would find a key position in today's DC. In Philadelphia, Jefferson's Declaration set the philosophical foundations of free men governing themselves; in Philadelphia, Madison's Constitution set up a system that if adhered to, followed, obeyed, practiced, maybe even just read, would give those free men, us, our "posterity" the tools to stay free that created a government "to secure" rights—life, liberty, property—for eternity.

Well, that eternity may not last as long as they hoped. Franklin's admonition, "If you can keep it," needs refreshing. The experiment cannot fail and must not be thrown on the heap of history. Free men have fought the revolution, the Civil War, and in the courts for the rights we have begun to either take for granted or more frequently squandered. Let's turn next to the struggle many have fought to stay free in a nation that has moved closer to Hamilton's America.

RIGHTS AND THE FIGHTS TO KEEP THEM

> No one may threaten or commit violence ("aggress") against another man's person or property. Violence may be employed only against the man who commits such violence; that is, only defensively against the aggressive violence of another. In short, no violence may be employed against a non-aggressor. Here is the fundamental rule from which can be deduced the entire corpus of libertarian theory.
> —Murray Rothbard

LET'S ENTER INTO the most controversial and sometimes contradictory subject of the American experiment. The God-given rights of man have often been transgressed (abused, stepped on) by government in its attempt at power. Government cannot stay small; power corrupts all who have. It must be controlled by the creators, We the People. The Bill of Rights is not a grant of those rights; it is a limit, or negative, against the state. All free men are enemies of the state, not anarchists, but enemies. Only the state can use force first. We need to be vigilant that that force is used to maintain the social contract for the general welfare, not for a select group. Like Obamacare, many of the laws burdening We the People Congress is exempt from, as are most government officials. Any law not applying to Congress, or for that matter ALL Americans, is a violation of the general welfare clause and therefore unconstitutional.

The courts have taken the responsibility on how to judge the violations of rights. Yet the debate over who is sovereign and the final voice in interpretations of the social contract continues today. It was not decided by the Framers whether the Supreme Court should be given the power of judicial review over the acts of the executive and legislative branches. To do so would give the judiciary the authority to declare acts of these branches of the national government unconstitutional.

This would mean giving one branch the power to ensure that the other branches did not exceed the limitations placed on them by the Constitution. The power to declare that legislative acts within the states had violated the state constitution already had been exercised by the courts in several states.

Some simply assumed that the judiciary would have the power to rule on the constitutionality of laws made by Congress. Nothing specific was decided on this subject at the Convention. This assumption, however, is one reason why the delegates rejected a proposal to let the Supreme Court and the president act as a committee to review bills passed by Congress and decide if they should become law. The only reference in the Constitution to the general powers of the judiciary is at the beginning of Article III: the "judicial power of the United States, shall be vested in one supreme court . . ."

The power of the Supreme Court to declare acts of Congress unconstitutional was clearly and surreptitiously established by the Supreme Court itself in 1803.

Judicial review is the power of the judicial branch of a government to declare acts of the legislative and executive branches to be in violation of the government's constitution. When a court makes such a decision, it orders that the decision made by the other part of the government be considered "null and void," which means that it is not to be obeyed or enforced. In the United States, the national judiciary, headed by the Supreme Court, now has this power over all parts of our government. State courts have this power over other branches of state governments.

Throughout our history, there have been great differences of opinion about whether the judicial branch should have this power and how it should be used. The controversy raises basic questions about representative government and majority rule on the one hand, and constitutional government and the protection of basic rights and unpopular minorities on the other hand. It is really a conflict of representative democracy and majority rule and the meaning of the social contract.

Should national courts have the power to declare acts of presidents or Congress or even the states unconstitutional?

One of the new ideas about government that developed in this nation was the idea that the Supreme Court and lower courts in the judicial branch should have the power to interpret the Constitution and decide what it means. In some situations, this means that the Supreme Court will order that a law passed by a majority in Congress or in a state legislature violates the Constitution and therefore is not to be obeyed or enforced.

Suppose you could go back to the Convention and decide whether a supreme court should be given the power of judicial review over acts of Congress. Look at the two options below and the results of each—which more closely would have been your choice?

> Option 1: Give a national Supreme Court the power to declare laws passed by Congress unconstitutional, null and void.
>
> Result: The Supreme Court would have the power to order a law that had been passed by a majority of representatives in Congress, who were elected by citizens to represent their interests, should not be obeyed or enforced. Would this be a violation of democracy?
>
> Option 2: Deny the Supreme Court the power to declare laws by the Congress unconstitutional.
>
> Result: This would mean that all laws passed by a majority of representatives in Congress must be obeyed and enforced by all citizens.

1. Does your choice conflict with principles of representative government and/or democracy's majority rule? If so, how?
2. Is your choice more democratic or more republican? If so, how?
3. Does your choice place our basic rights at the whim of temporary emotions and current popularity?

4. Does your choice allow the majority to tyrannize the minority? If so, how?

Where did judicial review come from?

If you read the Constitution, you will not find any mention of the power of judicial review. As you will see, however, soon after the beginning of the new government, the Constitution was interpreted to give the Supreme Court this power. Hamilton felt in *Federalist 78*,

> The interpretation of the laws is the proper and peculiar province of the courts. A constitution, is, in fact, and must be regarded by the judges, as a fundamental law. It therefore belongs to them to ascertain its meaning, as well as the meaning of any particular act proceeding from the legislative body. If there should happen to be an irreconcilable variance between two, that which has the superior obligation and validity ought, of course, to be preferred; or, in other words, the constitution ought to be preferred to the statute, the intention of the people to the intention of their agents.

The Convention was familiar with the idea that some part of government should be given the power to decide whether activities of the other parts of government had violated the "higher law" of a nation. Under British rule, the Privy Council, a group that advised the king, had the power to overrule decisions made by colonial courts if they violated English laws. Courts could nullify statutes originated in England with Chief Justice Edward Coke's 1610 opinion in Dr. Bonham's Case. In this case, Parliament enabled the London College of Physicians to levy fines against anyone who violated their rules. The college accused a doctor of practicing without a license and fined him accordingly. Coke found that their statutory powers violated "common right or reason" because "no person should be a judge in his own case."

Following the revolution, some state constitutions gave this power to the judicial branches of their governments. Even though the belief in legislative supremacy was strong, several state courts had declared laws made by their legislatures to be unconstitutional.

In addition, juries have always had the right to acquit criminal defendants who are technically guilty but who do not deserve punishment. It occurs in a trial when a jury reaches a verdict contrary to the judge's instructions as to the law. A jury verdict contrary to the letter of the law pertains only to the case before it. If a pattern of acquittals develops, however, in response to repeated attempts to prosecute a law violator, this can have the *de facto* effect of invalidating the statute. A pattern of jury nullification may indicate public opposition to an unwanted legislative enactment.

The Framers of the Constitution wanted to correct a basic weakness in the national government under the Articles of Confederation; under the Articles, the states had the right to decide whether they would obey and enforce the laws of the national government. To strengthen the new government, they wrote Article VI, which, in part, reads:

> This constitution, and the laws of the United States which shall be made in pursuance thereof; and all treaties made . . . under the authority of the United States, *shall be the supreme law of the land:* and the judges in every state shall be bound thereby, anything in the constitution or laws of any state to the contrary notwithstanding.

This section of the Constitution is known as the supremacy clause. It has been interpreted to mean that the Supreme Court can order that state laws not be enforced if they violate national laws or the Constitution. The First Congress also made this power clear in the Judiciary Act of 1789.

The Supreme Court first used its power of judicial review over state governments in the *Ware v. Hylton* case of 1796. After the Revolutionary War, the United States had signed a peace treaty with the British that said all debts owed by Americans to English citizens would be paid. However, the state of Virginia had passed a law that cancelled all debts owed by Virginians to British citizens. Since this law clearly violated the peace treaty, the Supreme Court ruled that the law could not be enforced because the laws and treaties of the national government are the supreme law of the land. Thus, the citizens of Virginia were responsible for paying their debts.

The question of whether the Supreme Court should have the power of judicial review over the legislative and executive branches of the national government was discussed during the Philadelphia Convention and the debates over ratification. But no decision was made that clearly gave the court this power. However, many historians believe that a majority of the Framers supported this idea. Some assumed that the court would have this power. Alexander Hamilton, for example, made this assumption in *The Federalist.*

The story of how the Supreme Court established its power of judicial review over the other branches of the national government involves one of the most famous cases in our history, the case of *Marbury v. Madison,* which was decided in 1803.

Marbury v. Madison

After Thomas Jefferson defeated the Federalist president John Adams in the election of 1800, Adams had several weeks remaining in office—lame duck. During this time, Adams feared the Jeffersonian radicalism and wanted to make sure the Federalists would continue to influence the government long after Jefferson and the Republicans took over. This is similar to Obama's appointees trying to sabotage and prevent a Trump success. The Federalists, who controlled Congress, passed a new judiciary act creating several new national courts. Adams filled these courts with Federalists; his secretary of state, John Marshall, became chief justice of the Supreme Court.

Jefferson did not disappoint the Federalists. In his first inaugural, he laid out what he considered the "essential principles of our Government:"

> Equal and exact justice to all men, of whatever state or persuasion, religious or political; peace, commerce, and honest friendship with all nations, entangling alliances with none; the support of the State governments in all their rights, as the most competent administrations for our domestic concerns and the surest bulwarks against antirepublican tendencies; the preservation of the General Government in its whole constitutional vigor, as the sheet anchor of our peace at home and safety abroad; a jealous care of the right of election by the people—a mild and safe corrective of

abuses which are lopped by the sword of revolution where peaceable remedies are unprovided; absolute acquiescence in the decisions of the majority, the vital principle of republics, from which is no appeal but to force, the vital principle and immediate parent of despotism; a well-disciplined militia, our best reliance in peace and for the first moments of war till regulars may relieve them; the supremacy of the civil over the military authority; economy in the public expense, that labor may be lightly burthened; the honest payment of our debts and sacred preservation of the public faith; encouragement of agriculture, and of commerce as its handmaid; the diffusion of information and arraignment of all abuses at the bar of the public reason; freedom of religion; freedom of the press, and freedom of person under the protection of the habeas corpus, and trial by juries impartially selected.

These principles form the bright constellation which has gone before us and guided our steps through an age of revolution and reformation. The wisdom of our sages and blood of our heroes have been devoted to their attainment. They should be the creed of our political faith, the text of civic instruction, the touchstone by which to try the services of those we trust; and should we wander from them in moments of error or of alarm, let us hasten to retrace our steps and to regain the road which alone leads to peace, liberty, and safety.

When Thomas Jefferson sat behind the desk in March 1801, some of the documents that officially gave many Federalists their new jobs as judges had not yet been delivered. John Marshall had apparently forgotten to do this in his last days as secretary of state before taking the position of chief justice. Jefferson was furious; he believed Adams and the Federalist Congress had abused their lame-duck time to undercut the will of the people. He did not want more Federalists, the rejected party, serving as judges; he ordered his secretary of state, James Madison, to destroy these documents.

One judge President Adams had appointed was William Marbury; he was to be a justice of the peace for the District of Columbia. Marbury wanted the legal job and was upset with Jefferson's decision not to give it to him. All rights violated have a remedy. He tried to find a way to get what he believed was rightfully his. He discovered that the Judiciary Act of 1789 gave him a remedy; the Supreme Court now had the power of *writ of mandamus*—a court order that forces an officer of the government to do something that person is supposed to do; in this case, deliver the appointment documents that had been congressionally approved.

Marbury knew that John Marshall, a Federalist, was chief justice, and he believed Marshall would be easily deal with his situation. He filed a suit to ask the Supreme Court to issue a *writ of mandamus* ordering Madison to deliver the document.

Marshall was stuck between a rock and a hard place. He did not want a political fight with President Jefferson; he knew that if he ordered Jefferson to order Madison to deliver Marbury's appointment, Jefferson would ignore him. Courts rely on the executive branch and citizens' respect for the law for the enforcement of law. If Jefferson refused to obey the Supreme Court's decision, it would make the court appear weak and powerless. On the other hand, if Marshall did not order Madison to deliver Marbury's document, he would put the court in a position of weakness and establish an inconsistent truth, or at least definition of constitutionality.

But Chief Justice Marshall was, and still is, considered the greatest chief justice. He used an ancient idea to avoid a confrontation with the president and, at the same time, establish the Supreme Court and lower courts with the power of judicial review. He asked three key questions of his fellow justices: Does Marbury have a right to be a judge? If he has a right to his appointment and that right has been violated, do the laws of the nation give him a way to have things set right? If the laws of the country give Marbury a way to deal with this problem, is that way a *writ of mandamus* from the Supreme Court?

Marshall answered yes to the first two questions and no to the third. His reasoning was as follows. Marshall reasoned that the appointment had been confirmed by the Senate, signed by the president, and sealed by the secretary of state; therefore, Marbury had the right to hold the office for five years as provided by law. He was certain, if law were to prevail, that the secretary of state is an officer of the government directed by the Constitution to faithfully execute laws made by Congress and to perform duties, legally assigned by Congress, such as delivering the documents. When Madison, under Jefferson's order, refused to do so, he broke the law and violated Marbury's rights. Each violation of your rights has a remedy. Marbury had the right to go to a court and ask it to order the secretary of state to deliver his document and to give him the job approved by the president.

But it was here that Marshall said no. He said the judiciary act that gave Marbury the right to ask the Supreme Court to issue a *writ of mandamus* was unconstitutional. The Constitution clearly limits the Supreme Court's original jurisdiction—that is, the cases it can hear without their first being heard by a lower court—to "cases affecting ambassadors, other public ministers and consuls, and those in which a state shall be a party." Marbury was not an ambassador, a minister, a consul, or a state; the Supreme Court did not have the power to hear his case unless it was first heard in a lower court and then appealed to the Supreme Court. The judiciary act gave Marbury rights he did not have; it gave the Supreme Court power it did not have. In essence, Congress had changed the Constitution. Since Congress did not have the authority to change the Constitution, the judiciary act was unconstitutional, or at least the portion granting extraconstitutional powers.

Chief Justice Marshall could not order Secretary Madison to deliver the appointments. Thus, the court avoided the almost certain embarrassment of having Jefferson refuse to obey the court's order. In the process, Marshall gained a much more important power for the Supreme Court. By declaring a part of the judiciary act unconstitutional, the Supreme Court took on the power of judicial review to declare acts of Congress and the president, and eventually the states, unconstitutional. By the way, Jefferson and Marshall were cousins, both from Virginia yet on opposite sides of history.

Before, I asked you to take a position on whether the Supreme Court should have the power of judicial review over acts of Congress. This is the question Chief Justice Marshall dealt with in the case of *Marbury v. Madison*, and he decided the court should have this power. When the people of this nation adopted the Constitution to be the supreme law of the land, they had consented to be governed by its rules, which included important limitations upon the powers of Congress. When Congress violates those limitations, it has violated the will of the people. If the Supreme Court were not to have the power of judicial review, there would be no effective way to enforce the limitations the people have placed upon the powers of Congress in the Constitution. Its powers would be unlimited, and we would no longer have a constitutional government. Marshall's voice from the bench:

> It is, emphatically, the province and duty of the judicial department, to say what the law is . . . So, if a law be in opposition to the constitution; if both the law and the constitution apply to a particular case, so that the court must either decide that case, conformable to the law, disregarding the constitution; or conformable to the constitution, disregarding the law; the court must determine which of these conflicting rules governs the case; this is of the very essence of judicial duty. If then, the courts are to regard the constitution, and the constitution is superior to any ordinary act of the legislature, the constitution, and not such ordinary act, must govern the case to which both apply.

Kentucky and Virginia Resolutions

The debate over the interpretation of the Constitution did not end with Marshall's decision. What if the Supreme Court itself agrees with a bad majority law? How do basic rights get protected then? The Kentucky and Virginia Resolutions were passed in opposition to the Alien and Sedition Acts by the Kentucky legislature on November 16, 1798, written by Thomas Jefferson, and by the Virginia legislature on December 24, 1798, written by James Madison, both were Founders, will be future presidents, and Madison was even the Father of the Constitution.

Though these resolutions came shortly before *Marbury*, they attacked the Federalists' interpretation of the Constitution, which extended the powers of the national government over the states. The resolutions declared that the Constitution only established an agreement and that the national government had no right to exercise powers not specifically delegated to it; should the national government assume such powers, its acts under them would be void. It was the duty and within the power of the states to decide as to the constitutionality of such acts.

The resolutions were submitted to other states for approval but with no real result. Their importance lies in that they were later considered to be the first statements of the States' Rights theory. In these Principles of '98, Jefferson considered these states' rights a much more important and effective guarantee of people's liberties than checks and balances. Using the Tenth Amendment the cornerstone of the Constitution: anything not given to central government or denied to the states are left to the states or the people. The states as protectors of the people from a central government would merely declare unconstitutional laws null and void. Laws are null and void if they are declared so and are then not to be obeyed.

Historical examples are plenty. Daniel Webster in the War of 1812, while New England was threatening secession over an illegal war, rose gallantly in Congress declaring that no Congress could declare a draft. Free men and conscription (draft) cannot exist together. Ohio, even after the Supreme Court said no, taxed the Bank of the United States. The courts of Wisconsin held the Fugitive Slave Act of 1850 unconstitutional and ordered the release of a prisoner who was prosecuted in the national district court for violation of the act. The Wisconsin court declared that the Supreme Court had no authority to review its decision. The Wisconsin legislature passed a resolution declaring that the Supreme Court had no jurisdiction over the Wisconsin court's decision. In language borrowed from the Kentucky Resolution of 1798, the Wisconsin resolution asserted that the Supreme Court's review of the case was void: the national government is not the exclusive judge of its own powers; that's despotism.

In the "Nullification Crisis," or "secession crisis," of 1828–1832, John C. Calhoun, Jackson's vice president, anonymously wrote the *South Carolina Exposition and Protest* to protest the Tariff of 1828, which South Carolina claimed was unconstitutional. In this essay, Calhoun stated that if the tariffs were not repealed, South Carolina would secede. He used the doctrine of nullification (i.e., the idea that a state has the right to reject national law), first introduced by Thomas Jefferson and James Madison in their Kentucky and Virginia Resolutions. Unfortunately for Calhoun, that's not what either Jefferson or Madison stated. They stated that any law "not pursuant to" the Constitution was to be nullified. Tariffs, even horrendous ones, or "abominable," were pursuant to the powers of Congress.

A constitution is, after all, only a piece of paper. It cannot enforce itself. Checks and balances among the executive, legislative, and judicial branches, a prominent feature of the Constitution, provide little guarantee of limited government, since these three central branches can simply unite against the independence of the states and the reserved rights of the people. Jefferson in a letter to a friend in 1825 continued to hold that the national government could never be trusted to control itself. "It is but too evident, that the three ruling branches of [the Federal government] are in combination to strip their colleagues, the state authorities, of the powers reserved by them, and to exercise themselves all functions foreign and domestic." Much more important than the feeble restraint of "checks and balances" is the ability of the states to interpose to prevent the enforcement of unconstitutional laws. That is a *real* check on national power. Today, many groups, Tea Party, Tenth Amendment Center, California's secessionist talk (CalExit), Montana, and Alaska are passing laws nullifying DC gun laws. These are states that are pressing their rights, which has a precedent that dates back over two hundred years.

Continuing controversies

Today most Americans believe that judicial review is a necessary power of the Supreme Court, though recently the Tenth Amendment doctrine of nullification has a growing audience. They do not always agree, however, on how the court should use this power. The Supreme Court often hears cases about which there are strong feelings and great controversy. The decisions of the court in these cases have important results that may affect the day-to-day lives of millions of citizens. Many of these cases involve disagreements about the proper role of our government and the meaning of the Constitution. Since the Supreme Court has taken the power to make final decisions about the interpretation of the Constitution, it is inevitable that some people will support its decisions, and some will criticize them. These disagreements are often over the methods used to interpret the Constitution.

Once the Supreme Court agrees to hear a case on a constitutional issue, the justices face the difficult question of deciding whether the national government or a state government has violated the Constitution. Understanding the meaning of some parts of the Constitution is fairly easy, since some parts of it are quite specific and their meaning is clear. For example, there is little disagreement about what is meant when the Constitution says that a person must be thirty-five years old to be president or no tax shall be placed on goods exported from a state.

However, as you will see, not all parts of the Constitution are so clear. For example, what does it mean when the Constitution says the following: Congress shall have the power to make laws that it decides are "necessary and proper" to carry out its responsibilities? Citizens are protected against "unreasonable searches and seizures"? No state shall "deprive any person of life, liberty, or property without due process of law"?

The Constitution is many things to many people. Undoubtedly, it is the framework for the Government of the United States of America, defining the three branches and clearly delineating the powers of the branches. It also undoubtedly grants certain power to the national government and leaves others to the states, and it undoubtedly guarantees the basic rights of the people.

The Constitution is short; it cannot and does not attempt to cover every eventuality. Even when it seems it is clear, there can be conflicting rights, conflicting spheres of power. When disputes arise, it comes time for people, and most importantly judges of the judicial branch, to interpret the Constitution. The concept of constitutional interpretation is foreign in some countries, where the constitution makes a reasonable effort to cover every eventuality. These constitutions are generally rigid and little changing, adapting slowly to advances in political views, popular opinion, technology, and changes in government.

The debate over how far the Congress or the presidency could stretch power can be seen in the first big issue facing the new Washington government, a central United States Bank. At the Convention, it was debated and soundly voted down to allow the national government the power to charter a national bank.

In 1787–88, the Nationalist forces pushed through a new Constitution replacing the "weaker" decentralist Articles of Confederation. The Nationalists were on their way to reestablishing the system they had just fought against, the mercantilist and statist British model. Yet the ratification was not certain; the Nationalists grudgingly accepted the Libertarian and majority-supported Bill of Rights as the price for the Anti-Federalists not to deny the Constitution or even call for a second constitutional convention, which may bring back the state-supporting articles.

The Nationalists began to install a British 2.0 upon the states: high protective tariffs, domestic taxes that included duties on land, alcohol, and even snuff, public works, direct aid to corporations, and a high public debt. These Hamiltonians had fought for in the Convention a strong central government, loose construction of the Constitution, the suppression of civil liberties, and an internationalist foreign policy. Sound familiar? John McCain, Hillary Clinton, Barack Obama.

The key, though, was Morris's control of our money. His mentee, Alexander Hamilton, as secretary of the treasury and now leader of the Federalist Party (duplicitous name taken by the Nationalists), put through Congress the First Bank of the United States (USB), a privately owned central bank, with the national government owning one-fifth of the shares.

Like modern-day FED chairs, he argued that an alleged "scarcity" of specie had to be overcome by infusions of paper money, to be issued by the new bank and invested in the public debt and in subsidies of cheap credit to manufacturers. The banknotes were to be legally redeemable in specie (gold) on demand, and they were supposedly to be kept at par with gold by the national government's accepting its notes in taxes, thus giving it a quasi-legal tender status; yet it soon became a mere promise broken many times it the USB's history. Money soon became a fiat currency of little to no value. The national government would also deposit its taxes into the USB. By the way, Morris's former partner, Thomas Willing of Philadelphia, was made president of the USB, a mere random coincidence of deep state control. Today's Federal Reserve (the FED) allows the deep state to fund wars, welfare, cronyism without telling the true costs to Americans; inflation is taxation without representation and without knowledge.

Hamilton convinced a Federalist-dominated Congress to allow it anyway; this produces the big split between the Jeffersonians and the Hamiltonians and to the first constitutional crisis of the new government. President Washington asked Secretary of State Thomas Jefferson and Treasury Secretary Alexander Hamilton for advice on whether he should veto the bill. After reading, Jefferson's opposition to the bank and Hamilton's support, he ends up signing it into law.

The majority of Americans, like today, I would suggest, followed the Republican Party, or Jeffersonians (not the modern-day party of Lincoln or the Busses), remembered what they had fought for: limited government, Federalism, sound money, low taxes and tariffs, no national debt, government separation from banks, no subsidies for business, a strict construction of the Constitution and a bill of protected liberties held by the people, and a noninterventionist, nonentangling foreign policy.

From this argument, political parties emerge, the Federalists under Hamilton and the Republicans under Jefferson, and the strict construction and loose construction of constitutional interpretation. Strict construction was if it is not in the Constitution, the national government cannot do it; loose construction was if it is not denied by the Constitution, the national government can do it.

The US Constitution, however, has been termed by some as a "Living Constitution"; in part, it should grow and adapt to internal and external pressures, changing from one era and generation to the next. When new situations arise, or even a new variation on an old situation, the Constitution is often looked to for guidance. It is at this point that the various interpretations of the Constitution come into play. Charles Evans Hughes, served on the court twice, resigning between two stretches to run for president, stated, "We are under a Constitution, but the Constitution is what the judges say it is." That's the equivalent of Hobbes's "What makes me happy is good."

There are many interpretations of the Constitution, and people often do not always stick to one interpretation. There are major divisions in interpretation; your own personal beliefs may fall into several of these categories. Jefferson felt "our peculiar society is in possession of a written constitution." Americans "must not make a blank paper by construction." Judge Joseph Story concurred, the Constitution "must have a fixed, uniform, permanent, construction . . . not dependent upon the passions or parties of particular times, but the same yesterday, to-day and forever."

Perspective of History

The Constitution contains basic ideas, principles, and values about government and the role that it should play in our lives. These include the natural rights philosophy, the principles of constitutionalism, and the values of republican government as they were understood by the Founders. The justices should base their decisions on these basic ideas, taking into account, however, the nation's history and the changes in morality and social policy that have taken place.

This modernist approach to constitutional interpretation looks at the Constitution as if it were ratified today. What meaning would it have today if written today? How does modern life affect the words of the Constitution? Justice George Sutherland, in *Village of Euclid v. Amber*, 1926, felt it must adapt to the present situation; situational ethics at the constitutional level.

> [W]hile the meaning of constitutional guaranties never varies; the scope of their application must expand or contract to meet the new and different conditions which are constantly coming within the field of their operation. In a changing world, it is impossible that it should be otherwise. But although a degree of elasticity is thus imparted, not to the meaning, but to the application of constitutional principles, statutes and ordinances, which, after giving due weight to the new conditions, are found clearly not to conform to the Constitution, of course, must fall.

Justices' decisions should be based upon their understanding of ideas such as freedom, justice, and equality, and what they mean today. The way we look at some of these ideas is very different from the way the Founders looked at them two hundred years ago, and the decisions of the Supreme Court should take these differences into account. It is these general, larger goals that the original patriots wanted to achieve, and the justices should do their best to adapt them to modern society. Modernists also contend that the Constitution is deliberately vague in many areas, expressly to permit modern interpretations to override older ones as the Constitution ages. It is this interpretation that best embodies the Living Constitution concept, sometimes called a liberal interpretation. The Constitution is flexible and dynamic, changing slowly over time as the morals and beliefs of the population shift.

However, opponents of this liberal argument believe it gives the justices too much freedom to decide cases according to their own political and moral preferences, the Charles Evans Hughes approach. Since there are no clear and precise ways to decide how to apply such ideas as freedom, justice, and equality to specific situations, justices would be free to apply them as they wished. This could mean a justice's position about what is just or fair might be different from the position of a majority of members of Congress. This would violate the basic idea of representative democracy by allowing a few justices to overrule the action of the majority of the legislature, which was elected by the people. Conservatives or originalists feel this does a disservice to the Constitution, that the people who wrote it had a pure and valid vision for the nation, and that their vision should be able to sustain us through any Constitutional question. Aaron Burr, late in life, felt the Constitution, if twisted away from its mooring, would set it adrift.

> When the Constitution was first framed I predicted that it would last fifty years. I was mistaken. It will evidently last longer than that. But I was mistaken only in point of time. The crash will come, but not so quick as I thought.

Democratic Interpretation

Related to the judges' interpretations is democratic interpretation. Democratic interpretation is known as normative or representation reinforcement. Changes in the Constitution that stem from this kind of philosophy will end up with principles of the population at-large while ensuring that the Framers still have a say in the underlying decision or ruling. This interpretation is seen to enhance democratic ideals and the notion of republicanism.

Democratic proponents advocate that the Constitution is not designed to be a set of specific principles and guidelines but that it was designed to be a general principle, a basic skeleton on which contemporary vision would build upon. Decisions as to the meaning of the Constitution must look at the general feeling evoked by the Constitution and then use modern ideals to pad out the skeleton.

As evidence, "democrats" point out that many phrases, such as "due process" and "equal protection," are deliberately vague, that the phrases are not defined in context. The guidance for interpretation must come from that basic framework that the Framers provided, but that to fill in the gaps, modern society's current morals and feelings must be taken into consideration.

However, the Constitution is a rule book for our government. The rules are the rules. They may not change when the players change.

The Literal Word

With this method of interpretation, the justices should consider the literal or plain meaning of the words in the Constitution or study what the words meant at the time they were written and base their decisions upon them. The court's decisions should be based, as closely as possible, on the words the writers used when creating the Constitution. If the meaning of the words is clear, then this is the best way to find out what they meant. Also, by relying on the plain language, the law becomes certain and predictable. The only thing one needs to interpret the Constitution is a literal reading of the words contained therein, with an expert knowledge in the eighteenth-century meaning of those words. The debates leading to the final draft are not relevant; *The Federalist* is not relevant, only the words—get a 1776 dictionary.

It is difficult to know the exact meaning of many of the words and important phrases in the Constitution. Meanings of words have changed over the years. Matter of fact, there was even disagreement about their meaning at the time of the Convention and shortly after it. The delegates came from different parts of the colonies, some recently from the mother country, Hamilton from the Caribbean. Consider, for example, the disagreements among Hamilton, Madison, and Jefferson over the meaning of the "necessary and proper" clause. Besides, the Framers and other Founders did not intend later generations to be restricted to eighteenth-century interpretations, since moral, social, and political standards do change. This is evident in James Madison's *Notes* from the Convention, which he hid and wanted destroyed after his death. Let every new generation "write" the Constitution in their words.

Original Intent

Well, what to do? How then does one look at Shakespeare four hundred years later? What did Jesus mean when he spoke of camels and needles? Many Americans have issues with "Herculean tasks"! The only interpretational approach if Jefferson's what is written is right.

The justices of the Supreme Court and of the lower courts should only make decisions based on how the Framers would have made them. To find how the original writers would have made the decisions, the justices should read the records of the Philadelphia Convention, Madison's *Notes*, the state conventions that ratified the Constitution—many of the Framers attended these conventions in their home states—and the congressional debates over amendments. *The Federalist* was written by three of the Framers.

This approach is the most faithful to the basic ideas and values contained in the Constitution. It limits the ability of justices to base their decisions not on their own personal preferences but the preferences in that room in Philadelphia. If the justices cannot find out what the Framers would have done with regard to an act of Congress or some other branch of government, they should not declare it unconstitutional, and that should be a political decision (left in the hands of the majority). I do not deny that on many questions about the meaning of the Constitution, it is difficult, if not impossible, to discover exactly what was intended.

First, this approach would require studying the ideas of the fifty-five men who attended the Philadelphia Convention and the ideas of the leaders of all the state conventions that ratified the Constitution. Then it would require deciding which of these ideas should be counted. Even when the intentions of some men were clear, the intentions of others were not, and there were often disagreements about the meaning of parts of the Constitution. Second, they had no idea about such twentieth-century developments as airline travel or wiretapping. They intended each generation to give its own meaning to the Constitution. Yet to rely solely on their intentions, which were formed two hundred years ago, might preserve outmoded ways of doing things and some practices that are no longer acceptable, such as slavery and racial segregation. To a black woman, how much trust can be placed in the thoughts of a white slave owner who's been dead for generations?

Judicial review since

Since the *Marbury* case, the Supreme Court has continued to stretch its power in extending the power of the state. Marshall was a true Federalist in the Hamiltonian mode; he began the misinterpretation of a centralized state within the Constitution; the states had to submit to the central government. With the early Marshall decision and Abraham Lincoln's war, the states were pushed into a position of mere administrative bodies of a consolidated national government. In *McCulloch v. Maryland* (1819), Marshall ruled that the national government could create a central bank. Though a bank is not specifically named as a power in the Constitution, he ruled that it was convenient, thus necessary and proper. Laws in the "spirit of the Constitution, are constitutional," not intent, which is difficult but a more nebulous spirit.

In *Dartmouth College v. Woodward* (1819), states were told they could not alter contracts regardless of the age. It appears this is a reiteration of the power of contracts, but in *Gibbons v. Ogden* (1824), contracts can be violated by the national government. Using the "commerce" clause, Marshall allowed the Congress to overrule a New York grant to a ferry company over the Hudson. In *Worcester v. Georgia* (1832), states could not regulate Indian nations or violate treaties; only the national government could do that. And then, quite arrogantly, in *Cooper v. Aaron* (1958), the Supreme Court went so far as saying its decisions are also supreme law of the land. Is this constitutional? Clearly not. Five in a distant city out of 326 million does not qualify as the final say.

In practice, justices tend to be influenced by many considerations. These include their interpretations of the language of the Constitution and the intent of the writers, the precedents justices have established in previous cases, current social policies and political and economic concerns, their personal and political beliefs, and where they went to law school.

Yet despite these influences, the justices are conscious of their responsibility to rule on the constitutionality of the issues involved and not based on their own personal feelings. This may mean that the Supreme Court will rule that a law is constitutional even if the justices feel that it is unwise. As Chief Justice Warren Burger stated, when reviewing an act of Congress:

Its wisdom is not the concern of the courts; if a challenged action does not violate the Constitution, it must be sustained . . . By the same token, the fact that a given law or procedure is efficient, convenient, and useful in facilitating functions of government, standing alone, will not save it if it is contrary to the Constitution (*INS v. Chadha*, 1983).

While it would be unrealistic to pretend that the personal preferences of justices never affect the decisions of the court, is it reasonable to claim that the continued authority of the court depends on its being faithful to both the language and spirit of the Constitution. John Hasnas, "The Myth of the Rule of Law," says no! Men makes decision, never the rule of law; court decisions are never objective, as we will see in the *Brown* decision of 1954.

The Supreme Court's decisions have been particularly controversial when they have attempted to define and protect certain basic rights, equal protection of the laws, due process of law, freedom of religion, or freedom of expression. Looking for the Supreme Court to protect people's rights against their government has become fanciful. The courts are the government; justice no longer rules the minds of justices. Recently, NPR's Nina Totenberg said justices of the court shouldn't be citing the Constitution in their decisions. Well? Huh?

Take a look

In the light of what you have learned about judicial review, which of the following positions of the Founders would you agree with? Makes some notes as to why you chose one over the other.

It is . . . of great importance . . . examine . . . the judicial power, because those who are to be vested with it, are to be placed in a situation altogether unprecedented in a free country . . . They are independent of the people, of the legislature, and of every power under heaven. Men placed in this situation will generally soon feel themselves independent of heaven itself. If the legislature pass any laws, inconsistent with the sense the judges put upon the constitution, they will declare it void; and therefore in this respect their power is superior to that of the legislature . . . (*Letters of Brutus,* 1787).

. . . The judiciary, from the nature of its functions, will always be the least dangerous . . . It may truly be said to have neither Force nor Will, but merely judgement (sic) . . . A constitution is, in fact, and must be regarded by the judges, as a fundamental law. It therefore belongs to them to ascertain its meaning . . . (Alexander Hamilton, *The Federalist, No. 78*, 1788).

. . . The opinion which gives to the judges the right to decide what laws are constitutional, and what not would make the Judiciary a despotic branch (Thomas Jefferson).

Which of the following statements by former justices of the Supreme Court do you agree with?

[The Constitution] is intended to endure for ages to come, and consequently, to be adapted to the various crises of human affairs (Chief Justice John Marshall).

We are under a Constitution, but the Constitution is what the judges say it is (Chief Justice Charles Evans Hughes).

As a member of this court I am not justified in writing my opinions into the Constitution, no matter how deeply I may cherish them (Justice Felix Frankfurter).

The case before us must be considered in the light of our whole experience and not merely in that of what was said a hundred years ago (Justice Oliver Wendell Holmes).

BILL OF RIGHTS

You have to remember, rights don't come in groups. We shouldn't
have "gay rights"; rights come as individuals, and we wouldn't
have this major debate going on. It would be behavior that
would count, not what person belongs to what group.
—Ron Paul

THE BILL OF Rights was ratified by the states on December
15, 1791, because of pressures from many of the ratification
conventions and opposition by the Anti-Federalist. It contains not a
grant of rights from the state; it is a list of prohibitions against the central
government. Many of these rights stem from English history, Magna
Carta, civil wars, the experience of English rule over the colonies, and
Greek, Roman, Medieval philosophies.

There are three different ways of coming at any "bill of rights." The
Hamiltonian, or natural law of both Locke and the Framers, was that a
bill of rights isn't needed; everyone knows the law of nature and man's
freedom. Hamilton, in *Federalist 84*, argued that a bill of rights was not
only unnecessary but dangerous as well. There were already numerous
limits; religious tests for office are forbidden, habeas corpus can only be
suspended during a time of rebellion, and all have the right to a trial by
jury. His second argument was that limited, enumerated governmental
powers removed the need for new safeguards against what it already did
not have the power to do. His most succinct argument was that bills of
rights "are not only unnecessary in the proposed constitution, but would
even be dangerous." If government is prohibited from doing *certain*
things but isn't prohibited from doing *everything* it isn't expressly told it
can do, then the danger is in its implications—that is, the government
can then do *anything* it's not expressly forbidden to do.

The Republicans fought England because of their perspective that
England abused the rights of all Englishmen had since time immemorial.

Madison wrote, "Although I know whenever the great rights, the trial by jury, freedom of the press, or liberty of conscience, come in question in that body [Parliament], the invasion of them is resisted by able advocates, yet their Magna Carta does not contain any one provision for the security of those rights, respecting which the people of America are most alarmed. The freedom of the press and rights of conscience, those choicest privileges of the people, are unguarded in the British Constitution."

Andrew Jackson decades later said, "As long as our government is administered for the good of the people, and is regulated by their will; as long as it secures to us the rights of persons and of property, liberty of conscience and of the press, it will be worth defending." That's the great experiment: can man rule himself if left alone from government oppression? The Bill of Rights and many of the later amendments are not there so you and I can know our rights. Freedom flows through our veins, lives in our dreams. The list of amendments shown below are to prevent government from stripping, abusing, abrogating, denying, or limiting our rights.

Amendment	Subject	Year	Time Required for Ratification
1st–10th	Bill of Rights	1791	2 years, 2 months, 20 days
11th	Immunity of States from certain lawsuits	1795	11 months, 3 days
12th	Changes in electoral college procedures	1804	6 months, 6 days
13th	Abolition of slavery	1865	10 months, 6 days
14th	Citizenship, due process, equal protection	1868	2 years, 26 days
15th	No denial of vote because of race, color, or previous enslavement	1870	11 months, 8 days
16th	Power of Congress to tax incomes	1913	3 years, 6 months, 22 days
17th	Popular election of U.S. Senators	1913	10 months, 26 days
18th	Prohibition of alcohol	1919	1 year, 29 days
19th	Woman suffrage	1920	1 year, 2 months, 14 days
20th	Change of dates for start of presidential and Congressional terms	1933	10 months, 21 days
21st	Repeal of Prohibition (18th Amendment)	1933	9 months, 15 days
22nd	Limit on presidential terms	1951	3 years, 11 months, 6 days
23rd	District of Columbia vote in presidential elections	1961	9 months, 13 days
24th	Ban of tax payment as voter qualification	1964	1 year, 4 months, 27 days
25th	Presidential succession, vice presidential vacancy, and presidential disability	1967	1 year, 7 months, 4 days
26th	Voting age of 18	1971	3 months, 8 days
27th	Congressional pay	1992	202 years, 7 months, 12 days

The Enlightenment expressed centuries of debate and struggles of rights. Where did they come from? Who had them? What happened if they were abused? As early as the Magna Carta in 1215, men compelled King John of England to agree to some governmental restrictions and protection his subjects' rights. With the Mayflower Compact of 1620, the Mayflower Pilgrims agreed to a set of laws governing behavior for the "good of the people." Some have always felt that rights are given by the state, or law giver. This positivism, with roots in Hobbes, bases law on the notion of sovereign power; law is understood to depend on the sovereign's will. No matter what a law's content, no matter how unjust it seems, if it has been commanded by the sovereign, then and only then is it law. But then that leads to tyranny of the majority. Rights cannot be based on whims of elections; slavery may still be legal.

The Declaration of Independence said all men created equal, that they had rights of life, liberty, and the pursuit of happiness that could not be violated. Governments are created by free men to protect their rights from violations, even from government itself. But what are rights? They are property; you own them as you own your life, liberty. This is sometimes referred to as the nonaggression principle, NAP. No one has a power to initiate violation—theft, murder, slavery—against another. Remember theft is stealing your stuff, your past you had worked at; murder is taking away any future; while liberty is your present to act or not act. You own your rights, given to you by God, like grace, freely without having to ask for them, again, not unconditionally but with responsibility. I had a catechism teacher when in school. His NAP was simple and to the point: "You have the right to hit someone in the nose until you touch it."

But what happens when the violator is the state? No man has the power to initiate violence—theft, murder, or slavery. What if it's the state that steals, kills, or enslaves—taxes, executions, drafts?

The War for Freedom produced thirteen state constitutions and bills of rights. The Framers in Philadelphia wrote of We the People and the blessings of liberty. The US Constitution contained Article I, Sections 9–10, powers denied to the central government or to the states. Article IV, Section 2, Clause 1 guaranteed citizens of each state shall be entitled to all privileges and immunities of citizens in the several states.

Article III created courts to protect citizens as well as a jury system for the accused. It was a limited government with few delegated powers.

The Anti-Federalists called for a Bill of Rights; it will outline and deny to the government the right to interfere. As Patrick Henry declared, freedom of expression was essential to freedom of government, without which republics cannot exist. During World War II while fighting totalitarian dictatorships, the courts in *West Virginia v. Barnette* (1943) would not allow even patriotism to overrule a man's freedoms. The Ninth Amendment makes it clear that the national government may not overrule a state-protected right. However, the courts may not create rights.

In *US v. Burr* (1807), the court stated unequivocally that the courts must protect individuals against the government. It was in this case that John Marshall again walked a fine line. Burr, no longer vice president under Jefferson yet not forgotten for his double-cross in the Chase impeachment trial, was accused by Jefferson of treason. Using forged letters, paid and bribed witnesses—as many as 140 "pardons" were issued to "witnesses" for the right testimony—letters to the editor of many papers, and even a little subtle arm-twisting of Marshall, Jefferson, in another abuse of power, precursor of Richard Nixon's "executive privilege," refused a subpoena of Marshall to turn other documents to the defense attorneys or himself appear in court. With no "overt act" or two witnesses in the court, as required under Article III of the Constitution, Burr walked away a free man.

It has not been an easy process; nor was it applied equally in the beginnings of this Republic. Blacks, women, and many others, such as enemies of the president, had been denied some fundamental rights. But Lincoln, himself a violator of habeas corpus, in the Gettysburg Address restated that this nation was "conceived in liberty" and dedicated to the ideal that "all men are created equal." But a "government of the people, by the people and for the people" was not finished. The goals of the Preamble have not been perfectly, even moderately, achieved. With the Civil War Amendments, the Thirteenth, Fourteenth, and Fifteenth, we began to fix the mistakes of history.

The courts and time have led to a better interpretation of civil liberties and rights. Civil liberties are also called "negative rights" because they limit the government. Individual liberties that are protected from government are articulated in the Bill of Rights. Civil rights are the attempts to give meaning to ideal of equality; while liberties are those freedoms to do things without government restraint. Civil rights, also called "positive rights," are protections provided by the government in amendment, legislation, judicial decision, and executive order.

People must know and use their rights because it is their responsibility more than the courts. Liberty lies in the hands of men, not in constitutions. But even rights are limited, they are not absolute; liberty does not and cannot equal license. Rights are relative to others' rights; they sometimes conflict. For example, which is greater, free press or fair trial (*Sheppard v. Maxwell* 1966)?

To whom are rights guaranteed—US citizens alone, or do the rights of man extend to aliens, even illegals (*Korematsu v. US*, 1944)?

The rights within the Bill of Rights rest upon the founding ideals and principles of the generation that created the Constitution. Though values have changed, the Constitution was written by them with these ideals forefront. These ideals come from many sources: puritan but also cavalier, free landholders but also working-class histories, centralized churches, and evangelicals. Without an understanding of these, many rights within the Bill of Rights and the debates over them seem random.

The Founders believed strongly that God is the source of all truth and the source of freedom. Freedom is the physical manifestation of acting and consequences of those actions, in the absence of coercion. Justice is the absence of injustice; it is achieved by securing individual rights. Natural law, or God's law, should be the foundation of all later laws. Religion, morality, and knowledge in the science of government are the pillars of human happiness and political prosperity. The Declaration of Independence declares the principles of freedom; the United States Constitution is the strategy for freedom. The Constitution was designed to control the national government. The national government was to deal with the states and other nations; the states and local governments were to deal with the people.

The Constitution was structured to recognize and protect separate and sometimes conflicting interests; it is the formula for freedom. Only those powers listed (enumerated) were given to the central government. There were checks and balances both vertically and horizontally. Vertical distribution of powers was Federalism; all power comes from the states, and some are delegated to a national government. Horizontal separation of powers and checks and balances among the branches assures no tyrant can emerge. The Framers intelligently designed the United States of America to be a complex constitutional representative republic, not a democracy. The first ten amendments, the Bill of (Individual) Rights, do not amend the original intent of the Constitution. They clarify the restraints placed on the national government, and they safeguard the rights of individuals. The Ninth and Tenth Amendments are the keystones to preserving freedom. To retain the divinely inspired Constitution, the "Miracle at Philadelphia," the great experiment, every generation must be educated in the divine science of government and be vigilant in its preservation.

Amending the Constitution

The Constitution provides for its own amendment—that is, for changes in its written words. Article V sets out two methods for the proposal and two methods for the ratification of constitutional amendments, creating four possible methods of formal amendment. After the Bill of Rights, there have been only seventeen amendments to the US Constitution. There have been over ten thousand amendments proposed by members of Congress or the States. Thirty-three passed the Congress by the two-thirds vote; six are still pending at the state level. This is the formal and only "constitutional" way to change the Constitution. However, over the years with Supreme Court's "logical tricks," presidential use of executive orders, and use of bureaucratic regulations, many "informal" amendments have changed the true intent of the great experiment. Felix Frankfurter, Oliver Wendall Holmes Jr., Hugo Black, John Roberts, some Progressive, some Conservative, have all believed the Constitution has been and can be changed by historical practices, precedents, falsely or correctly interpreted rather than by formal amendment.

There is currently a building movement to call for another constitutional convention. Under Article V, if two-thirds of states request a convention, it must be held; Congress cannot interfere or prevent. Currently there have been eleven states that have approved this convention, and it is pending in thirty-three others. That's forty-four; thirty-four are needed. The major impetus for a new convention is national spending and debt, misinterpretations by national courts, and other abuses of power. Today's deep state corruption and human nature to lean toward corruption—men are not angels—are precisely what both Founders and Framers feared. This convention is the only solution short of revolution. We have a duty to use it to save the experiment!

An informal amendment is a process by which over time many "changes" have been made in the Constitution, which have not involved any changes in its written word. The informal amendment process can take place by the passage of basic legislation by Congress, actions taken by the president, key decisions of the Supreme Court, the activities of political parties, custom, and traditions.

Presidential actions have produced several important informal amendments, such as the use of the military under the power of commander in chief. The term "executive action" itself is vague and can be used to describe almost anything the president calls on Congress or his administration to do. But many executive actions carry no legal weight. An executive order is one type of executive action. Other common types include presidential agreements, memoranda, and proclamations, which are also used to direct the operations of the executive branch. They can be invalidated by the courts or undone by legislation passed by Congress, though seldom have. A recent one was the Supreme Court's overruling an Obama action on immigration. On gun control, Obama issued his opinions as executive actions. But even the Obama White House acknowledged that most of the executive actions carried no legal weight. Here's what the administration said at the time the twenty-three executive actions were proposed: "While President Obama will sign 23 Executive Actions today that will help keep our kids safe, he was clear that he cannot and should not act alone: The most important changes depend on Congressional action."

An executive agreement is a pact made by the president directly with the head of a foreign state, Obama and his nuclear agreement with Iran, which as I write was violated with a launch of a missile that could reach Berlin. These are said to be within his power to conduct foreign affairs.

An executive order is a specific type of presidential action—an official, legally binding mandate passed down from the president to national agencies under the executive branch. Executive orders are printed in the Federal Register, and they're numbered consecutively for the sake of keeping them straight. Essentially, an executive order gives agencies instructions on how to interpret and carry out US law.

An executive memorandum is essentially an executive order. The difference is that for a memorandum, there is no established way on how the president orders it. Memoranda are not submitted to the Federal Register, making them difficult to track. President Obama utilized executive memorandum at least 407 times, including on DACA (the immigration policy), gun control, and the overtime rule. President Trump has already used this type of executive action eight times. Proclamations are the last form of executive actions. These are largely used for ceremonial purposes and usually don't carry any legal effect. For example, when a former justice of the Supreme Court dies, a president might issue a proclamation ordering American flags to be flown at half-staff.

During his term in office, a president may issue executive orders, which have in essence changed the Constitution during his term. Tradition has said these orders expire when he leaves office; however, many presidents have not cancelled their predecessor's actions. The last four presidents, Bill Clinton, George W. Bush, Barack Obama, and Donald Trump, have issued more than all previous presidents since George Washington. The terms "executive action" and "executive order" are not interchangeable. Executive orders are legally binding and numbered and published in the Federal Register, though they also can also be reversed by the courts and Congress. A good way to think of executive actions is a wish list of policies the president would like to see enacted; while an executive order is his acting without congressional agreement. So much for legislative supremacy.

Before his first cabinet meeting after a Republican landslide in 2014 elections, Obama made the statement he had a pen and would do what he felt was right, Constitution be damned!

> We are not just going to be waiting for legislation in order to make sure that we're providing Americans the kind of help that they need. I've got a pen, and I've got a phone. And I can use that pen to sign executive orders and take executive actions and administrative actions that move the ball forward in helping to make sure our kids are getting the best education possible, making sure that our businesses are getting the kind of support and help they need to grow and advance, to make sure that people are getting the skills

that they need to get those jobs that our businesses are creating . . . I've got a phone that allows me to convene Americans from every walk of life, nonprofits, businesses, the private sector, universities to try to bring more and more Americans together around what I think is a unifying theme: making sure that this is a country where, if you work hard, you can make it.

Are these in the Constitution? Well, yes and no. None of these terms are written in the Constitution. Most early presidents issued them as transparency, a term thrown around today yet seldom implemented, a way to keep the public in the loop, not to direct policy. Instead, Obama's "pen" comes from the "vesting clause" of the Constitution that grants the president "executive power"—an extremely vague term that, historically, has come to mean all the complicated administrative actions associated with the day-to-day operations of the government, FDR issued 3721. There has always been a debate about executive power, how the Framers envisioned its use, and what it means for presidents in the modern era. Constitutional experts generally agree that executive actions are legal as long as the president has authority in the policy area, and those policies are a reasonable interpretation of court precedent.

A recent development used by presidents, especially Clinton and Bush II, is the presidential signing statement. They are official pronouncements issued by the president when he signs a bill into law, commenting on his interpretation of the law's language as to how he sees its constitutionality, which is why he was given the veto power by the Framers, or his statement of what parts he will enforce based on his and his administration's philosophy of the government and the Constitution. They've been around since the early nineteenth century; however, today, they have altered anything the Framers could have imagined of executive power. Ronald Reagan began the practice to assert presidential authority and intent, issuing 250 signing statements; George H. W. Bush, 228 such statements; Bill Clinton, 381 statements; George W. Bush, though less with 161, combined many objections into less statements, actually objecting to Congress's legislative power, one thousand challenges to the majority chosen provisions of law; Obama, using executive orders more extensively, issued only thirty-seven signing statements. The greatest problem here is the near ignorance of the public that when a law is passed now in the Congress, it is no longer faithfully executed, or at least not as it was intended by Congress, nor understood by the voters. But is not what we should expect from a Hamiltonian system?

The nation's courts, most importantly the United States Supreme Court, interpret and apply the Constitution in many cases they hear. These actions are also unconstitutional but, without an assertive Congress, little stops recent presidents from expanding into imperial leaders. Or the Court from sitting *ex cathedra*.

The Bill of Rights was developed because many state ratifying conventions called for some list during 1787–1789. Virginia, under Patrick Henry's forceful oratory, was assured by James Madison that he personally would introduce a list of rights to be amended to the document if approved. It was this assurance that convinced Virginia and New York to ratify the Constitution. Basing his ideas on Virginia's Bill of Rights written by himself and George Mason, a list of twelve rights were developed by James Madison. He worked diligently to develop and assure passage of the document. They were accepted by enough states and became effective on December 15, 1791.

Many, however, believe these are not the amendments the Anti-Federalists truly wanted. These were added to the end of the document, in essence not changing anything that was to be ratified; they were "milk and water" amendments. Gerry wanted to change the structure and powers of the new government rather than a bill of rights! George Clymer wrote to Richard Peters on June 8, 1789:

> Madison this morning is to make an essay towards amendments but whether he means merely a tub to the whale, or declarations about the press liberty of conscience &c. or will suffer himself to be so far frightened with the antifederalism of his own state as to attempt to lop off essentials I do not know I hope however we shall be strong enough to postpone. Afternoon Madison's has proved a tub on a number of Amendments. But Gerry is not content with

them alone, and proposes to treat us with all the amendments of all the antifederalists in America.

Madison ended up—from the hundreds of suggestions, Virginia handed him thirty-one—with a proposal of twelve changes to be added. The first two did not make the cut in the states. Article I was a device to number Congress and allot representatives, no longer practical today. Article II will become the Twenty-Seventh Amendment limiting pay raises, passed in 1992. Thus, what we call the First Amendment was number three on the list.

The First Amendment protects a man's right to conscience, political speech, and the press; the right to alter his government; and the right to assemble. Both the Second and Third are historical amendments. The British at Concord and Lexington were trying to disarm the people so as to prevent true dissent and had already found a way to tax the people by requiring quartering of troops. The Fourth, Fifth, Six and Eighth are due process and protections against government accusations. The Seventh guarantees a right to trial if one is involved in civil suits. The often ignored and misunderstood Ninth and Tenth Amendments were specifically added so as to not appear as though only the rights mentioned are protected. The Ninth Amendment is a protection of rights not specifically enumerated in the Bill of Rights. While the Tenth Amendment restates Federalism that powers of states and people not given up are not taken away.

The next two amendments fixed mistakes that the Framers did not see coming. The Eleventh Amendment clarified state versus national courts jurisdictions. It is the responsibility of the state courts to decide disputes between individuals of different states or foreign nationals and citizens of the United States. The Twelfth adapted the Electoral College to rise of political parties. It determined that the Electoral College would vote two separate ballots, one for president and one for vice president. It also reminded the college that the vice president must possess the same qualifications as the president.

The United States then went decades without amending until the Civil War changed the makeup of the federal system. The Thirteenth outlawed slavery, something the Framers were incapable of doing. The Fourteenth, extending due process procedural protection in state actions, defined citizenship and began a process called equal protection of the substance of laws in the country. If you recall, all laws passed by Congress must be for the general welfare alone, never to harm or help one group over another; this most used amendment today attempted to state that more clearly (or so they thought!).

Amendments Fifteenth, Nineteenth, Twenty-Third, Twenty-Fourth, and Twenty-Sixth extended voting rights to many who had been denied suffrage in the early Republic, blacks, women, District of Columbia, the poor, and young adults.

The Sixteenth and Seventeenth Amendments will create what Hamilton wanted: high taxes and debt and national control over the states. The original Constitution had divided power between the states and the limited national government. With the use of revenue tariffs, taxation was voluntary. Don't buy the foreign products; don't pay the taxes. Yet for government to assist business, tariffs were relatively high; people bought less thus deposit less into the coffers of national tax collectors. This kept government small and noninvolved in much of the warfare and welfare of our time. With the Sixteenth Amendment, the government's ability to raise revenue has exploded. Using a progressive system of taxes (where the rich pay higher percentages), government can expand at the expense of class warfare and the constant bellwether of "They need to pay their fair share." The Seventeenth ended the federal system with direct election of senators. History has shown that elections are won by big money, national power money. With the state legislatures no longer able to control half of Congress, they have become merely enforcers of national laws standing in line to collect their portion of the handouts.

The rest outlawed (Eighteenth) and then allowed (Twenty-First) alcohol in a failed attempt by a consolidated government to regulate human behaviors. The Twentieth moved the date of office holding closer to elections; it established January 3 as the starting date for Congress and January 20 for the president's term inauguration. The Twenty-Second and Twenty-Fifth respectfully limited the terms of the president and finally placed into an amendment what happens if he dies or is incapable of serving his duties. And, finally, the Twenty-Seventh was passed in reaction to the continual arrogance of politicians to raise their own salaries and benefits in the face of the electorate falling behind. It required an intervening congressional election to occur before the raise took effect. In practice, it meant nothing because of the high percentage of incumbents (current officeholders) that are reelected.

A lost amendment?

Many consider the Bill of Rights as well as the Eleventh Amendment to be firm limitations on the national government's powers. States still possessed all powers not *specifically* taken away. The Twelfth was a fix as we noted on the new idea of an Electoral College in line with the new political party development the Framers did not see, or as Madison warned of factions.

The Framers distrusted—no, feared any sense of nonearned privileges. "Nobility" for them had a long history of abuse and excess against the man's natural rights. They wrote two clauses outlawing officeholders with "Titles of Nobility or Honor or emoluments" from external sources. All men according to Jefferson, and should be now to all Americans, are equal in the eyes of God. The 1775–1783 War was primarily waged to eliminate not only these abuses and excesses of the nobility but also any "monied classes" from the Republic. Yet the clauses in Article I, Section 9, Clause 8 of the Constitution had no consequences other than impeachment. Probably another Hamiltonian "correction" to the document.

As we see today with the deep state, elites tend to be treated with kid gloves. Cronyism, special "house arrests" for political crimes, and felonious "carelessness" of the elites are examples of exactly what the Framers and Founders feared. A title of nobility or honor was to set oneself apart from, or superior to, or possessing of any special privileges or immunities not available to any other citizen of the United States. To eliminate the widespread use of emoluments from lobbyists or foreign agents as bribery and/or graft was to assure laws were passed openly, and for the general welfare, not special interests.

To assure that politicians, civil servants, bureaucrats, and today's regulators stay unbiased, fair, and honest in service to the citizens, an amendment of enforcement was first proposed in 1810 by Sen. Phillip Reed of Maryland and ratified in 1819, adding a heavy penalty upon any person holding or accepting a title of nobility or honor, or emoluments from external powers by making that person would be "incapable of holding any Office of Trust or Profit under the United States"; but, more potently, anyone violating this amendment would "cease to be a citizen of the United States."

(March 12, Original 1819) Amendment XIII

> If any citizen of the United States shall accept, claim, receive, or retain any title of nobility or honour, or shall without the consent of Congress, accept and retain any present, pension, office, or emolument of any kind whatever, from any emperor, king, prince, or foreign power, such person shall cease to be a citizen of the United States, and shall be incapable of holding any office of trust or profit under them, or either of them.

This amendment was legally proposed and properly ratified and could be found published on contemporary US Constitutions until 1876, by which time it was quietly and fraudulently deleted, never repealed, during the period of Reconstruction after the Civil War when the Thirteenth Amendment was substituted.

Original records of the first Thirteenth Amendment were mostly burned when the British burned DC in the War of 1812; however, copies are being found in those states part of the Republic before the Civil War, as well as a copy in the archives of the British Museum. The Territory of Wyoming, 1876, was the last reference to it. An 1867 Colorado Territory edition includes both Thirteenth Amendments on the same page along with the then recent "ratified" Fourteenth Amendment.

On December 18, 1865, this "new" Thirteenth Amendment ended and quietly erased states' rights from history. Secretary of State William Henry Seward replaced and effectively threw down the black hole of history the original Thirteenth Amendment that had prohibited acceptance of "titles of nobility" and "honors" and "emoluments," and dishonest politicians have been bought and bribed and have treasonously accepted graft from external sources ever since, with no thought of penalty—Russian uranium sales, Saudi oil lobbyists, Ike's military-industrial complex—Hamilton had won.

What do you think?

1. Should any new amendments be added to the Constitution today?
2. What are the major issues facing our nation today? Are there some only solvable with a change in the way things are done? Some have suggested term limits of Congress, banning abortion, flag burning, balanced budgets. Can they be solved within the current system? How would you change it to solve those issues?

Many others have been suggested. In June 2005, the House of Representatives passed a proposed amendment (sixth time since 1995) to ban desecration of the American flag, balanced budget, end Electoral College, term limits for Congress like the presidential two terms, ban abortion, define marriage, allow non-native born citizens to be president, require national officials to obey the laws they pass—Obamacare.

RELIGION

The way liberals are interpreting the First Amendment today is that
it prevents anyone who is religious from being in government.
—Rush Limbaugh

THE IMPORTANCE OF freedom of religion to the Founders
can be seen by the fact that the first phrase of Amendment
I of the Bill of Rights says, "Congress shall make no law respecting
an establishment of religion, or prohibiting the free exercise thereof."
With gay marriage, Obamacare, LGBT bathrooms, let alone abortion
(which has become a mere health issue), all confronting other citizen's
religious faiths, the struggle is great than anytime in American history.
Americans have believed that freedom of religion is one of the most
important liberties to be protected by the Constitution.

The degree of religious freedom that you have today did not exist
in Europe, the colonies, or the states formed after the Revolutionary
War. Often only one official or "established" religious group could
practice its beliefs. Every subject/citizen had to attend its church, obey
its requirements, and pay taxes to support it.

Few of the earliest English colonies in North America allowed
religious freedom. In fact, in several colonies, especially those in New
England, a dominant and intolerant religious group insisted on strict
conformity to its own ideas of proper belief and worship. Dissenters
were persecuted. In the early days, some dissenters simply went off into
the wilderness and began new colonies of their own. Roger Williams
in 1635 fled Massachusetts and established Rhode Island. He gained a
charter from the king and soon thereafter instituted the first tolerance
law in 1663. This allowed Christians, not Catholics, Jews, or atheists,
to be left alone to freely exercise their own faith. Another was the
Reverend Thomas Hooker, who disagreed with the religious beliefs

in Massachusetts. He and his followers left the colony and settled in Connecticut. However, their new colony soon became as intolerant in its own way as Massachusetts. The only colonies that tolerated a relatively free expression of religious beliefs and practices were Pennsylvania, Rhode Island, Delaware, and New Jersey.

Anne Hutchinson, Puritan spiritual adviser, mother of fifteen, midwife, at a time when women had little to no existence but for her husband, was tried and convicted, excommunicated, and banished from the colony with many of her supporters. They will join Roger Williams in Rhode Island and establish the settlement of Portsmouth. When the Puritan Massachusetts Colony absorbed Rhode Island, Hutchinson moved totally outside the reach of Boston into the lands of the Dutch, today's New York City. She and all her children but the youngest and her entire household were massacred during Kieft's War with local native tribes. She is a key figure in the development of religious freedom in England's American colonies and the history of women in ministry. She challenged the authority of the ministers, exposing the subordination of women in the culture of colonial Massachusetts, "courageous exponent of civil liberty and religious toleration."

By the end of the colonial period, people had become more tolerant of religious differences. Many different religious groups existed together in the same communities and people became used to living and working with others who held different beliefs. In some of the colonies, most notably in New England, many people had become less strict about their own religious beliefs and were more willing to accept different points of view. Consequently, with an increased tolerance of religious differences, there came greater demands for genuine religious freedom, which were increasingly made by Quakers, Baptists, Catholics, and others.

There was also widespread opposition to the establishment of one church as the official national church. By the time of the ratification of the Constitution and the Bill of Rights, there was a widely held belief that the central government should not be allowed to establish an official church for the nation. Many agreed that an established church was harmful to religion and bad for the nation.

Finally, some leaders, notably Thomas Jefferson and James Madison, were greatly concerned about the dangers of religious intolerance. They understood throughout history, religious intolerance had often led to conflict rather than cooperation and to a violation of the basic rights of individuals. It was not that they were against religion, nearly all devoted believers in their personal faiths; they clearly did not wish to have some majority impose on the rest.

Even though many of the Founders believed strongly in religious tolerance, several state constitutions deprived members of some religious groups of the rights people who were members of other religious groups had. For example, some states did not allow Catholics or Jews to vote or hold public office. In Massachusetts and Maryland, only a Christian was allowed to become governor. For many years, New Hampshire, New Jersey, Massachusetts, and North Carolina required that officeholders be Protestants. Even Pennsylvania, which had a bill of rights protecting the "inalienable right of all men to worship God according to the dictates of their own conscience," still disqualified Jews and non-Christians from public office. New York and Virginia were the only states that did not have any restrictions on religious beliefs for persons serving in their state governments.

However, soon after 1776, important changes began to be made in those states in which religion had been established as an official part of the government. Between 1776 and 1789, New York, Virginia, and North Carolina eliminated state-established religion. Massachusetts, Connecticut, and New Hampshire decided to allow Anglicans and other Protestants to join Congregationalists as a part of the established church. In Maryland, the Constitution written in 1776 gave the legislature the right to tax citizens to support the Christian religion. However, each person was free to decide which denomination should receive his tax money. The Constitution of South Carolina, written in 1778, said that the Protestant Christian religion was to be the established religion of the state, and all Protestant groups would have equal rights and privileges including financial support from tax funds.

These changes meant that in some states, there was still an established religion, but it was not just one church or denomination. The established religion, however, was Protestant Christianity. Catholics, Jews, and members of other religions were not entitled to tax support. It was not until 1833 when Massachusetts changed its constitution to separate church and state that the last established religion in the states was eliminated.

Most of the Founders were religious people. Despite the history of intolerance, the influence of some of their religious beliefs resulted in promoting the freedom of religion, which we have today. They believed that you have certain natural rights simply because you are a human being. This belief developed in part out of the Puritan idea that God has given you a moral sense and the ability to reason, which enables you to tell the difference between what is right and wrong. Philosophers such as John Locke argued that society should allow you to live the way your moral sense, guided by the *Bible*, tells you is right. The best government, therefore, they believed, is the one that interferes as little as possible with your beliefs, including religious belief, although many did not support tolerance for you if you did not believe in God.

The Founders, it is important to remember, believed that religion is extremely important in developing the kind of character citizens of a free society needed to have to remain free. For example, George Washington said in his Farewell Address that virtue and morality are necessary for a government run by the people. He also believed that morality could not be maintained without religion. At the same time, he joined Thomas Jefferson and James Madison in opposing a bill introduced into the Virginia legislature, which would have used tax money to pay for religious teachers.

Yet there did not seem to be a death struggle between the law, science, and religion as there is today. In 2017, students were asked at the Ivy League schools their views on religion and Christianity more specifically. Sixty-eight percent believed that Christianity was more violent than others, including Islam. James Wilson, Franklin's friend, was adamant there was no conflict.

> Far from being rivals or enemies, religion and law are twin sisters, friends, and mutual assistants. Indeed, these two sciences run into each other. The divine law, as discovered by reason and the moral sense, forms an essential part of both.

A century later, Frederick Douglass, in many speeches across a healing America and Europe, stressed that without religion, Christianity, there would be no future United Sates.

I know there is a hope in religion; I know there is faith and I know there is prayer about religion and necessary to it, but God is most glorified when there is peace on earth and good will towards men.

I love the religion of Christianity—which cometh from above—which is a pure, peaceable, gentle, easy to be entreated, full of good fruits, and without hypocrisy.

The life of the nation is secure only while the nation is honest, truthful and virtuous.

Madison had been the author of the parts of the Virginia Declaration of Rights, passed in 1776, that provided for freedom of religion. Religion, he insisted, "can be directed only by reason and conviction." Jefferson later wrote the Act for Establishing Religious Freedom, which led to the end of an established church in Virginia. Both were acting on the basis of their belief that our right to liberty includes the liberty to believe as our conscience and reason direct. Established churches, they insisted, violate this basic right. It imposed on nonbelievers the burden to support an "untruth." They thought religion was an important part of the society. At the same time, they believed strongly that each person has a natural right to his or her own religious beliefs. The separation of the church and state required by the First Amendment is an expression of this belief.

The "establishment" and the "free exercise" clauses

The Framers thus included two clauses in the First Amendment that protect your religious freedom. These are the "establishment clause" and the "free exercise clause." The establishment clause prohibits the national government from establishing an official religion for the nation. This guards against establishing a mandated religion; in effect, this is freedom from religion. The Congress cannot favor one over another. Some have used a phrase by Thomas Jefferson to a friend, that this clause creates a "wall of separation between church and state." The rest of the letter does not justify that interpretation. It was merely to say that Baptists and other new evangelicals need not worry that they would be harassed by the government, as they were not "established faiths." Controversies have continued to arise in trying to decide what this separation of church and state should mean.

> Believing with you that religion is a matter which lies solely between Man and his God, that he owes account to none other for his faith or his worship, that the legitimate powers of government reach actions only, and not opinions, I contemplate with sovereign reverence that act of the whole American people which declared that *their* legislature should "make no law respecting an establishment of religion, or prohibiting the free exercise thereof," thus building a wall of separation between Church and State (Jefferson's Letter to Baptist Ministers Association January 1, 1802).

Some people have argued that it should be interpreted to mean that the government should have almost nothing to do with religion. This could mean anything from not allowing prayers in public buildings to eliminating tax exemptions for churches and to taking the phrase "in God we trust" off of all money issued by the government. Others argue that the Framers were only opposed to a single national church and the favoring of one religion over another. I want to come back to school and religion; having been denied free exercise for three decades may be why our schools are failing.

The free exercise clause protects your freedom to believe or not to believe as well as your freedom to act. It guards against the government interfering in the exercise of any religion; in effect, this is freedom *for* religion, while the establishment clause is freedom *from* religion. It protects the practice of one's faith. For example, if your religion requires you to wear certain kinds of clothing or not to eat certain foods, your freedom to practice these beliefs is protected. In past years, cases involving the free exercise of religious beliefs have involved a wide variety of religious groups such as Latter-Day Saints, Jehovah's Witnesses, the Amish, and Seventh Day Adventists; today it involves health care and contraceptives and baking cakes for queers and other faiths.

In some recent cases, the court has shown some sense. Based on *Widmar v. Vincent* (1981) at universities and *Board of Education v.*

Mergens (1990) for public schools, political and religious groups can meet in public schools same as any extracurricular groups and student religious groups allowed to meet in the school on the same basis as other student organizations. Under the United States Constitution, public school students have the right to express their faith. College students and high school students have the same rights as other groups of students to meet and associate with others during noncurricular times. This principle generally applies to junior high and elementary school student groups, although a few courts have denied equal access to such groups because of the students' maturity level and the associated establishment clause concerns.

Aaron, Melissa, and their five children live in Northwestern Oregon. In 2007, they fulfilled their dream of opening a family bakery called Sweet Cakes by Melissa. Aaron felt a family business "would be a great way to provide for our children." For Melissa, the bakery was an opportunity to express her creativity. They dreamed their children would be able to take over the shop one day—but that dream was shattered only a few years later. In 2013, a woman came to the bakery and requested a wedding cake for her same-sex wedding. The woman was a return customer who had come to the bakery with her partner months earlier to order a cake for another event. The women had such a positive experience at Sweet Cakes that they wanted Melissa to make their wedding cake. Melissa and Aaron are devout Christians who are committed to following the teachings of their faith. The Kleins explained to the women that by making a wedding cake, they would be endorsing something that violated their beliefs, which is something they could not do. The bakers were eventually fined $135,000, which they refused to pay; they were bombarded by protests and harassing Facebook posts and were boycotted by the Left. They appealed to SCOTUS in 2016.

Filed on April 25, 2016, First Liberty and Gray's appellate brief argues that Commissioner Avakian and the state of Oregon violated the Kleins' rights to free speech, religious freedom, and due process. And in the summer of 2017, the Supreme Court decided to take the case. Do business owners have the right to serve whom they wish? Well, the Fifth Circuit of Appeals decided Mississippi can enforce a law that allows merchants and government employees who cite religious beliefs to deny services to same-sex couples, but opponents of the law immediately pledged to appeal. This case will likely be attached to the Kleins' case. The brief states:

> One of America's founding principles is that state action "compel[ling] a man to furnish contributions of money for the propagation of opinions which he disbelieves and abhors" is "tyrannical" (Thomas Jefferson, A Bill for Establishing Religious Freedom, June 12, 1779). It is at least as tyrannical to compel people to use their time and talent to speak, or to carry, contribute to, or affiliate with others' expressions to which they do not ascribe and to which their religion forbids them from adhering.

Conflicts between establishment and free exercise

The problem of protecting religious freedom under the First Amendment is often complicated by the fact that at times there may be a conflict between the establishment clause and the free exercise clause. For example, consider the following problem from a case heard not too long ago by the Supreme Court (*Marsh v. Chambers,* 1983). A state legislature had used tax funds to hire a chaplain to open its sessions with a prayer. This was challenged as being a violation of the establishment clause requiring the separation of church and state. It was defended with the argument that to deny the legislators this right was to violate their right to the free exercise of their religious beliefs.

Article I of the Bill of Rights increased the protection of religious freedom. However, this protection was only from the actions of the central government, not those of the states. Since there were several state-supported churches, it was generally believed that the First Amendment left the state governments free to support religious groups if they wished to. And some people supported the First Amendment to protect the state religious establishments from interference by the national government.

In the late 1940s, however, the Supreme Court decided two cases that extended the First Amendment's protections of religious liberties against state action by incorporating them under the Fourteenth Amendment's guarantee of liberty. The interpretations of the Constitution in these cases increased the power of the national courts over state government's activities in the area of religion.

However, while you have the right to hold any religious belief you wish, this does not mean that the central government or state governments cannot make and enforce laws controlling your religious practices. Religious practices may be limited if they offend public morals, jeopardize public health, or in other ways endanger the common welfare. For example, according to court rulings, religious practices involving polygamy or handling rattlesnakes may be forbidden without violating citizens' constitutional rights. Couples who wish to marry may be required by state law to take blood tests before being given a marriage license. Children may be required to be vaccinated for small pox before being admitted to school, even if these requirements violate their religious beliefs. Actions that violate social duties or disrupt social order are not covered under the free exercise clause.

The most famous case is *Reynolds v. US* (1879); this is a case concerning polygamy in Utah. Reynolds, a Latter-Day Saint, said it was his religion that sanctioned polygamy. The United States won; if religion conflicts with a secular law with legitimate nonreligious purposes, law wins! Religion is not above law.

In 1961, the Supreme Court heard a case involving the state of Maryland. If you had been a citizen of Maryland at that time, you would have had to swear that you believed in God before you could hold a public office. The Supreme Court ruled that this part of Maryland's law violated the protection of freedom of belief guaranteed to every person by the First Amendment. This decision meant that each person has an absolute right to hold any or no religious belief and that no government in the United States has the right to force anyone to accept any religious beliefs or to censor such beliefs.

The issues surrounding religion and the state continue to be landmarks at the Supreme Court level. Prison rules, the draft, even Christmas have concerns in the practices and establishment of religions. In *Welsh v. US* (1970), a case of a conscientious objector to the Vietnam War that did not want to be drafted, the court said if it were a sincere belief, it would be a legal excuse to not serve. The practice of one's faith in prison: diet, length of hair, gatherings for Islamic faith must be accommodated. In July 2010, the Ninth Court of Appeals ruled on length of hair for Native Americans in prison. It was an unfair double standard for men and women.

The "Holiday" versus "Christmas" debate in a Christian country has reached comedic levels. It has become politically incorrect to refer to school vacations by their traditional Christian holydays. Winter break, instead of Christmas vacation; spring break, not Easter vacation; even holiday concerts and holiday trees, not the purpose for which those items are even celebrated. In a series of cases in the 1980s, the court went from intolerance of mainstream faiths to almost incomprehensible insanity. Beginning with *Lynch v. Donnelly* (1984), it allowed a display that was publicly -owned and privately displayed. Five years later, to finish the cabal *Allegheny County v. ACLU* (1989) made privately owned and publicly displayed unconstitutional and offensive. Nativity scenes OK if disclaimers are "clear and visible" or part of a seasonal display. This reindeer rule would place the burden on celebrants to not offend others by disrespecting their faith. Is a December music program in a public school constitutional if all the songs are religious and pertain to Christmas? Is the program saved by adding "Frosty the Snowman"? The *Allegheny v. ACLU* case prohibited an exclusively Christian holiday display yet, in *Pittsburgh v. ACLU* of the same year, allowed a multifaith holiday display.

In 2010, the Supreme Court overturned a lower court's injunction in *Salazar v. Buono* that prevented the national government from implementing a land transfer statute that would exchange a piece of land in the Mojave Preserve, US land, for a piece of private land of roughly equal value. The piece of public land to be exchanged for private land contained a controversial Latin cross that had been placed in the Preserve over seventy years ago by the VFW as a way of honoring the nation's war dead. The lower court viewed the proposed land transfer, clearly designed to defeat an establishment clause challenge to the cross, as in itself an unconstitutional establishment of religion. The Supreme Court disagreed. Writing the court's plurality opinion, Justice Anthony Kennedy said the cross was not a mere "reaffirmation of Christian beliefs" but a symbol that "evokes the thousands of small crosses in foreign fields marking the graves of Americans who fell in battles." As usual, it was a narrow opinion; four justices dissented.

In another, the court ruled unanimously in *Gonzales v. O Centro Espirita Beneficiente Uniao do Vegetal* (2006) that a small religious group who had argued that the Religious Freedom Restoration Act of 1993 required that they be free to use *hoasca*—an illegal drug under the Controlled Substances Act—for religious purposes was allowed. Chief Justice John Roberts wrote that the court had to review individual religious freedom of exercise claims and grant exceptions to generally applicable laws, the general welfare be damned.

In *Hein v. Freedom from Religion Foundation* (2007), the court ruled that taxpayers cannot bring establishment clause challenges against programs funded by the executive office. This came after the Bush administration created the Office of Faith-Based and Community Initiatives for the purpose of allowing religious charity organizations to gain national funding. Sounds establishment to me?

Schools and religion, the battle over our future

The position that there should be a "wall of separation" between church and state has been criticized by the leaders of some religious groups and strongly supported by others. This has been especially true in the sensitive area of education. The institution of education is by far what creates our future. Lincoln said the philosophy of the classroom in one generation is the philosophy of government in the next. To understand the importance of education none other than the best in centralization, as we saw before, Marx, Lenin, Stalin, and Mussolini, and add the American father of Progressive education, John Dewey.

> Children who know how to think for themselves spoil the harmony of the collective society which is coming where everyone is interdependent.

This is not a rant or tirade against today's educational system, which can be found elsewhere in many good places; see John Taylor Gatto. But the struggle for the souls of children is a struggle of momentous concern. We are going to examine some of the issues that arise regarding the relationship between religion and education and the ways in which they have been resolved by the Supreme Court. This should help you to understand the deeply divided opinions that Americans have on the meaning of religious freedom and the range of positions on the topic.

The court has developed some criteria in determining the constitutionality of laws affecting the relationship between religion and the schools.

To help you understand some of the current controversies over religion and education, below are some important questions constantly debated in many school districts. Chief Justice Warren E. Burger, who wrote the majority opinion in a 1971 case involving the establishment clause of the First Amendment, developed guidelines that are still used today by subsequent courts. This test is known as the "Lemon Test," since it was first written in a case called *Lemon v. Kurtzman* (1971). According to this test, for a law or action involving religion in the schools to avoid violating the Constitution, it must satisfy the following requirements.

1. The primary purpose of a law must be secular not religious. This means it must not have a religious purpose.
2. The principal or primary effect of the law must not be to advance or inhibit religion.
3. The law must not create an excessive government entanglement with religion.

How would you decide these issues regarding religion and the schools? Each of the following situations involves a law that might be considered a violation of the establishment clause of the First Amendment. Read them and use the three-part Lemon Test to decide if you think the laws should be declared unconstitutional.

1. Your state passes a law that allows your public school to have a daily one-minute period for silent prayer or meditation.
2. Your state passes a law that requires the textbooks used in your public school science or biology classes, which discuss evolution, to include an equal treatment of creationism.
3. Your state passes a law allowing your public school principal to post a copy of the Ten Commandments in every classroom.
4. Your state passes a law that gives parents who send their children to parochial schools a tax deduction for tuition, transportation, and educational materials.
5. Your state has a policy that allows your public school's algebra teacher to spend a part of the work day at a parochial school, giving remedial instruction to underachieving students.

6. A group of students at your public school requests permission to use an empty classroom after regular school hours for a voluntary prayer meeting. Should the principal be required to make the classroom available to them?

At the time the Constitution was written, public schools as we know them did not exist. Children who attended school usually received an education that included some degree of religious teaching. As public education became more important and widespread in the nation, sharp controversies over the extent to which religious teaching and practices should be supported in the public schools began to arise. The following are questions regarding the relationship between religion and the public schools that have been dealt with in Supreme Court cases since 1925.

Should national or state tax money be used to support private religious schools? The state government of Louisiana provides free textbooks for all students in parochial and public schools. In 1930, the Supreme Court decided this did not violate the "establishment" clause and was constitutional because it was an aid to schoolchildren rather than public assistance to church schools (*Cochran v. Louisiana State Board of Education,* 1930).

A New Jersey case involved a similar question. New Jersey at one time provided free bus transportation for schoolchildren traveling to either parochial or public schools. The Supreme Court, in a five-to-four decision in *Everson v. Board of Education of Ewing Township,* 1947, declared this law constitutional because it provided for public safety. Nevertheless, the court declared the following principle, which has dominated constitutional decisions for most of the past forty years. It declared that the First Amendment applies not only to the central government but to state governments as well (by incorporation through the meaning of "liberty" in the Fourteenth Amendment):

> The establishment of religion clause of the First Amendment means at least this: Neither a state nor the federal government can set up a church. Neither can pass laws which aid one religion, aid all religions, or prefer one religion over another . . . No tax in any amount, large or small, can be levied to support any religious activities or institutions,

whatever they may be called, or whatever form they may adopt to teach or practice religion.

In *Board of Education v. Allen* (1968), the court decided further that it was OK to give secular books to students in parochial schools using the "child benefit theory." The court now uses the Lemon test to determine what public funding of church-related schools is acceptable.

Should public schools provide certain periods of "released time" during the day when students can attend special classes to receive religious instruction from their own minister, priest, or rabbi? "Release time" means that students in public schools are released during a part of the normal school day to attend special classes where they are given religious instruction.

In 1940, members of the three largest religious groups in the United States-Roman Catholic, Protestant, and Jewish—joined together in Champaign, Illinois, to provide for the religious instruction of schoolchildren. Classes were held in the regular public school classrooms. Separate groups were taught by Protestant ministers, Roman Catholic priests, and Jewish rabbis. Students attended only with the consent of their parents, and those who did not choose to take religious instruction were required to stay in study rooms.

Mrs. Vashti McCollum, a parent, sued because she did not wish her child to be given religious teaching, nor did she wish him to be embarrassed because he was not receiving such instruction.

In a 1948 ruling, the Supreme Court ruled in favor of Mrs. McCollum, saying that a state may not use its public school system to promote religious education even though it aided all religions. Justice Hugo Black, speaking for the court, based the decision on the Everson opinion (*McCollum v. Board of Education*, 1948).

The *Everson* and *McCollum* cases stirred wide debate among interested church groups. It also led to debate among scholars, some of whom felt that the court had gone well beyond the intent of the First Amendment.

Four years after the *McCollum* decision, the court heard a case in which the New York public schools were releasing students during the school day, on parental request only, to go to religious centers for instruction. Those who were not released remained in the classrooms. No religious instruction was offered in the public school buildings.

Justice William O. Douglas, while supporting the idea of the separation of church and state, nevertheless upheld the New York system in which "the public schools do no more than accommodate their schedules to a program of outside religious instruction . . . We cannot read into the Bill of Rights . . . a philosophy of hostility to religion" (*Zorach v. Clausen,* 1952).

Should schools require students to take part in prayers or the reading of the Bible during regular public school hours? Some time ago, the New York State Board of Regents required a prayer as a daily exercise in New York public schools. The prayer was "non-denominational," written by state officials, and students who did not wish to participate in the exercise were permitted to remain silent or to be excused from the schoolroom.

In 1962, the Supreme Court held that the prayer required by the New York Board of Regents was unconstitutional (*Engel v. Vitale,* 1962). The court held that such an officially established prayer program violated the "establishment of religion" clause of the First Amendment.

The state of Pennsylvania had a law that called for "at least ten verses from the Holy Bible to be read without comment, at the opening of each public school on each school day." Any child was excused from the exercise upon written request of his parent or guardian.

In 1963, the Supreme Court declared this law an unconstitutional establishment of religion. The court said that the "establishment of religion" and "free exercise" clauses of the First Amendment require the government to be strictly neutral in matters of religion, "protecting all, preferring none, disparaging none" (*Abington School District v. Schempp,* 1963).

Kentucky passed a requirement to post the Ten Commandments in every classroom. In *Stone v. Graham* (1980), the court prohibited the commandments in schools.

In 1985, the Supreme Court declared unconstitutional an Alabama law that required a period of silence "for meditation or voluntary prayer in public schools" (*Wallace v. Jaffree,* 1985). In *Jager v. Douglas County School District* (1989), a lower court ruling in Georgia held that pregame invocations at high school football games are unconstitutional. Also, graduations were now included in the prayer ban in *Lee v. Weisman* (1992).

The Supreme Court's decisions in the school prayer cases have stirred heated controversy in the press, among church groups, in Congress, and in state legislatures. Some religious organizations have been strongly in favor of adding an amendment to the Constitution that would take away the Supreme Court's power to review state legislation regarding religious practices in the public schools. They argue this is necessary so that schoolchildren will not be deprived of their religious heritage or denied moral instruction.

On the other hand, spokespersons of the major religious groups have generally supported the Supreme Court's position that government should be neutral with respect to religious activities. The separation of church and state, they point out, does not prevent people from praying at any time or going to the church of their choice.

The teaching of evolution in public schools has always been a major controversy for those teaching and those advocating creationism, sometimes called intelligent design. This controversy first became a national issue with the Scopes trial of 1927. "Scientific creationism" using "Flood geology" was taught in many school science classes as support for a purely literal reading of Genesis. In *Epperson v. Arkansas* (1968), an Arkansas statute forbade teachers in public schools from teaching the "theory or doctrine that mankind ascended or descended from a lower order of animals." This was ruled contrary to the freedom of religion mandate of the First Amendment and in violation of the Fourteenth Amendment. The court ruled that a state may not eliminate ideas from a school's curricula solely because the ideas come in conflict with the beliefs of certain religious groups.

After the legal judgment of the case, *Daniel v. Waters* (1975) ruled that teaching creationism in public schools was a violation of the establishment clause. The content was stripped of overt biblical references and renamed creation science. When the court case *Edwards v. Aguillard* (1987) ruled that creation science similarly contravened the constitution, all references to "creation" in a draft school textbook were changed to refer to intelligent design, which was subsequently claimed to be a new scientific theory. The *Kitzmiller v. Dover* (2005) ruling concluded that intelligent design is not science and contravenes the constitutional restriction on teaching religion in public school science classes.

Compulsory education was challenged in Wisconsin with a case of religion versus education. In *Wisconsin v. Yoder* (1972), Amish parents were taking their children out of school at age fourteen when the state said they must be in school until age sixteen (now eighteen). The court ruled in the middle; Amish needed their children at home for work and to learn a trade. Yoder wins; Amish are not required to attend school past eighth grade. Yes, education is a state responsibility but can be done by parents as well. Secondary schooling was not as important as religion to the Amish. This is the beginning of an explosion in the homeschool movement, which today accounts for over two million students ages five to seventeen.

The state of Washington refused to honor its contract with a student obtaining a Promise Scholarship. Joshua Davey was promised in junior high that if he graduated, there would be a scholarship waiting for him at a state university. When Josh asked for his money, he was denied because of the fact he was pursuing a religious degree. In *Locke et al. v. Joshua Davey* (2004), the court ruled that Washington did not violate the free exercise. It appears that if government wishes to discriminate or has an agenda, well, don't worry about it. *Christian Legal Society v. Martinez* (2010) provides another example. The court ruled that a student organization at a public university was not free to limit their members to those who shared their belief system if that resulted in discrimination on the basis of sexual orientation.

In 2014, the absurdity of the justices reached, well, absurd levels. The court had recently ruled that a New York town meeting could open its meetings with prayer; Congress does daily. The issue was that town had relied predominantly on Christian ministers to deliver the prayers. This case relates to the case of Elmbrook School District in Wisconsin. This small town brought the court's various tests for evaluating whether a government practice violates the First Amendment's prohibition on a government establishment of religion to argumentum ad absurdum.

In *Elmbrook v. Doe* (2014), the full US Court of Appeals for the Seventh Circuit, in Chicago, ruled 7–3 in 2012 that the school district's use of a Christian church for its high school graduation ceremonies resulted in government endorsement of religion and coercion of students in violation of the establishment clause. Yes, you read that right. The defendant, Doe, felt they were being coerced to convert, I assume, by being in the church. Doe believed the establishment clause prohibits the government from conducting public functions such as high school graduation exercises in a church building, even if the function has no religious content and the government merely selected the church reasons of secular convenience.

Oh, it gets better. Doe also believed the government was still "coercing" religious activity in violation of *Lee v. Weisman* and *Santa Fe Independent School District v. Doe* by being merely exposed to religious symbols and that government "endorses" religion even when it engages in a religion-neutral action that incidentally exposes citizens to a private religious message. The petition for a *writ of certiorari* was denied. The appellate court's decision stood; Doe was saved from coercion.

But there is the issue that has caused apoplexy by originalists and conservatives. Instead of doing its job, the court has become the lawmaker, similar to the presidential "pens." Since *Brown*, and we will look at *Brown v. Board of Education, Topeka, Kansas,* the court has attempted to create a society they felt it should be, acting where the legislature—lawmaker!—should act.

The late justice Antonin Scalia, along with Justice Clarence Thomas, joined in a dissent they may put this issue into perspective. I will leave it with these two brilliant scholars of the Constitution.

> Some there are—many, perhaps—who are offended by public displays of religion. Religion, they believe, is a personal matter; if it must be given external manifestation, that should not occur in public places where others may be offended. I can understand that attitude: It parallels my own toward the playing in public of rock music or Stravinsky. And I too am especially annoyed when the intrusion upon my inner peace occurs while I am part of a captive audience, as on a municipal bus or in the waiting room of a public agency. My own aversion cannot be imposed by law because of the First Amendment. Certain of this Court's cases, however, have allowed the aversion to religious displays to be enforced directly through the First Amendment, at least in public facilities and with respect to public ceremonies—this despite the fact that the First Amendment explicitly favors religion and is, so to speak, agnostic about music.

Christmas, the twelve rules

Public school students' written or spoken personal expressions concerning the religious significance of Christmas (e.g., T-shirts with the slogan "Jesus is the Reason for the Season") may not be censored by school officials absent evidence that the speech would cause a substantial disruption.

As long as teachers are generally permitted to wear clothing or jewelry or have personal items expressing their views about the holidays, Christian teachers may not be prohibited from similarly expressing their views by wearing Christmas-related clothing or jewelry or carrying Christmas-related personal items.

Public schools may teach students about the Christmas holiday, including its religious significance, so long as it is taught objectively for secular purposes such as its historical or cultural importance, and not for the purpose of promoting Christianity.

Public school teachers may send Christmas cards to the families of their students so long as they do so on their own time, outside of school hours.

Public schools may include Christmas music, including those with religious themes, in their choral programs if the songs are included for a secular purpose such as their musical quality or cultural value or if the songs are part of an overall performance including other holiday songs relating to Chanukah, Kwanzaa, or other similar holidays.

Public schools may not require students to sing Christmas songs whose messages conflict with the students' own religious or nonreligious beliefs.

Public school students may not be prohibited from distributing literature to fellow students concerning the Christmas holiday or invitations to church Christmas events on the same terms that they would be allowed to distribute other literature that is not related to schoolwork.

Private citizens or groups may display crèches or other Christmas symbols in public parks subject to the same reasonable time, place, and manner restrictions that would apply to other similar displays.

Government entities may erect and maintain celebrations of the Christmas holiday, such as Christmas trees and Christmas light displays, and may include crèches in their displays at least so long as the purpose for including the crèche is not to promote its religious content and it is placed in context with other symbols of the holiday season as part of an effort to celebrate the public Christmas holiday through its traditional symbols.

Neither public nor private employers may prevent employees from decorating their offices for Christmas, playing Christmas music, or wearing clothing related to Christmas merely because of their religious content so long as these activities are not used to harass or intimidate others.

Public or private employees whose sincerely held religious beliefs require that they not work on Christmas must be reasonably accommodated by their employers unless granting the accommodation would impose an undue hardship on the employer.

Government recognition of Christmas as a public holiday and granting government employees a paid holiday for Christmas does not violate the establishment clause of the First Amendment.

The Pledge or National Anthem

Written in 1892 in celebration of Columbus Day, Francis Bellamy, a Socialist, published the Pledge in a youth magazine the *Youth's Companion*. It was accepted as a national pledge during WW II by the US government. However, even before the war challenges began. In 1940, in a case called *Minersville School District v. Gobitis*, SCOTUS, Supreme Court, said it could be required. Three years later, in *West Virginia State Board of Education v. Barnette*, SCOTUS changed its mind and ruled that requiring a person to say the pledge is in violation of the First and Fourteenth Amendments, if against one's religious beliefs.

When Pres. Dwight D. Eisenhower asks Congress to add "under God" to the Pledge the battles became angrier and more often. *Lipp v. Morris* ruled in 1978 that school officials in New Jersey violated the First Amendment when they punished a student for refusing to stand during the Pledge, but in 1992, the Seventh Circuit in Chicago said it was OK to make them in *Sherman v. Community Consolidated School District 21*.

The longest and most convoluted battle began in 1998 when Dr. Michael Newdow filed suit against the school board of Broward County (Florida) to get the phrase "under God" removed from the Pledge; his suit was dismissed for lack of standing. Sandy Banning, the mother of the girl, says that her daughter is not an atheist and has not been harmed by saying the pledge in school. When his daughter transferred in 2000 to the Elk Grove school system in California, he brought suit again. The Ninth Circuit Court of Appeals decided that reciting the Pledge in public schools is an unconstitutional "endorsement of religion" because of the phrase "under God." In 2004, the school appealed, and SCOTUS dismissed again because of Newdow not have legal standing.

Not one to give up, Newdow with eight coplaintiffs filed suit in a Sacramento national court seeking to remove "under God." Also in 2005, two cases, one on the East Coast, one on the West, contradicted each other. In the Fourth Circuit Court of Appeals, a Virginia law that requires public schools to recite the Pledge every day was upheld; it rejected a claim that its reference to God is an unconstitutional promotion of religion; the Pledge is not an affirmation of religion similar to a prayer but simply a patriotic exercise. This suit is raised by a father of three Edward Myers of Sterling, Virginia; he felt his children should not have to say "one nation under God." In Sacramento, reciting the Pledge in schools was ruled unconstitutional by US district judge Lawrence Karlton; he stated that the phrase "under God" violates the children's right to be "free from a coercive requirement to affirm God." And in 2009, in *Frazier v. Alexandre*, the eleventh Circuit Court of Appeals tried to compromise issuing a ruling that with a parents' written request, schools can excuse a student from reciting the pledge regardless of the student's personal beliefs.

Back to Newdow, now suing the Rio Linda Union School District, he loses his case to remove the words "under God" from the Pledge, and US money. Judge Carlos T. Bea writes, "The pledge is one of allegiance to our republic, not of allegiance to the God or to any religion."

The final word, I doubt it, came in 2014. Based on previous cases, the Supreme Judicial Court of Massachusetts, a similar case in New Jersey, ruled the Pledge does not discriminate against atheists, saying that the words "under God" represent a patriotic not a religious exercise.

WHAT IS DUE PROCESS OF LAW?

But where says some is the King of America? I'll tell you Friend, he reigns
above, and doth not make havoc of mankind like the Royal Brute of
Britain . . . let it be brought forth placed on the divine law, the word of
God . . . we approve of monarchy, that in America THE LAW IS KING.
—Tom Paine

DUE PROCESS IS mentioned twice in the Constitution:
the Fifth and the Fourteenth Amendments. The essence of
these two clauses is considered one of the most important ideas in the
Constitution. It has been the basis for many of the Supreme Court's
decisions limiting the authority of both national and state governments
to protect the basic rights of the people. There are two types of due
process: substantive and procedural. Each protects your rights to life,
liberty, and property though in different methods. Many of the original
protections of the Bill of Rights have been incorporated into state law
by the Fourteenth Amendment.

The due process clause of the Fourteenth Amendment says,

> . . . Nor shall any State deprive any person of life, liberty, or
> property, without due process of law . . .

That same clause appears in the Fifth Amendment. But the Fifth and
the rest of the Bill of Rights applied only to the national government. For
more than the first hundred years of the history of our nation, the Bill of
Rights was not applied to the acts of state governments. Gradually, after
the Fourteenth Amendment was approved, not ratified, this changed,
and today most of your protections under the Bill of Rights are also
protections imposed on state governments through interpretations of
the due process clause of that amendment.

What is due process of law?

It is impossible to give an exact definition of the phrase "due process of law." The term was first used in England in 1354, in a rewording of the Magna Carta. Its first use in America was the Constitution's Fifth Amendment as part of the wording recommended by James Madison. There was no discussion of its meaning at that time. The Supreme Court in the various cases that have come before it has interpreted it to mean, in a general sense, the right to be treated fairly by government. The due process clause, as interpreted by the courts, requires that the content of laws passed by legislatures be fair and reasonable. This is called "substantive due process." It also requires that the procedures for conducting hearings, collecting evidence, and enforcing and applying those laws be fair and reasonable. This is called "procedural due process."

There have been different ways the Supreme Court has interpreted the due process clauses when asked to decide whether the content of the laws is fair and reasonable. In other words, do the laws place an unfair burden or limitation on people's rights to life, liberty, or property? The Supreme Court has used the due process clause to attempt to ensure fairness in the procedures used by the executive and judicial branches in enforcing laws made by the legislatures. Art. I, 9, 3 forbids the use of laws that are passed and then used to punish previous offenders. These are *ex post facto* (after the fact); states are denied *ex post* powers under Art. I, 10, 1.

Property Rights

From the 1880s to the 1930s, the Supreme Court used the idea of substantive due process to protect the property rights of citizens from what it considered unreasonable and unfair treatment by state legislatures. The court's interest focused upon that phrase of the Fourteenth Amendment that says, ". . . Nor shall any State deprive any person of . . . property without due process of law." This emphasis, which lasted over fifty years, led to increasing conflicts and eventually the court changed its interpretation of the phrase.

During the late 1880s, America was changing drastically. Cities became a driving force in politics and law. Because of the rapid growth of American industry in large factories and mass production, many small craftsmen and merchants, Jeffersonians, were left behind, as were farmers and laborers. The farmers' interests were often endangered by large railroad companies, which controlled the cost of sending produce to market. The factory workers were often forced to work long hours, in dangerous conditions, for very low pay. Child labor in factories was common in some states.

To protect the interests of the farmers, laborers, and children, the state legislatures passed many laws. Some laws limited the rates the railroad owners could charge farmers for sending their products to market. Other laws required factory owners to improve working conditions, limited working hours, and established minimum wages. Laws were also passed outlawing or regulating child labor.

When the state legislatures passed these laws, they claimed they were promoting the common welfare of the people. Critics disagreed. They thought the best way to promote the common welfare was for government to leave the economy alone. This policy, you recall, was known by the French phrase *laissez-faire*. The people who supported *laissez-faire* argued that laws that regulated various forms of economic activity and working conditions did not promote the common welfare but instead furthered the interests of some groups at the expense of others. The laws, they claimed, protected the interests of farmers and laborers at the cost of violating the property rights of those who owned the railroads and factories, and the consumer. More specifically, these state laws violated the right to contract. All men should have the right to enter voluntary agreements without the extra power of the government on their side.

Many believed the growing pains of a free market would heal themselves. Child labor was fading as more Americans moved into the middle class. The market was raising wages faster than any time in history. The takeoff phase on a modern industrial, mass production, consumer-dominated society was right around the corner.

The Supreme Court from 1880 to 1937 was composed for the most part of justices who considered limitations on the market as unreasonable and unfair citizens' rights to property. They interpreted the due process clause of the Fourteenth Amendment in a way that found unconstitutional state laws enacted to limit working hours, establish minimum wages, regulate prices, and bar employers from firing workers for belonging to labor unions. For example, in 1905, the

Supreme Court declared a New York law unconstitutional because it limited the work week of bakery employees to sixty hours. It claimed that this was an unreasonable limitation on the freedom of contract. The court consistently found laws that limited people's property rights to be unconstitutional except in situations where it was convinced that the laws were absolutely necessary to protect public health or safety.

When the Supreme Court decides that a law is unreasonable and unfair and thus unconstitutional, the question is raised as to what is "reasonable" and "fair." The problem is that what one person thinks is reasonable and fair may be considered unreasonable and unfair by another person. Opinions on such matters often depend, at least in part, upon a person's knowledge and experience and upon the person's economic, social, and political views.

In a republic, elected members are supposed to be responsible for taking into account people's differing ideas of what is reasonable and fair when they pass and enforce laws that place limitations on your "life, liberty and property" to protect the common welfare. Critics of the Supreme Court have often argued that when the court decides that its interpretation of what is reasonable and fair is correct and that a law passed by a state legislature is unreasonable and unfair, it is acting like a "super legislature." The critics claim that in our system, the Congress and state legislatures have the responsibility to decide what the nation's economic policies should be rather than the Supreme Court. As a result of political and economic changes and new appointments to the Supreme Court, the court stopped holding laws regulating property rights and the economy unconstitutional under the due process clause.

During the 1930s, the Supreme Court began to interpret the due process clause of the Fourteenth Amendment in another important way, an expansive and unconstitutional way. This change occurred for two specific reasons. The first, FDR threatened to remake the court by adding another member after a justice reached the age of seventy. This would allow him to place, with Senate confirmation of course, six more justices up to a panel of fifteen. This would give him a majority of Progressives, and the "Conservatives" would no longer have "pro-property" control. The second was the movement of the Democratic Party joining the Republican Party in believing in the Progressive movement of government as the solution to society's problems. For the last eighty years, these two parties have been the right wing (Republicans) and the left wing (Democrats) of the same bird, a hovering vulture. It reminds me of Latin American banana republics; two groups of elites alternating the chains of power over the population with a façade of democratic voting and choice.

This change focused on the meaning of the words ". . . nor shall any state deprive any person of . . . liberty . . . without due process of law . . ." The court's attention had shifted to concern with the civil liberties of the people, and the property clause lost its equality. Using the popularity of Progressive largesse to the voters, something that will explode in the years to come, the word "liberty" in the due process clause of the Fourteenth Amendment has been interpreted by the court to include, gradually, almost all the rights guaranteed in the first eight amendments of the Bill of Rights. The process of making these rights apply to state governments is called incorporation. In this process, the various rights contained in the Bill of Rights have been held to be incorporated, one by one, into the Fourteenth Amendment and therefore applicable to the states. Controversy arose, and continues today, over how this section of the due process clause should be interpreted. John Marshall and Hamilton, the Federalists, the Whigs, the Republicans, and today's Democrats would be proud.

> The subject is the execution of those great powers on which the welfare of a nation essentially depends . . . This provision is made in a Constitution intended to endure for ages to come and, consequently, to be adapted to the various crisis of human affairs (*McCulloch v. Maryland*, 1819).

What rights?

Most of the disagreements involve the meaning of the individual rights listed in the Bill of Rights and the extent to which they can be limited by Congress or state legislatures. Like most of the Constitution's clauses, the individual rights listed need to be interpreted. For example, the First Amendment contains the statement that "Congress shall make no law . . . abridging the freedom of speech . . ." What is meant by "speech"? Is wearing black armbands to protest a war a form of speech? Do laws that prevent people from using loudspeakers to advertise in neighborhoods at night violate free speech? Does the protection of freedom of religion mean that the state cannot control any religious practices?

These are the kinds of questions that arise in deciding whether laws made by Congress and state legislatures violate the protections of your rights listed in the Bill of Rights. Ultimately, these questions are decided in the Supreme Court. Can the court create rights, ones the Framers would not have thought of? Cloning? Sex changes? What bathrooms one may use?

Among the rights that have been protected by decisions of SCOTUS under the due process clause is the right to travel to foreign countries, even though it is not a right specifically listed in the Bill of Rights. The Supreme Court has found laws passed by Congress restricting that right to be unconstitutional. In a 1958 case, Justice William Douglas stated,

> The right to travel is a part of the "liberty" of which the citizen cannot be deprived without due process of law under the Fifth Amendment . . . In Anglo-Saxon law that right was emerging at least as early as the Magna Charta . . . Freedom of movement across frontiers in either direction, and inside frontiers as well, was a part of our heritage . . . It may be as close to the heart of the individual as the choice of what he eats, or wears, or reads. Freedom of movement is basic in our scheme of values . . . Our nation . . . has thrived on the principle that, outside areas of plainly harmful conduct, every American is left to shape his own life as he thinks best, do what he pleases, go where he pleases.

Let's take procedural due process first. This includes searches, arrests, trial procedures, punishments. Many lawyers today complain that because of television crime dramas, many jurors know too much wrong information on due process. Procedural due process is the requirement that the procedures used by your national and state governments be reasonable and fair. The requirements of procedural due process apply in some degree to all the branches and functions of government. However, I'll focus specifically on one of their most important applications—that is, to criminal procedures. By showing how these procedural protections might apply to you, I hope to increase your understanding of their importance as part of your rights to life, liberty, and property.

The Founders knew, and we see it daily, that throughout history, governments had used their power to enforce criminal laws in ways that had violated the most basic rights of citizens. This was a lesson they had learned from long and painful experience in both England and in the colonies. The criminal law had often been used as a political weapon. This frequently results in punishment of the innocent and unfair and inhumane treatment of the guilty. For this reason, the Framers included in the Constitution and the Bill of Rights several rights that were specific limitations designed to prevent the possible abuse of power by government. These limitations are safeguards to protect long-accepted ideas of human freedom, privacy, and dignity from the kinds of attacks they had been subjected to by past governments.

And with the Fourteenth Amendment, most of the procedural protections guaranteed to you by the Constitution and Bill of Rights, which originally applied only to the central government, now apply to state governments as well. These protections, taken together, are called procedural due process or due process of law. To understand their importance, let's see how they protect you.

Suppose you are suspected of a crime, arrested, imprisoned while awaiting trial, tried, convicted, and sentenced to prison by a court. What rights are guaranteed to you under the Constitution at each step of that process? How did these rights come to receive the protection of the Constitution? And what is their importance to you and the rest of society? Remember these rights are not given to you by the government; rather, they are God-given. The limits on government behavior is to prevent them from taking away these rights.

You are suspected of a crime

Suppose a law enforcement officer suspects you of having committed a crime. How does the right to due process of law protect you from unfair treatment? The Fourth Amendment guarantees that law enforcement officers cannot search you or your property, arrest you, or take your property unless they can show a good reason for doing so.

This amendment has been interpreted to mean that, except in certain emergencies where they must act quickly, law enforcement officers, actually any agent of the government, TSA, DHS, a school principal, must get the permission of a judge (in the form of a warrant) to search you or your property, arrest you, or take your property. Further, the judge can only give this permission if the police officer can present reasonable evidence that you may be guilty of a crime and can describe the evidence being sought, probable cause. As you can imagine, applying these protections in specific situations can lead to considerable disagreement over such questions as to whether a search or arrest is "reasonable." Many cases decided by the court try to make sense of when and when not you can be arrested or searched without a warrant. No warrants are required for movable vehicles, or a protective sweep, but only for dangerous persons. Those on parole and probation, or those who are stopped and frisked (Terry Search) are not protected as strongly by the Fourth. For the protection of police or possible victims in immediate danger, warrants are seen as impractical. Evidence in plain view or thrown away is also fair game; no need to search if it can be seen.

The prohibition against unreasonable searches has a long history in English and colonial experience. It dates back to the seventeenth and eighteenth centuries when judges placed restrictions on the right of police to search people and their homes. The judges had decided this right was necessary when they learned that police had been unreasonable and unfair in searching the homes and meeting places of people with unpopular political and religious beliefs. In the last years of the colonial period, there was a public outcry against searches made by British troops, which had been made possible by the detested general warrants known as "writs of assistance." The main purpose of the Fourth Amendment was to place strict limits on the issuing of search warrants by judges, yet recently the courts have leaned more toward the police and used weak excuses to do so: national security, terrorism, for example.

James Otis, Mercy Otis Warren's brother, is considered the "father of the Fourth Amendment." Otis fought for decades the British use of "blanket search warrants," the writs of assistance; they allowed customs officials to enter any business or home without advance notice, probable cause, or reason. Otis stated in defiance that they were unconstitutional.

Otis worked for the Crown in a vice admiralty court, primarily prosecuting smuggling. Otis changed from prosecutor to defense attorney, resigned, and began representing Boston merchants at no cost. In a case he lost, he spoke for over five hours on the violation of the natural rights of man to be secure in his own home. Sadly, he died before his ideal of freedom in one's home was added as the Fourth Amendment.

Today the words of James Otis seem to be mute as the fourth Amendment gets chipped away in a digital no-place-to-hide world. He believed we "are by the law of nature free born." Government, according to Jefferson later, was to secure rights, to provide for the security, the quiet and happy enjoyment of life, liberty, and property.

> Can there be any liberty where property is taken away without consent? . . . A man's house is his castle; and whilst he is quiet, he is as well guarded as a prince in his castle. This writ [of assistance] . . . would totally annihilate this privilege. Custom-house officers [police] may enter our houses when they please . . . break . . . everything in their way; and whether they break through malice or revenge, no man, no court may inquire . . . Everyone [any government] with this writ [power] may be a tyrant . . . [Even] if every prince . . . had been a tyrant, it would not prove a right to tyrannize. There can be no prescription old enough to supersede the law of nature, and the grand of God almighty; who has given to all men a natural right to be free. Tyranny of all kinds is to be abhorred . . .

When the Framers placed the protection against "unreasonable searches and seizures" in the Constitution, they could not know of the technological advances that would allow government agents to engage in search methods such as electronic eavesdropping on conversations, drones, or e-mail scanning. Yet the basics are still fundamental. A reasonable search still must be with a warrant, based on probable cause, signed by a judge and specific to what searched for, where searching, and for what purpose searched.

What is "probable cause"? A mere gut feeling, suspicious? How about seeing a police officer and walking the other way? In March 2017, the Supreme Court of Kansas allowed a search because a kid slouched down in the seat of his car. John Whitehead surmises that you can be stopped for any reason.

> The ruling in *State v. Howard* follows in the wake of other court rulings in recent years upholding warrantless searches and seizures by police for such "suspicious" behavior as having acne scars, driving with a stiff upright posture, having car windows that are too heavily tinted, driving too fast, driving too slow, failing to maintain speed, following too closely, improper lane changes, distracted driving, screeching a car's tires, leaving a parked car door open for too long, avoiding a traffic light by driving through a parking lot, driving near a bar or on a road that has large amounts of drunk driving, driving a certain make of car (Mercedes, Grand Prix and Hummers are among the most ticketed vehicles), having anything dangling from the rearview mirror (air fresheners, handicap parking permits, troll transponders or rosaries), or displaying pro-police bumper stickers.

The Supreme Court has dealt with such changes by interpreting your due process protections to mean that you should be given reasonable protections against government eavesdropping. For example, the Supreme Court has ruled that the police must get a warrant before they can tap your phone and listen to your conversations, but that warrant may be secret. DNA samples, cell phone listening, and pat down searches at airports are continual struggles.

Evidence that is gotten illegally by the police is to be excluded in a trial. This goes back to *Weeks v. the United States* in 1914. Fremont Weeks was using the mail for a lottery. The police searched his room, obtained papers, and took letters and envelopes without a search warrant. The court praised the police for bringing guilty people to punishment; but as privacy is a fundamental right, that evidence, though necessary, should have meant the police knew it essential. To allow private documents to be seized and then held as evidence against citizens would have meant that the protection of the Fourth Amendment declaring the right to be secure against such searches and seizures would be of no value whatsoever. This was the first application of what eventually became known as the "exclusionary rule."

The key issue in many cases is what is "unreasonable." Blood tests are reasonable, but pumping a stomach for swallowed evidence goes too far? Anything illegally searched or seized cannot be used. But . . . there's the "good faith exception," the "inevitable discovery rule," and the "no knock rule" if they believe one is in danger or a danger to others. In the "good faith exception," if police make mistakes if they accidentally, say, go to 305, instead of 503, and discover illegal evidence, that evidence is not excluded; it's a reasonable search. With the "inevitable," the court stretches even further. If the evidence would have been found with a warrant, then the search is reasonable. Then get the warrant! The "no knock" emerged in the "war" on drugs in which police feared evidence of drug use, possession, production, selling could be destroyed by Billy as Johnny answers the door and checks the warrant. Battering rams and SWAT teams can enforce the Constitution better this way.

Do you have a right to see the warrant? Well, the Fourth Amendment was applied (incorporated) to the states in *Mapp v. Ohio* (1961) on this very issue. Dorlee Mapp supposedly had information about a suspected bomber. Police knocked, she asked for a warrant, they handed her a piece of paper, she shoved it into her bra, and they retrieved it. Yet no piece of paper was produced for her or at trial. In the search, the police found pornographic materials that were used against Mapp at trial for child abuse. The court ruled the Fourth Amendment was applicable to state searches; the "exclusionary rule" applies to states by the Fourteenth Amendment.

There have been many recent additions to warrantless searches. School searches to control drugs and students' behaviors have become easier for staff. Phone taps, both wired and wireless, are less protected since 9/11; garbage can be searched for evidence by police. But most disturbing is the current policy because of homeland "security," the Foreign Intelligence Surveillance Act (1978) allowed warrants to be issued after the evidence found. The Protect America Act of 2007 allows wiretapping calls that originate in or end in a foreign country without FISA court approval. What about facial recognition scanners at stop lights? GPS locating to track someone's driving and stopping behaviors? iPhones turning themselves on the "listen in" on private conversations? Edward Snowden's leaking made us aware of the government collecting "metadata" on every purchase, e-mail, phone call, Facebook comments, likes, check-ins, IRS, postal service, drones, iris scans, drive-by scanners that hear into your home. WHAT FOURTH AMENDMENT? But Justice Anthony Kennedy stated what James Otis stated two hundred years ago, "Someone arrested for a minor crime has their whole existence exposed."

As I write this, a blip on the screen caused me to stop and read. Excerpts from this article copied and pasted below, written by a recent high school graduate Olivia Donaldson for FEE.org, could not summarize the current situation better. Thanks, Olivia!

Imagine you are in the middle of your typical day-to-day activities. Maybe you are driving, spending time with family, or working. If you are like most people, your phone is at your side on a daily basis. Little do you know that, at any time, police and law enforcement could be looking at information stored on your phone. You haven't done anything wrong. You haven't been asked for permission. You aren't suspected of any crime.

Police have the power to collect your location along with the numbers of your incoming and outgoing calls and intercept the content of call and text communication. They can do all of this without you ever knowing about it.

How? They use a shoebox-sized device called a StingRay. This device (also called an IMSI catcher) mimics cell phone towers, prompting all the phones in the area to connect to it even if the phones aren't in use.

The police use StingRays to track down and implicate perpetrators of mainly domestic crimes. The devices can be mounted in vehicles, drones, helicopters, and airplanes, allowing police to gain highly specific information on the location of any particular phone, down to a particular apartment complex or hotel room.

Quietly, StingRay use is growing throughout local and federal law enforcement with little to no oversight. The ACLU has discovered that at least 68 agencies in 23 different states own StingRays, but says that this "dramatically underrepresents the actual use of StingRays by law enforcement agencies nationwide."

Information from potentially thousands of phones is being collected every time a StingRay is used. Signals are sent into the homes, bags, and pockets of innocent individuals. The Electronic Frontier Foundation likens this to the Pre-Revolutionary War practice of soldiers going door-to-door, searching without suspicion.

Richard Tynan, a technologist with Privacy International notes that, "there really isn't any place for innocent people to hide from a device such as this."

The StingRay clearly violates [Fourth Amendment] standards. The drafters of the Constitution recognized that restricting the government from violating privacy is essential for a free society. That's why the Fourth Amendment exists. The StingRay is creating a dangerous precedent that tells the government that it's okay for them to violate our rights. Because of this, freedom is quietly slipping out the window.

Law Enforcement is using StingRays without a warrant in most cases. For example, the San Bernardino Police Department used their StingRay 300 times without a warrant in a little over a year.

In 2010, the Tallahassee Police Department used a StingRay in a warrantless search to track down the suspect of a crime. A testimony from an unsealed hearing transcript talks about how police went about finding their target. The ACLU sums it up well:

> Police drove through the area using the vehicle-based device until they found the apartment complex in which the target phone was located, and then they walked around with the handheld device and stood "at every door and every window in that complex" until they figured out which apartment the phone was located in. In other words, police were lurking outside people's windows and sending powerful electronic signals into their private homes in order to collect information from within.

A handful of states have passed laws requiring police and federal agents to get a warrant before using a StingRay. They must show probable cause for one of the thousands of phones that they are actually searching. This is far from enough.

Additionally, there are many concerns that agents are withholding information from federal judges to monitor subjects without approval—bypassing the probable cause standard laid out in the Constitution. They even go as far as to let criminals go to avoid disclosing information about these devices to the courts.

If the public doesn't become aware of this issue, the police will continue to use StingRays to infringe on our rights in secret and with impunity.

Many seem to welcome this attack on rights. Ironically, the Patriot Act of 2001, extended in 2011, 2015, until 2019, gives authorization of indefinite detentions of immigrants; the permission given law enforcement officers to search a home or business without the owner's or the occupant's consent or knowledge; the expanded use of National Security Letters, which allows the Federal Bureau of Investigation (FBI) to search telephone, e-mail, and financial records without a court order; and the expanded access of law enforcement agencies to business records, including library and financial records, and forbids a citizen from telling someone you got one of these self-written warrants. We'll address other portions of this law under freedom of expression. But without reservation, the Patriot Act is the worst law since the Alien and Sedition Acts of John Adams.

The National Security Agency, the FBI, even our local police know more about us than our families. The NSA, with Apple, Google, Twitter, surveilles and reports on us 24/7. Every credit card purchase, all banking and finance activities, they know.

Edward Snowden is an American computer professional, former CIA employee who copied and leaked classified information from the National Security Agency in 2013. These revealed numerous global surveillance programs, many run by the NSA with the cooperation of telecommunication companies and governments. He is, as I type, living in asylum someplace in Russia. Snowden is called a hero, a whistle-blower, a dissident, a traitor, and a patriot.

Edward Snowden believed that the government fundamentally "had noble intents," as did the American people. However, admitting he was naïve, he came to believe the upper echelons of government and the corruption and hubris toward the Constitution and against those that defend it led him to do what he did—whistle blow on mass surveillance programs.

Snowden insists that the importance of the citizen in having the right to know and understand the policies that govern us—namely, one in particular, surveillance—and that this right is vital to our democratic functioning. Most of Congress knew nothing about the programs maintained and instituted; nor was the Senate and House fully briefed on covert actions. He points out the political unwillingness, post 9/11, to confront difficult questions about what was right and wrong in this regard. Why didn't the public have the opportunity to participate in debate about their security and well-being? Why were top officials unaware of this? Only a small handful of officials knew of these ongoing policies. These actions by those making the decisions have "essentially degraded our society. Our democratic processes have eroded away, not allowing us to know about the *issues,* let alone policy that is still being engaged in . . . We have lost the freedom to associate with our judgement. And that in itself, is where the real danger rests."

And today, March 7, 2017, the most unbelievable happened. Julian Assange of *WikiLeaks* released "Vault 7," nearly nine thousand documents revealing even more than Snowden's revelation. Included were programs to make what they were doing was "Russian hacking." *Umbrage* covered spying on cell phones, smart TVs, wireless routers that had malware installed, turning these devices into microphones even when powered off! Fourth Amendment be damned! "Collecting evidence" was shared around the room when "interesting" or "funny" conversations were found. The epitome of invasion of privacy, and all done without court-issued warrants. And as judge, jury, and executioner, literally, CIA has the ability to take control of a vehicle's computer system and "assassinating" without being present.

You've been arrested and taken to jail

Your arrest, like searches, are covered the same under the Fourth Amendment. But once arrested, it is the Sixth Amendment guarantees you the right to know why you have been arrested; it contains the "notice clause," which says that you must be informed of the "nature and cause of the accusation" for which you have been arrested. The main purpose of this protection is to give you the information necessary to answer the charges and to prepare to defend yourself. The Sixth also guarantees you the right to have a lawyer help you answer the accusation and your rights through the courts. It guarantees you the right to the "assistance of counsel" for the defense in front of judge or jury later. If you are like most people, you probably know a little about the law, or about the rights, you are entitled to while being held in jail, or about court procedures, such as those that deal with examining witnesses. You would be at a great disadvantage trying to answer charges against you even if you were innocent and had been arrested by mistake.

Until about fifty years ago, the right to counsel was interpreted to mean that you were merely free to hire a lawyer to help you if you wanted one. Since that time, the Supreme Court has interpreted the right to counsel to mean that if you are accused of a crime and are too poor to hire a lawyer, the government must provide one at public expense to represent you at all stages of the criminal proceeding. It was an appeal by a poor serial criminal, Clarence Earl Gideon, in Florida. He was arrested for a minor offense, breaking and entering a poolroom. Without assistance at the trial, something he asked for numerous times, he was convicted and because of his record got five years! From the prison library, he penciled his request for the court to change its mind and force all states to give adequate defense to all. In 1963, SCOTUS 9-0 stated that the Sixth Amendment applied to the states in regard to assistance of counsel.

Recently, funding has been short at both the state and national levels for public defenders. Wait time for a competent lawyer can be six to eight months, while innocent citizens languish in jails all over the country. One extreme example is in Colorado, where eighty thousand accused wait for disgustingly overburdened 370 public defenders. Due process? Not hardly!

The Fifth Amendment guarantees that you have the right to remain silent both at the time of your arrest and throughout your trial. This right protects you from being forced to give evidence against yourself. It is contained in the "privilege against self-incrimination clause," which says that a person cannot be "compelled in any criminal case to be a witness against himself." The right has its origins in the English common law system dating back at least to the 1500s. The Framers knew that throughout history, it had been common practice to torture people to make them confess to crimes. Even if you were innocent, you might confess to a crime if you were tortured or given the "third degree." This protection also reflects the belief that even if you were guilty, you should be treated with dignity and not be subjected to cruel and inhumane treatment by your government. The cases of *Escobedo* and *Miranda* in the early 1960s guaranteed your rights to attorneys while questioned and gave responsibility to the government to remind of these rights.

Suppose you think that the police have arrested you without having a good reason for doing so, that they are keeping you in jail unfairly, or that they have denied you one of your other basic rights to due process. What can you do? Article I, Section 9 of the Constitution guarantees you the right to have a judge hear your story and decide if you are being treated unfairly.

This guarantees you the protection of the writ of habeas corpus, or the "Great Writ of Liberty" as it was known by the Framers. This protection, included in the Magna Carta, has its origins in the English common law and is considered one of the most important safeguards of freedom in the British and American governmental systems. It means that if you are being held in jail, you or someone acting for you may get an order from a court requiring the police to take you to court so you can argue before a judge that you have been unfairly arrested and should be set free. The police would have to present the evidence they had against you to the judge to justify their actions. If the judge agreed with you, you would be set free. If not, you would be held for trial.

The purpose of habeas corpus is to protect you from being held in jail for a long time without being tried and convicted. The Framers knew that it was a common practice for governments to arrest people and put them in jail without ever giving them a fair trial. Today, the writ has also been interpreted to protect you if you have been convicted and are being held in a state or US prison and can argue that your conviction had been unfairly obtained. It gives you the right to have a judge review your case to see if you have been treated unfairly. It is not guaranteed during times of "rebellion or invasion"; nor does it seem to be for those suspected of "terrorism." Many suspected terrorists have been held in secret prisons since the 9/11 bombings.

The National Defense Authorization Act of 2012 allows the president to hold "enemies of the state" indefinitely. Hidden deep in subsections 1021–1022 of Title X, Subtitle D, titled "Counter-Terrorism," the president as commander in chief is authorized to indefinitely detain under military arrest persons the government suspects, not convicts, of involvement in terrorism, including US citizens arrested on American soil. Although President Obama and the Senate maintain that the Authorization for Use of Military Force (AUMF) already grants presidential authority for indefinite detention, the act states that Congress "affirms" this authority and makes specific provisions as to the exercise of that authority. The detention provisions of the act were appealed but dismissed on a technicality, thus the president's power still exists under NDAA.

There are two other issues that relate to unfair detention in violation of habeas corpus. The first is the government using the expense of proving innocence or the fear of "longer" sentences to gain plea agreements and convictions. Unfortunately, this has filled jails with innocent people. The other is police confiscation of property of arrestees before trial, without trial, and even of the innocent.

At trial

The right to trial, we'll look at shortly, is the most important difference between tyranny and the American system of justice, at least traditionally. Today many trials never "go to trial." Costs and the desire for convictions have caused many district attorneys and US prosecutors to plea bargain; nine out of ten national and state criminal defendants now end their cases by pleading guilty. Many will say, "Great. It decreases caseload for stretched judges, saves the taxpayers money, gets the bad guys off the streets." But in recent years, many US prosecutors threaten defendants by offering them shorter prison terms if they plead guilty. Sometimes they will state that the costs of defense and time to get to and through the trial will bankrupt most defendants. Or they will exaggerate that if there is a trial, the sentence may be "so excessively severe, they take your breath away." The average sentence in national drug cases was sixteen years at trial, while five years and four months for plea bargainers. Such abuse and violations of due process, especially in drug cases, have filled jails with the innocent.

Recently, the issue of civil asset forfeiture has emerged as a major concern of the new presidency of Donald Trump and his attorney general, Jeff Sessions. The original idea was to prevent big drug lords and other from using their resources to buy judges, bribe juries, or escape the country. It was presented to the legislatures as a way to "handcuff" large-scale criminal enterprises by confiscation of their resources. But today, aided by unconstitutional national and state laws, many national and states police departments use civil asset forfeiture to pad their budgets, seizing property when arresting but not returning at acquittal; many times it has been sold and money deposited into department coffers. To regain one's property, the costs and time are prohibitive. In 2015, according to the Institute for Justice, the Treasury and Justice departments deposited more than $5 billion into their respective asset forfeiture funds. That same year, the FBI reports that burglary losses topped out at $3.5 billion. The Treasury Inspector General for Tax Administration (TIGTA) reports 91 percent of IRS asset confiscation were innocent or were never charged. When the leading thief is the guy that's supposed to protect us from theft, time for a new sheriff. In April 2017, the court finally began to stop this in a Colorado case, *Nelson v. Colorado*, under Fourteenth Amendment due process clause.

In poor nations, police may stop your car for a "missing headlight" and ask for *la mordida*, a bite, a bribe, his lunch money. Or a busload of tourists will be pulled over because of a "faulty" brake light, each will contribute five pesos. I myself had to pay one hundred pesos to have a secretary at the American embassy to retype a border pass to reenter the US in the 1980s. George Will shared an example of how bad it's become in the United States. In a December 2016, he related a case that began a nightmare for one family in 2014 Philadelphia.

> The [Chris and Markela] Sourovelises' son, who lived at home, was arrested for selling a small amount of drugs [$40] away from home. Soon there was a knock on their door by police who said, "We're here to take your house" and "You're going to be living on the street" and "We do this every day." The Sourovelises' doors were locked with screws and their utilities were cut off. They had paid off the mortgage on their

$350,000 home, making it a tempting target for policing for profit. Nationwide, proceeds from sales of seized property (homes, cars, etc.) go to the seizers. And under a federal program, state and local law enforcement can partner with federal authorities in forfeiture and reap up to 80 percent of the proceeds. This is called—more Orwellian newspeak— "equitable sharing." No crime had been committed in the Sourovelises' house, but the title of the case against them was *Commonwealth of Pennsylvania v. 12011 Ferndale Street*. Somehow, a crime had been committed by the house. In civil forfeiture, it suffices that property is suspected of having been involved in a crime. Once seized, the property's owners bear the burden of proving their property's innocence. [At this point, the home, the case, is still unresolved!]

In *Honeycutt v. United States* (2017), the court finally said asset forfeiture is limited to property the defendant himself actually acquired as the result of the crime only, not friends or family not related to the crime. Honeycutt never received any property as a result of the crime, thus cannot lose his property because of his brother's crimes.

OK, let's get back to the trial. Suppose after you have been arrested, a judge decides that there is enough evidence that you may be guilty to justify holding you for trial. What rights do you have? The right to an attorney continues; also self-incrimination still pertains. The Eighth Amendment guarantees the right to be free on reasonable bail while you wait for your trial.

It says that "excessive bail shall not be required." This idea has a long history in English common law dating back to the Magna Carta. It was a part of the legal tradition that the colonists brought from England. Bail is an amount of money left with the court to guarantee that an accused person will return to court to be tried. It is an attempt to reduce the harm done by imprisonment between arrest and trial. Such imprisonment may punish in advance someone who is eventually found innocent, may cause someone to lose a job or be unable to fulfill family duties, and may make it more difficult to prepare a defense.

The "right to bail" is limited to those who can afford to pay the amount set by the court, which is not considered "excessive" or unreasonable if it is the amount normally charged for a particular offense. If you don't have the money for bail, you may have to remain in jail until your trial. Also, if a judge decides, for example, that you would not show up for your trial or that if you were free you might endanger others, you might be refused the right to be set free on bail. Two groups have consistently been denied bail by the courts, juveniles and gangsters, terrorists, and gang members.

The Sixth Amendment adds a guarantee to a speedy and public trial in the area where accused. This serves two purposes. First, it protects you from being kept in jail for a long time even though you have not been convicted, habeas corpus. Second, it protects you from being tried in secret where members of government might treat you unfairly and no one would ever know about it. The Framers knew that governments had used secret trials to unfairly convict people of crimes for which they probably would not have been convicted in a public trial by a jury of their peers.

The Framers knew that the right to a trial by jury was one of the greatest protections from unfair treatment by the king and his judges that the people of England had developed. In England, the jury was traditionally made up of twelve persons selected from the community at large; they were not members of the government. Juries are mentioned in the Constitution four times. The purpose of a jury trial is to provide an unprejudiced group to determine the facts and to provide fair judgments about guilt or innocence. Requiring a jury trial is a way of making sure that the criminal justice system is democratic and involves citizens of the community. The Constitution forbids Bills of Attainder wherein lawmakers could punish whom they feel to be offenders with legislation, not a trial. Juries are also empowered to judge the law itself; juries may challenge the constitutionality of the laws themselves.

The Sixth Amendment guarantees you the right to be confronted with the witnesses against you. Suppose a secret informer tells the police you committed a crime but that person is not required to face you and your lawyer in court. You don't know who the person is and have no chance to challenge the accusation. You and your lawyer must have the right to face and question anyone who has given evidence against you that may be used to convict you. The amendment also guarantees you the right to compel witnesses to testify in your favor. Suppose you know someone who knows something that might help you with your case or who even might have evidence to show you are innocent, but the person won't testify for you for one reason or another. Thus, you might be convicted of a crime you didn't commit. This right says that in such situations, the government must do everything it can to bring witnesses who may be in your favor to court to testify for you. The court will issue a subpoena on your behalf for the witness to appear.

You have been convicted of a crime

The Eighth Amendment guarantees that you may not be subjected to cruel and unusual punishment. This protection has been interpreted to mean that the punishment shall not be "barbaric." Such punishments as branding or whipping are prohibited. The punishment shall not be "excessive." For example, you cannot be given, as happened in the past, the death sentence for stealing a loaf of bread. The court has recently decided that capital punishment and even life for juveniles is excessive. Yet in the case of Marvin Williams in Texas, the court allowed the state to decide what it considers "mental disability."

The Fifth Amendment guarantees you the right to be free from being tried again for the same crime. The protection against "double jeopardy" is the oldest of the procedural protections that were included in the Constitution. It has its roots in ancient Greek and Roman law, it is in English common law, and it is found in the laws of many nations. It is intended to prevent the government from abusing its power by trying you again and again for the same crime of which you have been found innocent. To allow the government to do this would be to subject you to continued embarrassment, expense, anxiety, and insecurity, and the possibility of eventually being found guilty even though you are innocent. The protection against double jeopardy also protects you, if you have been found guilty, from being punished more than once for the same crime.

Controversies over procedural due process have not been over the rightness or wrongness of the basic rights themselves but rather over how they should be interpreted and applied. The court's interpretations of these rights show how it has tried, under changing and often difficult circumstances, to balance your rights as an individual against the responsibility of government to protect all of us from people who break the law and who may endanger our lives, liberty, or property. Since the protection of your individual rights is the main purpose of constitutional government, the problem of balancing these interests is one of the most difficult problems of a limited government.

While controversy remains over the interpretation and extent of particular rights and how they are to be protected, all justices have agreed that fairness in the procedures by which a person is accused and tried for a crime is a cornerstone of our constitutional democracy. The guarantees of procedural fairness or justice are among the most important of your rights contained in the Constitution and Bill of Rights.

In *In re Gault* (1967) [*in re* is Latin for "in reference to"], juveniles were guaranteed the rights of trial. Prior to this time, many states assumed control over juveniles more as parents than as government and assumed that juveniles were the "property" of their parents. Two boys were arrested for making prank calls. Parents were not notified of the arrests, charges, or where the boys were being held. There were no records kept of the proceedings. Charges were dropped against one of the boys who was moving out of state. The woman receiving the calls never appeared as a witness. In addition, Gault received tougher sentence than an adult. The court felt that juvenile courts ruled like "kangaroo courts." Adding to *Gault*, in 1970, the court's decision of *In re Winship* added the concept to the juvenile due process of "beyond a reasonable doubt." Samuel Winship, twelve, had already been labeled a juvenile delinquent when he was again arrested for stealing $112 from a woman's pocketbook. The trial court used a "preponderance of the evidence," a civil law legality. The judge in his case acknowledged the evidence did not establish his guilt beyond a reasonable doubt, but he "must have done it because he was that type of kid."

Some scholars have said that procedural due process is the "keystone of liberty." Others have called it the "heart of the law." Some scholars have said that the degree of due process protections a nation provides for its citizens is an important indicator of whether the nation has a constitutional government or an autocratic or dictatorial government.

What if the juvenile is a repeat offender, one who knows the system? Morris Kent, sixteen, who had been on probation since he was fourteen for burglary and theft, was arrested and charged with three home burglaries, three robberies, and two counts of rape in Washington DC. Because of the seriousness of the charges and Morris's previous criminal history, the prosecutor asked to waive him to adult court. His attorney wanted his case tried in juvenile court, where the penalties were much less severe; he had planned to argue that Morris had a mental illness that should be taken into account when deciding where he would be tried. Without a hearing, the judge sided with the prosecutor and sent Morris to adult court, where he was found guilty and sentenced to thirty to ninety years in prison. Morris appealed, arguing that the case should have remained in juvenile court.

The court in *Kent v. Morris* (1966) ruled against Morris and said that a minor can be tried and punished as an adult. However, the decision stated that in deciding whether to remove a case from juvenile court, judges must weigh a variety of factors, including the seriousness of the crime, the juvenile's age, and the defendant's criminal background and mental state. How the courts treat juveniles in the legal system varies from state to state. In many states, those under eighteen can be tried as adults for crimes such as murder, sexual assault, or possession or sale of drugs, with punishments that range up to life in prison without the possibility of parole. In 2005, the Supreme Court abolished the death penalty for juvenile offenders, saying it violated the Eighth Amendment's protection against "cruel and unusual punishments."

DUE PROCESS: EQUAL PROTECTION OF THE LAWS

If you're not ready to die for it, put the word
"freedom" out of your vocabulary.
—Malcolm X

THE FOURTEENTH AMENDMENT to the Constitution was ratified in 1868, just after the Civil War. The equal protection clause of this amendment has become the most important protection in the Constitution used to prevent unfair discrimination against people by the national and state governments. Equal protection is substantive due process; is the law itself fair? The history of the attempt to use this clause is filled with conflict. Is it equal opportunity, equal results? What's equal, or equity? The courts in recent years have seemingly resulted in abolishing a great deal of discrimination in our society; however, many believe the courts have often gone too far in their attempts to correct the effects of past discrimination.

The civil rights movement was a long, primarily nonviolent struggle for one people, brown, fighting to join the experiment, the American dream. The movement has had a lasting impact on United States society, in its tactics, the increased social and legal acceptance of civil rights, and in its exposure of the persistence and costs of racism in two ways. First, in denying the qualified to join the dream but, in addition, denying the dream their qualities.

Discrimination?

Before looking at the history of the equal protection clause, take a look at the following examples of discrimination. Each illustrates an issue involving the equal protection clause that has been dealt with by the national courts. Explain which of these examples of discrimination by a government you think should be considered unconstitutional.

1. Your state has a law that says that you and all students of your race must go to separate schools from the other students in your community.
2. Your city has an ordinance saying that you and your family cannot live in certain sections of town because of your religious beliefs.
3. Your state has a law saying that you can only marry someone of the same race.
4. Your state passes a family law that unwed fathers cannot gain custody of their children if mother passes away.
5. Your city fire department will not hire you because you are a woman.
6. You and a friend of the opposite sex work for the state and do the same type and amount of work. Yet you discover that you are paid considerably less than your friend.
7. A ban has been put in place profiting entry to a group of people.
8. You are a member of the local school board, and the board voted to deny access to bathroom based on the self-identity of three students, not their DNA identity.
9. You've been fined because your team is called "The Redskins."

The history of the Fourteenth Amendment, which limits the powers of state governments, begins shortly after the Civil War ended slavery in America. At that time, three amendments, commonly called the Civil War Amendments, were added to the Constitution. The Thirteenth Amendment abolished slavery in the United States, the Fourteenth Amendment granted the newly freed slaves national and state citizenship, and the Fifteenth Amendment guaranteed to the new citizens the right to vote—well, at least the males.

The amendment, addressed to the states, contains two clauses that many scholars consider among the most important in the entire Constitution: due process clause, we've dealt with this one; the other is the equal protection clause. These clauses have been the basis for some of the most important interpretations of the Constitution the Supreme

Court has made—interpretations that have affected the lives of all of us. But is it even constitutional?

The purported fourteenth amendment—small *a*—to the United States Constitution is and should be held to be ineffective, invalid, null, void, and unconstitutional. The joint resolution proposing said amendment was not submitted to or adopted by a constitutional Congress per Article I, Section 3, and Article V of the US Constitution; similar to Obamacare, it was run through the backdoor process. The resolution was not submitted to the president for his approval as required by Article I, Section 7 of the US Constitution; he was the Democrat Andrew Johnson who surely would have vetoed it; Johnson stated so in his message on June 22, 1866.

The "approved" fourteenth amendment was rejected by more than one-fourth of all the states; then in the Union, and it was never ratified by three-fourths of all the states in the Union as required by Article V of the US Constitution.

The Constitution is clear in Article I, Section 3. "The Senate of the United States shall be composed of two Senators from each State," and Article V provides: "No State, without its consent, shall be deprived of its equal suffrage in the Senate." The fact that twenty-eight senators had been unlawfully excluded from the US Senate, to secure a two-thirds vote for adoption of the joint resolution proposing the fourteenth amendment is shown by resolutions of protest adopted by many state legislatures. Hence, this "amendment" was proposed by "two-thirds of both Houses" of a legally constituted Congress and is not, constitutionally or legitimately, before a single legislature for ratification.

> If the votes of these States are necessary to a valid ratification of the amendment, they were equally necessary on the question of proposing it to the States; for it would be difficult, in the opinion of the Committee, to show by what process in logic, men of intelligence could arrive at a different conclusion.

Article I, Section 7 of the Constitution states that not only every bill that shall have been passed by the House of Representatives and the Senate of the United States Congress but also that every Order, Resolution, or Vote to which the Concurrence of the Senate and House of Representatives may be necessary (except on a question of Adjournment) shall be presented to the President of the United States; and before the Same shall take Effect, shall be approved by him, or being disapproved by him shall be repassed by two-thirds of the Senate and House of Representatives, according to the Rules and Limitations prescribed in the Case of a Bill.

Therefore, the joint resolution did not take effect.

Regardless of the above failed process, fifteen states out of the then thirty-seven states of the Union rejected the proposed fourteenth amendment between the date of its submission to the states by the secretary of state on June 16, 1866, and March 24, 1868, further nullifying the resolution and making it impossible for its ratification by the constitutionally required three-fourths of such states, as shown by the rejections thereof by the legislatures of the following states: Texas, Georgia, Florida, Alabama, North Carolina, Arkansas, South Carolina, Kentucky, Virginia, Louisiana, Delaware, Maryland, Mississippi (all slave states, though not all secessionist), Ohio, and New Jersey, two northern states.

There was no question that all of the southern states that rejected the fourteenth amendment had legally constituted governments were fully recognized by the national government and were functioning as member states of the Union at the time of their rejection.

That Congress itself recognized all these governments when they ratified the Thirteenth Amendment by December 8, 1865, undoubtedly supplies this official proof. If the southern states were not member states of the Union, the Thirteenth Amendment would not have been submitted to their legislatures for ratification and also would not be a part of the Constitution.

The Thirteenth Amendment was ratified by twenty-seven states of the then thirty-six states of the Union, including southern states of Virginia, Louisiana, Arkansas, South Carolina, Alabama, North Carolina, and Georgia. Without the votes of these seven state legislatures, the Thirteenth Amendment would have failed. There can be no doubt, but that the ratification by these seven southern states of the Thirteenth Amendment again established the fact that their governments were duly and lawfully constituted and functioning as such under their new postwar constitutions.

When the state of Louisiana rejected the fourteenth amendment, making the tenth state to have rejected the same, or more than one-fourth of the total number of thirty-six states of the Union as of that date, thus leaving less than three-fourths of the states possibly to ratify the same, the amendment failed ratification in fact and in law; it could not have been revived except by a new joint resolution of two-thirds of the Senate and House of Representatives in accordance with constitutional requirement.

Faced with the positive failure of ratification of the fourteenth amendment, both houses of Congress passed over the veto of the president three acts known as Reconstruction Acts to remove with "military force" the lawfully constituted state legislatures of the ten southern states of Virginia, North Carolina, South Carolina, Georgia, Florida, Alabama, Mississippi, Arkansas, Louisiana, and Texas.

These states were again "in rebellion," Lincoln believed secession illegal; thus if they were states, the national government, once the rebellion was over, has no right to dictate to them. If they were not states; they could not ratify amendments. So which is it, states that rejected or territories that can't ratify?

As states, they had ratified one amendment that required the vote of twenty-seven states of the thirty-six then composing the Union. When the requisite twenty-seven votes were given in favor of that amendment—seven of which votes were given by seven of these ten states—it was proclaimed to be a part of the Constitution of the United States, and slavery was declared no longer to exist within the United States or anyplace subject to their jurisdiction. If these seven states were not legal states, it follows as an inevitable consequence that in some of the states, slavery must still exist. It does not exist in these seven states, for they have abolished it also in their state constitutions; but Kentucky not having done so, it would remain in that state. But in truth, if we assume these states had no legal governments, then the abolition of slavery by these illegal governments binds no one, for Congress now denied to these states the power to abolish slavery by denying to them the power to elect a legislature, or to frame a constitution for any purpose, even for such a purpose as the abolition of slavery.

As to the other constitutional amendment having reference to suffrage, it happens that these states did not accept it. The consequence is that it has never been proclaimed or understood, even by Congress, to be a part of the Constitution of the United States.

The constitutional requirements set forth in Article V of the Constitution permit the Congress to propose amendments only whenever two-thirds of both houses shall deem it necessary—that is, two-thirds of both houses as then constituted without forcible ejections.

There is no such thing as *de facto* amendment, no such thing as amendment by waiver, no such thing as amendment by acquiescence, and no such thing as amendment by any other means whatsoever except the means specified in Article V of the Constitution itself.

It is not a valid argument to say that there have been hundreds of cases decided under the fourteenth amendment to supply the constitutional deficiencies in its proposal or ratification as required by Article V. If hundreds of litigants did not question the validity of the fourteenth amendment or questioned the same poorly without submitting documentary proof of the facts of record that made its purported adoption unconstitutional, their failure cannot change the Constitution for the millions in America.

To ascribe constitutional life to an "amendment" that never came into being according to specific methods laid down in Article V cannot be done without doing violence to Article V itself. This is true, because the only question open to the courts is whether the alleged fourteenth amendment became a part of the Constitution through a method required by Article V. Anything beyond what a court is called upon to hold to validate an amendment would be equivalent to writing into Article V another mode of amendment that has never been authorized by the people of the United States.

For now, we will for this text use "public opinion" concerning the Fourteenth Amendment and move on from here. Yet only an aroused public sentiment in favor of preserving the Constitution and our institutions and freedoms under constitutional government, and the future security of our country, will break the political barrier that now prevents judicial consideration of the unconstitutionality of the Fourteenth amendment.

Equal protection clause

The equal protection clause of the Fourteenth Amendment (let's assume it's an amendment from now on, but . . .) says: "No State shall . . . deny to any person within its jurisdiction the equal protection of the laws." At the time of its ratification, in 1868, this clause, like the rest of the Fourteenth Amendment, was intended to prevent discrimination against blacks and to guarantee them the rights that go along with equal citizenship. But as we shall see, it did not begin to serve this purpose until almost one hundred years later.

It should be noted that after the Civil War, when Congress was considering the amendments to free the slaves, grant them citizenship, and guarantee them the right to vote, women leaders of the antislavery movement, including Susan B. Anthony, asked that the right to vote for women be included in the amendments. The male antislavery leaders refused to do so. Instead, they specifically included the term "male citizen" for the first time in the Constitution, in the second section of the Fourteenth Amendment.

In addition, the Fourteenth Amendment was selectively enforced by the courts, as well as the states, depending on the race or benefit to sitting officeholders. In California and other western states, the amendment was ignored or in reality "nullified." Blacks were a small minority in California, thus not needed by the Republican majority after the Civil War. In 1870, it was Chinese Americans that held the largest minority status after Mexicans, about 9 percent. In 1870, the "radical" Republicans passed its first of a series of immigration laws to keep out Asian immigrants.

The 1870 Naturalization Act guaranteed blacks the right to become naturalized citizens and, as such, to own property, but specifically excluded other "non-white" immigrants. It was sponsored by two New York Republicans; passed overwhelmingly 33–8 in the Senate and 132–53 in the House, and signed by President Grant. In 1878, in *In re Ah Yup,* national circuit court ruled that Chinese Americans could not become naturalized citizens.

Like today, the debate now centered on the children of Chinese immigrants born here. The Fourteenth Amendment was very clear that anyone born in the nation was a citizen of the state and the country.

California had ratified the Fourteenth yet now took specific actions to ignore it.

First, the state proposed to Congress the 1875 Page Act preventing Chinese women immigrants. Then California made it illegal for Chinese to marry whites, thus still no route to citizenship as Chinese American. Third, the state of California in *People v. Brady (40 Cal. 198–1870)* ruled the Fourteenth Amendment didn't apply to California because it was a "sovereign state." California, following the Jeffersonian and Madisonian Kentucky and Virginia Resolutions, nullified a portion of the Constitution that it did not like, not merely a law, but an actual piece of the Constitution. The Republican, and later Democratic, congresses did nothing to prevent this legal racism and constitutionally disobedience. By 1950, Chinese consisted of less than 2 percent of California's population.

But like today's illegals having children here while in the country, Wong Kim Ark was born to Chinese immigrants in California, went to first his parents who had returned to China, and was not allowed to enter—I mean reenter the United States on his trip back in 1890. The essential question was how does one become a citizen? Naturalization rules have changed since the first in 1790, as politics, economics, or frankly prejudices changed. In *Dred Scot*, the Supreme Court had said being born in America and black did not grant citizenship. In *Elk v. Wilkins,* the court said an Indian born on a reservation did not acquire United States citizenship at birth (because he was not subject to US jurisdiction per the Fourteenth Amendment), even if he had later moved off the reservation and renounced his tribal citizenship. So in *United States v. Wong Kim Ark* (1898), when they decided "a child born in the United States, of parents of Chinese descent, who, at the time of his birth, are subjects of the Emperor of China, but have a permanent domicil (*sic*) and residence in the United States, and are there carrying on business, and are not employed in any diplomatic or official capacity under the Emperor of China," automatically became a citizen at birth, Wong was granted his wish, to stay American. Now that did not end the issue of race in immigration. Today the issue still is controversial: are illegals—Wong's parents were legally here—born here citizens?

In the years following the passage of the Fourteenth Amendment, however, blacks found it difficult as well to gain the equal rights guaranteed to them by this addition to the Constitution. Many state governments passed "Jim Crow" laws requiring blacks to use separate schools and other public facilities. The states claimed that such laws did not violate the equal protection clause because the separate facilities were equal. The Supreme Court considered this argument in two famous cases.

Plessy v. Ferguson (1896)

Suppose your state passed laws saying that because of your race, you could not use the same public bathrooms, water fountains, seats on buses or trains, or other public facilities that other citizens could use. However, separate facilities that were supposed to be equal to those used by others were set aside for your use. Would you say that your state was providing you with the "equal protection of the laws"?

The case of *Plessy v. Ferguson* involved this "separate but equal" argument—that is, that a state government was treating blacks equally when it required them to use segregated facilities if the facilities were equal.

The state of Louisiana had passed a law requiring railroad companies to provide "equal but separate" cars for white and black passengers. A committee was formed by black leaders to test the constitutionality of the law. They chose Homer Plessy to make their test case. He looked white, but everyone in town knew his status. Plus, he traveled alone; blacks that traveled with whites—say, a nanny—could sit in the "white cars." Thus, it wasn't color alone that mattered, if at all. Homer was "white" but couldn't sit in the car; nannies were blacks and could. It was really the relationship of the black to the white—subservient, OK; independent, no! He bought a ticket, but he insisted on riding in the cars for whites and refused to ride in the cars for blacks. Plessy was arrested and convicted in the state courts, and eventually, his case was appealed to the Supreme Court. The court was asked to decide whether the law requiring "separate but equal" treatment of blacks was unfair discrimination by the state government in violation of the equal protection of the laws clause of the Fourteenth Amendment.

The Supreme Court held that the Constitution had not been violated. The court said that to separate the races did not in itself suggest one race was inferior to the other. Since the law required that blacks and whites be provided equal facilities, the court concluded there was no discrimination, and, therefore, the law was constitutional.

Justice John Marshall Harlan (kind of foresighted to name a future justice after a chief justice; good job, Mom and Dad!) disagreed and wrote a strong dissenting opinion. He argued that the segregation law, passed by whites who dominated the state government in Louisiana, was unfair to blacks and implied that they were inferior. Therefore, it was clearly in violation of the Constitution. He said the promise of "equal" facilities was a false promise made to avoid providing blacks the equal protection of the laws, which they were supposedly guaranteed by the Constitution.

The "separate but equal" argument contained in *Plessy v. Ferguson* was the Supreme Court's position on racial segregation for next sixty years. Congress and state legislatures continued to tolerate and, in some cases, encourage discrimination against minorities. Don't forget until the 1930s, the court's interpretations of the Fourteenth Amendment gave little responsibility or power to the central government to protect citizens from racial discrimination by state governments or by private citizens. Since 1954, however, there have been significant changes in the way the Supreme Court has viewed the equal protection clause of the Fourteenth Amendment. The landmark in this shift came in the case of *Brown v. Board of Education*.

Brown v. Board of Education (1954)

Suppose your state passed a law saying that you were not allowed to go to certain public schools because of the color of your skin. Instead, you and all students like you were forced to attend special schools for your group, which were supposedly equal in physical facilities and quality of teaching to the schools attended by other students but separated from them. Would you say that your state was providing you with the "equal protection of the laws"?

Nine-year-old Linda Brown lived five blocks from a neighborhood elementary school, but because of her race, she was to attend the school for black children twenty-one blocks away. Her parents sued the school board of Topeka, Kansas, for denying their seven-year-old daughter admission to a neighborhood school set aside "for whites only." The Browns were represented by an attorney for the National Association for the Advancement of Colored People, Thurgood Marshall, later justice of the Supreme Court. Marshall argued that the practice of having segregated public schools violated the equal protection clause because it placed black children at a severe disadvantage.

In hearing the argument in this case, the Supreme Court asked the attorneys to address themselves to two questions:

- What historical evidence was there that the authors of the Fourteenth Amendment intended it to prohibit the segregation of public schools?
- If the intention of its authors is not clear, was it within the power of the court to abolish public school segregation if the court concluded that the state was violating the equal protection clause of the Fourteenth Amendment?

As you can see, the justices used the ideas about how to interpret the Constitution we discussed before in making their decision in this issue of racial segregation. In deciding to overrule *Plessy v. Ferguson,* they agreed, under pressure from Chief Justice Earl Warren, to reject the "separate but equal" theory, which had stood for nearly sixty years.

The court decided, contrary to massive historical evidence, contrary to jumping into a legislative power, contrary to the *Federalist,* which stated this was the to be the weakest branch, that it was impossible to determine if the authors of the Fourteenth Amendment intended it to prevent racial discrimination in public schools. Warren's court also decided that it was within the power of the court to abolish discrimination based on the principles of the equal protection clause because the members felt times had changed, and if the authors of the amendment were alive today, they would have decided this way too. The court began its intent to fill in the blank of the original writers of the Fourteenth Amendment, even if that "blank" was intentional; they never meant to provide schooling; that was up to the states, not a national concern. On May 17, 1954, Earl Warren delivered the unanimous decision of the Supreme Court.

> To separate [children] from others of similar age and qualifications solely because of their race generates a feeling of inferiority as to their status in the community that

may affect their hearts and minds in a way unlikely ever
to be undone . . . Whatever may have been the extent of
psychological knowledge at the time of *Plessy vs. Ferguson,*
this finding is amply supported by modern authority . . .

Any language in *Plessy vs. Ferguson* contrary to this finding
is rejected . . . Separate educational facilities are inherently
unequal . . . [We] hold that the plaintiffs . . . [are] deprived
of the equal protection of the laws guaranteed by the 14th
Amendment.

National Troops to enforce the law

Most southern states resisted the court's order to integrate their
schools "with all deliberate speed" in a second Brown case *Brown
II* (1955). In so doing, they raised the issue of how far the national
government can, or should, go to be sure that the decisions of the
Supreme Court are carried out. In one case, when the governor of
Arkansas refused to obey a court order and tried to stop black students
from entering a previously all-white public high school in Little Rock,
Pres. Dwight Eisenhower ordered the United States Army to go to that
city to prevent the state from continuing its segregation policies.

While the Supreme Court was trying to end racial discrimination
in the public schools, Congress, the executive branch, and many groups
in the general public were also working to end racial discrimination. As
early as 1947, the report of Pres. Harry S Truman's Committee on Civil
Rights called for an end to racial discrimination in education, housing,
employment, voting, and all other areas of American life. Over the
next twenty years, great efforts were made to end racial discrimination
and guarantee all citizens equality of opportunity. The 1954 decision
in the *Brown*, important as it was, dealt only with the issue of racial
segregation in the schools. It did not protect blacks from other forms of
public and private discrimination. In the 1960s, sit-ins, freedom rides,
and mass demonstrations by blacks and some whites played a key role in
mobilizing public opinion in support of the elimination of other forms
of discrimination against blacks.

In response to the pressures for social change of the 1960s, and the
policies of presidents John F. Kennedy and Lyndon B. Johnson, the Civil

Rights Acts of 1964, 1965, and 1968 were passed. Their purpose was to implement the ideals of the Thirteenth, Fourteenth, and Fifteenth Amendments—almost a hundred years after their passage, though none of those amendments would apply if read by the writers of them. The Act of 1964 was to stop segregation and discrimination in public accommodations; it also was to prohibit employment discrimination against minorities. The 1965 Act was the Voting Rights Act, which protected the voting rights of blacks. The 1968 Act was the Fair Housing Act, which prohibited discrimination in the rental, sale, and advertising of housing.

In response to public pressure, Congress has continued to take steps to prevent other forms of discrimination. The Equal Employment Opportunities Act passed by Congress in 1968 has been used to prevent discrimination in job opportunities based on sex or age. And Title IX (Education Act, 1972) bans discrimination based on sex in any educational program that receives central government aid. The Americans with Disabilities Act of 1990 forbids discrimination against those deemed "disabled," though that term has never really been defined.

What is discrimination?

The attempt to eliminate discrimination and provide equal opportunities to all citizens is a continuing and controversial process. Today, disagreements continue about how much power, as well as responsibility, the central government should have to prevent discrimination. Some of the important issues today involve claims by a variety of groups that they are still the victims of both public and private discrimination.

The issue of discrimination is a difficult one. Sometimes there are good and fair reasons for treating certain groups of people differently. For example, few people would argue that a law that says that people under the age of sixteen may not be licensed to drive is unreasonable and unfair, even though there may be some individual fifteen-year-olds—or even fourteen-year-olds—who are capable of driving skillfully and safely. The state has the responsibility to protect its citizens, and the courts hesitate to declare laws unconstitutional if the laws are reasonable ways to do this.

Since the Progressivism of the last hundred years, something has happened. The Fourteenth Amendment said equal protection of persons, not groups. There is no classification in US liberty. This change in attitude began in the failure of Progressives, let's say it, Marxists, to discredit the economic miracle of a free America, using tactics of Saul Alinsky in his rules for radicals, and other Marxists. These groups began as races spread to gender, abilities, preferences. None of these exist, only three hundred plus million individuals. Alinsky said, the activist's "job is to create the issues or the problems," not to solve by dividing, conquering, and destroying legitimacy in the institutions.

Thus, the courts have allowed "classes" of people to exist, and when a law treats a group of people differently from others without good reason, it may be found to be a violation of the equal protection of the laws and thus unconstitutional. Laws that deprive people of rights just because of their race, sex, age, or ethnic background most likely violate the principle that we have needs that have become "rights" regardless of any of these factors.

Depending on the classification, the court has set levels of scrutiny (amount of review) of the discriminatory laws. The highest level of scrutiny is strict scrutiny. There are two basics of strict scrutiny: does it deal with "fundamental" constitutional rights (voting, travel, First Amendment), and are those the law is applied to a "suspect classification" (race or national origin). If so, the law or policy must satisfy three prongs, tests:

- compelling governmental interest
- narrowly tailored
- least restrictive means

It must be to protect a compelling governmental interest. Though never actually defined, the court's decisions have been based on something necessary or crucial, not just preferred. Compelling state interests include national security, order, safety, preserving the lives of a large number of individuals, or preventing violating explicit constitutional protections.

Narrowly tailored means to achieve that goal or interest, the government cannot be overbroad. The action must also address essential aspects of the compelling interest, or it is not considered narrowly tailored.

Last, the strict scrutiny test requires a law or an action to be the least restrictive means for achieving that interest. If there is a less restrictive way to do it, that's the way it must be done.

Gender discrimination is one of the most difficult to decide. In "intermediate standard of review," the action of the state is unconstitutional unless it is "substantially related." Is there an "important" rather than "compelling" reason for the courts to allow discrimination? The court has upheld males being drafted but not females. It knocked down an Alabama law requiring husbands but not wives to pay alimony. As you can see, it is a case-by-case process, without any real clarity sometimes.

In dealing with categories on some other basis, such as age, wealth, sexual orientation, or mental disabilities, the rational-basis test is the level of scrutiny. The law or policy must be "reasonably related" to a "legitimate" government interest. Discrimination must be a reasonable way to satisfy that interest. In the case of *Gregory v. Ashcroft* (1991), it was OK to make mandatory retirement ages for some fields and not others.

The most recent case of discrimination is the 2017 Trump executive order "banning" Muslims into the United States for 120 days. Better analysts than I have done great work on this, but let's address the issue of discrimination. First, it's not an order that applies to American citizens or even illegals within the United States, only to those entering as an immigrant or refugee from seven specific nations. Many have argued this is a violation of the free exercise clause of First Amendment. Again, these are not citizens, and they have not yet entered the nation. Others say it prevents American citizens from bringing over family members from these countries. No discrimination again. Do nonresidents have rights under the Fourteenth Amendment? No! But residents, legal or illegal, do. Before deporting even illegals—yes, they are criminals—they have rights even under a "compelling" interest of government to, say, prevent crime or protect national security. The Fourteenth Amendment says, "No State shall . . . deny to any person within its jurisdiction the equal protection of the laws." Illegals are "any person." But the ban doesn't affect internal, only external immigrants; thus, it is not discrimination. It's a matter of policy, and the court itself has said "political questions" are not within our jurisdiction; well, that's what they've said. As of this writing, the "ban" is still working its way through the matrix.

What about during wartime or martial law? Martial law has been a major topic in the months since Trump relieved Obama of duty. Riots, property destruction, blocking of highways and thoroughfares, even emergency room entrances, violence toward opponents, even superintendents of schools firing pro-Trump teachers, all have become the norm, though a sliver of support, leftists and the media have amplified the impact. This has caused many to suggest, even call for martial law. Leftists called for it to prevent Trump's inauguration; rightists to stop leftist destruction. Sorry, I'm going to say it, trigger warning . . . these snowflakes weren't alive in the 1960s when martial law was imposed on campuses, cities, and helped destroy the awe for the experiment; also, it gave evidence that maybe the Founders and Framers were wrong—we can't rule ourselves.

Yet we endured that as we will endure this. In the actual Civil War, Justice David Davis, in *Ex parte Milligan*, 1866, a case against Lincoln's suspension of habeas corpus, was adamant.

> The Constitution of the United States is a law for rulers and people, equally in war and peace, and covers with the shield of its protection all classes of men, at all times, and under all circumstances. No doctrine, involving more pernicious consequences, was ever invented by the wit of men than that any of its provisions can be suspended during any of the great exigencies of government.

One attempt at "fixing" discrimination is affirmative action, a set of procedures designed to eliminate unlawful discrimination between applicants, remedy the results of such prior discrimination, and prevent such discrimination in the future. Applicants may be seeking admission to an educational program or looking for professional employment. We saw with *Plessy*, the court upheld "separate but equal," separation of the races in schools, public transportation, and elsewhere so long as the opportunities were equal.

Many believed that past discriminations, labels as illiterate, ex-slave, or missed opportunities, as well as the mere separation, handicapped many. They looked for a way to "catch up" with the mainstream

American dream. The idea of affirmative action was reborn on June 25, 1941, when Pres. Franklin Roosevelt—fearing a march on Washington organized by civil rights pioneer A. Philip Randolph—issued Executive Order 8802 requiring defense contractors to pledge nondiscrimination in employment in government-funded projects, though the military itself was segregated.

In 1947, Harry S. Truman's President's Committee on Fair Employment Practices found many "wartime gains of Negro, Mexican-American, and Jewish workers . . . began to disappear as soon as wartime controls were relaxed." In 1961, Pres. John F. Kennedy issued Executive Order 10925, requiring not only that national contractors pledge nondiscrimination but also that they "take affirmative action to ensure" equal opportunity under penalty, suspension of contracts for noncompliance. Pres. Lyndon Johnson added Executive Order 11246, creating the Office of Federal Contract Compliance in the Department of Labor to enforce its nondiscrimination and affirmative action requirements and complaints, amended in 1967 to include prohibitions on sex discrimination. The Vietnam Era Veterans Readjustment Assistance Act of 1972 called for "the preferential employment of disabled veterans and veterans of the Vietnam era . . . who are otherwise qualified." In 1973, the act added employment and promotion for people with disabilities.

As usual good intentions turned into that road to hell. Under Richard Nixon's "Philadelphia Plan," quotas and reverse discrimination became the new issue. From *Bakke* (1978) in California to *Grutter* (2003) in Michigan to *Fisher* (2016) in Texas, the court has validated affirmative action but with varying enthusiasm, especially in education.

Affirmative action in college goes back to James Meredith at Ole Miss in the early 1960s. Allan Bakke was denied in the 1970s a spot at UC-Davis School of Medicine even though he was more qualified than many of the candidates that were accepted. It upheld affirmative action, allowing race to be one of the several factors in college admission. The court ruled that specific racial quotas, such as the sixteen out of one hundred seats set aside for minority students by the University of California, Davis School of Medicine, were impermissible.

In 1997, Barbara Grutter, a white Michigan resident, was denied admission to the University of Michigan Law School. Grutter, who had a 3.8 undergraduate grade point average and good standardized test scores, sued the university, which considered race as a factor in admissions. Grutter claimed that Michigan admitted less-qualified minority applicants in violation of national civil rights laws and the Fourteenth Amendment's equal protection.

The court continued Bakke, the use of affirmative action "is a compelling state interest that can justify the use of race in university admissions." But race cannot be the major, only one of many, qualifications, and any racial quota system must not be used. By the late 1990s, three states, California, Washington, and Michigan, have banned affirmative action in public education, in state government hiring, and the awarding of state contracts.

Abigail Fisher applied to the University of Texas under the "race-neutral" policy of top 10 percent. Dating from 2004, that plan makes some use of race in deciding which students are chosen to enter each year, but race is only taken into account by admissions after 80 percent of each freshman class is already filled. Most of each class is chosen automatically; any student in the top 10 percent of her high school graduating class in Texas is entitled to entry. The remaining vacancies are filled competitively on evaluations of each applicant as an individual by a "holistic" method, looking at academic and other achievements, life experience, and overall potential for success—and in a measure that is not a hard-and-fast percentage, no quota, race.

Abigail, not in her class's top ten, had to compete in that smaller pool. She has claimed in all the cases, it was heard twice by the Supreme Court, she was not admitted because of her race; the university has argued she would not have qualified for admission in any event because she did not measure up. Though the court, after hearing the Fisher case in *Fisher I* (2013) and *Fisher II* (2016), allowed Texas's policy, it cautioned universities to constantly check data of their student bodies to see if they've met their goals of a "diverse" community. Affirmative action, past discrimination, slavery reparations continue to be things we struggle with as a nation.

In *Matal v. Tam*, First Amendment and discrimination banged into each other. A musical group headed by Simon Tam tried to register the band's name, "The Slants," as a trademark with the Federal Trademark Office. The Supreme Court's unanimous 8–0 decision of summer 2017—new justice Neil Gorsuch did not vote—reversed a century of legal precedent since the Lanham Act, which prohibits registration of a mark that may "disparage . . . or bring . . . into contemp[t] or disrepute" any "persons, living or dead." The office denied it based on the idea that "trademarks are private, not government, speech" and that "powerful messages can sometimes be conveyed in just a few words." Because of this, it is improper for the Trademark Office to refuse registrations on the grounds that they are, or might be taken as, disparaging or insulting. A major victory for the First Amendment for private not just government speech. By the way, Tam is an Asian American.

A good ending to this topic may be a quote from a famous black American, Booker T. Washington, a former slave, university professor, and foreseer of a stolen civil rights movement. This is taken from chapter 5 of his 1911 *My Larger Education*.

> There is another class of colored people who make a business of keeping the troubles, the wrongs, and the hardships of the Negro race before the public. Having learned that they are able to make a living out of their troubles, they have grown into the settled habit of advertising their wrongs, partly because they want sympathy and partly because it pays. Some of these people do not want the Negro to lose his grievances, because they do not want to lose their jobs.

VOTING, A RIGHT OR A DUTY?

> Democracy must be something more than two wolves
> and a sheep voting on what to have for dinner.
> —James Bovard

SUFFRAGE—THAT IS, THE right to vote—has been a subject of controversy throughout our history. During our colonial period and the early years of our nation, voting was generally restricted to white men who owned property. While the majority of white males qualified for suffrage, other people such as women, blacks, American Indians, and members of certain religious groups were usually denied the right to vote. We are not going to discuss the Electoral College, or the "will of the people," or primaries. We will look at how the right to vote has been extended over the last two hundred plus years to almost every person over eighteen years of age, the extension of representative democracy; the extension of the right to vote is related to most of the fundamental ideas and principles about constitutional government under the control of We the People. Without the right to vote, citizens are ruled only; subjects, never rulers, free men.

In ancient Greece, since at least 508 BC, the earliest forms of "democracy" appeared. Each year, a negative election was held. Each citizen cast a vote for politicians; the votes were written on broken pots (*Ostraka*). If the politician received enough votes, he had to leave the city; he was ostracized. This "democracy" was clearly not a true democracy. In many city-states, six thousand votes of male landowners were the electorate. In Medieval Venice, the Great Council of forty members performed "approval voting." Electors cast one vote for every candidate they find acceptable; none for those whom they deem unacceptable. Thus, the winner was acceptable to largest number of voters.

At the Philadelphia Convention, the Framers could not agree on who should be given the right to vote. Thus, the Constitution only stated that members of the House of Representatives were to be elected by the people in each state who, under state law, were eligible to vote for the lower house of their state legislature. They left to each state government the power to decide who could vote. As a result, many of the early battles over suffrage took place at the state level. Some of the most important steps in this struggle to end discrimination in suffrage are described below.

> You require that a man shall have sixty dollars' worth of property, or he shall not vote. Very well, take an illustration. Here is a man who today owns a jackass, and the jackass is worth sixty dollars. Today the man is a voter and he goes to the polls and deposits his vote. Tomorrow the jackass dies. The next day the man comes to vote without his jackass and he cannot vote at all. Now tell me, which was the voter, the man or the jackass? (Thomas Paine, 1737–1809).

White men had the right to vote and take part in government, but usually, they had to meet certain property qualifications. This was the idea that taxation without representation and representation with taxation were coequal ideas, two sides of the same coin. However, even before the Civil War, especially since Thomas Jefferson's and Andrew Jackson's democracy, there was a marked increase in the number of white men who did gain the right to vote. As we moved west across North America, freedom spread and widened.

During the Revolutionary War, six state governments eliminated all property requirements and gave the right to vote to all white males, rich or poor. But at the same time, three other state governments increased the property requirements, limiting the right to vote. In some states, the right to vote included the requirement that a person belong to a particular religious group. Following the election of Thomas Jefferson as president in 1800, many states began to eliminate the property restrictions for voting. Between 1812 and 1821, six western states became part of the Union, and these gave the vote to all white males. During the same period, four of the older states that had property requirements abolished them. Andrew Jackson ran for president in 1828. His support came from many men who had just won the right to vote. During this period, suffrage continued to be extended to more white males. And by the 1840s, almost every state government had given all white males the right to vote. Only two states still had any significant property qualifications. Restrictions on voting by Catholics and non-Christians were eliminated. In a few states, even immigrants not yet naturalized were given the right to vote. The last state to change, North Carolina, abandoned its property test in 1856.

It should not be assumed that the gains that were made during this period were easily achieved or that feelings did not run high. The situation in Rhode Island, where over half the white males were denied the right to vote, led to Dorr's Rebellion of 1842. This unsuccessful struggle is an example of the difficulty of expanding the right to vote during the first part of the 1800s. Despite the gains, it should not be forgotten that the right to vote was still restricted to white males and only those over twenty-one years of age.

The Civil War

The Fifteenth Amendment was added to the Constitution in 1870, just after the Civil War. It says,

> Section 1: The right of citizens of the United States to vote shall not be denied or abridged by the United States or by any State on account of race, color, or previous condition of servitude.

> Section 2: The Congress shall have the power to enforce this article by appropriate legislation.

The intent of this amendment was to give black males the right to vote. Unfortunately, just changing the Constitution or passing a law does not necessarily mean that what you wish to happen will. During the early part of this period, the Supreme Court left to the state governments the responsibility for protecting most of the basic rights of their citizens. There were many people in the United States who did not want black males to have the right to vote or to have a role in the government. Although the Fifteenth Amendment guaranteed the right to vote to black males, the state governments passed laws that made it almost impossible for them to exercise their newly won right.

Some state governments passed laws that required citizens to pay a tax before they could vote. These were called "poll taxes." Since most former slaves were very poor, they were unable to pay the tax; this eliminated many immigrants, and farmers recently moved to cities and migrant workers. Yet in a number of the states, poor white men were allowed to vote even when they could not pay the poll tax. Some of the state governments also passed laws requiring men to take tests to prove that they could read and write before they were allowed to vote. These were called "literacy tests" and were very difficult for many Americans, black and immigrants, who had not had an opportunity to get an adequate education, to pass. By manipulation, literacy tests also eliminated educated blacks because they were administered unfairly so that blacks would fail and whites, even though illiterate, would pass; many of the test givers could not pass the tests. Another method called "grandfather clauses," used to stop blacks, specifically, from voting, was the use of laws that stated that people could only vote who were descendants of those who had previously had the right to vote. This obviously did not include former slaves.

Other methods used to deprive black citizens of their rights were those that were not employed directly by state governments but by private individuals and organizations who were usually not prosecuted by state authorities for their illegal activities against blacks. Among these were torture and murder, carried out by groups like the Ku Klux Klan, bosses threatening unemployment, to terrorize black citizens so that they would not try to exercise their constitutional rights.

Some of the restrictive voting laws that were enacted by state governments were not declared unconstitutional by the Supreme Court until 1915, over forty-five years after the Fifteenth Amendment had been passed. Many of the laws that limited the right of blacks to vote lasted even longer than that.

As a result of the civil rights movement of the 1950s and 1960s, the national government began using its power to protect the rights of blacks against political discrimination. In 1964, the Twenty-Fourth Amendment was added to the Constitution prohibiting the use of poll taxes as a means of denying the right to vote in national elections.

The following year, Congress passed the Voting Rights Act, which gave additional protection for voting rights by authorizing the national government to take over registration of voters in areas where state officials had regularly prevented blacks from registering to vote. President Johnson urged Congress to pass this act after Martin Luther King Jr. led a demonstration in Selma, Alabama, against restrictive policies. There were more than fifteen thousand blacks that were eligible to vote, but only 335 had been able to register successfully. The Voting Rights Act established age, residence, and citizenship as the only valid criteria for voter eligibility, rather than literacy or approval of a person's character.

In 1966, the Supreme Court ruled that the use of poll taxes in state elections was a violation of the equal protection clause of the Fourteenth Amendment (*Harper v. Virginia Board of Elections*). Thus, by the mid-'60s, great progress had been made in ensuring that blacks could enjoy the right to vote, which had been guaranteed in the Fifteenth Amendment almost a century earlier.

Women

Closely linked with the struggle of blacks for both freedom and equality was the struggle for women's rights. It took even longer for women to win the legal right to vote than it did for blacks. For most of the history of the United States, women did not have the right to vote or take part in government. Women were the largest group of people ever denied the right to vote in our Republic. That struggle for was long and difficult. It involved a challenge to strongly held traditional beliefs about what the role of women should be in society.

The following events illustrate this struggle. The Fourteenth Amendment includes the following: "All persons born or naturalized in the United States, and subject to the jurisdiction thereof, are citizens of the United States and of the State wherein they reside." In 1874, people in favor of women's rights argued in the Supreme Court that this clause gave women the right to vote. The Supreme Court denied their claim saying that being a citizen does not automatically give a person the right to vote and that it was not unconstitutional for states to deny the vote to women.

In 1876, Susan B. Anthony led a delegation of women to the Philadelphia Centennial Celebration of the Declaration of Independence. Although no women had been invited to participate in the program, Anthony's protest including reading the Women's Declaration of Rights:

> Yet we cannot forget, even in this glad hour, that while all men of every race . . . have been invested with the full rights of citizenship under our hospitable flag, all women still suffer the degradation of disfranchisement.

Wyoming gave women the right to vote while it was still a territory. The story is told that when certain members of Congress argued against this "petticoat provision," the Wyoming legislature said it would prefer to stay out of the Union one hundred years rather than join it without allowing women to vote. Wyoming was allowed into the Union. After Wyoming, other western states quickly extended the right of suffrage to women. By the end of World War I, over half of the states had given women the right to vote. Pressure for a women's suffrage amendment mounted during World War I as women entered the workforce in record numbers, replacing men drafted into the war. In 1918, Pres. Woodrow Wilson announced his support for the proposed amendment.

The uncertainty and slowness of state-by-state victories encouraged women to push harder for a constitutional amendment that would give them the right to vote. In 1920, even though there was still considerable opposition to granting women this right, the Nineteenth Amendment was finally ratified. Women had the right to vote after being denied that right for over 130 years.

> The right of citizens of the United States to vote shall not be denied or abridged by the United States or by any State because of gender.

> Congress shall have the power to enforce this article by appropriate legislation.

Eighteen-year-olds

Before 1971, only Alaska, Georgia, Hawaii, and Kentucky had allowed persons younger than twenty-one to participate in elections. In 1970, Congress, in amending the Voting Rights Act, included a section that said no one should be denied the right to vote on the grounds of age that was eighteen years old or older. This law was challenged in the case of *Oregon v. Mitchell,* and the Supreme Court justices were divided in their opinions. Four justices decided that Congress had the power to lower the voting age to eighteen; four other justices concluded that Congress had no such power. Justice Hugo Black cast the decisive vote. He ruled that Congress could regulate the voting age in national elections but not in state elections. He argued that the Constitution leaves to the states the power to regulate the elections of their own public officials. The Congress does have the authority, however, to lower the voting age in national elections.

Within six months of the court decision, the Twenty-Sixth Amendment was ratified by the required number of states. It lowered the voting age to eighteen.

> Section 1: The right of citizens of the United States, who are eighteen years of age or older, to vote shall not be denied or abridged by the United States or by any State on account of age.
>
> Section 2: The Congress shall have the power to enforce this article by appropriate legislation.

This amendment reduced the voting age from twenty-one to eighteen in response to protests from young people who complained that, even though they were old enough to be drafted, they were not considered responsible enough to vote. The Nixon administration worried that opposition among these new voters to the war in Vietnam would severely hamper the president's chances for reelection. But to Nixon's great relief, few eighteen-year-olds even bothered to register, and of those that did register, not many actually voted.

Today almost every citizen of the United States eighteen years of age or older has the right to vote and take part in government. States can, however, pass some laws restricting the right to vote.

- **Citizenship**. The Constitution does not mention citizenship as a requirement for voting. In the past, as you know, some states allowed noncitizens to vote. Today, however, all states make citizenship a requirement of voting. This became a serious issue in 2016 when it was reported that Hillary Clinton won the popular vote with as many as four million illegals voting for her.
- **Residence**. All states have a residency requirement for voting. This means persons must live in the state and locality for a period before they can vote. The time that is required is not a long one, however, usually only thirty days—because the Supreme Court has held longer periods to be unconstitutional. Some states' ten days' residency meets the requirement.
- **Age**. No state can prevent anyone over eighteen years of age from voting based on his or her age. Although none has done so, states can permit younger citizens to vote. There have been many calls to allow seventeen-year-olds to vote if they would turn eighteen before the candidates took office.
- **Registration**. All states except North Dakota need to register with election officials and provide such information as name, age, and address to vote. The trend over the years has been to make this process easier and less time-consuming, even Election Day registration, online or drive-throughs.
- **Other qualifications**. States also have several laws that can disqualify voters. For example, persons who are judged to be mentally incompetent, under the influence of drugs or alcohol, have been convicted of serious crimes or election fraud, or have been dishonorably discharged from the armed forces maybe denied the right to vote.

Part of the Progressive centralization, in 1913, the Seventeenth Amendment allowed citizens to vote directly for their senators for the first time. Before this amendment, senators were chosen by the individual state legislatures. This amendment destroyed a major ideal of Federalism woven into the Constitution. Now senators were state-elected, under massive pressure from national lobbyists, and a major nail in the coffin of a republic. The amendment carried to the national scene direct democracy, mob rule. The state-controlled Senate was a major compromise in Philadelphia, but Progressives distrusted of representative government and "chaffed against the institutions of the Founders since the beginning of the republic." C. H. Hoebeke, librarian at the University of Virginia and fellow in Constitutional History at the Center for Constitutional Studies, did a spectacular piece on the failure of the Seventeenth Amendment:

> The fact most Progressives failed to acknowledge or to come to terms with was that the underlying premise of direct Senate elections, and of the direct democracy movement in general, was the complete antithesis of the founding idea of government. Having in the short span of eleven years experienced the violent swing of the political pendulum from abusive monarchy to abusive majoritarianism, and in the process discovered that life, liberty, and property were no more secure under the latter than they had been under the former, the Constitution's Framers saw the will of the people as a force to be restrained and refined, not unleashed and encouraged. Unseduced by the egalitarian speculations of Jean-Jacques Rousseau and Thomas Paine, they knew first hand that the simplicity of one man, one vote did not of itself engender a greater harmony of interests. "Theoretic politicians," James Madison observed, "have erroneously supposed that by reducing mankind to a perfect equality in their political rights, they would, at the same time, be perfectly equalized and assimilated in their possessions, their opinions, and their passions." On the contrary, liberty brought about a diversity of interests, which in turn brought conflict. Hence, faction, rather than originating in the inequalities of the social order, was "sewn in the nature of man" and could not be removed. The putative existence of a wide chasm separating "the interests," on the one side, and "the people," on the other—which provided the rationale for unceasing agitation by subsequent generations of reformers—turns out to have been a fiction of the Enlightenment.

A system of government based solely on equality of political expression, therefore, had the paradoxical result of creating another form of inequality, because it gave the majority an absolute power over the rights of the minority. "Who," asked Madison, "would rely on a fair decision from three individuals if two had an interest opposed to the third?" Whether it was three or three hundred million, impartiality would not be increased, "nor any further security against injustice be obtained, than what may result from the difficulty of uniting the wills of a greater number."

After more than twenty-one hundred years of Western political evolution, the classical solution was to balance the rights and powers of the many against those of the few and the one, much as the British government struck a balance among Commons, Lords and Crown. Any act of government that could get the support of all three achieved a reasonable approximation of political justice. Much as the stability of that system was admired by the delegates in Philadelphia, however, the creation of hereditary elements was neither practicable nor politic in the former American colonies, and was never seriously considered. But without such checks, the stronger central authority that the Founders thought necessary for the effective governance of a growing nation would only increase the potential tyranny of a numerically superior faction. The dilemma, as pronounced in *The Federalist*, was "to secure the public good and private rights against the dangers of such a faction, and at the same time to preserve the spirit and the form of popular government."

In 1964, Congress looked to itself and freed its own principality slightly. The Twenty-Third Amendment permits citizens in the District of Columbia to vote for electors for president and vice president. However, they are still unable to send voting representatives or senators to Congress. Recently, statehood has been suggested. Maybe statehood would solve the problems of crime and education in the District, respectively the highest and the lowest among the states.

The District constituting the seat of Government of the United States shall appoint in such manner as the Congress may direct: A number of electors of President and Vice President . . . entitled if it were a State . . . [three electors make it 538 electoral votes].

Since almost all citizens now have the right to vote, the question of the suffrage is no longer seems important or as controversial as it once was. Those who are concerned about the fate of representative democracy have turned their attention to other questions. Why do so many people who have the right to vote fail to exercise that right? How can the citizen acquire sufficient information to vote intelligently when government has become so complex? These are only two of the questions.

However, the 2016 presidential election proved that suffrage was still a concern. From rigged primaries to popular versus electoral vote to protests and "Not my President" to a sitting president using executive power to leak information, fake the reports, campaigning for his choice, paid protesters, before, during and after the election, illegal wire taps of one candidate to discredit with leaked "press releases." Even though the US government, CIA, FBI, or NSA has interfered with many foreign elections, many are indignant that it maybe happened here.

FREEDOM OF EXPRESSION(S)

If liberty means anything at all, it means the right to
tell people what they do not want to hear.
—George Orwell

THE FOUNDERS PLACED great importance on freedom of
expression. Under the First and the Fourteenth Amendments,
neither national nor state governments, can place unreasonable or unfair
limitations upon this right. This means that there are very few situations
in which the government can interfere with your right

- to discuss anything you wish;
- write, publish, or read anything you wish;
- gather together to associate with whomever you wish; and
- petition your government to correct wrongs.

There are hundreds of cases dealing with expression, speech,
press, assembly, and the religious issues we've seen already. Freedom of
expression consists of assembly, petition, press, and speech, spoken and
written, graphic or symbolic. It is protected to ensure to all persons a
full, wide-ranging discussion of public affairs to hear all.

The historical events that led to the American Revolution and
helped develop the First Amendment give foundation to arguments in
support of freedom of expression. Criteria by the court have been used
over the last two hundred years to determine when it is reasonable and
fair to limit freedom of expression in favor of other important values
and interests.

The Founders and freedom of expressions

The importance the Framers placed on your right to freedom of expression is made evident by the following phrases in the First Amendment to the Constitution.

> Congress shall make no law . . . abridging the freedom of speech, or of the press; or the right of the people peaceably to assemble, and to petition the Government for a redress of grievances.

It is not surprising that the Founders, the Framers, and Americans today place(d) so much importance upon freedom of expressions, given their experiences and knowledge of history. They knew that attempts to restrict freedom of expressions had often occurred in the past to limit the people's access to ideas and information. Some were political, others religious, yet all were attempts to be outside of the "acceptable" standards.

In England, about 1600, there were laws that required all people to believe in the same religious doctrines. People opposed to these laws spoke, wrote, and distributed materials criticizing them. Members of the government knew that one of the best ways to stop these dissenters from spreading their ideas was to limit their right to print and distribute them. So they passed laws that said that all printing in England could only be done in three cities and that before being printed, all books had to be approved by the archbishop of Canterbury and the bishop of London. Today these are called copyright laws. Many today believe it is to protect the authors' "intellectual property." In fact, it was to control authors not approved for publication. We will see that in the digital world, control is nearly impossible. "Fake news" labels and governments' "assistance in protecting" us from it, which is the original intent of copyright laws, control freedom of expressions.

In the colonies, those controls followed. In 1682, in the Colony of Virginia, a printer named John Buckner was accused of printing the laws of the colony without the governor's permission. The next year, the governor made a law that no person in the colony would ever be allowed to use a printing press. The governor said, "Printing has encouraged [the people] to learn and even criticize the best governments. God keep us from free schools and printing."

In the colony of New York, in 1735, a newspaperman named John Peter Zenger wrote in his newspaper that the governor had rigged elections, that his officials were incompetent, and that the colony was in danger of becoming a dictatorship. The governor had Zenger arrested and brought to trial for making these criticisms. After a lengthy trial, the jury decided that since Zenger's charges against the governor were true, he should be set free.

In some cases, repression of freedom of expression had tragic results. In ancient Athens, in the year 399 .C, that great philosopher of truth, Socrates, was accused of corrupting the youth with his teaching. Athenian judges warned Socrates that unless he agreed to stop teaching, they would order his execution. In response, Socrates replied that no official could order him what to think or what to teach, he answered to a higher authority. Thus, he was condemned to death; look back at *Crito* on page 29.

In colonial Massachusetts, in the year 1660, Mary Dyer taught that all men and women were equal before God and that slavery, war, and capital punishment were evil. She was hanged by the Puritans in the city of Boston for preaching beliefs that were different from those of other members of the colony.

In addition to their knowledge of history, the Founders believed in natural rights and representative democracy. They believed that your right to hold and express your beliefs is one of your "inalienable rights" that is crucial if you are to be a responsible and capable citizen.

Your right to develop, hold, and express ideas is an important part of your intellectual, moral, and social development. So, of course, is your right to hear and consider the views of others. Further, a respect for your dignity and abilities requires you having the right to gain knowledge and express your beliefs and opinions. If man is to rule himself, she must be free to be human, unique, but with all the tools needed to be happy. It is through the free competition of different ideas and beliefs that the truth is most likely to be found. As Justice Oliver Wendell Holmes Jr. put the argument, "The best test of truth is the power of the thought to get it accepted in the competition of the market." Scientific discoveries and intellectual developments seem more likely to come about when it is possible for ideas to be discussed and debated freely. In the "free marketplace of ideas," all points of view, even those with which you may disagree, have the right to be heard, and it is important to hear them.

The ultimate power of our government rests with you and the rest of the people. If you are to judge wisely and to make informed choices about candidates and policies, you must be able to get the information you need and be able to discuss it freely. Freedom of expression is also important for providing a way for you to check on how well members of government are doing their jobs and to let them know if you approve or disapprove of their actions.

Having the right to express yourself freely gives you an opportunity to "blow off steam." You may be more willing to accept decisions made by government if you have at least had a fair opportunity to be heard and to participate in the decision-making process. You may also be more willing to use democratic means of attempting to influence your government rather than resorting to violence, a state of nature. The lessons of history are clear, that when governments gain the power to place unreasonable and unfair limitations upon your freedom of expression, they become arbitrary and despotic, violate basic principles of justice, and deprive you of fundamental human rights. The result, even per Jefferson, is violence, destruction of lives, liberty, and property.

The importance of freedom of expression to the protection of all of your rights and of our free society itself has led scholars and justices to say it should be protected more carefully than many of your other basic rights. The Supreme Court has held that freedom of expressions can only be limited when it very clearly endangers other important values and interests.

When should freedom of expression be limited?

Although the First Amendment appears to say that there cannot be any laws limiting your right to freedom of expression, this does not mean that you can freely say absolutely anything. For example, you do not have the right falsely to shout "Fire!" in a crowded theater because you might cause a panic in which people could be injured or killed. You do not have a right to tell military secrets to foreign nations because of the requirement of national security—that is, our need to protect our entire nation. What about WikiLeaks? Some have blamed the e-mails posted by WikiLeaks as causing Americans to have "too much information" and torpedoing the campaign of Hillary Clinton in 2016.

Given our strong belief that our right to express ourselves on political matters is vital to the preservation and improvement of our constitutional republic, you can imagine the problems that arise when decisions are made about when it is reasonable and fair for the government to limit this freedom. Most people, including the Supreme Court, believe that your right to freedom of expression must be balanced against other important values and interests of our society such as public safety or national security. This means that your right to express yourself freely may be limited in certain situations if it would seriously endanger other very important values and interests.

For example, suppose you try to convince other people to rise up and overthrow our government by violent means such as the Founders used to overthrow the British government. And suppose you believe that our government should be replaced with one that severely restricts those basic rights this nation was founded to protect. Under what conditions do you think your government should be able to arrest, try, and convict you for expressing such beliefs?

Over the years, the Supreme Court has developed different guidelines or "tests" to use in deciding when it is reasonable and fair to limit freedom of expression. The following three tests have been developed by the court at different periods to decide when freedom of expression may be limited in situations or cases that involve what is called sedition, conduct or speech inciting people to rebel against the authority of a state, situations in which a person tries to convince others to engage in the overthrow of our government.

Read these tests and be prepared to apply them to the cases that follow that involve issues of sedition.

1. **The clear and present danger test.** The government may limit your freedom of expression if its result is that people will break the law so soon after you have expressed your ideas that there will be no opportunity for full discussion of the consequences of what you are suggesting.

2. **The dangerous tendency test.** The government may limit your freedom of expression if it creates a dangerous tendency among

others to break a law. The government does not have to wait until an unlawful act is about to happen.

3. **The incitement test.** The government may limit your freedom of expression if it can show that your speech is directed to inciting or producing immediate unlawful action and is likely to cause that action to happen.

When reading the cases, keep in mind the same questions the justices asked when deciding.

1. Should the person in the case have his or her right to freedom of expression limited?
2. Which of the three tests you have just studied should be used to decide the case? Be prepared to explain why you have made your decision.
3. Explain which of the tests seem to provide more and which less protection of your right to freedom of expression.

Schenck v. the United States (1919)

In 1917, the United States was involved in World War I. Congress passed the Espionage Act, which made it unlawful to make statements intended to interfere with the armed forces of the United States or to obstruct the recruitment or enlistment of personnel in the armed forces; it added the Sedition Act 1918 to punish anyone, including the press, who "willfully utter, print, write, or publish any disloyal, profane, scurrilous, or abusive language about the form of government of the United States, or the military or naval forces of the United States, or the flag." Not much left except Aunt Mabel's birthday, so long as she wasn't a German.

Charles Schenck, the general secretary of the Socialist Party during World War I, was against the United States entering the war. He sent out letters to about fifteen thousand young men eligible to be drafted into the army. The letters strongly stated Schenck's opinion that the war was only being fought in the interests of the rich people in our country and that the national government did not have the right to draft men to be in the army. Schenck encouraged the men to speak out and try to get the draft laws repealed.

Schenck was arrested because his letters might make people disobey the laws even though his letters didn't actually recommend this. He was tried, convicted, and imprisoned. He appealed his case to the Supreme Court claiming that the Federal Espionage Act was a violation of his First Amendment right to freedom of expression.

Gitlow v. New York (1925)

During World War I, some of the Russian people revolted against the Czar and overthrew the government. The leaders who finally took over were Communists who believed the workers of all countries should also take over their governments. During the 1920s, there were Communists in the United States who wished to overthrow the government by force. In New York, a man named Benjamin Gitlow printed a Communist pamphlet and sent sixteen thousand copies through the mail to people in this country. The pamphlet said that the workers of the United States should begin a Communist revolution, have large strikes, and destroy the United States form of government.

Gitlow was arrested under the 1902 New York Criminal Anarchy Law, which made it a crime to advocate the violent overthrow of the government. He was tried, convicted, and imprisoned. He appealed his case to the Supreme Court. He claimed that his right to freedom of expression had been unfairly limited because there was no evidence that his pamphlets had made anyone break the law.

Dennis v. United States (1951)

In 1940, Congress passed a law known as the Smith Act, which made it illegal to teach or print materials advocating the overthrow of the government of the United States by force or violence. It was aimed to stop the rise of an American Fascism. After World War II, with Soviet-American tensions rising, the government began prosecution of Communists under the Smith Act. In 1948, the Smith Act was used against Eugene Dennis and ten others. Dennis was secretary general of the Communist Party of the United States. He and the others were charged with conspiring to form groups to teach the overthrow of the government by force and violence. They were tried, convicted, and imprisoned. They appealed to the Supreme Court claiming that the Smith Act violated their rights to freedom of speech, of the press, and of association.

Yates v. United States (1957)

In 1951, fourteen members of the Communist Party in California were arrested for violation of the Smith Act. Again, this act made it illegal to teach or print materials advocating the overthrow of the government of the United States by force or violence. The government accused the Communists of writing and publishing articles and conducting schools that promoted the overthrow of the government. In violation of the Smith Act, all fourteen persons were arrested, tried, convicted, and sentenced to prison for five years. They appealed their case to the Supreme Court claiming that the law violated their freedom of expression.

Brandenburg v. Ohio (1969)

A local leader of the Ku Klux Klan, Clarence Brandenburg, spoke at a rally of the Klan held on a farm in rural Ohio, near Cincinnati. The rally was attended by twelve members of the Klan and a reporter and cameraman from a local television station. The film showed the twelve persons carrying guns gathered around a burning cross. Clarence told the group that if the national government continued to suppress the white race, ". . . there might have to be some revenge taken. We are marching on Congress July the 4th, four hundred thousand strong." He was arrested and convicted under a 1919 Ohio law, which prohibited unlawful means of terrorism as a means of accomplishing political reform. He was tried, convicted, and sentenced to ten years in prison. He appealed his case to the Supreme Court claiming that the Ohio law violated his right to freedom of expression.

Let's see how you did? To preface, I see no harm in any of the previous cases; all defendants should have been acquitted under the Constitution. The court was unanimous; Schenck's criminal conviction was constitutional. The law only applied to successful obstructions of the draft; Oliver Wendell Holmes Jr., who wrote the opinion, believed prosecution for attempts that were dangerously close to success was constitutional. Attempts made by speech or writing could be punished like other attempted crimes; the First Amendment did not protect speech encouraging men to resist the draft because, "when a nation is at war, many things that might be said in time of peace are such a hindrance to its effort that their utterance will not be endured so long as men fight, and that no court could regard them as protected by any constitutional right." In other words, the court held, wartime allowed greater restrictions than would be allowed during peacetime, if only because new and greater dangers are present.

> The most stringent protection of free speech would not protect a man in falsely shouting fire in a theatre and causing a panic . . . The question in every case is whether the words used are used in such circumstances and are of such a nature as to create a *clear and present danger* [emphasis mine] that they will bring about the substantive evils that Congress has a right to prevent.

Yet his flimsy, even illogical, logic is so obvious to us simple, nonlitigating types as to be sophomoric. The handouts Schenck was distributing began ironically with "LONG LIVE THE CONSTITUTION." Holmes abused the First Amendment to give leeway to the commander in chief during wartime. But "clear and present," later called "national security," is as arbitrary as the executive behind the desk in the Oval Office. Could one yell "FIRE" in a crowded on-fire theater? Isn't a fire drill as dangerous to the moviegoers? If anything, theater yellers could be prosecuted as a property rights violator, disrupting the owners of tickets as well as the owner of the movie house; but as a Progressive, Holmes had no problem expanding national power.

What is most ironic of the Holmes's opinion is his lack of historical context. Daniel Webster in 1812 was an echo of Scheck's 1917 leaflets. Webster called the draft no better than slavery; on the floor of Congress, he stated the draft caused a citizen to be no more than a convicted criminal. A man in the military "is deprived of his liberty and of his right to think and act as a free man; the draft was, and is, unconstitutional. Fort that Charles T. Schenck received thirty years in prison.

In *Abrams v. United States* (1919), Holmes appears to clarify, even reverse his *Schenck* opinion. He dug up the common-law principle that freedom of expression, speech, and press, and opinion was central to a republican system because competition in the "marketplace of ideas" was the best test of truth; he was, however, in the minority. In *Whitney v. California* (1927), concerning a conviction for seditious speech forbidden by California law, Holmes joined a concurring opinion written by Justice Louis D. Brandeis, again explaining the clear-and-present-danger standard for criminal attempts in these terms, and reiterated political speech was protected because of the value of democratic deliberation; expressions of honest opinion were entitled to near absolute protection, though expressions made with the specific intent to cause a criminal harm, or a "clear and present danger" of such harm, could be still be punished.

The court upheld Benjamin Gitlow's conviction; state governments may suppress or punish speech that advocates the duty, need, or appropriateness of overthrowing government by force or violence. Justice Edward Terry Sanford attempted to clean up the "clear and present danger" test of *Schenck*. He suggested the "bad [dangerous] tendency test" found in *Shaffer v. United States* (1919), which held that a "state may punish utterances endangering the foundations of government and threatening its overthrow by unlawful means" because such speech clearly "present[s] a sufficient danger to the public peace and to the security of the State." Sanford stated a "single revolutionary spark may kindle a fire that, smoldering for a time, may burst into a sweeping and destructive conflagration." He said the Gitlow's words contained "the language of direct incitement" and were not "the expression of philosophical abstraction."

Holmes, dissenting again, wrote that he believed it was still the appropriate test to employ in judging the limits of freedom of expression. Joined by Brandeis, he argued that Gitlow presented no present danger because only a small minority of people shared the views presented in Gitlow's manifesto and because it directed an uprising at some "indefinite time in the future." He responded to Sanford's kindling metaphor that "eloquence may set fire to reason, but whatever may be thought of the redundant discourse before us, it had no chance of starting a present conflagration."

The court continued to allow convictions for seditious speech in a series of prosecutions of leftists, however, culminating in *Dennis v. United States* (1951), in which the justices divided over convictions for the leaders of the Communist Party. Judge Learned Hand in his lower court decision and Chief Justice Fred Vinson for only a plurality used *Schenck* and a new "clear and probable danger" test. "In each case [courts] must ask whether the gravity of the 'evil,' discounted by its improbability, justifies such invasion of free speech as necessary to avoid the danger." The court ruled that Dennis did not have the right under the First Amendment to exercise free speech, publication, or assembly, if that exercise involved the creation of a plot to overthrow the government. In his dissent, Black wrote,

> These petitioners were not charged with an attempt to overthrow the Government. They were not charged with overt acts of any kind designed to overthrow the Government. They were not even charged with saying anything or writing anything designed to overthrow the Government. The charge was that they agreed to assemble and to talk and publish certain ideas at a later date: The indictment is that they conspired to organize the Communist Party and to use speech or newspapers and other publications in the future to teach and advocate the forcible overthrow of the Government. No matter how it is worded, this is a virulent form of prior censorship of speech and press, which I believe the First Amendment forbids. I would hold 3 of the Smith Act authorizing this prior restraint unconstitutional on its face and as applied . . .
>
> So long as this Court exercises the power of judicial review of legislation, I cannot agree that the First Amendment permits us to sustain laws suppressing freedom of speech and press on the basis of Congress' or our own notions of mere "reasonableness." Such a doctrine waters down the First Amendment so that it amounts to little more than an admonition to Congress. The Amendment as so construed is not likely to protect any but those "safe" or orthodox views which rarely need its protection . . .

There is hope, however, that in calmer times, when present pressures, passions and fears subside, this or some later Court will restore the First Amendment liberties to the high preferred place where they belong in a free society.

In 1957, the Court in *Yates v. United States* pulled back a little from *Dennis*; the Smith Act did not prohibit advocacy of forcible overthrow of the government as an *abstract* doctrine. While *Yates* did not overrule *Dennis*, it handcuffed the Smith Act's conspiracy provisions basically unenforceable.

In 1969, *Brandenburg v. Ohio* held "mere advocacy" of violence was protected speech. *Brandenburg*, in essence, overruled *Dennis*, raising the criterion to incitement to an "imminent lawless action" to prohibit speech.

Many believe *Brandenburg* has thrown into the court's trashcan the clear-and-present-(or probable)-danger standard of *Schenck* and *Dennis* and moved closer to Holmes, Brandeis, or Black dissents; nevertheless, the court has repeatedly used *Schenck*'s precedent in holding that the destruction of a draft card could be prosecuted as a violation of Selective Service regulations even though carried out as a protest (*United States v. O'Brien*), but that burning an American flag at a protest could not be prosecuted because it posed no danger of causing a harm that the legislature had the power to forbid (*Texas v. Johnson*).

In 2010, the Supreme Court rejected the argument of Holmes's *Abrams* dissent. The facts in *Holder v. Humanitarian Law Project* were similar to those in *Abrams*: persons who planned to advocate the causes of Sri Lankan and Kurdish organizations, designated terrorist groups, had a reasonable fear of prosecution under the Patriot Act 2001 in providing material support for terrorist organizations. The court held that such prosecutions were not barred by the First Amendment, expressly rejecting the argument that a "specific intent" to assist terrorist acts was required, rejecting also the claim of the dissenting justices that the case was governed by the concurrence in *Whitney,* or by the standard stated in *Brandenburg*. Finally, in *Citizens United v. FEC,* the court's majority rejected the argument made by the dissenters that the First Amendment was premised on the value of democratic deliberation in the "marketplace of ideas." Instead, they held the First Amendment rights are individual, not based on communitarian considerations.

As the precedents stand at present, therefore, it appears that *Schenck* is still good law. Criminal attempts may be prosecuted even if carried out solely through expressive behavior, and a majority of the justices continue to view such prosecutions in the light of the majority opinion in *Abrams*; the court has relied on legislatures' judgments, at least in national security matters, that some forms of political advocacy may be prosecuted.

The rights of expressions and peaceful protest are crucial in a republic; information and ideas help to inform political debate and are essential to public accountability and transparency in government. Teddy Roosevelt in 1918 was adamant: "Free speech, exercised both individually and through a free press, is a necessity in any country where people are themselves free." Free speech would mean nothing if it were not used in public places. The rights to speech, press, protest, and to form and join associations or groups are without exception, the building blocks of the experiment of self-rule. These rights have been limited by law, the court, and executive actions to protect the interests of others (life, liberty, or property), but only when the limitation is proportionate and necessary in a republican society. The right to free expression will not protect a person from prosecution who tries to spread hateful lies against another, but it will protect fair comment. The right to protest won't protect violent gatherings, but it will protect peaceful protest.

In recent years, we have seen a variety of attempts to undermine the right of expression. Laws intended to combat antisocial behavior, terrorism, and serious crime are routinely used against legitimate protesters. Vague antiterrorism legislation that prohibits "encouragement" or "glorification" of terrorism threatens to make careless talk a crime. Membership of certain organizations can be banned under antiterror laws even if the organization is nonviolent and political; the IRS and conservative groups, Tea Party types. Hate speech laws have been extended in a piecemeal way to ban ever-expanding categories of speech. Broad antiterrorism powers of stop and search have been used to harass and stifle peaceful protesters. Free speech zones have been established to severely restrict assembly and protest around public officials. Even the Supreme Court, the "protector" of the minorities, forbids demonstrators within earshot of its chambers.

John Whitehead of the Rutherford Institute, a nonprofit civil liberties law firm, defending a protester, Harold Hodge, arrested in

January 2011 for standing on the plaza wearing a three-by-two-foot sign that said, "The U.S. Gov. Allows Police to Illegally Murder and Brutalize African Americans and Hispanic People," stated,

> If citizens cannot stand out in the open and voice their disapproval of their government, its representatives and its policies without fearing prosecution, then the First Amendment is little more than window-dressing on a store window—pretty to look at but serving little real purpose. Through a series of carefully crafted legislative steps and politically expedient court rulings, government officials have managed to disembowel this fundamental freedom.

All the issues raised by the First Amendment protection of freedom of expression cannot be raised here; there is a myriad of conflicting rights, powers of government, and rationales with many of the important questions of free speech and public safety, freedom of the press and fair trials, and freedom of association.

Clearly, your right to be free to express your views is one of the most important of those inalienable rights of which Jefferson spoke. As with other rights, it implies a corresponding duty; the recognition and zealous devotion to the protection of the same right for others, even for those with whom you disagree.

Generally, governments have a free hand in how they want to go about regulating these areas. Some may or may not trigger a constitutional protection; some may or may not involve situations that encroach upon the rights of others (protestors who block entrances), burdens on government functions (free flow of passersby); some forms of expression may or may not take a violent form or lead to criminal activity. In these areas, the court has set down few strict rules.

Freedom is not what we think it is! Whitehead sees we may merely be fooling ourselves if we think the expression is still free.

This holds true whether you're talking about the right to criticize the government in word or deed, the right to be free from government surveillance, the right to not have your person or your property subjected to warrantless searches by government agents, the right to due process, the right to be safe from soldiers invading your home, the right to be innocent until proven guilty and every other right that once reinforced the founders' belief that this would be "a government of the people, by the people and for the people."

Not only do we no longer have dominion over our bodies, our families, our property and our lives, but the government continues to chip away at what few rights we still have to speak freely and think for ourselves.

If the government can control speech, it can control thought and, in turn, it can control the minds of the citizenry.

The unspoken freedom enshrined in the First Amendment is the right to *think freely* and openly debate issues without being muzzled or treated like a criminal.

In other words, if we no longer have the right to tell a Census Worker to get off our property, if we no longer have the right to tell a police officer to get a search warrant before they dare to walk through our door, if we no longer have the right to stand in front of the Supreme Court wearing a protest sign or approach an elected representative to share our views, if we no longer have the right to protest unjust laws by voicing our opinions in public or on our clothing or before a legislative body—no matter how misogynistic, hateful, prejudiced, intolerant, misguided or politically incorrect they might be—then we do not have free speech.

What we have instead is regulated, controlled speech, and that's a whole other ballgame.

Protest laws, free speech zones, bubble zones, trespass zones, anti-bullying legislation, zero tolerance policies, hate crime laws and a host of other legalistic maladies dreamed up by politicians and prosecutors are conspiring to corrode our core freedoms purportedly for our own good.

In the name of "public safety and limiting economic damage," eighteen states regulate to discourage speech not wanted by the bureaucrats. A few examples of the most unconstitutional follow.

- In Arizona, police would be permitted to seize the assets of anyone involved in a protest that at some point becomes violent.
- Oregon lawmakers want to "require public community colleges and universities to expel any student convicted of participating in a violent riot."

- A proposed North Dakota law would give drivers the green light to "accidentally" run over protesters who are blocking a public roadway. Florida and Tennessee are entertaining similar laws.
- Pushing back against what it refers to as "economic terrorism," Washington wants to increase penalties for protesters who block access to highways and railways.
- A North Carolina law would make it a crime to heckle state officials. Under this law, shouting at a former governor would constitute a crime.
- Missouri wants to make it illegal for anyone participating in an "unlawful assembly" to intentionally conceal "his or her identity by the means of a robe, mask, or other disguise."
- Oklahoma wants to create a sliding scale for protesters whose actions impact or impede critical infrastructure. The penalties would range from $1,000 and six months in a county jail to $100,000 and up to ten years in prison. And if you're part of an organization, that fine goes as high as $1 million.
- Michigan hopes to make it easier for courts to shut down "mass picketing" demonstrations and fine protesters who block entrances to businesses, private residences, or roadways up to $1,000 a day. That fine jumps to $10,000 a day for unions or other organizing groups.

Whitehead continues,

Every despotic measure used to control us and make us cower and fear and comply with the government's dictates has been packaged as being for our benefit, while in truth benefiting only those who stand to profit, financially or otherwise, from the government's transformation of the citizenry into a criminal class.

Remember, the Patriot Act didn't make us safer. It simply turned American citizens into suspects and, in the process, gave rise to an entire industry—private and governmental—whose profit depends on its ability to undermine our Fourth Amendment rights.

So, too, these protest laws are not about protecting the economy or private property or public roads. Rather, they are intended to muzzle discontent and discourage anyone from challenging government authority.

These laws are the shot across the bow.

They're intended to send a strong message that in the American police state, you're either a patriot who marches in lockstep with the government's dictates or you're a pariah, a suspect, a criminal, a troublemaker, a terrorist, a radical, a revolutionary.

Yet by muzzling the citizenry, by removing the constitutional steam valves that allow people to speak their minds, air their grievances and contribute to a larger dialogue that hopefully results in a more just world, the government is deliberately stirring the pot, creating a climate in which violence becomes inevitable.

One of the purposes of these freedoms of expression—speech, assembly, petition, press, and, yes, religion—are the key to a republic, the experiment. But it is also the safety valve, a release for grievances. When there is no safety release, "there is no one to hear what the people have to say, because government representatives have removed themselves so far from their constituents," violent revolution is soon to follow. Today, from Ferguson to UC-Berkeley to Chicago in flames to highways being closed what is "for our best interest" may be leading to our destruction. Jack Kennedy and Marin Luther King Jr. both saw the future when dissent is caged. "Those who make peaceful revolution impossible will make violent revolution inevitable" (Kennedy), while Martin saw the "spontaneous explosion of anger by various citizen groups" and inevitable suppression by the government.

In March 2017, violence took the lead over free speech. Charles Murray was scheduled to speak at Middlebury College in Vermont. Murray is the writer of *The Bell Curve* in which he and fellow author Richard Herrnstein argue that intelligence is a better predictor than parental socioeconomic status or education level of many individual outcomes such as income, job performance, pregnancy out of wedlock, and crime. But the mob prevented his presentation—"white supremacy" wasn't welcome. Murray was attacked and was run out to another venue; his host, a political science professor, was assaulted and needed medical care.

I went onstage, got halfway through my first sentence, and the uproar began.

First came a shouted recitation in unison of what I am told is a piece by James Baldwin. I couldn't follow the words. That took a few minutes. Then came the chanting. The protesters had prepared several couplets that they chanted in rotations—"Hey, hey, ho, ho, white supremacy has to go," and the like.

Although Murray was able to present in the new site, yelling and screaming and pounding on the walls outside that room continued the whole speech. As he tried to leave, protesters wearing ski masks blocked him. Campus security were needed to escape.

> If it hadn't been for Allison and Bill keeping hold of me and the security guards pulling people off me, I would have been pushed to the ground. That much is sure. What would have happened after that I don't know, but I do recall thinking that being on the ground was a really bad idea, and I should try really hard to avoid that.

Murray stated he was afraid that

> the intellectual thugs will take over many campuses. In the mid-1990s, I could count on students who had wanted to listen to start yelling at the protesters after a certain point, "Sit down and shut up, we want to hear what he has to say." That kind of pushback had an effect. It reminded the protesters that they were a minority. I am assured by people at Middlebury that their protesters are a minority as well. But they are a minority that has intimidated the majority. The people in the audience who wanted to hear me speak were completely cowed. That cannot be allowed to stand. A campus where a majority of students are fearful to speak openly because they know a minority will jump on them is no longer an intellectually free campus in any meaningful sense.

Similar tactics have become the norm. Taking right from Marcuse, free speech will not be allowed to the intolerant, the differing of opinion, opinions that may hurt others' feelings, the Fascist. Congressional local town meetings with their constituencies have become mob scenes but not by voters, rather paid, full-time protesters. Many of the same who protest *Citizens United* for allowing corporations to "protest" with millions of dollars in PAC monies are now using paid professional to disrupt elected government.

Thierry Meyssan of Voltairenet.org, on March 1, 2017, issued a warning to the American electorate that their opinions are being manipulated by a vast conspiracy to undermine the voters' decision, the media, and the Republic. Meyssan is a French intellectual, founder and chairman of Voltaire Network and the Axis for Peace Conference. His columns specializing in international relations feature in daily newspapers and weekly magazines in Arabic, Spanish, and Russian. His last two books published in English, *9/11 the Big Lie* and *Pentagate,* deal with the shadow government that is as Lofgren said keeps a façade of a republic. But this time it is a vast "scientifically organized" to undermine the newly elected president Trump and the very system that selected him.

From the Women's March two days after his inauguration, riots at Berkeley against Milo Yiannopoulus, Anne Coulter, and Ben Shapiro (all conservative speakers invited by student groups), and the Middlebury event of Charles Murray, to a worldwide March for "Science" all to show Donald Trump as "not only a misogynist but also an obscurantist" and literally unfit to hold any office. The man behind this organization is an ex-Republican operative that did the same against Bill Clinton—Troopergate, the Whitewater affair, and Monica Lewinsky—and Mitt Romney after switching sides. Hired by the Obama-Clinton-Soros triad, David Brock "cleared" Hillary of her role in the assassination of the US ambassador in Benghazi and ruined Bernie Sanders in the Democratic primaries of 2016, which have now been acknowledged by the Democratic National Committee. The *National Review* called him "a right-wing assassin who has become a left-wing assassin."

Who paid Brock to switch teams? Meyssan is adamant, the deep state. It is the same group that used Watergate to stop Nixon (deep throat, later identified as Mark Felt, assistant to and taking orders from J. Edgar Hoover) and to force Bill Clinton to engage in conflict in Yugoslavia.

The current effort against Trump and his outsiders and "Drain the Swamp" campaign was assembled before he even took office. With a budget of nearly $100 million, three hundred specialists in social media, IT, espionage, riot organizations, and hundreds of "snowflake" volunteer workers, the goal is to destroy the image of not just this president but the very presidency and institutions of the "land of Liberty" by creating racial conflicts, chaos on college campuses, and warfare between police and paid provocateurs.

The big four in this conspiracy are the following:

- *Media Matters* is to watch, listen, read everything the president does, and scour for any mistake. You read their reports every day in your local newspapers. He said this when he should have said that. "He can't be trusted—he spelled coverage 'covfefe.'" Media Matters also "contributes" its media to public schools for free. I had a young Boy Scout cheer when I was talking about the three branches, telling them that if President Trump dies, Mike Pence is next in line. Dinesh D'Souza's new book, *The Big Lie,* says the Progressives have the big three institutions under their control: media, education, and Hollywood. Here Media Matters gets two for one!

- *American Bridge 21st Century* is to collect all video on the current administration. They have over two thousand hours of Trump and nearly twenty thousand members of the cabinet. And like a Facebook junkie, it uses Department of Defense software to cut and paste and create a new reality. It can also compare old video with new to point out contradictions in any statement.

- *Citizens for Responsibility and Ethics in Washington* (CREW) is a DC law firm whose job is to look at anything that may be or become a scandal. Most are *pro bono* Democratic supporters working with Democratic legislators to impeach or invoke the Twenty-Fifth Amendment of incompetence as president. This is the same group that prepared the case against Trump's immigration decree, Executive Order 13769.

- *Shareblue* is an electronic media company that claims 140 million viewers per month with newsletters and thirty-second videos. It will base itself on two other groups—a company that makes documentary videos, *The American Independent*, and a statistical unit, *Benchmark Politics,* producing and spreading preordained themes. Recent headlines show a contradiction with their website's stated purpose—"optimistic, honest, and unafraid."

After Black Voters Win Alabama Election, GOP Declares Their Votes Don't Count

Trump Is under the Influence of Vladimir Putin

Trump Is a Weak and Quick-Tempered Personality, He's Manic-Depressive

Trump Was Not Elected by the Majority of US Citizens and Is, Therefore, Illegitimate

His Vice-President, Mike Pence, Is a Fascist

Panicked GOP Rushes to Make Secret Tax Deal before Alabama Seats Its New Dem Senator

Half the Country Now Believes Trump Has Groped and Harassed More Than a Dozen Women

Trump Is a Billionaire Who Will Constantly Be Faced with Conflicts of Interest between His Personal Affairs and Those of State

Trump Is a Puppet of the Koch Brothers, Who Are Famous for Sponsoring the Extreme Right

Trump Is a White Supremacist and a Threat to Minorities

GOP Plans to Make California Fire Victims Pay for Billionaires' Tax Cuts

The Anti-Trump Opposition Just Keeps Growing outside Washington

Overthrowing Trump Will Take Time, So Don't Let's
Weaken Our Resolve

Semiprotected speech

Fake news, "leaks," generated news with software to splice and delete
segments, even words, make it harder and harder to obtain real press.
If someone feels she has been defamed of her character in a publication
of a known falsehood, she can bring a civil action of libel against the
offending party and collect both compensatory and punitive damages.
Truth is the only defense to libel; good motives don't matter; half-truths
are as bad as lies. The same applies to Internet posts, phone texts,
Tweets, and spoken defamations. Unfortunately, those in the public eye
have much less protection. False statements are not necessarily libel or
slander if, say, given by an anonymous tip, and the media published it
without malice, intent to harm; it's not defamation per *New York Times
v. Sullivan* (1964).

In *Stanley v. Georgia* (1969), it was OK to possess literature that is
obscene but not for minors. Thus, it was OK to punish those who use
the mail to send it.

In *Cohen v. California* (1971), the court was asked if "fighting
words" could be put on a sign or clothing, in this case the F-word on a
jacket. The test is whether others can avert their eyes easily enough and
do not experience a direct insult in terms of offensiveness. The court
allowed it; free speech protects racist, sexist, or violent clothing. In 1914,
as the Great War heated up, the famous historian of the Constitution,
Charles Beard resigned in protest over the firing of antiwar professors
at Columbia University. Today's alt-right, alt-left, Antifa thugs could
use his advice.

> If we have to suppress everything we don't want to hear, this
> country is resting on a pretty wobbly basis . . . I was among
> the first to urge a declaration of war by the United States,
> and I believe that we should now press forward with all our
> might to a just conclusion. But thousands of my countrymen
> do not share this view. Their opinions cannot be changed
> by curses or bludgeons. Arguments addressed to their reason
> and understanding are our best hope.

What about in the case of police and speech? Speech that directly threatens the officers' safety ("I'm coming down to the station and kill you") or clearly hinders the officers' performance of their duties is criminal? Yet certain types of profanity, name-calling, and obscene gestures are now constitutionally protected if directed to the officials. There are too many examples to list them all, but most of the unprotected language involves those four-letter words like "Damn you" and "F*** you." Recently, Hollywood entertainers have edged toward the line of unacceptable. Madonna threatened to blow up the White House. In a profanity-laced speech at the Women's March in January 2017, the fifty-eight-year-old pop singer said she was "angry" and "outraged" over Trump becoming the forty-fifth president. Many called for her indictment as threatening the president.

> Yes, I have thought an awful lot about blowing up the White House. But I know that this won't change anything. We cannot fall into despair.

Though, later without addressing her original ballistics, tweeted, it was out of context,

> My speech began with "I want to start a revolution of love." ♥ I then go on to take this opportunity to encourage women and all marginalized people to not fall into despair but rather to come together and use it as a starting point for unity and to create positive change in the world.
>
> I spoke in metaphor and I shared two ways of looking at things—one was to be hopeful, and one was to feel anger and outrage, which I have personally felt. However, I know that acting out of anger doesn't solve anything. And the only way to change things for the better is to do it with love.

In today's politically correct world, many issues have started to revolve around what is hateful, mean, or derogatory speech, triggers, microaggressions. The court has struggled with these all. The Framers wanted all speech, even speech many find disgusting, to be protected. Even conservative justices try to strangle speech by stating the Founders were concerned with absolute freedom of "political speech." But again, where does the line lie? In 1964, the court in *Garrison v. Louisiana* said hate-motivated speech will be protected if the speaker honestly speaks out of hatred. In *RAV v. City of St. Paul* (1992), teenagers burned a cross inside the yard of an African American family. The teens could not be punished under an overbroad hate crimes statute and that since the conduct contained a political message, even more so. How easy will it be to determine when a KKK cross-burning is a statement of group solidarity (protected by the First Amendment) rather than an unprotected attempt to arouse the fear of racial or religious minorities?

The court has had plenty to say about everything from a free speech at school to teenagers' rights in the legal system. We saw in the *Gault* case, the court ruled that teenagers have distinct rights under the Constitution. Since *Gault*, the court has decided many cases concerning those under eighteen—from speech, press, dress codes, and privacy at school.

In the United States, public school students have certain rights when it comes to what they wear to class. For instance, in the 1996 case *Pyle v. School Committee of South Hadley*, two brothers, Jonathan and Jeffrey Pyle, wore T-shirts that the school's dress code prohibited. What started out as a simple issue turned in a series of confrontations between two brothers, their father, a constitutional college professor, and an unprepared school district. A gym teacher told Jeffrey he could not wear "Coed Naked Band: Do It to the Rhythm." Twice Jeffrey requested that the school formally draft a dress code, which it did not have; like many decisions at the school level, it is based on the boss's values, too vague and arbitrary to enforce. The school finally wrote a dress code, but the boys continued to push to destroy the school's authority in violating the First Amendment. Shirts were banned, and then unbanned, as the school struggled to implement its own dress code against the challenges of the Pyle family. Ultimately, only the Coed Naked shirt that originally sparked the conflict and another worn by Jonathan ("See Dick Drink. See Dick Drive. See Dick Die. Don't Be A Dick.") were banned under the new policy. The court held that a student had a First Amendment free speech right to wear the shirt as long as it was not actually disrupting her classes.

US law on student dress codes clearly states that schools can create "reasonable" dress code rules. However, many court cases have depended on what the word "reasonable" means. Courts have ruled that school dress codes are "reasonable" if they promote hygiene, prevent disruptions, promote safety, or reduce violence. Particular dress code rules that courts have approved include prohibiting cleats or metal shoe plates, prohibiting shorts, and prohibiting hats or head wraps in class; some have used the rationale that girls' short shorts or skirts disrupt learning because it distracts young boys. The dress code ruling derived from three essential cases dealing with students' rights of expression.

A case during the Vietnam War, *Tinker v. Des Moines* (1969) dealt with students wearing black armbands in protest of the war. In late 1965, John and Mary Beth Tinker and their friend Chris Eckhardt wore the black armbands to school in Des Moines, Iowa; school officials told them to remove the armbands, and when they refused, they were suspended (John, fifteen, from North High; Mary Beth, thirteen, from Warren Harding Junior High; and Chris, sixteen, from Roosevelt High). As juveniles, they had their parents sue, claiming a violation of their First Amendment right of speech.

The court sided with the students. Students or teachers don't "shed their constitutional rights to freedom of speech or expression at the schoolhouse gate." However, it was not an infinite license of expression; the First Amendment needs balance with school order: As long as an act of expression doesn't disrupt classwork or school activities or invade the rights of others, it's acceptable. The Tinkers "deviation consisted only in wearing on their sleeve a band of black cloth," symbolic speech. "They caused discussion outside of the classrooms, but no interference with work and no disorder."

Tinker was used in the following case, *Bethel*, when the school punishes a vulgar speech of Matthew Fraser. *Tinker* is still used by many lower court rulings on school attire, allowing nose rings and dyed hair, for example, but disallowing a T-shirt displaying a Confederate flag. The court used Tinker to allow in *Morse v. Frederick* (2007) schools to limit student speech that seems to advocate illegal drug use. The case concerned Joseph Frederick, an eighteen-year-old senior at Juneau-Douglas High School in Alaska who was suspended in 2002 for holding a banner that said, "Bong Hits 4 Jesus," while standing across the street from the school during the Olympic torch relay.

Schools have more leeway in both speech and press because schools are areas or learning, not just public spaces. In *Bethel School District v. Fraser* (1986), Matthew Fraser gave a speech nominating a fellow student for student office. It was made during school hours as a part of a school-sponsored educational program in self-government. Fraser had been warned by two teachers who told him they thought his prepared speech was not appropriate. The school felt it was sexually and profanely written, and Matthew was suspended for three days for having violated the school's "disruptive conduct" rule. Fraser sued. The court said schools have a right to regulate what is curriculum and how it is delivered. It also concluded that the First Amendment did not prohibit schools from prohibiting vulgar and lewd speech, since such discourse was inconsistent with the "fundamental values of public school education," as well as not pure political speech.

Cathy Kuhlmeier, Leslie Smart, and Leanne Tippett, juniors at Hazelwood East High School in St. Louis, Missouri, helped write and edit the school paper, *The Spectrum*, as part of a journalism class. *Hazelwood School District v. Kuhlmeier* (1988) brought the girls' articles on pregnancy and divorce in the school newspaper before the court.

The principal objected, and the two pages containing the articles in question as well as four other articles previously approved by the principal were deleted, saying they were too sensitive for younger students and contained too many personal details. The court held that educators did not "offend the 1st Amendment by exercising editorial control over the style and content of student speech in school-sponsored expressive activities, so long as their actions are reasonably related to legitimate pedagogical concerns."

Schools may censor newspapers and restrict other forms of student expression, including theatrical productions, yearbooks, creative writing assignments, and campaign *(Bethel)* and graduation speeches. But the court's ruling in *Hazelwood* encourages schools to look closely at a student activity before imposing any restrictions and to balance the goal of maintaining high standards for student speech with students' right to free expression.

Your belongings can be searched in school but not arbitrarily. TLO (Terry), a fourteen-year-old freshman at Piscataway High School in New Jersey, was caught smoking in a school bathroom by a teacher. The principal questioned her and asked to see her purse. Inside was a pack of cigarettes, rolling papers, and a small amount of marijuana. The police were called, and Terry admitted selling drugs at school. Her case went to trial, and she was found guilty of possession of marijuana and placed on probation. Terry appealed her conviction, claiming that the search of her purse violated her Fourth Amendment protection against "unreasonable searches and seizures."

Using the idea of *in loco parentis*, the justices ruled in favor of the school. Students do have a "legitimate expectations of privacy," but because of the school's responsibility to maintain "an environment in which learning can take place," they have the rights of parents to protect their charges from harm. The initial search of Terry's purse for cigarettes was reasonable based on the teacher's report that she'd been smoking in the bathroom; the rolling papers and marijuana found was also reasonable; anything found in a reasonable search is also reasonable.

TLO v. New Jersey (1969) is a major case of search and seizure at school. Basically, school officials may search a student's property if they have a "reasonable suspicion" rather than "probable cause" that a school rule has been broken or a student has committed or is in the process of committing a crime.

This "reasonable suspicion" standard can also be used in schools to subject a group to searches. James Acton, a twelve-year-old seventh-grader at Washington Grade School in Vernonia, Oregon, wanted to try out for the football team. The district required all student athletes to take drug tests at the beginning of the season and on a random basis during the school year. James's parents refused to let him be tested because, they said, there was no evidence that he used drugs or alcohol. The school suspended James from sports for the season. He and his parents sued the school district, arguing that mandatory drug testing without suspicion of illegal activity constituted an unreasonable search under the Fourth Amendment.

The school district won the court's opinion. Schools must balance students' right to privacy against the need to make school campuses safe and keep student athletes away from drugs. The drug-testing policy required students to provide a urine sample if involved in athletics. The test was only a limited invasion of privacy. "Students who voluntarily participate in school athletics have reason to expect intrusions upon normal rights and privileges, including privacy."

The court noted that all students surrender some privacy rights while at school: they must follow school rules and submit to school discipline. But student athletes have even fewer privacy rights, the justices said, and must follow rules that don't apply to other students. Joining a team usually requires getting a physical exam, obtaining insurance coverage, and maintaining a minimum grade point average. And athletes must be willing to shower and change in locker rooms, further reducing their privacy. "School sports are not for the bashful," *Vernonia School District 45J v. Acton* (1995). In 2002, the court has ruled any student involved in any school activity could be required to take random drug testing (*Board of Education v. Earls*).

Now, what about the discipline if "caught"? Teachers can use corporal (physical) punishment if allowed by school district policy. James Ingraham, a fourteen-year-old eighth grader at Drew Junior High School in Miami, was taken to the principal's office after being accused by a teacher for being rowdy in the school auditorium. The principal decided to give him five swats with a paddle, but James said that he hadn't done anything wrong and refused to be punished. He was subsequently held down while given twenty swats. Corporal punishment was permitted in the school district. James suffered bruises that kept him out of school for ten days, and he had to seek medical attention. James and his mother sued the principal and other school officials, claiming the paddling had violated Eighth Amendment protections against "cruel and unusual punishments."

The court in *Ingraham v. Wright* (1977) ruled against James. Reasonable physical discipline at school does not violate the Constitution. The Eighth Amendment was designed to protect convicted criminals from excessive punishment at the hands of the government—not schoolchildren who misbehave, *in loco parentis*. They did direct teachers and principals to be cautious and use restraint when administering corporal punishment and consider the seriousness of the offense, the student's attitude and past behavior, the age and physical condition of the student, and the availability of a less severe but equally effective means of discipline. Nineteen states currently permit corporal punishment in public schools; thirty-one banned the practice.

Before we leave the rights of juveniles, there is one case that I have struggled with since decided. I had two sons about the time this case was in the courts. Parents should have the right—many power is better—to educate, raise, and discipline their children without state inference. Yet the issue is murky when the parents should not have become parents. Today, mainly because of government welfare programs condoning dysfunctional families, many parents have become breeders, not nurturing parents. In 1989, the state of Wisconsin became the battle ground over the rights of parents and the duty of the state over a child.

Four-year-old Joshua DeShaney lived with his father, who physically abused him, in Neenah, Wisconsin. At one point, the State Department of Social Services took custody of Joshua but drastically returned him after three days. Later, Joshua was hospitalized with bruises all over his body and severe brain damage. He survived but was permanently paralyzed and mentally disabled. His father was convicted of child abuse and sent to prison. Joshua's mother, incompetent as a parent herself, now sued the Department of Social Services for returning him to his father. She argued that the department had a duty to protect her son under the Fourteenth Amendment, which forbids the state from depriving "any person of life, liberty, or property, without due process of law." The court ruled against Joshua and his mother. It said essentially that the Constitution does not protect children from their parents and that therefore the government was not at fault in Joshua's abuse. The court has consistently respected parents' rights to discipline their children. But even though the government isn't required under the Constitution to protect children, all states assume this responsibility through child protection laws; they generally defer to state and local governments to enforce these laws and to intervene in cases of mistreatment, *DeShaney v. Winnebago County Social Services* (1989).

The court was formed to protect the weak, "losers" in a democratic vote, minorities, outsiders, disenfranchised. As of late, the court appears to be more a Hamiltonian/Marshall court of bolstering government over We the People. From forcing firms to serve customers to creating a "tax" on health care to allowing interference in contracts to unlimited search power of the state, the court has become a major legislator rather than an arbitrator. Justice Ruth Ginsburg believes her "dissenting opinions, like [her] briefs, are intended to persuade. And sometimes one must be forceful about saying how wrong the Court's decision is." Her opponent and best friend on the court, Justice Antonin Scalia, disagrees on trying to legislate through the courts: "Persuade your fellow citizens it's a good idea and pass a law. That's what democracy is all about. It's not about nine superannuated judges who have been there too long, imposing these demands on society."

The court in its 2017 term is venturing further into areas where its jurisdiction does not allow under the instruction manual. How much education is enough education? Does gender exist, or is it just a felling, an attitude? What doors will be opened if someone feels like sixty-five—can they collect social security? Can I drive at twelve—I feel I'm good enough—with a booster seat? Are police officers legally liable for their actions or merely agents of the government, thus immune from responsibility? What if they violate constitutional rights? What is excessive force? Does the "child benefit" decisions of public funding of private schools allow safe playground equipment to be supplied by the state? Does a state have the power to "take" your property by denying improvements or sale of land? Does the Constitution cross borders? Location, location, location—can a plaintiff search for the best judge to hear his case?

A case that crosses into criminal procedures is a case dealing with convicted sexual predators. In *Packingham v. North Carolina* (2017), the Supreme Court decided that a law that bars sex offenders from using sites like Facebook or Twitter was unconstitutional. In its decision, the court recognized the fundamental nature of the Internet and social media to exercising one's First Amendment rights and found North Carolina's law to be far too broad. The court's logic is simple; a state cannot stop legal and natural rights to prevent a possible illegal activity—an important protection of free expression online.

FEDERALISM

Be assured that if this new provision [the Fourteenth Amendment] be engrafted in the Constitution, it will, in time, change the entire structure and texture of our government, and sweep away all the guarantees of safety devised and provided by our patriotic Sires of the Revolution.
—Orville Browning

THE NATIONAL GOVERNMENT is often the key in many studies of civics or government, even economics at the macrolevel. Yet man in the state of nature created government at local levels to protect his rights. As former speaker of the house, Tip O'Neill from Massachusetts once said, "All politics is local." Most Americans, until the takeover by the Progressives at the beginning of the twentieth century, knew national government as the post office may be military if they were drafted. Government in Washington DC seldom touched people's lives. Yet elections, debates, and even world issues were dealt with by citizens at the town governmental level. States were for most the government they understood and controlled. When the Progressives took away the Senate, added national income taxes, and created the Federal Reserve, the national government began a growth unintended by the Framers and antithetical to Jefferson's and Madison's philosophy. Let's look closely at not only the true idea of Federalism as proposed by the Framers but also how again Hamilton's consolidated government prevailed.

In 1787, the Framers of the Constitution created our federal system of government. They created this system to solve a tough political problem; however, they needed to convince fiercely independent states to join to create a stronger central government.

James Madison explained the dilemma in a letter to George Washington before the start of the Constitutional Convention. He said the creation of "one single republic" excluding the states would be "unattainable." Madison, in trying to address the problem, said, "I have sought for a middle ground which may at once support a due supremacy of national authority, and not exclude (the states)." Federalism was the answer.

To answer the many opponents, Robert Yates of New York, Elbridge Gerry of Massachusetts, Luther Martin of Maryland, arising in the ratification conventions of the states, in *Federalist 45*, Madison stated that the powers delegated by the proposed Constitution to the national government are few and defined: "war, peace, negotiation, and foreign commerce; with which last the power of taxation will, for the most part, be connected." Those that are to remain in the state governments are numerous and indefinite: the "ordinary course of affairs, concern the lives, liberties, and properties of the people, and the internal order, improvement and prosperity of the States." States have all the powers not restricted to them by Article I, Section 10 of the constitution, their own state constitutions, and the will of the sovereign people within each state; in essence, other than limits placed on it by their citizens, states have unlimited powers.

Federalism today means the division of governmental powers between the national and state governments. Both levels of government may act directly on citizens through their own officials and laws. The national government derives its power to act from our Constitution; the states from the people. Each level of government has certain subjects over which its powers are supreme. Both levels of government must also agree to any changes in the US Constitution.

Like the states, the sovereignty of Indian tribes was decided in *Worcester v. Georgia* (1832) as inherent to their peoples; *Worcester* granting national protection to the Cherokee nation from the actions of the state governments. Indian tribes are subject to national, not state law. Each tribe has a unique form of government, laws, and citizenship.

One key idea of Federalism is that two levels of government—national and state—each have independent powers to act on the citizens of the United States. Under Federalism, for example, the state of Wisconsin has formal authority over its residents, but so does the national government in Washington DC. Wisconsin's residents must obey Wisconsin's laws as well as those passed by the national government. And, unfortunately, these same residents must also pay taxes to both the state of Wisconsin and the national government.

This is a very different approach to government from the two forms known to the Framers in 1787—the confederation and the unitary government. Remember in a unitary government, all formal political power rests with a central government. The central government acts directly on the people. Today, France and Japan are examples of unitary governments. Unitary governments have geographical subdivisions, but the subdivisions do not have any real power of their own. They are the local offices for the central government. They may also be abolished at any time. France, for example, is divided into units called "departments." Each department is set up and run, however, by the central government in Paris.

The other form of government known to them in 1787 was a confederation. A confederation is an alliance of independent states. In such an alliance, the states create and operate a national government. The national government handles certain limited jobs for the states, usually foreign affairs, war, and post offices. This national government can only do what the states permit. The national government does not act directly on the people. The Articles of Confederation, in operation from 1781 to 1788, established a confederation form of government. As we saw, the powers of the national government were limited. It could not directly tax the people, for example; only the states had this power.

The Framers of the Constitution drew on ideas from both the unitary and confederation forms of government to create a federation or "federal republic." No one at the Philadelphia Convention was quite sure what this new idea of a federal system would look like. At that time, few delegates used the term "Federalism" to describe the plan they were designing. These people were sure, however, that the powers of government had to be divided in a fresh way between the national government and the states. Federalism is just another check and balance. While the checks between the branches are "horizontal," the checks by the states on the central government are "vertical."

Since 1787, many nations have adopted a federal system of government. Canada, India, Australia, Brazil, Nigeria, Germany, and Mexico have federal forms of government. In each system, the exact arrangements between the states and the central governments vary.

Yet all true forms of federal systems share four common characteristics. These characteristics reflect ideas from both the unitary and confederation forms of government. Federal systems give the national government and the states some powers to exercise directly over the people. The member states retain certain powers beyond the control of the national government. Federalism guarantees each state has a right to exist and that the states in the Union are equal under the law. Each state has the right to be treated equally regardless of its size or population. Last, if disputes erupt between the two levels of government, a judicial branch interprets the meaning of their constitutions and their laws as well as settles disputes between the nation and the states.

Both the national government and the states have powers in our federal system. These powers and how they are divided are explained in the Constitution.

Article I, Section 8 of the Constitution lists the powers that belong only to the national government. Sections 9 and 10 of Article I list the powers that the national government and the states, respectively, are forbidden to exercise. The Tenth Amendment reserves for the states traditional powers over areas such as public health, education, fire and police protection, local elections, and marriages and divorces, among others. In addition, the Tenth Amendment is an explicit reminder that the powers not given to the national government or specifically denied to states are state powers.

Since both the central government and the states are able to pass laws to carry out their powers, the Framers wrote Article VI of the Constitution to prevent the states from ignoring or contradicting national laws made with constitutional. Article VI says that "this Constitution and the Laws of the United States . . . shall be the supreme law of the land." This statement, known as the supremacy clause, is supposed to guarantee Federalism. Though the *supremacy clause* was used in the *McCulloch v. Maryland* (1819) decision, we saw Madison objected to Marshall's opinion. The court ruled that state governments could not impose a tax on the central government. But more importantly to the Hamiltonian interpretation of government, Marshall established that the Constitution grants to Congress implied powers greater than understood by the ratifiers. You notice the quote above, it is missing a key element, "Laws of the United States which shall be made in pursuance thereof . . ." Madison and Jefferson both agreed all those *made in pursuance thereof* shall be the supreme law of the land. Like we discussed before, a good law disobeyed is a crime, a bad law obeyed is a sin. Congress may only pass laws with a connected constitutional power.

In December 1787, Roger Sherman, at the Connecticut Convention, was clear that the "excellency of the constitution" was "when the government of the united States acts within its proper bounds it will be the interest of the legislatures of the particular States to Support it, but when it leaps over those bounds and interferes with the rights of the *State governments* [my emphasis] they will be powerful enough to check it."

Hamilton, in *Federalist* 33, wrote that the new Congress could only pass laws expressly pursuant to the Constitution. In the fall of the following year, at North Carolina's ratifying convention, James Iredell stood and spoke, "Congress passes a law consistent with the Constitution, it is to be binding on the people. If Congress, under pretense of executing one power, should, in fact, usurp another, they will violate the Constitution."

For creating a functional national government, Article I, Sections 8–10 must be uncloudy, uncluttered. States may not pass law interfering with the valid constitutional powers of the national government. State law may not conflict with national law. The supremacy clause means that although the powers of the national government are limited, they are, nevertheless, supreme. The states cannot ignore these laws. Nor can they pass laws that conflict with the Constitution or laws made by the national government pursuant to the Constitution.

Changing division of powers

In many cases, the division of powers between the national government and the states is quite clear. No one disputes that only the national government has the power to coin money. However, in other areas, the division of powers is not so clear-cut.

For example, state governments have the power to regulate commerce within their states. The national government has the power to regulate commerce between the states. This distinction has become blurred. Recently, the national government passed a law allowing double-trailer trucks to travel on the nation's highways. Many states, however, had earlier passed laws to prohibit these types of trucks from traveling on some state roads. The question arose as to whether the states had the right to regulate traffic on their roads or whether the national government had this right because the trucks travel between the states. The national government and the states have battled for years over the regulation of commerce. Such questions concerning commerce and Federalism are often settled by the Supreme Court, since Marshall is primarily on the side of national government.

Because the division of powers between the states and central government is subject to the court's review, these powers are not permanently fixed. In fact, the role of the national government and the state governments, and the positions of the Supreme Court on this issue have changed many times in the last two hundred years. For example, in the early 1800s, any attempt by the national government to regulate the working conditions in a local factory would have been considered a violation of state's rights and Federalism. Today, because of court decisions and governmental actions, this regulation is widely accepted.

Originally, Federalism was "dual Federalism." This is a system whereby the national and the state governments are cosovereigns, each having supreme control over its own sphere of operation. It is also referred to as "layer cake Federalism." The national government was to be limited by specific, enumerated rules and purposes defined by the Constitution. There is a strict division of power between national and state governments. Dual Federalism was dominant from the 1790s up to the 1930s.

Because of the Great Depression, FDR used the crisis—never let a good crisis go by—to extend national power over states' power. "Cooperative Federalism" is a concept of government in which national, state, and local governments work together to solve problems interactively and cooperatively. It is also known as "marble cake Federalism." National and state governments share functions and collaborate on major national priorities. This relationship has predominated since the 1930s.

In relation to this cooperative relationship, "fiscal Federalism" is an approach to government spending concerned with understanding which levels of government are most efficient with specific taxation and expenditure policies. Fiscal Federalism focuses on national-to-state transfer payments and block grants, though, which the national government shares revenue with state and local governments. When the money is there, states tend to jump on board quickly with hands out. Yet, often, money from the national mandate disappears, and the states are left with a requirement from above with no funding. These are called unfunded mandates. Recently, more and more states are beginning to realize the costs to their taxpayers and refusing to buy in.

Since the days of the struggle between Jeffersonians and Hamiltonians as to which is greater, states or a consolidated central government, through the Civil War and into the present, states' rights, should be powers, only humans have rights, has been a rallying call for both sides. The centralizers have consistently labeled the states' rights advocates as traitors, secessionists, even racists. To men like Daniel Webster, Andrew Jackson, and Abe Lincoln, talk of states' rights have brought threats of and eventually acts of war. The famous debate between Webster and Robert Hayne of South Carolina over definition of the nation (Webster favoring a unified, indivisible contract, Hayne basing his "state's rights" arguments on Jefferson, Madison, and the ratifying conventions of the original thirteen) was clearly won by Hayne. Yet secession is only the final option for frustrated Jeffersonians. With the "secession" of Great Britain in 2016 from the European Union (BREXIT), talk has resurfaced in America of leaving the Union. After the Trump victory, a small yet vocal minority in California has called for secession (CALEXIT)!

Thomas Jefferson and James Madison, in the Kentucky and Virginia Resolutions of 1798, believed states each have "an equal right to judge for themselves" if laws are just or not. As the states created the Constitution, they could determine its power. We have seen already where states denied the central government's authority. In the War of 1812, Daniel Webster advocated that the states ignore the draft; something Charles Schenck will go to prison for in 1917. The South Carolina Nullification Crisis of 1832 was a protest against taxation. Even the Progressive state of Wisconsin was willing to take up arms against the national government rather than enforce an immoral Fugitive Slave Act.

Erosion of states' powers was always a Hamiltonian desire, using the implied powers clause (Art. I, Sec. 8, Cl. 18), "elastic clause" John Marshall, in *McCulloch v. Maryland* (1819). Under the "protection" of contracts, Marshall in *Dartmouth* College: *The Trustees of Dartmouth College v. Woodward* (1819), took from New Hampshire the power to cancel contracts within its borders. Yet in *Charles River* (1837),

Massachusetts in violation of its contract with Charles River Bridge Company granted a second contract to a competing bridge. Marshall now cancelled the original contract in favor of the "public good."

As late as 1820, Thomas Jefferson was still warning against courts as only interpreters of the law. Writing to William Charles Jarvis in September 1820, the sage of Monticello said,

> To consider the judges as the ultimate arbiters of all constitutional questions; [is] a very dangerous doctrine indeed, and one which would place us under the despotism of an oligarchy. Our judges are as honest as other men, and not more so. They have, with others, the same passions for party, for power, and the privilege of their corps.

Jefferson could see the future of what will later be called states' rights. As Americans closed in on Civil War, James Buchanan (one of the most qualified for the office, one of the worst users of the office) signed a resolution to avoid war on March 2, 1861, two days before Lincoln's inauguration. It read,

> Resolved by the Senate and House of Representatives of the United States of America in Congress assembled, That the following article be proposed to the Legislatures of the several States as an amendment to the Constitution of the United States, which, when ratified by three-fourths of said Legislatures, shall be valid, to all intents and purposes, as part of the said Constitution, viz:
>
> ARTICLE THIRTEEN, No amendment shall be made to the Constitution which will authorize or give to Congress the power to abolish or interfere, within any State, with the domestic institutions thereof, including that of persons held to labor or service by the laws of said State.

President Buchanan had signed a resolve that would have forever permitted slavery and upheld states' rights. Only one state, Illinois, Lincoln's home state, had ratified this proposed amendment before the shots at Fort Sumter in 1861. Two more state legislatures ratified it, beginning with Ohio on May 13, 1861, followed by Maryland on January 10, 1862.

But the violence of Lincoln's unconstitutional war allowed the leadership to convince the citizens then and now that the Republic was more in danger from the states than the national government. "You never let a serious crisis go to waste. And what I mean by that it's an opportunity to do things you think you could not do before" (Rahm Emanuel). And so, after more than seventy years of national life, the people, by the currently accepted Thirteenth Amendment and the Fourteenth and Fifteenth, eviscerated the Jeffersonian states and created the Hamiltonian states restrictions, which a few years before would have been impossible, and unchained the deep staters' and monied interests.

In the destruction of property, lives, and Union after Lee's surrender, the original thirteenth amendment was removed from our Constitution. Congress resolved to amend dated December 5, 1864, approved and signed by President Lincoln, February 1, 1865, another amendment numbered XIII (which prohibited slavery in Section 1 and ended states' rights in Section 2) was sent to the states.

The Civil War forced national supremacy over the states. States were now under the thumb of consolidation. The Fourteenth Amendment granted Americans national citizenship and protection of "privileges and immunities" common to all Americans regardless of the laws of their individual state. Since the 1950s, states too slow for redress of grievance have been forced to take 5–4 opinions of the court as "new" state law.

Missouri v. the US: Whose law for ducks?

In *State of Missouri v. Holland* (1920), states lost the power to regulate their wildlife if it violated a national treaty. Central power is greater (Art. VI) in foreign affairs, and with an international treaty involved, states are secondary, even to foreign nations.

Ray P. Holland, a national game warden, stood before the Supreme Court of the United States in 1920 as the symbol of a power struggle. As a US government officer, he had tried to enforce national game laws in Missouri. But Missouri claimed it was none of his business.

The specific problem was about birds. Each autumn, ducks, geese, and dozens of other types of birds surged over Missouri's boundaries in their passage south from summer homes in the northern US and Canada. Missouri claimed the right to regulate the shooting, capture, and sale of the birds by its own state laws. The state's lawyers argued that US Game Warden Holland should be prevented from enforcing laws that Congress had made to support a US birdlife treaty with England.

Under all traditions of English and American law, they said, government held "absolute control of wild game." The Constitution had not delegated this control to the national government (in Art. I, Sec. 8) or denied it to the states (in Art. I, Sec. 9). Thus, according to the Tenth Amendment, the control of wildlife was one of the things "reserved to the states respectively." Missouri concluded, its legislature was "the representative of the people in their common ownership of the wild game within the borders of the state." Missouri appeared to have strong grounds for its arguments.

Several years earlier, conservationists in the United States and Europe had become concerned about the slaughter of migrating birds by hunters. In 1913, Congress was convinced by their arguments. It passed a national law that limited the hunting seasons and the number of migratory birds that could be killed. The Supreme Court, however, had agreed that hunting regulations were the business of the states. The law was overthrown.

But in 1916, the United States signed a treaty with England. This treaty committed the nation, with Canada (part of England at the time), to work out plans to limit the destruction of migratory birds. According to the Constitution (Article VI), such treaties are "the supreme law of the land." In 1918, the new migratory bird law was passed by Congress.

Missouri's lawyers protested that Congress should not be allowed to do anything under a treaty that it could not do without the treaty. They asked the court to wipe out the new law, as it had the old one. The question was did a treaty to do what the national government couldn't do, now overrule state powers under the supremacy clause? Or did the treaty infringe upon powers reserved to the states by the Tenth Amendment?

No. In a 7–2 decision, written by Holmes again, the court held that the national interest in protecting the wildlife could be protected only by national action. The court noted that the birds the government sought to protect had no permanent habitats within individual states and argued that "[b]ut for the treaty and the statute there soon might be no birds for any powers to deal with." The court thus upheld the exercise of the treaty power. The only limit on a treaty is that they may not violate the Constitution. And Holmes said there was no violation of the Tenth Amendment.

Holmes said that the Constitution may very well never included powers of regulation Congress or the executive are now exercising. He even felt that the national government could now claim powers it had been denied specifically in Article I, Section 9, as well as the ninth and Tenth Amendments because—get ready for this—of its unpredictable growth.

> . . . When we are dealing with words that also are a constituent act, like the Constitution of the United States, we must realize that they [words? Or the Framers?] have called into life a being the development of which could not have been foreseen completely by the most gifted of its begetters. It was enough for them to realize or to hope that they had created an organism; it has taken a century and has cost their successors much sweat and blood to prove that they created a nation. The case before us must be considered in the light of our whole experience, and not merely in that of what was said a hundred years ago. The treaty in question does not contravene any prohibitory words to be found in the Constitution. The only question is whether it is forbidden by some invisible radiation from the general terms of the Tenth Amendment. We must consider what this country has become in deciding what that Amendment has reserved.

When it comes to treaties, the Senate and the president are the sole limits on their powers. As we've seen with laws and regulations, the people are to be cared for by a benevolent government, with little, if any, restrictions.

Today, most of the economy, not just flying ducks, is regulated by both the state governments and the national government. One major aspect of Federalism was its flexibility. The states could experiment with dealing with issues that directly touched its citizens, divorce, marriage, adoption, education, welfare, and funding for roads and other infrastructure. The system could change as the country and conditions of the economy change. The national government has quite frankly bullied states with bribes, threats of cuts in spending, or placement of national projects in states that tolled the line.

Commerce clause

Much of the abuse of national powers upon the states comes from a rather ambiguous clause in the Constitution, the commerce clause (Art. I, Sec. 8, Cl. 3). From Obamacare to eating your own garden produce, the national government has imposed its version of the world rather than letting citizens of the individual fifty states to determine how to deal with issues important to them.

Walter Williams, economist at George Mason University, answers a question of one of his readers to his blog on the "infamous" commerce clause growth and manipulation by the Hamiltonians.

> Several weeks ago, under the title "Is It Permissible," I discussed how Congress systematically abuses the Constitution's "welfare clause" to control our lives in ways that would have been an abomination to the Framers. Quite a few readers pointed to my omission of Congress's companion tool to circumvent both the letter and spirit of the Constitution, namely the "commerce clause."
>
> The Constitution's Article I, Section 8, paragraph 3 gives Congress authority "To regulate Commerce with Foreign Nations, and among the several States, and with the Indian Tribes." During the war, the thirteen colonies formed a union under the Articles of Confederation (1778) whereby, "Each state retains its sovereignty, freedom, and independence, and every power, jurisdiction, and right, which is not by this Confederation expressly delegated to the United States, in Congress assembled." The Treaty of Paris (1783) that ended the war between the colonies and Great Britain recognized thirteen sovereign nations.
>
> A key failing of the Articles of Confederation was the propensity of states to erect protectionist trade barriers. When the Framers met in Philadelphia in 1787 and wrote the Constitution that governs us today, they addressed that

failure and through the commerce and the privileges and immunities clauses that created a national free-trade zone. Thus, the *original purpose of the commerce clause was primarily a means to eliminate trade barriers among the states* [emphasis mine]. They didn't intend for the commerce clause to govern so much of our lives. Indeed, as James Madison, the father of our Constitution, explained, "The powers delegated by the proposed Constitution to the federal government are few and defined. Those which are to remain in the State governments are numerous and indefinite."

For most of our history, the Courts foiled congressional attempts to use the "commerce clause" to sabotage the clear meaning of the Constitution, particularly the 9th and 10th Amendments. The Courts began caving in to congressional tyranny during the 1930s. That tyranny was sealed in 1942 by a little-known U.S. Supreme ruling in *Wickard vs. Filburn*. Mr. Filburn was a small farmer in Ohio. The Department of Agriculture had set production quotas. Mr. Filburn harvested nearly 12 acres of wheat above his government allotment. He argued that the excess wheat was unrelated to commerce since he grew it for his own use. He was fined anyway. The Court reasoned that had he not grown the extra wheat he would have had to purchase wheat; therefore, he was indirectly affecting interstate commerce.

If there's any good news, it's the tiny step the U.S. Supreme Court took in its in *U.S. vs. Lopez* (1995) ruling. In 1990, Congress passed the Gun-Free School Zones Act, citing their powers under the "commerce clause." Namely, the possession of a firearm in a local school zone substantially affected interstate commerce. Why? Violent crime raises insurance costs and those costs are spread throughout the population. Violent crime reduces the willingness of individuals to travel to high-crime areas within the country. Finally, crime threatens the learning environment thereby reducing national productivity. While all of this might be true, the relevant question is whether Congress had constitutional authority to pass the Gun-Free School Zones Act. The U.S. Supreme Court ruled it didn't saying, "If we were to accept the Government's arguments, we are hard pressed to posit any activity by an individual that Congress is without power to regulate." In other words, the hours children spend studying, the amount of rest they get and what they eat has something to do with learning. Congress could easily manufacture a case for the regulation of these activities based on their perverted interpretation of the "commerce clause."

While the *Lopez* ruling is a tiny step in the right direction, there's much more to be done. Constitution-respecting Americans should demand the impeachment of congressmen and other elected officials who ignore their oath of office to uphold and defend the Constitution.

Dennis Brady, in his opinion on *Lopez*, added,

The abuse of the commerce clause has been continuing ever since [*Wickard v. Filburn*]. Some recent examples is [are] new regulations giving the FTC power of yard sales (See my May 3, 2010 article: "You're Not My Mother, -The Rise of the "Nanny State" in America" on this [BradyReports.com] site) even though these private transactions do not cross state lines. Also the FDA has been targeting small farmers (including the Amish) that sell raw milk to individual citizens even though the vast majority of these small transactions do not cross state lines. There is even a proposal by the Obama administration for a federal tax on car owners on the amount of miles driven. I personally think this proposal violates the commerce clause since it does not involve the sale of a commodity (Such as gasoline) that has crossed state lines. How can the federal government tax miles that are driven within a particular state? This proposal if enacted will require every car to be fitted with a tracking device to record the amount of miles driven which in my opinion is also a violation the 4th Amendment.

The most recent and most overreaching is the Health Care Reform Act otherwise known as ObamaCare and its mandate for individuals to buy health insurance. This extreme view of commerce clause not only applies to some in the current congress or president but even by some Supreme Court Judges. This view was expressed during a recent exchange between Senator Tom Coburn (R-OK) during a committee hearing asked now Supreme Court judge Elena Kagan; "do you think the government through the Commerce Clause could regulate you eat three vegetables a day?" Her response was, yes. I can list several others here but I hope you get the point. The Federal Government current use and interpretation of the commerce clause as illustrated by Representatives Clyburn's statement [*There's nothing in the Constitution that says the federal government has anything to do with most of the stuff we do {Rep. James Clyburn (D-SC), 2009}]* at the beginning of this article would have shocked and sickened James Madison and the other Framers of the Constitution.

Yet today many states are starting to stand up to this grabbing of power by the central government. A national ID card law was passed by Congress, so many states refused to enforce it that the national government backed down. TSA pat-downs are being resisted, and a new call for nullification from Jefferson's and Madison's Kentucky and Virginia Resolutions is growing. The Tenth Amendment Center out of Los Angeles has pushed in all the states to nullify unconstitutional laws by state legislatures and local juries.

Since the infamous *Wickard vs. Fliburn* case, the feds use the commerce clause to justify virtually unlimited intrusion into nearly every corner of American life. From regulating the nation's entire health care system to waging a "war on drugs," federal agents wield power over the states and the people via the commerce clause.

Rep. John Yarmuth reluctantly admitted the truth during a radio interview in August 2010. The show host asked the Kentucky Democrat: what can't the federal government do if it can mandate Americans must purchase health insurance.

It really doesn't prohibit the government from doing virtually anything—the federal government. So I don't know the answer to your question, because I am not sure there is anything under current interpretation of the commerce clause that the government couldn't do, Yarmuth replied.

Of course, the commerce clause was never intended to grant such sweeping power. It was meant to allow the feds to regulate trade across state lines with some ancillary power to regulate shipping and transportation. That's it. It didn't grant the federal government the power to regulate manufacturing or agriculture, and it certainly wasn't meant to allow the feds to interfere with commerce engaged in strictly within a state's own borders. James Madison alluded to the limits of the commerce regulating power.

It is very certain that [the commerce clause] grew out of the abuse of the power by the importing States in taxing the non-importing, and was intended as a negative and preventive provision against injustice among the States themselves, rather than as a power to be used for the positive purposes of the General Government.

Some states are beginning to fight back against federal intrusion into intrastate commerce. Legislatures in Iowa, Florida and New Hampshire will consider bills during the 2012 session that seek to reestablish the states' control over commerce within their borders. And the Tenth Amendment Center expects a number of other states to follow suit this year.

House File 380 in Iowa reaffirms that the Constitution grants the federal government the power to regulate commerce among the several states, but the power to regulate intrastate commerce is reserved to the states or the people under the Ninth and Tenth Amendments. The bill goes on to declare:

All goods produced or manufactured, whether commercially or privately, within the boundaries of this state that are held, maintained, or retained within the boundaries of this state shall not be deemed to have traveled in interstate commerce and shall not be subject to federal law, federal regulation, or the authority of the Congress of the United States under its constitutional power to regulate commerce.

If the bill passes into law, any agent attempting to enforce federal law in violation of the act would be guilty of an aggravated misdemeanor and subject to appropriate penalties.

The Iowa bill, sponsored by Rep. Kim Pearson (R-Pleasant Hill), was initially filed in Feb. 2011 and will carry over into the 2012 session. Senate File 272, introduced at the same time by Sen. Kent Sorenson, serves as the companion bill.

A second Senate bill, Senate File 385, with 11 co-sponsors, proposes even stricter penalties. It would make it a class D felony to enforce any federal law interfering with intrastate commerce—that's commerce **within** Iowa's borders.

Rep. Matt Caldwell (R-Ft. Meyers) and Sen. Greg Evers (R-Crestview) sponsor the Florida version of the Intrastate Commerce Act. The bills' language reads similar to Iowa's, and the Florida act also makes it a felony for any agent to enforce federal law on intrastate commerce within Florida.

The New Hampshire General Court will consider HB1406. The bill, sponsored by Rep. Richard Ockerman (R-Rockingham) and Marc Tremblay (R-Berlin), declares, "all goods produced or manufactured, whether commercially or privately, within the boundaries of the state that are held, maintained, or retained within the boundaries of the state shall not be deemed to have traveled in interstate commerce and shall not be subject to federal law, federal regulation, or the authority of the Congress of the United States under its constitutional power to regulate commerce."

The New Hampshire Intrastate Commerce Act does not stipulate penalties for agents attempting to enforce federal law on intrastate commerce.

But the New Hampshire General Court will take up stronger intrastate commerce legislation applying specifically to food grown in the state. HB1650-FN exempts any food grown or produced, and consumed in New Hampshire from federal regulation, providing that "any public servant of the state of New Hampshire as defined by RSA 640:2 that enforces or attempts to enforce a federal act, order, law, statute, rule, or regulation upon a foodstuff labeled 'Made in New Hampshire,' that is produced commercially or privately in New Hampshire, and that remains within the state of New Hampshire shall be guilty of a class B misdemeanor."

Six legislators have signed on as sponsors of this bill.

And Utah will also consider an agriculture-centric version of the Act—Senate Bill 34 "prohibits federal regulation of an agricultural product that remains in Utah after it is made, grown, or produced in Utah, and addresses the designation of a Utah agricultural product."

Putting a stop the federal government's abuse of the commerce clause would fundamentally change the way the feds do business. Intrastate commerce acts establish a beachhead. The states must stand up and say, "No! We will no longer sit back and allow you to push us around!" It is our hope the legislatures in Florida, New Hampshire and Iowa will get these bills passed, and that other states will follow suit.

Brady adds,

There are a few states passing "State Sovereignty Resolutions" reaffirming their rights under the 10th Amendment which [is a] good first step but it does not have the "teeth" to "Punish" the federal government for overstepping its bounds under the Constitution. Four states tired of the federal government ignoring the Constitution are in the process this year of passing Intrastate Commerce

Act [2011]. This arises from the recent abuses from both the Congress in passing last year's healthcare reform bill and the rise in abuses by federal agencies in intra-state commerce under both Bush and Obama Administrations. The most recent state is Arizona with its bill (SB 1178) which will amend the Arizona Revised Statutes in order to provide that all goods grown, manufactured or made in Arizona and all services performed in Arizona, when such goods or services are sold, maintained, or retained in Arizona, shall not be subject to the authority of the Congress of the United States under its constitutional power to regulate commerce.

The bill even goes a step further by penalizing the federal government if they violate the statute:

A. Any official, agent, or employee of the United States government or any employee of an entity providing services to the United States government that enforces or attempts to enforce an act, order, law, statute, rule or regulation of the government of the United States in violation of this chapter is guilty of a class 6 felony, except that any fine imposed shall not exceed two thousand dollars.

B. Any public officer or employee of this state who enforces or attempts to enforce an act, order, law, statute, rule or regulation of the United States government in violation of this chapter is guilty of a Class 1 misdemeanor, except that any fine imposed shall not exceed five hundred dollars.

If passed by the legislature (and it looks like it will) and signed by the governor [this] should send a warning shot to remind Congress and the President that the states are sovereign entities under the Constitution and not mere provinces. The very fact that we as a federal republic have gotten to this point says how far we have come from the original intent of the Framers. This should awaken every American Citizen and state government that it is our duty to reign in the power of the national government to what was intended under our Constitution.

The Bill of Rights was added to protect citizens from the new national government. Yet these guarantees apply only to the national government, not the governments of the states. The Supreme Court held that the Bill of Rights only restricts the national government in *Barron v. Baltimore,* in 1833. Beginning in the 1950s, most especially with *Brown v. Board of Education, Topeka Kansas* (1954), the Supreme Court has used the Fourteenth Amendment's due process clause to say that no state can "deprive any person of life, liberty or property, without due process of law . . ." The writers of the Amendment in 1868 clearly never envisioned this broad of extension.

The extension of the commerce clause has gone even further to regulating individual behaviors within a state, between individuals, and in areas its writers also never intended. So as an individual, whose law do you obey? George Mason was furious over the inclusion of the commerce clause and the power of Congress to expand with a simple majority. In his *Objections to the Constitution*, he foresaw the danger of a majority commerce clause to the South, to minorities, to the states.

> By requiring only a majority to make all commercial and navigation laws, the five Southern States, whose produce and circumstances are totally different from that of the eight Northern and Eastern States, may be ruined, for such rigid and premature regulations may be made as will enable the merchants of the Northern and Eastern States not only to demand an exorbitant freight, but to monopolize the purchase of the commodities at their own price, for many years, to the great injury of the landed interest, and impoverishment of the people; and the danger is the greater as the gain on one side will be in proportion to the loss on the other. Whereas requiring two-thirds of the members present in both Houses would have produced mutual moderation, promoted the general interest, and removed an insuperable objection to the adoption of this government.

In the court's 2010–2011 calendar, a decision few watched yet few should ignore. It was a simple case of a spurned wife getting even with her best friend that slept with her husband. Carol Bond found out her best friend and her husband had an affair, and her friend was now pregnant. Carol decided to get even, spreading toxic chemicals on her friend's car and mailbox; minor chemical burns resulted.

She was arrested by the FBI, not local authorities, for "violating" the Chemical Weapons Convention (1998); the law banned nonpeaceful use of chemicals that "cause death, temporary incapacitation or permanent harm." She challenged the law as an unconstitutional violation of the Tenth Amendment, which provides that "powers not delegated to the United States . . . are reserved to the States respectively, or to the people." She felt the law was so vague and elastic and infringed on state criminal law, and was not "necessary or proper" to execute national powers, in this case, treaty power.

Robert Levy, of the Cato Institute, continues,

> An appellate court decided, however, that Bond did not have legal standing to assert a 10th Amendment right. After all, she sought to vindicate her personal interests, not the state's; no state was party to her lawsuit; and yet the 10th Amendment is presumably about federal intrusion on state authority. Enter the Supreme Court, which unexpectedly transformed a tedious legal issue—standing to sue—into an energetic discourse on the meaning of federalism.
>
> Many Americans believe federalism is synonymous with states' rights [powers]. Indeed, states do have some rights [powers] under the Constitution. For example, the Supreme Court has barred the federal government from "commandeering" the states to enforce federal gun laws and waste disposal regulations. States' rights are part of what federalism is about. Others think of federalism as conferring state powers. That, too, is part of the story. But the 10th Amendment confers no specific powers. It simply reserves to the states or the people all powers not granted to the national government. Whether a state can exercise a particular power depends on the state's constitution and laws—the legal pact between the state and its own citizens.

Federalism goes beyond states' rights and powers. Its essence is dual sovereignty—the Framers' ingenious system of shared authority between federal and state governments with each sovereign checking the other. The purpose of that check is to shield individuals from concentrations of power. Federalism is first and foremost a device to safeguard personal freedom. Justice Anthony Kennedy's opinion in Bond put it this way: Federalism "protects the liberty of all persons within a State by ensuring that laws enacted in excess of delegated governmental power cannot direct or control their actions . . . By denying any one government complete jurisdiction over all the concerns of public life, federalism protects the liberty of the individual from arbitrary power."

All nine members of the Court agreed: "States are not the sole intended beneficiaries of federalism . . . An individual has a direct interest in objecting to laws that upset the constitutional balance between the National Government and the States . . . Fidelity to the principles of federalism is not for the States alone to vindicate." Justice Kennedy also reminded us that "state sovereignty is not just an end in itself: Rather, federalism secures to citizens the liberties that derive from the diffusion of sovereign power."

So, Carol Bond will have her day in court to argue that her indictment for a local crime oversteps the federal government's treaty powers. "The individual," said the Supreme Court, "can assert injury from governmental action taken in excess of the authority that federalism defines." That principle extends, of course, to other matters the Court will be considering—including various challenges to President Obama's healthcare scheme now percolating through the appellate courts.

Here is the logic: (1) The federal government is precluded from commandeering the states to carry out federal regulatory programs. (2) States and the people are treated equivalently by the 10th Amendment. (3) All current justices acknowledge that an overriding goal of the 10th Amendment is to secure individual rights. Therefore, (4) individuals, like states, cannot be commandeered to carry out federal regulatory programs.

Those principles may not be reconcilable with a federal mandate ordering individuals to purchase medical insurance to implement President Obama's healthcare agenda. In declaring the mandate unconstitutional, the U.S. Court of Appeals for the Eleventh Circuit pointedly noted that the Constitution's "structural limitations are often discussed in terms of federalism, [but] their ultimate goal is the protection of individual liberty."

WHAT DO WE NOW DO?

> Increasingly I found myself spending time with people of means—
> law firm partners and investment bankers, hedge fund managers
> and venture capitalists . . . I found myself avoiding certain topics
> during conversations with them, papering over possible differences,
> anticipating their expectations . . . I know that as a consequence of
> my fund-raising I became more like the wealthy donors I met, in the
> very particular sense that I spent more and more of my time above
> the fray, outside the world of immediate hunger, disappointment, fear,
> irrationality, and frequent hardship of the other 99 percent of the
> population—that is, the people that I'd entered public life to serve.
> —Pres. Barack Obama, *The Audacity of Hope*, 2006

NOW WE KNOW how the Republic, created over two hundred years ago, is to work, the reasons why the Founders fought a war against the *ancien régime* and why the Framers were afraid of too little government—a state of nature and insecure rights—and too much government—an all-encompassing police state. We know the rules, but can we still play the game or even wish to? It seems as though the system *is rigged*; thus, many have abdicated the people's control to a secret cabal of leaders, mostly unelected or even known by the people. Today many young people, college-educated, even a majority of Americans, cannot name all three branches; many don't know their own representatives—senators, governors, mayors. Who is chief justice? Who is the vice president? Who is speaker of the house? When asked, many respond that the "C-word"—capitalism—is the cause of inequality, poverty, lack of quality health care, corruption, and environmental decay.

Where did the America the Patriots created in 1787 go?

Justice Louis Brandeis called citizenship the "most important office" in the land. Brandeis was acknowledging one of the oldest principles of the American Republic, part of the nation's legacy of classical republicanism. Our nation's experiment in self-government depends foremost not upon presidents, members of Congress, or justices, but upon each of us as "citizens." Citizens of this nation, the United States, this great experiment, is of special importance. The idea of citizenship in America is not nationality but rather a common ideal of man, as men and women, living not as a subject but as the ruler. We are a land of immigrants from many nations, histories, languages, yet the experiment is at the heart of humanity. We cannot fail the world in failing in our experiment.

From its beginnings, America was strongly influenced by the ideals of classical republicanism. The early American colonies of the seventeenth century were political communities in which civic virtue would be exercised. Many of these colonies were called commonwealths, a word that meant something like a republic—that is, self-governing communities of equals whose members were expected to help serve the good of all. In the Mayflower Compact, the pilgrims declared their intent to "covenant and combine themselves together into a civil body politic."

The American Founders admired the civic virtue of the ancients and the classical models of republican government. They also were influenced by the natural rights philosophy of John Locke. The natural rights philosophy at times seems to conflict in several important ways with the ideals of classical republicanism. Instead of the common good, it stressed the importance of individual rights and self-interest. Society and government, according to Locke, were established to protect the rights of the individual. Government's job was to protect individuals from foreign and domestic thugs. Human communities do not exist for their own sake but rather to protect the individuals within them, each of whom is free to pursue his or her own interest so long as it does not interfere with the interests of others.

That self-interest will lead to what's best for the community. My profits as a business, without government protection, are greatest when I serve my customers well. As a property owner, I am able to use my property best when I respect the property of others. In voting, I have always voted for the candidate that serves the ideals of the Constitution, thus securing my rights as Jefferson stated was the purpose of government.

The Founders were influenced by both these theories of government. They had to compromise in adapting this intellectual inheritance to the conditions in America. They established a limited government of checks and balances that not only allowed civic virtue to flourish but also could prevent abuses of self-interest when it did not.

They realized that the classical republicanism of the ancient city-states could not be easily adapted to a country as large and diverse as America might become. They also recognized that republican self-government required a greater measure of civic virtue than did other forms of government. Civic virtue, therefore, was essential. But how was civic virtue to be promoted in this new experiment in republican self-government?

This experiment is what makes America exceptional. The exceptionalism of America is what draws many here. We are a nation of immigrants, but there'd be no immigration if others did not believe they could come here and participate in the dream of mankind. Dinesh D'Souza, an immigrant himself from India, says that we all have an innate tendency to stay put, to live in misery even, if close to home and family and the familiar. The experiment is greater than our human fear of moving. And there's still room for those wishing to join, to try, to be free.

The Founders looked to two solutions: religion and education. They themselves had different religious beliefs. Many were wary of the dangers that religious orthodoxy, or a state-imposed religion, posed to individual freedom. At the same time, however, they acknowledged the value of organized religion in promoting virtue. Virtuous behavior, which enabled people to control their passions, would produce upright, responsible citizens.

The second solution that they recognized was the importance of education to good citizenship. For the American experiment in republican self-government to succeed, each of its citizens had to be schooled in the ideals and principles upon which that experiment was based. Formal schooling, together with a free unbiased press, became a priority in the early years of the new Republic. Public or "common schools" developed rapidly to prepare Americans not only as workers in a growing economy but also as citizens committed to the principles of self-government. As nineteenth-century American educator Horace Mann observed, "Schoolhouses are the republican line of fortifications." Today, less than 25 percent of students taking the NAEP (National Assessment for Educational Progress) civics test, 40 percent in the economics test, and—ready?—12 percent in Unites States history, passed.

> The average NAEP science scores for the nation increased 4 points between 2009 and 2015 at both grades 4 and 8, but did not change significantly at grade 12.

George Washington, in many ways, was and remains the model of what it means to be an American citizen, a Republican. He embodied the civic virtues that Madison described as indispensable for a self-governing republic. In his First Annual Address to Congress, he was adamant that "the people must be taught to know and to value their own rights; to discern and provide against invasions of them; to distinguish between oppression and the necessary exercise of lawful authority . . . to discriminate the spirit of liberty from that of licentiousness—cherishing the first, avoiding the last; and uniting a speedy but temperate vigilance against encroachments, with inviolable respect to the laws."

George Carlin and Bob Marley—great political scientists in their own right—second Washington's sentiment but go further. Marley's "Get Up, Stand Up":

> It's not all that glitters is gold;
> 'Alf the story has never been told:
> So now you see the light, eh!
> Stand up for your rights. Come on!

> Rights aren't rights if someone can take them away. They're privileges. That's all we've ever had in this country, is a bill of temporary privileges. And if you read the news even badly, you know that every year the list gets shorter and shorter. Sooner or later, the people in this country are gonna realize the government . . . doesn't care about you, or your children, or your rights, or your welfare or your safety . . . It's interested in its own power. That's the only thing. Keeping it and expanding it wherever possible (Carlin).

In his farewell address, delivered as he moved from war hero, father of his country, to retirement, he said, "Promote then as an object of primary importance, institutions for the general diffusion of knowledge. In proportion as the structure of a government gives force to public opinion, it is essential that public opinion should be enlightened." He knew that republican government required the participation of enlightened citizens to survive. In his first inaugural, he described what was, and still is, at stake: "The preservation of the sacred fire of liberty and the destiny of the republican model of government are justly considered, perhaps as deeply, perhaps as finally, staked on the experiment entrusted to the hands of the American people."

The Framers built into the Constitution a number of mechanisms that would curb the power of a national government, making it difficult for government to violate the liberties and rights of citizens—separation of powers, checks and balances between the three branches, staggered elections and varying terms of office, and Federalism. As important as these improvements were over past governments, however, they were at best "auxiliary precautions," according to James Madison, in *Federalist 51*: "A dependence on the people is no doubt the primary control on the government."

The primary responsibility for keeping American government within the cage of the Constitution, protecting the liberty of the American people, belongs to the people themselves. Or again, as Ben quipped, "if they can keep it!" H. L. Mencken went a step further:

> The most dangerous man to any government is the man who is able to think things out for himself, without regard to the prevailing superstitions and taboos. Almost inevitably he comes to the conclusion that the government he lives under is dishonest, insane, and intolerable . . .

Citizens have a number of ways to maintain control over the government. The most obvious way is voting into office candidates who will defend the Constitution. But citizens can also influence those officials already in office by writing them letters or e-mails, or calling them on the telephone; there are apps now to directly mail your representatives as each bill is placed on the calendar—*Countable, iCitizen, VoteSpotter*.

Run for office, challenge the deep state incumbents. And, finally, if a government persists in violating the rights of citizens, and there is no peaceful way (such as free elections) for citizens to redress their grievances, citizens might choose to exercise their natural right of revolution, overthrowing the current government and replacing it with a government more likely to protect their rights. With all these options and so many ways of exercising each of them, how is a person supposed to know what he should do? How, for example, should he vote in an upcoming election, or what kind of letter should he write to his representative or senator? Questions such as these point to the first kind of civic virtue, civic knowledge.

First and foremost, citizens must understand what the Constitution says about how the government works and what the government is supposed to do and what it is not to do. That's what the first part of this book was to do. We must understand the basis of our responsibilities as citizens, no less than our rights. We must be able to recognize when the government or another citizen infringes upon our rights. This civic knowledge was to form the core of education for young people. In the Northwest Ordinance of 1787, for example—the first national law governing the western territories—it was stated that "religion, morality, and knowledge, being necessary to good government and the happiness of mankind, schools and the means of education shall forever be encouraged."

Washington and other Founders knew that for citizens to live in a free society with limited government, knowing was not enough, each citizen must also be able to control or restrain himself; otherwise, we would need a police state—that is, a large, unlimited government—to maintain safety and order. Yet it must be very clear, no government, no economic system can fix the failing nature of man. That is the duty of family, church, and other voluntary associations.

When he was sixteen years old, Washington copied a list of "Rules of Civility and Decent Behavior" into his school notebook. Most of these 110 rules deal with common etiquette. The last rule reads: "Labor to keep alive in your breast the little spark of celestial fire called conscience." By "conscience" he meant our ability to understand and reason about moral right and wrong. In that First Inaugural, he declared, "The foundation of our national policy will be laid in the pure and immutable principles of private morality . . ." Continuing, "There is no truth more thoroughly established that there exists in the economy and course of nature, an indissoluble union between virtue and happiness." To be truly happy requires one to be a virtuous or moral person; remember Aristotle's "On Happiness"? The "happiness" that comes from doing things that are wrong—drugs, theft, reckless or irresponsible behavior—is not liberty but license, not happiness but hedonism. If one continues to engage in such behavior, she will not discover happiness, but misery—jail, sick, friendless.

Washington both believed and practiced what he declared for his nation; individual or private morality and virtue are necessary for the country to prosper: "The propitious smiles of heaven can never be expected on a nation that disregards the eternal rules of right and order, which heaven itself has ordained . . ." Given all the freedom that comes with a limited government, a people that live rightly and virtuously will end up living happily with all the goods, material and otherwise, that make the difference between living and living well. If a people violate the "rules of right and order which heaven has ordained," they will end up living unhappily, with little to ease their misery.

Washington's self-restraint was displayed consistently during and after the Revolutionary War. Instead of asking for a high office or political power, Washington relinquished power as commander in chief of the army. He wrote a circular letter to the state governments and asked only that he be allowed to return to his private life at Mount Vernon, as he turned in his sword to the Confederation Congress. After serving two terms, he retired a second time to his wife and his farm.

But when the ideals of the nation, the rights of citizens are infringed, free men must have the courage to stand up in public and defend their rights. Sometimes a government may usurp the very rights that it was created to protect. In such cases, Thomas Jefferson wrote in the Declaration of Independence, "It is the right of the people to alter or abolish" that government. George Washington asserted himself in the American struggle against the British government. As a young man, he had served in the British army and considered himself a loyal British subject, yet later he became convinced of the need to end British rule over the colonies. Although at first reluctant to take up arms against the British, Washington boldly wore his military uniform to the First Continental Congress, where he was selected as commander in chief of the Continental Army. As the Second Continental Congress finished its work on the Declaration of Independence in July 1776, Washington was in the field with our first army. He challenged his men to assert themselves in defense of liberty against their British enemy:

> Our cruel and unrelenting enemy leaves us no choice but a brave resistance, or the most abject submission. This is all we can expect. We have therefore to resolve to conquer or die. Our own country's honor, all call upon us for a vigorous and manly exertion, and if we now shamefully fail, we shall become infamous to the whole world . . . Let us therefore animate and encourage each other, and show the world, that a freeman contending for liberty on his own ground is superior to any slavish mercenary on earth.

After the Revolutionary War, we saw it was Washington that brought together at his home at Mount Vernon Madison in 1785 delegates from Virginia and Maryland on the verge of war to settle a dispute over river travel. He stepped forward to preside at the Constitutional Convention and assured ratification of the new Constitution with his endorsement. He then left a comfortable retirement at his beloved Mount Vernon to serve for eight years as the nation's first president. When the Whiskey Rebellion threatened the stability of the young Republic, Washington asserted his authority as president to raise an army and preserve the rule of law, yet instead of listening to Hamilton, to hang them all, the president pardoned them all. Both in war and peace, this man repeatedly demonstrated the civic virtue of self-assertion in the service of his country when he could have been king or a wealthy retired landowner.

To be truly free, citizens must be able to provide the basic necessities of life for themselves and their families. But as we saw, nearly two-thirds of Americans know little to nothing of the system of economics under which we work, play, and enjoy life. Citizens who cannot provide for themselves will need a large government to take care of them. And as soon as citizens become dependent on government for their basic needs, the people are no longer in a position to demand that government stay limited within the confines of the Constitution. Self-reliant citizens are free citizens in the sense that they are not dependent on others for their basic needs. They do not need a large provider government, which has the potential to become an intrusive or oppressive government, to meet those needs.

George Washington understood the need for citizens to be self-reliant. In a letter to a recent immigrant, he lauded the benefits available in America to self-reliant, virtuous citizens: "This country certainly promises greater advantages, than almost any other, to persons of moderate property, who are determined to be sober, industrious, and virtuous members of society." Washington knew, and our national experience has shown, that only a strong, self-reliant citizenry is able to fully enjoy the 'blessings of liberty."

Thomas Jefferson understood the importance of striving, not complacency, of independence, not enslavement. As governor of Virginia, he abolished two of the greatest sins of the Middle Ages, primogeniture and entailment. Being the firstborn, common law rule of inheritance was the oldest male child has the right to succeed as heir to the estate to the exclusion of older other siblings, both male and female, as well as all other relatives. By the time of the Revolution, nearly three-fourths of Tidewater land and perhaps a majority of western lands were under primogeniture as well as entailed.

Entailment, as defined by *Webster's Collegiate Dictionary*, refers to the restriction of property by limiting the inheritance to the owner's lineal descendants or to a particular class thereof. Although it was feudal in origin, an entail was a legal device to prevent a landed property from being broken up and from descending in a female line. The law was simply an extension of the practice of leaving the bulk, if not all, of one's wealth to one's heir, the eldest son.

Thus, entailed property was usually inherited by male primogeniture (by the nearest male-line descendant of the original owner). The law also prevented a father from disinheriting his eldest son, as the law prescribed that the son was his rightful heir. Furthermore, women only inherited if there were no male heirs left, and if there was more than one daughter, then they were all equal coheiresses, and the land was subdivided evenly among them all.

Both entailment and primogeniture stymied innovation and created a two-class system of landed gentry and a landless lower class. Though Jefferson was of the landed elites, he knew that a republic of many dependent on a few would not last the ages.

Alexis de Tocqueville was a young French aristocrat who visited the United States in the 1830s, at a time when the spirit of Jacksonian democracy was helping to bring about greater equality and more widespread participation in the nation's political life. He was curious about and impressed by America's experiment in self-rule and how well it worked. After finishing his tour of the United States, he recorded his impressions in a very influential book, *Democracy in America*.

Tocqueville found much both to admire and to criticize as he traveled the country. Though impressed by the equality of opportunity in this new Republic, he wondered how a society so devoted to materialism and the pursuit of individual self-interest could produce the civic spirit needed for self-government. He believed the answer was to be found in the qualities he admired in Americans: traditions of local self-government and habits of free association.

The New England townships were tiny models of classical republicanism, where the habits of citizenship were developed. Tocqueville observed that a citizen of one of these American towns

> . . . takes part in every affair of the place; he practices the
> act of government in the small sphere within his reach . . .
> and collects clear practical notions on the nature of his duties
> and the extent of his rights.

This tradition of local self-government also encouraged voluntary association. Nothing so impressed Tocqueville about America as the fondness American citizens had for banding together to address problems of common interest. While Europeans would prefer to allow government to address all public problems, Americans preferred to do it themselves, as citizens. This spirit of association remains a distinctive characteristic of American society today. Such traditions of local self-government and habits of free association, Tocqueville concluded, provided a way for teaching citizenship in the American Republic. He wrote,

> The most powerful and perhaps the only means that we still
> possess of interesting men in the welfare of their country is
> to make them participate in the government. At the present

time, civic zeal seems to be inseparable from the exercise of political rights.

Like the Founders, Tocqueville realized that the civic virtue of the ancients was not practical in the United States. Republican citizenship, he believed, would have to depend on something else, yet he did not believe there had to be a contradiction between self-interest and civic-mindedness. In a land of equality and widespread participation in political life, each citizen could see a connection between self-interest and the common good. American citizens are willing to devote themselves to public ends, Tocqueville believed, because they realize that the fulfillment of their private ambitions depends in large part on the success of the republican society. Good citizenship for Tocqueville, therefore, was nothing other than enlightened self-interest.

The natural rights philosophy and classical republicanism provide different answers to this question.

The natural rights philosophy emphasizes the elective nature of citizenship. Each citizen has a choice whether to remain a citizen of the United States. Each citizen possesses certain natural rights, and it is the primary purpose of government to protect these rights. In choosing a government to protect these rights, citizens follow their self-interest in making sure that government does its job. We pay attention to how well the people we choose to govern us are doing their jobs. We participate as citizens, therefore, to ensure that government complies with its contractual obligations to us as individuals.

The classical republican philosophy, on the other hand, emphasizes our obligation to the society into which we were born or naturalized. Classical republicanism emphasizes the common good and the obligation of each citizen to serve the good of the whole community. Citizenship requires that we put this general good before our own self-interest, especially when the two conflict. In practice, of course, the American civic tradition includes both concepts of citizenship. One of the enduring challenges you face as a citizen is sorting out for yourself the conflict between them in many different situations.

The conflict between the common good and self-interest is not the only problem you face as a citizen. Sometimes it is difficult to determine what the common good or your own self-interest actually is. In some situations, the common good may be quite clear as, for example, the need to protect the community from criminals, foreign enemies, and air pollution. In other situations, however, citizens strongly disagree about what the common good is and what policies are needed to serve it. For example, some would argue that laws strictly limiting human activity in environmentally sensitive areas are necessary to preserve the future well-being of our natural resources. Others claim that such restrictive policies can endanger the economy and may violate property rights. It is not always easy to know how our individual interests are served. What may appear to be self-interest in the short run might not be in our best long-term interest.

The conflict, what do you think?

Is the common good the greatest happiness of the greatest number? If so, what does that phrase mean? Should the measurement of the greatest number be a minimum of 51 percent, or should the percentage be higher? What would be the danger in determining the common good according to this principle? What about the 49 percent, 25 percent, that one person harmed?

Is the common good the goals that all people in the nation share? If so, how do we find out what those goals are?

If you find that you and your fellow citizens cannot agree on what the common good is, should you just pursue your own interests and forget about what is good for all? What alternatives might there be?

Who is a citizen?

In our country, anyone who is born here or is born to citizens of the United States is a citizen. The term used for noncitizens who legally reside in the United States is resident aliens. By satisfying certain requirements, resident aliens may become naturalized citizens.

Both resident legal aliens and citizens who live in the United States must obey the laws—taxes, speed limits, jaywalking. They also receive the protection of those laws. Legal resident aliens are guaranteed most of the rights possessed by citizens. If they are tried in a court of law, for example, they are guaranteed the same rights to due process detailed through history and the Constitution.

There are two important rights, however, that citizens have and aliens do not—voting and holding public office. Having these rights is what separates the citizen from the noncitizen. Many add that possessing these rights requires of citizens special responsibilities toward their country that noncitizens do not.

From the very beginning, America has been what the poet Walt Whitman called a "nation of nations," peopled by millions of immigrants of different races, religions, languages, and ethnic backgrounds. One of the greatest challenges to the American experiment in republican government has been to form a common bond out of such diversity. That common bond is provided by the ideal of American citizenship and a commitment to the Constitution and its ideals and principles. Though they could not foresee how diverse the immigration to this country would become, many of the Founders recognized that the new country would continue to take in people of different origins. For them, becoming American was primarily a matter of allegiance to the political ideals of the great experiment. In the early nineteenth century, Congress required five years as the minimum time required for immigrants to learn these ideals and to become naturalized citizens.

As George Washington told the members of the Touro Synagogue of Newport, Rhode Island, in 1790,

> Happily, the government of the United States that gives to bigotry no sanction, to persecution no assistance, requires only that they who live under its protection should demean themselves as good citizens in giving it their effectual support.

For Washington and other Founders, good citizenship meant responsible conduct and acceptance of the nation's political principles. For much of our nation's history, however, becoming an American meant something more. It represented a fresh start, a new beginning, leaving the injustices and prejudices of the old world behind.

"What then is this American, this new man?" asked Crevecoeur, an eighteenth-century French immigrant to America. Americans had, and have, left behind a world they knew with values and lifestyles they understood, and came to a new world the take a chance at freedom, wealth, and a better life. They brought their different origins behind but became "a new race of men." Perhaps the most famous metaphor for this ideal of Americanization was written by Israel Zangwell in his 1908 play, *The Melting Pot*, "America is God's crucible, the great melting pot where all the races of men are melting and re-forming."

Is America really a melting pot? Not completely at all times. Throughout our history, the absorption of different peoples from different religions, cultures, histories into the new American experiment of classical republicanism is a common culture. Some immigrants to their new land were reluctant to give up their heritages they brought with them. They were proud of both their "Americaness" and the cultural inheritance they carried from the Old World.

As a nation of immigrants, we have come to appreciate the benefits of this great mixture of heritages; they have enriched American life in many ways. This diversity of the nation's cultures has sometimes met with opposition, from the Alien and Sedition Acts of 1790s to the Know-Nothing Party before the Civil War to Japanese incarceration during World War II to calls today for a wall. Social, economic, and political unity depends on the ability of the ideal—the civic culture all Americans, whatever their particular origins, share in common—to hold us together as a nation. We need to ensure all newcomers understand what they are joining, a great experiment of freedom of man to live the dream of happiness.

Citizenship has meant different things at different times in history and in different places. Totalitarian states and dictatorships also have citizens, though these "citizens" lack the rights and responsibilities of true citizens—due process, bearing arms, voting, and/or holding office. Your role as a citizen in a republic differs fundamentally from a citizen—a subject—living under unlimited or arbitrary government where obedience, unquestioning loyalty, and fear. As a citizen of a republic, you are expected to be a critical and participating member of the political community. Citizens of republic need information—free press and speech—to have a reasoned loyalty, patriotism, and obedience to constitutionally fair laws. Criticism of one's government requires knowledge of history, law, philosophy of man, and government; to disobey laws you believe are unjust laws, unconstitutional, is not an easy choice, but patriotism requires courage. Think of the struggles of the civil rights movement and its heroes.

What rights and responsibilities do you as a citizen have?

As you consider the rights of citizenship, it is important to distinguish between civil rights and political rights. Civil rights protect us in our private lives from the arbitrary and unfair actions of government. Political rights allow us to participate in our own governance. Since noncitizens living in this country are granted the same civil rights that citizens enjoy, political rights are to a large extent what define our status as citizens. You must be a citizen to exercise the rights to vote or serve in government. The Supreme Court in June 2017 declared illegal entries do not have these civil rights, say, due process, attorneys, or trials.

Your rights always come with obligations. In exercising our rights as individuals, we must respect other citizens' use of those same rights. Some obligations are legal, imposed by laws commonly agreed upon—obey the law, pay taxes, serve on juries. Other obligations are moral requirements. Some argue you have a duty, as well as a right, to vote. Even though the law no longer requires American citizens to perform military service, many Americans believe it is a duty to defend one's country or to assist it in other emergencies.

Citizenship is both an inheritance because of the luck of birth and an honor for performance as law abider, taxpayer, voter, community member, player in the marketplace, officeholder, or even Facebook writer.

WHEN THE STATE SEEMS GREATER
THAN WE THE PEOPLE

> I think I can say, and say with pride, that we have some
> legislatures that bring higher prices than any in the world.
> —Samuel Clemens

What do you think?

Is civil disobedience ever justified in political participation?
Think about the anti-Trump protestors.

Are there any circumstances when a citizen in a republic has
a right to violate a law?

What power is proper for a government against someone
who, for reasons of conscience, breaks the law?

Do you agree with Thomas Jefferson that "a little rebellion"
now and then is healthy for government? If so, what form
might a little rebellion take?

CITIZENSHIP IN A free society is not always easy. Freedom
requires us to live as self-reliant individuals, to think for
ourselves, to solve our own problems, to cope with uncertainty and
change, and to assist and respect others. Today it is even harder with a
Panopticon of control—NSA mass surveillance of all citizens, current
presidents interfering in elections, facial recognition at traffic stops,
your own TV turning you into a paranoid "traitor." The Panopticon of
Jeremy Bentham was an all-seeing, all-hearing, all-knowing government,
similar to Hobbes's deep-state Leviathan.

I've got nothing to hide; I've got nothing to fear. Everyone has something to hide. Somewhere, sometime, you've said or done something you regret or wouldn't want the world to know. And you probably said or did it within a few feet of your smartphone, your laptop, or your television. Maybe nobody was listening or watching. Or maybe someone was. The only plausible conclusion from the Vault 7 disclosures is that you should assume the latter.

Vault 7 confirms that as a state entity, the CIA answers to philosopher Anthony de Jasay's inevitability. As a business acts to maximize profits, the state and its arms act to maximize their own discretionary power. Even if it doesn't do some particular thing, it requires the option, the ability to do that thing. It seeks omnipotence. The abuses of our privacy implied by the WikiLeaks dump aren't an aberration. They're the norm. They're what government does.

I am not arguing some historical necessity, some inexorable dynamics which must cause any state, if sound of mind, to become totalitarian. On the other hand, I would not accept that, like Plato's Republic on its way from democracy to despotism, the state "degenerates" in the process. If it has improved its ability to fulfil *its* ends, it has not degenerated, though it may well have become less apt to serve the ends of the observer, who would then have every reason to be alarmed by the change. I am arguing, though, that it is rational in a higher, "strategic" sense of rationality different from the "tactical" sense of optimal adjustment, for the state generally to become more rather than less totalitarian to the extent that it can get away with it, i.e. maintain majority support at the stage where it still needs it. It is also rational for a rival for power to propose, under democracy, a more totalitarian alternative if this is more attractive to the majority though more unattractive to the minority. Hence, there is in competitive, democratic politics, always a latent propensity for totalitarian transformation. It manifests itself in the frequent appearance of socialist policies within non-socialist government and opposition programmes, and in socialist streaks in the liberal ideologyAnthony de Jasay, "The State"). would not accept that, like Plato's Republic on its way from democracy to despotism, the state 'degenerates' in the process. If it has improved its ability to fulfil its ends, it has not degenerated, though it may well have become less apt to serve the ends of the observer, who would then have every reason to be alarmed by the change. I am arguing, though, that it is rational in a higher, 'strategic' sense of rationality different from the 'tactical' sense of optimal adjustment, for the state generally to become more rather than less totalitarian to the extent that it can get away with it, i.e. maintain majority support at the stage where it still needs it. It is also rational for a rival for power to propose, under democracy, a more totalitarian alternative if this is more attractive to the majority though more unattractive to the minority. Hence, there is in competitive, democratic politics, always a latent propensity for totalitarian transformation." would not accept that, like Plato's Republic on its way from democracy to despotism, the state 'degenerates' in the process. If it has improved its ability to fulfil its ends, it has not degenerated, though it may well have become less apt to serve the ends of the observer, who would then have every reason to be alarmed by the change. I am arguing, though, that it is rational in a higher, 'strategic' sense of rationality different from the 'tactical' sense of optimal adjustment, for the state generally to become more rather than less totalitarian to the extent that it can get away with it, i.e. maintain majority support at the stage where it still needs it. It is also rational for a rival for power to propose, under democracy, a more totalitarian alternative if this is more attractive to the majority though more unattractive to the minority. Hence, there is in competitive, democratic politics, always a latent propensity for totalitarian transformation."

Jasay's "pessimism" is not my own; nor is Hobbes's or the conspiracy theorists' or survivalists'. I was born with liberty in my soul, the liberty of man. Yet citizens are made, not born. Like the ancient Greeks and Romans, the Founders placed great importance on the role of education in preparing each generation for citizenship. Your education will help provide you with the knowledge and skills to function effectively as citizens of a republic. Practical experience has been as important as formal schooling in preparing Americans for citizenship. Americans learn the skills of citizenship through the many opportunities to participate in public affairs.

The necessity of sacrifice to a higher call is best presented in a short letter in 1942 by Dietrich Bonhoeffer. Though our situations are much different, the struggle is the same.

We have been silent witnesses of evil deeds: we have been drenched by many storms; we have learnt the arts of equivocation and pretence; experience has made us suspicious of others and kept us from being truthful and open; intolerable conflicts have worn us down and even made us cynical. Are we still of any use?

Only the one for whom the final standard is not his reason, his principles, his conscience, his freedom, his virtue, but who is ready to sacrifice all these, when in faith and sole allegiance to God he is called to obedient and responsible action: the responsible person, whose life will be nothing but an answer to God's question and call.

We must begin the process of learning to be citizens in early childhood. At home and in the classroom, we must think for ourselves, to express our own opinions, and to respect the opinions of others. Through such activities as student government, school projects, sports, and community and club activities, we begin to acquire the skills of teamwork, organization, and debate. In short, many of the qualities that we need for citizenship begin to develop early in our lives.

In dealing with the problems of our communities and the nation, we have different possibilities. We may engage in social action or we may engage in political action, or we may do nothing and hope to die before all hope is crushed. We may, of course, choose to engage in both political and social actions. In dealing with the problems of crime in the community, we might join a neighborhood watch. Alternatively, we might organize other members of the community to present the problem to the city council in an effort to get more police officers on the streets. The first is an example of social action; the second, an example of political action. These two courses of action are not mutually exclusive. We might decide to engage in both at the same time.

One of the issues we must decide as citizens is how each particular problem is most effectively solved. The decision we make depends on our analysis of the problem, our estimate of the possible solutions, and our own values. Making these decisions lies at the heart of the practice of responsible citizenship with the correct skills and philosophy of liberty.

A new movement in American higher education aims to transform the teaching of civics. "New Civics" redefines civics as Progressive political activism. Rooted in the radical program of the 1960s New Left, the New Civics presents itself as an up-to-date version of volunteerism and good works. Though camouflaged with soft rhetoric, the New Civics, properly understood, is an effort to repurpose higher education.

The New Civics seeks above all to make students into enthusiastic supporters of the New Left's dream of "fundamentally transforming," not restoring America—decarbonizing the economy, massively redistributing wealth, intensifying identity group grievance, curtailing the free market, expanding government bureaucracy, and elevating international "norms" over American Constitutional law.

Most importantly, it is to diminish, disparage, and destroy our common history and ideals. New Civics advocates argue among themselves which of these transformations should take precedence, but they agree that America must be transformed by "systemic change" from an unjust, oppressive society to a society that embodies social justice. The New Civics hopes to accomplish this by teaching students that a good citizen is a radical activist, and it puts political activism at the center of everything that students do in college, including academic study, extracurricular pursuits, and off-campus ventures.

It builds on "service-learning," which is an effort to divert students from the classroom to vocational training as community activists. By rebranding itself as "civic engagement," service learning succeeded in capturing nearly all the funding that formerly supported the old civics. In practice, this means that instead of teaching college students the foundations of law, liberty, and self-government, colleges teach students how to organize protests, occupy buildings, and stage demonstrations. These are the new forms of "civic engagement," not political action within the system, not social action among neighbors, but antisystem at all costs.

Since the summer of 2016, the two most important names in the Democratic Party were Obama and Clinton. Yet these two are disciples of Richard Cloward and Francis Fox Piven.

Most people have never heard of these two; nor the names Saul Alinsky or Herbert Marcuse. Chuck Norris, in an op-ed for *World Net Daily*, explained that the two people were professors at Columbia

University who came up with the "new civics" as a plan for Socialism in the United States.

Norris said that "the Cloward-Piven strategy" is a political plan created in 1966 by two Columbia University sociologists to overload the US public welfare system, the goal being to replace it with a national system of "a guaranteed annual income and thus an end to poverty."

> I echo again that it's neither a coincidence that Obama graduated from Columbia University nor that others who espoused the Cloward-Piven strategy were a group of radicals who have been a part of his life and education: Bill Ayers, Saul Alinsky, Bernardine Dohrn, George Wiley, Frank Marshall Davis, Wade Rathke and George Soros, among others.

What's also not a coincidence is how close Hillary ran in the same circles.

> Robert Chandler, a retired Air Force colonel and former strategist for the White House…explained in the *Washington Times* that "much of (the Cloward-Piven) strategy was drawn from Saul Alinsky." There's no doubt that Alinsky's life and work served as the coach and plan for Cloward and Piven.
>
> Hillary's similar discipleship devotion was clearly seen by her 92-page college thesis paper on Saul Alinsky, which is a glimpse behind the present veil of her politically savvy and guarded gloss into the heart of her true ideologies . . . No surprise that in 1993, the Clintons asked officials at her alma mater to hide Hillary Rodham's senior thesis from Clinton biographers.

Norris writes that the "Motor Voter" law, a Bill Clinton "legacy," was a Cloward and Piven tactic. Barbara Ehrenreich, a friend Cloward and Piven, hoped the law "was dedicated to the idea that if citizens were allowed to register to vote when they apply for aid from government programs or for drivers' licenses, some of the historic administrative encumbrances on the right to vote could be overcome . . . The poor in particular, who often lack the time for voter registration, would be effectively enfranchised."

Norris continues,

> What's not surprising is how the "Motor Voter" law has morphed to incorporate more Cloward-Piven-Clinton strategies . . .

> For example, in Oregon, legislators have just enacted a subsidiary law that registers a person to vote when they obtain or renew a state driver's license. That might sound all fine and dandy, too, until one realizes that a stone's throw away in neighboring states like California, they are doling out licenses to 1.5 million illegals over the next three years. How long will it be until California's Motor Voter laws extend voting rights to illegals, too?

> A first-year political student can easily see where a Hillary presidency will take Cloward-Piven strategies. You see, the plan to "fundamentally transform the United States of America" has a successor, and she must be stopped.

In contemporary urban and rural America, violence by and against young people is receiving increased social and political attention, as well as daily coverage on television and in newspapers. Statistically, the incidence of youth violence has not increased during the last decade; the deadliness of it has. More young people carry guns or other weapons and use them as a means of settling disputes or intimidating others.

Is this how to control the people? Martin Luther King Jr. saw and John Whitehead sees the purposeful using of miseducated youth to disrupt a system and then become their own destroyers.

> You sow discontent and fear among the populace. You terrorize the people into believing that radicalized foreigners are preparing to invade. You teach them to be non-thinkers who passively accept whatever is told them, whether it's delivered by way of the corporate media or a government handler. You brainwash them into believing that everything

the government does is for their good and anyone who opposes the government is an enemy.

You acclimate them to a state of martial law, carried out by soldiers disguised as police officers but bearing the weapons of war. You polarize them so that they can never unite and stand united against the government. You create a climate in which silence is golden and those who speak up are shouted down. You spread propaganda and lies. You package the police state in the rhetoric of politicians.

And then, when and if the people finally wake up to the fact that the government is not and has never been their friend, when it's too late for peaceful protests and violence is all that remains to them as a recourse against tyranny, you use all of the tools you've been so carefully amassing—the criminal databases and surveillance and identification systems and private prisons and protest laws—and you shut them down for good.

The government—at all levels—could crack down on virtually anyone at any time.

"Police, national guard and other armed bodies are feverously preparing for repression," King wrote shortly before he was assassinated. "They can be curbed not by unorganized resort to force . . . but only by a massive wave of militant nonviolence . . . It also may be the instrument of our national salvation."

Militant nonviolent resistance.

"A nationwide nonviolent movement is very important," King wrote. "We know from past experience that Congress and the President won't do anything until you develop a movement around which people of goodwill can find a way to put pressure on them . . . This means making the movement powerful enough, dramatic enough, morally appealing enough, so that people of goodwill, the churches, laborers, liberals, intellectuals, students, poor people themselves begin to put pressure on congressmen to the point that they can no longer elude our demands.

"It must be militant, massive nonviolence," King emphasized.

In other words, besides marches and protests, there would have to be civil disobedience. Civil disobedience forces the government to expend energy in many directions, especially if it is nonviolent, organized and is conducted on a massive scale. This is, as King knew, the only way to move the beast. It is the way to effect change without resorting to violence. And it is exactly what these protest laws are attempting to discourage.

We are coming to a crossroads. Either we gather together now and attempt to restore freedom or all will be lost. As King cautioned, "everywhere, 'time is winding up,' in the words of one of our spirituals, corruption in the land, people take your stand; time is winding up."

Not playing the part of violent paid destroyers of the experiment but stopping the machine. Remember Mario Savio at Berkeley in 1963?

We have an autocracy which runs this university [government]. It's managed . . . But we're a bunch of raw material[s] that don't mean to have any process upon us, don't mean to be made into any product, don't mean to end up being bought by some clients of the University, be they the government, be they industry, be they organized labor, be they anyone! We're human beings!

[*Applause*]

There is a time when the operation of the machine becomes so odious, makes you so sick at heart, that you can't take part; you can't even passively take part, and you've got to put your bodies upon the gears and upon the wheels, upon the levers, upon all the apparatus, and you've got to make it stop. And you've got to indicate to the people who run it, to the people who own it, that unless you're free, the machine will be prevented from working at all!

Politics, from West Virginia to Afghanistan

From Lofgren's *Deep State*, more defeatism, pessimism against a growing leviathan. Under the guise, of fear, national security, what is our best interest, of they know more than we, the members of the deep state are no longer our representatives. We are bled dry through taxation, while our needs are ignored.

In January 2014, toxic chemicals spilled into the Elk River in West Virginia, contaminating the drinking water of a nine-county area surrounding the state capital and forcing residents to drink bottled water for two months. It was found that the leaking storage tanks had not been inspected a government agency for fifteen years, and, as it turned out, the law did not require them to be inspected, even though they lay near the river, upstream of the intakes of a drinking water filtration plant.

Do the citizens of the world's oldest constitutional republic consciously decide with their votes that the safety of their drinking water is a lesser priority than delivering suitcases of off-the-books cash, reportedly totaling tens of millions of dollars, to a corrupt satrap running Afghanistan named Hamid Karzai—an extraordinary act of philanthropy that failed to make him any easier to work with? More to the point, do their representatives and senators in Washington deliberately prioritize the stated requirements of the Pentagon and CIA above the most basic needs of their constituents? Yes, if those legislators have developed the unfortunate tendency to go into a trance every time someone utters the magic phrase "national security." In truth, it happens often enough, and many times over the course of my career I saw Congress respond to that occult incantation like iron filings drawn to a magnet. But the problem is not quite so simple.

Congress has abdicated a lot of control over foreign policy to the executive branch, but it still retains the constitutional power of the purse. So why do congressmen keep funding extravagances like a $7 billion sewer system in Baghdad and not take care of matters closer to home? And what does the public at large think of this behavior?

Public trust in government has with temporary fluctuation steadily declined from a high of around 75 percent in the mid-1960s to a level of distrust near 80 percent in 2010. One 2013 survey result from Public Policy Polling ranked Congress below head lice or cockroaches in public esteem, although it did manage to pull in ahead of the Kardashians and North Korea. The American people clearly believe that something is wrong, and something plainly is. Adjusted for inflation, median household income peaked in 1973, and has been stagnant or falling ever since. The 2008 financial crash merely exacerbated already existing long-term trends and resulted in a further drop in the American standard of living. The public knows from its own material condition that governmental decision making is defective, yet the same decision makers keep getting elected. Why?

They search us, tax us, and play us as fools. Now is the time we take back the Republic. Franklin was wrong; we can keep it. It is not going to be easy. Many know little of the ideals of this experiment; many are afraid. Who will build the rods? How will know if we are safe in a plane?

Frédéric Bastiat, in his short but great book *The Law* (1850), published shortly before his death of tuberculosis, asked the same questions summarized in the simplest form. What, then, is law?

> It is the collective organization of the individual right to lawful defense . . . [I]t follows that a group of men have the right to organize and support a common force to protect these rights constantly. Thus the principle of collective right—its reason for existing, its lawfulness—is based on individual right. And the common force that protects this collective right cannot logically have any other purpose or any other mission than that for which it acts as a substitute.
>
> [L]aw cannot operate without the sanction and support of a dominating force, this force must be entrusted to those who make the laws . . . This fact, combined with the fatal tendency that exists in the heart of man to satisfy his wants with the least possible effort, explains the almost universal perversion of the law.

Yet today's politicians live behind a shadow. They come out once in a while during election season, talking public school reforms, while their children attend $45,000-a-year private schools, arguing over our best health care and insurance while never being covered by it. Urban reform, the ills of slums, discrimination, low-skilled jobs, fair trade, trade restrictions, banks too big to fail, evil Wall Street, Black Lives Matter, bullying, drug use, guns in school, welfare, housing shortages, unfair lending practices, student loans, and on *ad nauseam*. Mike Lofgren again,

> [They] engage in sonorous generalities about jobs, faith, family, and so forth, once the issues move from the ethereal realm of sloganeering into specific policies, they do not seek to identify with the desires of the majority, except insofar as those desires happen to overlap with the preferences of those who are footing the bill. Single-payer health care, tax breaks for hedge fund managers, minimum wage policy—on these and a host of other issues, the American public lines up on one side and wealthy elites on the other. And every time, the position favored by those elites prevails. Most of the art and science of politics these days consist of camouflaging a politician's real stance on an issue.

Joachim Hagopian, a West Point graduate and former US Army officer, has written a manuscript based on his unique military experience titled "Don't Let the Bastards Getcha Down." He examines and focuses on US international relations, leadership, and national security issues. His greatest concern is the inability of Americans to make these decisions on their own and will let the deep state (the odious machine) lead them to war, enslavement, or both.

Utilizing Goebbels's infamous mantra that if you repeat telling a lie long enough, eventually it will convince and effectively brainwash a docile, gullible (US) population into misbelieving the designated enemy is a threat to its very existence; thus, the Russians, Chinese, and Iranians (terrorists, immigrants) have been conveniently relabeled cold war enemies whose fabricated "aggressions" in self-defense must be stopped through all-out war. The fake stream news has relentlessly been working overtime on the American population, prepping US citizens into acquiescence and acceptance of the inevitability of World War III.

Though the war is far from over, the elite's diabolical, violently destructive agenda has been thoroughly exposed like never before. The unstoppable truth is now stripping away the layers of filthy lies that have survived under the cover of darkness with which the Washington traitors and their partner-in-crime—fake stream press—have flourished for so long. But those days are now over. A growing counterinsurgency army comprised of a citizen investigator uprising is leaving no stone unturned, letting the truth be their guide while they uncover the previously protected and hidden criminal cabal cockroaches, with perhaps a president on their side who may finally go after the pervs. Honest, truth-seeking citizens of the world are becoming more empowered as they take back their cherished planet from the true villains before they destroy everything in life that we cherish. Our time has come for the truth to shine in setting us all free while locking up the traitors.

A PLAN OF ACTION

Rebellion against tyrants is obedience to God.
—Benjamin Franklin

YOU KNOW HOW Americans have adapted the idea of citizenship to a nation of immigrants, people from many lands and cultures, bound together by a commitment to a common set of political values. The American ideal of *E Pluribus Unum*—"Out of Many, One"—has usually been able to balance the benefits of a diverse society with the unifying influence of a common civic culture. One of the major challenges you face as an American citizen is to sustain that balance in a society that is becoming far more diverse and complex.

America at the time of the founding was a nation of 3.5 million inhabitants—three million free whites and half a million enslaved Africans. Most of the white population were northern European in ancestry. The young Republic also was overwhelmingly Protestant. Today America is a microcosm of the world. It has become one of the most ethnically diverse countries on earth. You see evidence of this diversity everywhere. More than one hundred languages are spoken by students in the Los Angeles school district. The results of recent immigration to this country have been dramatic. Of the million immigrants since 1965, 85 percent have come from non-European countries. During the 1980s, immigrants to the United States came from 164 different lands. By the turn of the century, one in every four Americans was either Hispanic, African American, or Asian. By the year 2030, one-half of the country's population will belong to one minority group or another. In a sense, there will no longer be a traditional majority group. In 1995, only 15 percent of Americans identify themselves as descendants of British immigrants, who once comprised a large majority of the population. The faces of "We the People" have changed considerably over the course of two hundred years and will continue to change during your lifetime. What consequences will the change toward a more diverse society have for us as citizens?

Americans today disagree about the answers to this question. To some, today's America is no different from what has happened throughout American history. The mix of people has strengthened American society and reaffirmed our commitment to ideals that are the property of man, not a particular ethnic group. As with their predecessors, most recent immigrants have adapted to American society, enriching the nation's economic life, culture, and educational institutions.

Others worry that there are limits to how much diversity the country can absorb without losing the common bonds that unite us. Today's immigrants are holding on to their own religions and cultures with little assimilation. Many fear that in an increasingly diverse society, self-interests may prevail over the common good. Our challenge, as it was for all previous generations, is balancing the *unum* with the *pluribus* in America.

Modern technology has expanded the possibilities for participatory citizenship. Skype, Facebook, Snapchat, and Instagram have caused revolutions in many countries. Talk radio broadcasts twenty-four hours a day from every political direction you can imagine. Some futurists see revolutionary implications in this technology. They envision the possibility of a "teledemocracy" in the years ahead. This term means a new version of direct democracy, where citizens can participate to a much greater extent in the affairs of government with less reliance on their elected representatives. National plebiscites also have become a practical option. By use of online computerized voting, each citizen could register his or her views on particular issues, with the results instantly tabulated. "Going to the polls" could become an outmoded custom. Citizens could exercise their political rights from a computer workstation at home or in public facilities like libraries or the post office.

The Framers believed that classical republicanism in its purest form was impractical in a country as large and diverse as the American Republic. Some people believe that teledemocracy overcomes many of these impracticalities. The computer makes possible an electronic city-state in which citizens scattered across the country can join together to participate more effectively in public affairs.

The movement of people, as well as information, has helped bring about global interdependence. Improved transportation has been a key factor in increased immigration to the United States. People go where there is economic opportunity, and they can go more easily and much farther than in the past. The movement of people across national borders will continue to increase. Such migrations help to reduce cultural and other differences that have historically divided nations. They also create new problems for governments, which have the responsibility for providing for the well-being of citizens and other residents.

One important consequence of the communications revolution has been America's increased interaction and interdependence with the rest of the world. Issues of national importance in the United States have an impact beyond our borders. Conversely, events and developments elsewhere in the world are becoming more significant in the lives of American citizens.

The achievements of modern technology are turning the world into a global village, with shared cultural, economic, and environmental concerns. National corporations have become international. Economic decisions made in Tokyo or London affect the things Americans buy and the jobs they seek. Environmental concerns also transcend national boundaries. Entertainment—music, sports, and film—command worldwide markets. The culture that we live in is becoming cosmopolitan—that is, belonging to the whole world.

Citizenship in modern history has been defined largely in terms of nation-states. The idea of being a citizen, however, developed in many different political contexts throughout history, from tiny city-states to large empires. In the American experience, citizenship has changed in its patterns of allegiance and loyalty. Before the Civil War, many Americans would have defined their citizenship in terms of loyalty to their respective states rather than to the United States.

Although national citizenship is likely to remain fundamentally important in the future, the issues confronting American citizens are increasingly international. Issues of economic competition, the environment, and the movement of peoples around the world require an awareness of political associations that are larger in scope than the nation-state.

Returning to fundamental principles

George Mason said, "No free government, or the blessings of liberty can be preserved to any people, but by frequent recurrence to fundamental principles." The key element of a restoring of the experiment of self-rule is being able to reeducate old Americans and educate new ones in the fundamental principles and ideas of our government, great ideas, and principles that have shaped our constitutional heritage. Some of these ideas contradict each other. American constitutional history has witnessed many conflicts between competing principles of equal merit—for example, the conflict between majority rule and minority rights, between sovereign power and fundamental rights, liberty and order, unity and diversity.

Mises, in his "The Argument of Fascism" in *Liberalism* (1927), argued that violence must be stopped with greater violence. But the key for Republicans—he called them by the original name, Liberals, eighteenth-century Liberals, classical liberals—are ideas. As Lincoln said, "The philosophy of the classroom in one generation will be the philosophy of government in the next." Remember citizens are not born; they must be taught freedom.

> Now it cannot be denied that the only way one can offer effective resistance to violent assaults is by violence. Against the weapons of the Bolsheviks, weapons must be used in reprisal, and it would be a mistake to display weakness before murderers. No liberal has ever called this into question. What distinguishes liberal from Fascist political tactics is not a difference of opinion in regard to the necessity of using armed force to resist armed attackers, but a difference in the fundamental estimation of the role of violence in a struggle for power. The great danger threatening domestic policy from the side of Fascism lies in its complete faith in the decisive power of violence. In order to assure success, one must be imbued with the will to victory and always proceed violently. This is its highest principle. What happens, however, when one's opponent, similarly animated by the will to be victorious, acts just as violently? The result must

be a battle, a civil war. The ultimate victor to emerge from such conflicts will be the faction strongest in number. In the long run, a minority—even if it is composed of the most capable and energetic—cannot succeed in resisting the majority. The decisive question, therefore, always remains: How does one obtain a majority for one's own party? This, however, is a purely intellectual matter. It is a victory that can be won only with the weapons of the intellect, never by force. The suppression of all opposition by sheer violence is a most unsuitable way to win adherents to one's cause. Resort to naked force—that is, without justification in terms of intellectual arguments accepted by public opinion—merely gains new friends for those whom one is thereby trying to combat. In a battle between force and an idea, the latter always prevails.

The English economist John Maynard Keynes once remarked that "in the long run it is ideas and not men who rule the world." If the upheavals of the last two centuries have taught us anything, it is that ideas have consequences, sometimes for good, sometimes for evil. We like to believe that in the end, good ideas will prevail over bad. Whatever the case, ideas do matter. One of the twentieth century's most compelling images comes from the Chinese student uprising of 1989. It was the photograph below of a young man, armed only with the moral authority of his cause, confronting a column of armored tanks. The picture moved and inspired the world; it hangs above my desk as I write. One man with the right ideas can change the world, can change America, and can destroy the deep state.

You will remember that this book began with the observation that the American experiment in self-government was an adventure in ideas. The individuals who founded our government cherished and respected ideas. They were excited about them. Ours is a nation that was created by ideas. It is not the product of a common culture or geography or centuries of tradition. The United States began as an experiment to see if certain ideas about government—never before tried on such a scale and in such a way—would work.

I had a recent e-mail from a colleague, Deidre McCloskey, that made me rethink the deep state as not so much an actual parallel or shadow government. She stated it is more of an ideology. F. A. Hayek said the same. He said many believe it's the system that produces dictators. The state cannot solve our problems, never could; but those that see themselves as saviors "soon have to choose between disregard of ordinary morals and failure. It is for this reason that the unscrupulous and uninhibited are likely to be more 'successful' in a society tending toward totalitarianism."

The Soviet dictator Joseph Stalin once disparaged the influence of religion by asking, "How many divisions does the Pope have?" It is one of the great ironies of this century that the fall of Stalin's Communist empire began in Poland, in a revolution inspired in large part by the religious faith of the Polish people and supported throughout by the moral influence of the papacy. "An invasion of armies can be resisted," said the French novelist Victor Hugo, "but not an idea whose time has come."

When George Mason spoke of the importance of a frequent recurrence to fundamental principles, he was invoking an old idea associated with republican government. The ancient Greeks and Romans believed that a government established with the purpose of serving the public good and involving the participation of all citizens could not survive unless each generation was reminded of that government's reason for being and the principles by which it operated.

"If a nation means its systems, [families or education or economic or] religious or political, shall have duration," said a federal farmer, "it ought to recognize the leading principles of them in the front page of every family book." What is the usefulness of a truth in theory unless it exists constantly in the minds of the people and has their assent?

It is doubtful that these Founders had in mind an uncritical acceptance of the "wisdom of the past." In revisiting these principles, each generation must examine and evaluate them anew. Indeed, it is probable that they would be somewhat surprised at the reverence in which they and their writings have been held by subsequent generations of Americans.

They themselves were vigorous critics of the wisdom they inherited and the principles in which they believed. They were articulate, opinionated individuals who loved to examine ideas, to analyze, argue, and debate them. They expected no less of future generations. They would expect no less of you. To go back in thought or discussion to first principles requires us to make principled arguments and ground our opinions in ideas of enduring value. It is what citizenship in a free society is all about. This book is an attempt to redefine—no, revive, the ideology of America.

Liberty versus order

One of the most enduring and important challenges in our constitutional system of government is how to balance order with liberty. Today, this challenge is focused on the issue of crime. Violent crime is widespread in the nation's inner cities, but few areas of our society feel safe. Violence even has become a problem for our schools. Terrorism is abroad and here, near our homes. Recently, in response to the issue of immigration, ICE, Immigration and Customs Enforcement, has been rounding up all suspected illegal immigrants. In the early 1990s, because of large-scale crime problem in a housing project of one of the nation's largest cities, officials used similar techniques doing police "sweeps" of apartments in 1988 in Chicago and other major cities in search of illegal weapons. These searches, like the ICE searches, were without search warrants or probable cause. After a judge struck down the public housing searches as an unconstitutional violation of the Fourth Amendment, the city required prospective tenants in public housing projects to waive their Fourth Amendment rights as a condition of renting.

Critics doubt the constitutionality and worry about the consequences of such a policy requiring citizens to give up their natural rights to be sheltered. Many states have recently gone to drug testing for welfare recipients. Those in favor point to the dangerous conditions that such tenants may live in. What good is a constitutional right in a violent world, a state of nature? Didn't Locke, Hobbes, and Jefferson state the purpose of government is to provide the security of an orderly society? If government is to protect rights of its citizens seems ironic, the Department of Defense has developed contingency plans that order supersedes liberty.

In an excerpt from a released Department of Defense report on zombies—yes, fighting zombies—it becomes apparent We the Zombies need to be controlled. John Whitehead of the Rutherford Institute believes this is no laughing matter. The DOD's "CONOP 8888" is "how to put down a citizen uprising or at least an uprising of individuals "infected" with dangerous ideas about freedom . . . beginning with martial law."

CONOP 888 outlines five steps to "shape, deter, seize initiative, dominate, stabilize and restore civil authority."

Phase 0 (Shape): Conduct general zombie awareness training. Monitor increased threats (i.e., surveillance). Carry out military drills. Synchronize contingency plans between federal and state agencies. Anticipate and prepare for a breakdown in law and order.

Phase 1 (Deter): Recognize that zombies cannot be deterred or reasoned with. Carry out training drills to discourage other countries from developing or deploying attack zombies and publicly reinforce the government's ability to combat a zombie threat. Initiate intelligence sharing between federal and state agencies. Assist the Dept. of Homeland Security in identifying or discouraging immigrants from areas where zombie-related diseases originate.

Phase 2 (Seize initiative): Recall all military personal to their duty stations. Fortify all military outposts. Deploy air and ground forces for at least 35 days. Carry out confidence-building measures with nuclear-armed peers such as Russia and China to ensure they do not misinterpret the government's zombie countermeasures as preparations for war. Establish quarantine zones. Distribute explosion-resistant protective equipment. Place the military on red alert. Begin limited scale military operations to combat zombie threats. Carry out combat operations against zombie populations within the United States that were "previously" U.S. citizens.

Phase 3 (Dominate): Lock down all military bases for 30 days. Shelter all essential government personnel for at least 40 days. Equip all government agents with military protective gear. Issue orders for military to kill all non-human life on sight. Initiate bomber and missile strikes against targeted sources of zombie infection, including the infrastructure. Burn all zombie corpses. Deploy military to lock down the beaches and waterways.

Phase 4 (Stabilize): Send out recon teams to check for remaining threats and survey the status of basic services (water, power, sewage infrastructure, air, and lines of communication). Execute a counter-zombie ISR plan to ID holdout pockets of zombie resistance. Use all military resources to target any remaining regions of zombie holdouts and influence. Continue all actions from the Dominate phase.

Phase 5 (Restore civil authority): Deploy military personnel to assist any surviving civil authorities in disaster zones. Reconstitute combat capabilities at various military bases. Prepare to redeploy military forces to attack surviving zombie holdouts. Restore basic services in disaster areas.

How much of the George Soros-sponsored "riots" are to spark the implementation of CONOP 888?

What is your position on this issue? How do the following statements apply to this situation? What principles and ideals are implied in each statement? How, if at all, do these principles conflict with each other?

The right of the people to be secure in their persons, houses, papers, and effects, against unreasonable searches and seizures, shall not be violated, and no warrants shall issue, but upon probable cause . . . (Fourth Amendment).

The good of the people is the highest law (Cicero).

Authority without wisdom is like a heavy axe without an edge, fitter to bruise than polish (Anne Bradstreet).

For a man's house is his castle (Edward Coke).

They that can give up essential liberty to obtain a little temporary safety deserve neither liberty nor safety (Benjamin Franklin).

Since the general civilization of mankind, I believe there are more instances of the abridgment of the freedom of the people by gradual and silent encroachments of those in power, than by violent and sudden usurpation (James Madison).

Every successful revolution puts on in time the robe of the tyrant it has deposed (Barbara Tuchman).

Liberty, too, must be limited in order to be possessed (Edmund Burke).

The great and chief end, therefore, of men's uniting into Commonwealths, and putting themselves under Government, is the preservation of property [i.e., life, liberty, and estate] (John Locke).

. . . That order and progress can only come when individuals surrender their rights to an all-powerful sovereign . . . (Barack Obama).

Rights of the accused

Americans are worried about the drug problem. A recent poll indicated that a substantial percentage of American citizens would be willing to give up some protections of the Bill of Rights to control illegal drug use. Presidents Bush and Obama have made it very clear that security comes with less freedom.

Several years ago, Congress passed a law authorizing US authorities to confiscate the property of individuals suspected of trafficking in drugs. Such property could be seized on mere suspicion. Civil asset forfeiture has been opposed by Charles Koch, Justice Clarence Thomas, and Chuck Norris. Individuals whose property had been seized could appeal and seek a return of their property, but the burden of proof rests on them to prove their innocence contrary to Fifth and Fourteenth Amendments of due process. Advocates of this law argued its constitutionality because the government was not acting against the suspected individuals, only against their property. Since only individuals, and not property, enjoy the protection of the Bill of Rights, they said the law did not violate the Constitution.

How do the following statements apply to this situation? What principles and ideals are implied in each statement? How, if at all, do these principles conflict with each other?

No person shall be . . . deprived of life, liberty, or property, without due process of law . . . (Fifth Amendment).

It is better that ten guilty persons escape than one innocent person suffer (William Blackstone).

Man's capacity for justice makes democracy possible, but man's inclination to injustice makes democracy necessary (Reinhold Niebuhr).

The mood and temper of the public in the treatment of crime and criminals is one of the most unfailing tests of civilization of any country (Winston Churchill).

Criminals should not get to keep money, property or other ill-gotten gains from illegal activity. But criminals aren't criminals until they have been convicted. That's what "innocent until proven guilty" means (Derek Draplin and Kahryn Rileyc).

Unity versus diversity

Is a common language essential to the survival of the great experiment? One of the most controversial aspects of diversity in America has to do with language or cultural assimilation. Throughout our history, English has been the principal language of the country. For millions of immigrants, learning English was an important first step to becoming a US citizen. It has been left to public education to teach immigrant children who speak other languages to speak, write and read, and communicate in English. Educators differ about how best to accomplish their tasks. The largest percentage of recent immigrants uses Spanish as their first language. In certain areas of the country, Spanish is as commonly spoken as English. Are we becoming a bilingual nation?

More importantly, are we at times speaking the same language, same words, but with different meanings? In "A Solution for a Fragmented America" by John Horvat of the *Imaginative Conservative*, the cause may be in today's struggle with the ideal of freedom. Is a common "language" necessary to American citizenship?

> In his masterwork, *The City of God*, Saint Augustine offers a definition of a people that can shed some light on why we are so fragmented today. He states that a people is "a gathered multitude of rational beings united by agreeing to share the things they love."
>
> If there is one thing that has always united, and can even still unite Americans, it is our love for freedom. Indeed, the mere mention of freedom has always served as an inebriating rallying cry that opens up seemingly infinite possibilities of realizing dreams. This concept is found in our myths and is intertwined in our national narratives. Soldiers fight and die for freedom.
>
> However, the idea of freedom that so united us in the past now divides us. Freedom used to be the means by which we celebrated our diversity. Today, it splinters us up and set us in radical discord with each other. It has become the point of contention that is tearing the country apart.
>
> Freedom presupposes a moral order that helps us discern the good. Freedom buttresses the rule of law; it does not undermine it.
>
> Perhaps a better way to understand freedom is that which allows us to live fully inside a broad framework of family, community and faith. These social institutions serve as benevolent handrails not odious fetters upon our future. They facilitate freedom and enable us to be a people by helping us unite to "share the things we agree to love."

America was founded in this context of ordered liberty. It served as a point of unity that allowed Americans to prosper and express themselves with amazing variety. Inside this context, it is also understood that freedom is not without cost. It must often be bought with sacrifice and even blood.

The traditional notion of freedom has long been in conflict with the more modern ideal that came from the Enlightenment. This concept is a freedom without rules or restraint best expressed in the rambling impressions of French philosopher Jean-Jacques Rousseau.

Rousseau saw freedom as obedience to the law one gives oneself. Law originates in the individual who is the supreme judge of right and wrong. Each is deemed autonomous and self-determining. The ultimate goal in life is the remaking of the "self" to achieve self-realization and self-fulfillment. There is a denial of any limits or boundaries to experience; nothing is forbidden.

This distorted vision of freedom repudiates social institutions as obstacles that inhibit individual expression. It proclaims a freedom from God and His law. It is constantly undermining its foundations by introducing elements of chaos and frenetic intemperance, which it labels diversity. This freedom denies duty and demands entitlement.

Thus, we are fragmented because this second notion of freedom now dominates the culture. We can no longer live off the legacy of ordered liberty, a fruit of Christian civilization that has sustained our society. Our social capital has been spent. Things are breaking down.

With the splintering of society, many Americans are searching for what we lost. If we are to be a people once again, we must rally around what Russell Kirk called those "permanent things" that we once loved and agreed to share.

America is God's crucible, the great melting pot where all the races of Europe are melting and reforming! (Israel Zangwell).

Immigrants are not refuse; rather, they are the sinew and bone of all nations . . . Education is the essence of American opportunity, the treasure that no thief could touch, not even misfortune or poverty (Mary Antin).

Our political harmony is therefore concerned in a uniformity of language (Noah Webster).

We have room for but one language here, and that is the English language, and we intend to see that the crucible turns our people out as Americans, and not as dwellers of a polyglot boardinghouse (Theodore Roosevelt).

In world history, those who have helped to build the same culture are not necessarily of one race, and those of the same race have not all participated in one culture (Ruth Fulton Benedict).

We have become not a melting pot but a beautiful mosaic. Different people, different beliefs, different yearnings, different hopes, different dreams (Jimmy Carter).

America is not a melting pot. It is a sizzling cauldron (Barbara Mikulski).

Unless you speak English and read well, you'll never become a first-class citizen . . . but when you say "official," that becomes a racial slur (Barbara Bush).

The individual...does not exist for the State, nor for that abstraction called "society," or the "nation," which is only a collection of individuals (Emma Goldman).

Individual rights versus sovereignty of the people

One of the great conflicts of principles you have struggled with in this book is that between fundamental rights of the individual and the sovereign power of the state. It is not a new debate; it was key in the American Revolution and in the Civil War. A fundamental right, as you remember, is one that cannot be revised or taken away by any power, it is inalienable, given by God. Sovereignty is that power within a state beyond which there is no appeal—whoever has the sovereign power has the final say, such as the supreme law of the land, the Constitution in America.

In 1990, the Supreme Court ruled in *Texas v. Johnson* that the burning of an American flag as a political protest, however distasteful, unpatriotic, even treasonable an act to many Americans, was protected under the free speech provision of the First Amendment. The court's decision prompted calls for a constitutional amendment prohibiting the desecration of "Old Glory." President George Bush publicly endorsed such an amendment.

Were the proposed amendment to be added, it would in effect exempt some speech from protection. This is not the first or the last attempt to end objectional speech. There were the Alien and Sedition Acts under our second president, arrests of critics, even imprisonment for those voting against our sixteenth officeholder; attempts in the 1980s to use "hate speech" as a crime enhancer were allowed in some cases, rejected in others. The most famous was the case of Todd Mitchell beating into a coma a young white boy as revenge for lynching he had seen in the movie *Mississippi Burning*. Today, there are calls for speech codes on college campuses, riots or calls for banning of speech that offends minorities of listeners. All of these have represented a limitation on one of the essential freedoms guaranteed in the Bill of Rights. Yet we need to remember that it is within the sovereign authority of the American people to revise or abolish entirely the Bill of Rights.

What do you think about the protection of rights in a republic? Does it suggest that the theory of fundamental rights is irrelevant? What does it suggest about the relevance of the natural rights philosophy? How do the following statements apply to this situation? What principles and ideals are implied in each statement? How, if at all, do these principles conflict with each other?

> We the People of the United States . . . do ordain and establish this Constitution . . . (Preamble).

> Congress shall make no law . . . abridging the freedom of speech (First Amendment).

> All lawful authority, legislative, and executive, originates from the people. Power in the people is like light in the sun, native, original, inherent, and unlimited by anything human (James Burgh).

Those who desire to give up freedom in order to gain security will not have, nor do they deserve, either one (Thomas Jefferson).

You have rights antecedent to all earthly governments; rights that cannot be repealed or restrained by human law; rights derived from the Great Legislator of the Universe (John Adams).

Those who surrender freedom for security will not have, nor do they deserve, either one (Benjamin Franklin).

No one cause is left but the most ancient of all, the one, in fact, that from the beginning of our history has determined the very existence of politics, the cause of freedom versus tyranny (Hannah Arendt).

When I refuse to obey an unjust law, I do not contest the right of the majority to command, but I simply appeal from the sovereignty of the people to the sovereignty of mankind (Alexis de Tocqueville).

The dangers of "energetic" government

One of the major issues of today is health-care reform. In addition to the many complex aspects of health care itself, there also is a philosophical aspect to this issue: the benefits and dangers of government power. Obamacare was a substantial expansion of the national government's involvement in the private sector. Health-care services now comprise about one-seventh of the nation's economy.

Advocates of comprehensive health-care reform argue the need for government to take charge of what has become a serious problem in contemporary America. They would point to precedents such as the Social Security System that was created in 1935 as part of the New Deal.

Critics of Obamacare, on the other hand, express concern about any substantial increase in government bureaucracy. A national health-care system administered by the government, they believe, constitutes a potential threat to individual liberty. Yet when asked by a reporter of the constitutionality of health care forced on the people, Speaker of the House Nancy Pelosi's response shows utter contempt for the Constitution itself: "Are you serious? Are you serious?"

Do not be discouraged by many that will agree with Hamilton that man cannot rule himself. As California Congressman Adam Schiff opines on the releasing of memos, one on FISA and one from the House Intelligence Committee under Devin Nunes, on the abuses of power by our CIA, FBI, DOJ, NSA, that We, the People are not competent, lack the intelligence, don't understand how things work. We can retake the Republic.

The deep state assumes we are mere "inert matter, passive particles, motionless atoms, at best a kind of vegetation indifferent to its own manner of existence." Bastiat writing this fifty years before the Progressives take over America, that we are incapable of understanding who we are, what we are to do, from food consumption, medical decision, or working without the permission of government. Remember Rousseau's program to create the new man. With the complexities and demands of modern American society, what are the proper limits to an energetic government? What criteria should the citizen employ in evaluating the benefits and dangers of government regulation? Who decides? How do the following statements apply to this situation? What principles and ideals are implied in each statement?

> . . . [to] promote the general Welfare (Preamble).

> To make all Laws which are necessary and proper for carrying into Execution the foregoing Powers (Constitution, Art. I, Sec. 8, Cl. 18).

> If, my countrymen, you wait for a constitution which absolutely bars a power of doing evil, you must wait long, and when obtained it will have no power of doing good (Oliver Ellsworth).

> A government ought to contain in itself every power requisite to the full accomplishment of the objects committed to its care, and to the complete execution of the trusts for which it is responsible, free from every other control, but a regard

to the public good and to the sense of the people (Alexander Hamilton).

I own I am not a friend to a very energetic government. It is always oppressive (Thomas Jefferson).

I agree with Paul Ryan when he said we are a free country and we have the right to purchase something or not purchase it. I profoundly, utterly, inexorably disagree with him when he says it's our job, meaning the federal government, to make health care affordable. That is not the job of the federal government. That is not in the Constitution. It is nowhere in law. That is a self-assumed job on the part of the Congress because they are afraid to take away benefits that Obamacare unconstitutionally gave out (Andrew Napolitano).

Capital punishment and the Eighth Amendment

When it comes to Supreme Court opinions, church and state conflicts rank number one in volume and discord. Next is the constitutional interpretation and the role of the judges in making such interpretation as the death penalty. In 1994, Justice Harry Blackmun announced that he could no longer in good conscience vote in favor of allowing the death penalty. While he did not exactly say that capital punishment was unconstitutional, his remarks suggested that because the death penalty had become so repugnant to him, he could no longer have anything to do with its enforcement. Does "repugnancy" make it unconstitutional? Does a change in social mores change constitutionality?

Justice Blackmun's remarks were controversial, in part because of the strong opinions on the death penalty issue in the United States. They also were controversial because of what they suggested about how the words of the Constitution should be interpreted and the degree to which a judge's personal opinions should influence that document's meaning.

Is the death penalty constitutional? Its opponents say no. They maintain that the penalty itself violates the "cruel and unusual punishment" of the Eighth Amendment—not only both the manner of taking life but also, somewhat contradictorily, the long delays that many death row inmates face. Opponents also have argued that implementation of capital punishment violates the equal protection clause of the Fourteenth Amendment because a greater percentage of death penalty recipients are male, poor, and minority. Other critics claim it doesn't act as a deterrent to future murderers.

While proponents and even some who are opposed to the death penalty as a policy say it is constitutional. The text of the Constitution, they argue, makes clear that the Framers clearly intended to allow for capital punishment. It is up to the people through their representatives—and not to judges—to decide on whether to employ this option. We see this in the Constitution itself in dealing with treason—the only crime specified in the document—"Congress shall have power to declare the punishment of treason." And if more minorities and the poor are executed, is it merely they commit more capital offenses?

How do the following statements apply to this situation? Is taking the life of another a violation of "life, liberty, property"? What about the nonaggression policy of causing no harm? Does the state have power to eliminate the socially destructive?

> . . . *N*or cruel and unusual punishments inflicted (Eighth Amendment).

> No punishment has ever possessed enough power of deterrence to prevent the commission of crimes (Hannah Arendt).

> No person shall be . . . deprived of life, liberty, or property, without due process of law . . . (Fifth Amendment).

> Then thou shall give for a life, eye for eye, tooth for tooth . . . (Exod. 21:23–24).

> Thou shalt not kill (Exod. 20:13).

All of these issues, all of politics, all of life are based on costs and benefits, trade-offs, rights versus responsibility. Before laying down a plan of action, let's, like government, limit our actions by a list I have had hanging in my classroom for nearly thirty years. I do not know where I got this list. Online, the best source I could find was Freedoms Foundation out of Valley Forge. This list, clearly stemming from Washington's "110 Rules," is for citizens who are determined to make a difference, to hopefully move back to the Jeffersonian experiment, the great experiment of self-rule, or self-reliance, self-control.

Preamble to the Bill of Responsibilities:

Freedom and responsibility are mutual and inseparable; we can ensure enjoyment of the one only by exercising the other. Freedom for all of us depends on responsibility by each of us. To secure and expand our liberties, therefore, we accept these responsibilities as individual members of a free society.

Bill of Responsibilities

To be fully responsible for our own actions and for the consequences of those actions. Freedom to choose carries with it the responsibility for our choices.

To respect the rights and beliefs of others. In a free society, diversity flourishes. Courtesy and consideration toward others are measures of a civilized society.

To give sympathy, understanding, and help to others. As we hope others will help us when we are in need, we should help others when they are in need.

To do our best to meet our own and our families' needs. There is no personal freedom without economic freedom. By helping ourselves and those closest to us to become productive members of society, we contribute to the strength of the nation.

To respect and obey the laws. Laws are mutually accepted rules by which, together, we maintain a free society. Liberty itself is built on the foundation of law. That foundation provides an orderly process for changing laws. It also depends on our obeying laws once they have been freely adopted.

To respect the property of others, both private and public. No one has a right to what is not his or hers. The right to enjoy what is ours depends on our respecting the right of others to enjoy what is theirs.

To share with others our appreciation of the benefits and obligations of freedom. Freedom shared is freedom strengthened.

To participate constructively in the nation's political life. Democracy depends on an active citizenry. It depends equally on an informed citizenry.

To help freedom survive by assuming personal responsibility for its defense. Our nation cannot survive unless we defend it. Its security rests on the individual determination of each of us to help preserve it.

To respect the rights and to meet the responsibilities on which our liberty rests and our democracy depends. This is the essence of freedom. Maintaining it requires our common effort, all together and each individually.

Our plan of action

What would fix the experiment? What must be done to fully achieve what the Founders and Framers saw for "ourselves and our posterity"? Some of these actions are social, some political, some quite revolutionary. But all must be achieved if we are again to be the City on the Hill, the Light of Liberty shining from that Old North Church through the flyover states to the Golden State. These are not in order of when or importance; priority will develop by events and reactions from the opposition. My preference is to defeat the incumbency, as that is the stumbling stone of reform. While the beneficiaries of the deep state are in power, the rest will be difficult.

The rule book must be studied, learned, and taught. We see little civic education being taught any longer, and what it is, is a watered-down social justice, Progressive agenda. Sen. Mike Lee, in his *Written Out of History,* states that all governments that are to do their job of protecting individual rights need a rule book with specific powers and limitations spelled out.

In the United States, we set out the rules and the limitations in our Constitution. To the extent we have as a nation adhered to that document, we have prospered as a result. The opposite is also true: when we neglect the Constitution, we lose its protections and the benefits that flow from them.

It concerns me greatly that some of our most significant constitutional protections—particularly structural features like federalism and the separation of powers, but also many of the substantive limitations found in the Bill of Rights—have been neglected and weakened over the last eighty years. While it is easy to blame the Supreme Court or certain presidents for this neglect, it is a saving grace of our Republic that the people can remedy the problems created by the Courts of the chief executive.

But in order to do that, the people first have to understand the Constitution, and then reinstate it as the centerpiece of American political discourse.

Most Americans are not inclined to willingly disregard the wisdom of our founding documents. Some, however, want to do precisely that; they consider the document quaint, outdated, and an unnecessary impediment to expanding the size, reach, and cost of the federal government.

Accordingly, if we want to preserve, protect, and defend the Constitution—and the many blessings of liberty that come from a government that follows it—the best thing we can do is to keep ourselves (and our fellow citizens) informed about what that document says, how it came into existence, and the nature of the threats facing it. In other words, in the American Republic, knowledge—specifically, a deep and widespread knowledge of the Constitution—is the greatest way to safe guard freedom.

Such knowledge, however, is not transmitted from one generation to another through the bloodstream. It must be taught, learned, and followed in each generation. And whenever that fails to happen, the Constitution—and with t, the liberty and prosperity of the American people—is left unprotected.

Term limits are the first order of business. I have always been against limiting the people from choosing its representatives. The philosophy the Framers hoped for, a dedicated servant of the people, the "best and the brightest" ruling for us, has been lost. Today the average senator serves a little over two terms; while the most powerful, fifty-seven years. In the house, the average representative serves about nine years; John Dingell of Michigan was there before I was born, nearly sixty years, retiring 2015.

We changed the rule for presidents in 1950s to get the people back in charge; we need the same for Congress. Two terms for a senator, the average, and three for members of the house must be added to the Constitution. This would eliminate the professional politician, many of which are now millionaires with only a $174,000-per-year salary. As an economist, I'm not really good at math, but twelve years (two terms) at $174,000, that only equals a million, if no income taxes, no food, clothing, shelter. Harry Truman once said, "You can't get rich in politics unless you're a crook."

End all private money in elections would ease many people's minds. Solving many of the problems that are criticized by both sides of politics, except the recipients of the billions doled out from lobbyists, PACs, and corporations, a set amount to run a campaign would allow politicians to be representatives of the people not leeches of them.

The list of "crimes" to the Republic is long and immense, but many stem from the buying of elections. It would shorten the campaign to one month, maybe two, September to November. This, like term limits, was hard for me to accept at first, yet this with term limits may be the only way to stop the deep state, the George Soros, even the issue of unlimited corporate monies OK'd by *Citizens United v. FEC* (2010). The court allowed independent political expenditures by a nonprofit corporation. The principles articulated by the Supreme Court in the case have also been extended to for-profit corporations, labor unions, and other associations.

Citizens United, a nonprofit conservative group, wanted to air a film critical of Hillary Clinton and to advertise the film during television broadcasts shortly before the 2008 Democratic primary election in which Clinton was running for US president. This supposedly would violate a national law prohibiting certain electioneering communications near an election. The court found the law prohibiting corporations and unions from making such electioneering communications to conflict with the Constitution.

The key to the case, however, is the dissent by Justice John Paul Stevens. He argued that the ruling "threatens to undermine the integrity of elected institutions across the Nation. The path it has taken to reach its outcome will, I fear, do damage to this institution . . . A democracy cannot function effectively when its constituent members believe laws are being bought and sold."

Pseudo-isolationism is not the 1920s but is George Washington's "no entangling alliances." Trillions of dollars and thousands of lives, ten thousands scarred should be enough to satisfy the warmongers of the hawkish deep state. We need to be prepared to fight when fought against, but policeman of the world needs rethinking. Simply war, and as we've seen the military-industrial-digital Panopticon, sucks more and more every year. We are fighting or stationed or protecting in places, frankly, Americans cannot pronounce, for people who pray for our downfall.

The billions, and now the new budget proposed today asks for $54 billion more, would be the true "peace dividend" we've heard about, looked for, never realized that can be used for the updating of infrastructure politicians have mentioned every two years, while potholes continue to grow. Schools, roads, rural "internalization" all are well than $600 billion spent on defense in 2016. If conservatives feel that infrastructure is a local issue, national taxes could be cut by one-third or block grants to each state based on population of miles of roads. Like Washington, James Madison knew the dangers of war to a republic.

> Of all the enemies of true liberty, war is, perhaps, the most to be dreaded, because it comprises and develops the germ of every other. War is the parent of armies; from these proceed debts and taxes; and armies, and debts, and taxes are the known instrument for bringing the many under the domination of the few.

Taxes the same for all is contrary to all since the debacle of the Sixteenth Amendment. Murray Rothbard, a great Austrian economist and founder of the original Libertarian Party with Charles and David Koch in the 1970s, believed that the more tax deductions the better; less money going to the government. But these are emergency times. As I write, the debt limit has again been exceeded, $20 trillion; no one of sound mind can accept that, let alone envision it. That is the weight on the shoulders of our children; we spent it, we need to pay it.

Here goes, buckle your seat belts, pull your damn pants up, wait until you see it all before I get your e-mails. First, no more tax exemptions; you want children you pay for them. Second, no more tax-exempt foundations; lots of PAC money comes from these. No more mortgage interest deductions; why should renters pay so you can own? Are homeowners better Americans? Is it government's job to pick winners and losers? NO! All entities pay the same, corporations, nonprofits, individuals, partnerships, no deductions, no loopholes, 10 percent flat tax. It should take minutes, even seconds to write down total income, move the decimal, mail the postcard, or hit "send" digitally. I made $95,000, I owe $9,500; I made $14,000, $1,400; Donald Trump $156,000,000, write the check, it's $15.6 million, not $58 million. After the debt is paid, maybe reduce the rate to 8 percent. OK, now yell and scream.

Cut the budget is related to the tax issue. With a $1.1 trillion budget proposed by the Trump administration for its first budget cutting snippets around the edges, some see hope, others devastation. But snippets are not going to be enough. These are emergency times, remember. And as a previous occupant of the office used to say, "Don't let a good crisis go by." Again, hold your breath, cut to twelve because that's the number of departments about to disappear.

We need to cut to those departments specifically mentioned by power in the Constitution; that leaves four! Officially, as of 2009, the national government employed 2.8 million individuals out of a total US workforce of 236 million—just over 1 percent of the workforce. But it's not quite as simple as that. Add in uniformed military personnel, and the figure goes up to just under 4.4 million. The Department of State deals with foreign affairs; stay out of domestic issues. The budget is $48 billion with sixty-nine thousand employees. This could be cut too, especially aid to our enemies in the billions, but let's start small.

Department of Defense, getting $54 billion more next year, like state, is to deal with foreign affairs; no defense intelligence in my iPad either. The budget is near $600 billion for both civilian (742,000) and military (2.1 million). Pseudo-isolation could drop this budget too. But that's a policy decision of a strong defense; remember, offense, first-strike, starting a war, hitting first violates nonaggression policy and the Constitution. Government's job to keep the foreign and domestic bad guys away; must be doable, quick, efficient, and costs and lives saving.

Attorney general, Department of Justice, is the president's enforcer of the law. There is no execution of the law without an enforcer. To "faithfully execute the law," the Justice Department has 114,000 employees spending $28 billion. Here great cuts could be made and still faithfully execute the law. Civil Rights, Antitrust, Tax, War, Civil, Criminal, Management, Environmental National Security Divisions, each with a deputy. Maybe we have too many laws?

The Treasury Department is needed to collect taxes and pay the bills. With eighty-six thousand people and $14 billion, we ought to balance a budget. Hitting the debt ceiling of twenty dollars too much spent is not good math.

That's it! All other employees you have six months to find a job; we'll cover income and insurance until then. All of you are college graduates; all are pretty smart, you'll have no problems.

Federalism needs to be reestablished, maybe even be rebuilt. With the Fourteenth Amendment incorporation, Seventeenth Amendment to break Congress away from the states, even the "New Federalism" of Nixon with block grants and revenue sharing. Yet from 1937 to 1995, SCOTUS did not void a single congressional action for exceeding Congress's power under the commerce clause of the Constitution; instead, the court has held that anything that could conceivably have even a slight impact on commerce was subject to national regulations.

The court kind of wavered in *Gonzales v. Raich* (2005) but still allowed the national government to outlaw the use of marijuana for medical purposes under the commerce clause even if the marijuana was never bought or sold and never crossed state lines. How broad a view of state power under the Tenth Amendment will the court take in future decisions remains unclear. This needs to end.

Louis Brandeis, in a dissenting opinion (maybe we should read dissenting opinions more carefully), *New State Ice Co. v. Liebmann* (1932), said,

> It is one of the happy incidents of the federal system that a single courageous state may, if its citizens choose, serve as a laboratory; and try novel social and economic experiments without risk to the rest of the country.

Let the citizens decide. States are 100 percent empowered in all areas not specifically taken from them by the Constitution. Domestic issues are primarily state issues—education, family, wills, property regulations—and should be allowed to experiment to solve their own problems. This leads to the next, local control of the government.

Local control of government is the locus of our power—cities, school boards, towns, and counties. It is here that we can make the biggest difference. Learn everything you can about your local government. This will take some effort and mainly to shift your focus of politics from the national to the local scene. Most reading this book know Trump, Ryan, McConnell yet can't tell you the name of one of their local county supervisor/commissioners, alderperson, president of school board, or even the mayor. We need to reverse this; read the headlines of the national stuff, react if necessary, but focus, focus, focus on learning the local stuff. Learn your local representatives' names, backgrounds, beliefs, values, career history, and voting records.

Learn the organization of your local government, learn the schedules of all relevant board and commission meetings, know when they meet, and show up for important issues.

Learn how to find and obtain all publicly available information: meetings, agendas, budgets, revenues, expenditures, bondholders and financiers, contracts, projects, land use plans, rezoning efforts, constitution, and bylaws—everything. You will find that information gathering in itself will begin to breed questions. Numbers and budgets and legal memos have their own way of whispering. You may discover corruption or questionable practices your officials wish to remain quiet or hidden. You may find that a board member is working to give himself or herself special privileges for their career advancement or profit. Maybe not. But the more information you have, the more transparent and accountable the government can be forced to be.

Don't trust "minutes" of meetings alone; locally where I live, I have attended meetings, read the minutes, and no jiving between the two. As Sir Humphrey of an old BBC comedy *Yes, Prime Minister!* once said, "The purpose of meetings is not to record events, it is to protect people"—"people," meaning the government agents involved! Go for everything you can find or have a desire to get. Good idea to record the meetings for later use.

Then start a blog, Facebook page, or website dedicated to making your local government as public and transparent as possible. You can be as detailed or selective as necessary, as long as it's honest and open. Post everything you can, video, notes taken, and those bogus minutes. Show any clear connections; show every cent that is taxed, how it is assessed and collected, how it is spent; show every cent borrowed and who profits from borrowing against future taxation and who holds the bond. Show how much elected officials and public employees of all sorts are paid and what their public pension benefits look like. This is all perfectly legal. Share it online, especially with others doing the same elsewhere.

A great resource is *OpentheBooks.org*. Salaries of all local officials, government paychecks, farm subsidies of local farmers. It would be great to have at least one such website dedicated to ultimate transparency in each of America's three thousand plus counties. It would better to have several in each county. Variety, choice, and competition will make them better and more effective. These would make fabulous projects for students; but, really, *anyone* could do this, and *everyone* should.

The point is to have a clear and open public record, and get the word out to as many people, and make everything about local government as accessible and understandable to as many people as possible. This will lead, eventually, to the election of board members, judges, sheriffs, assessors, collectors, etc., who better represent a greater percentage of the population, and better represent local values; it will increase accountability, and it will help end corruption, self-serving, and waste. Taxes will decrease in many localities, choices will open up, and people will be freer.

Resist national regulations and laws that conflict with local values. This will lead to court battles and possibly intimidation from higher governments, but the fact is Jefferson, Madison, the Tenth Amendment agree that sovereignty exists with the people, and the vision for local sovereignty is growing and can be implemented. The fight is only begun, but it has begun.

Some states have declared all national gun regulations and laws "null and void" within their boundaries for guns or ammo manufactured there. There is at least a dozen or more areas in which states currently are nullifying national laws. And as these attempts become more prevalent, it will only make moral sense to extend it to counties. Local sovereignty, county sovereignty, will grow more viable as well.

This is, after all, the foundation of American freedom: the first American declaration of independence was not that of 1776 but was written by a single county. Mecklenburg County, North Carolina, formally declared independence from Great Britain on May 31, 1775, saying that "the Authority of the King or Parliament, are annulled and vacated." They proceeded to set up an interim government all by their lonesome until (as they expected) the rest of the colonies should catch up. If it takes one secession—say, California, say, Shawano County, say, the village of Cecil to do this—so be it.

One way to stop the Hamilton screwup is to take to heart the last two paragraphs of McClanahan's book *How Hamilton Screwed Up America*:

> Think locally, act locally should be the political slogan of the twenty-first century. Hamilton's America, the "one nation indivisible" beaten into our heads since we were five, would work well for a homogenous population, but Americans have never—never—enjoyed that. From the colonial period to the present, Americans have been a diverse lot. Cavalier Virginians and Puritan Massachusettians never saw eye to eye on government policy. They in fact hated each other, but a union with very limited power in the central authority allowed each people to develop their political community as they saw fit. It would be immoral for one group of people to tell another how to live, yet this type of cultural imperialism is foisted upon Americans, both left and right, on a daily basis in Hamilton's American "nation."
>
> We live in Hamilton's America, but if we want an America that reflects who we are and have been as a people,

Hamilton's America needs to be buried next to the bastard from Nevis. The only way to "make America great again" is to rid the people of the states of Hamilton's curse and take government into our own hands at the state and local level. Maybe then, Hamilton, Marshall, Story, and Black could cease screwing up the original federal republic.

Cases of local freedom—individuals asserting control over corrupt local officials—are occurring as well. In one case, a small-town council in South Carolina had very quietly been paying itself an extremely rich pension package. When a few local business owners found out, they were outraged. At least one council member was opposed, and the businessmen approached him with a plan. They then showed up impromptu at a council meeting with video camera running. They got the members to confirm the terms of the rich package and then asked for a show of hands on the council of all those who disapproved of it. The lone honest member of the council jetted his hand high, and the rest were caught on video exposed. The businessmen then simply thanked the council and left with the video. The council was so scared that it called a recess and chased the inquirers into the parking lot, trembling, asking what they were going to do with the video! They knew good and well—publish it!

In a similar case, a seventeen-year-old kid exposed the appointment of a school superintendent whom a school board tried to rush through because he would be a big spender on behalf of the district. By simply showing up at both the interview process and the board meetings with a digital recorder, the corrupt thugs were caught and were trembling in fear.

Dr. Joel McDurmon, from whom I took these examples, tells of a friend of his dealing with the decay of property and community values because of government housing projects.

> He's watched his community deteriorate with a combination of Federal Section 8 housing and corrupt local investment trusts, much of which came about only after an influx of "free school lunch" programs and Title I status gained for local public schools to receive massive federal aid. There is much to discern and sort out here, but the bottom line is

corrupt local fat cat officials using government grants to empower and enrich themselves. And they are protected by liberal politicians above them, for several reasons. My contact said he started attending board meetings to record what was said. Very early on, one of these fat cats approached him with suspicious questioning and threatening demeanor—essentially threatening to wreck his career. The man is now very paranoid, because he has seen how deeply the corruption goes in his area, and how serious some of the insiders are about keeping it that way. There is work to be done here.

The deep state has fingers everywhere. Dr. McDurmon continues,

Another man wrote me telling how he won a seat on his local commission because the local conservatives were raising taxes and spending like crazy. He simply took a strong "TEA-party" stand against spending and corruption, and he was elected—despite overwhelming opposition from the local papers, labor unions, and even the local Chamber of Commerce. The local Chamber opposed him because it was dominated by big businesses that favor big-government for their corporate welfare. In other words, the local Chamber itself was corrupted by the forces of wealth redistribution. It had taken the cheese, and was now entrapped. My friend won the election nevertheless, but still faces an uphill fight against complacent and complicit officials, and, as he put it, "the grip that federal grants place on local units."

If we can't dismantle tyranny locally, you can forget it happening at the state level, let alone in DC. "But this is what is encouraging about the successes we're seeing: we in fact *can* have an effect locally, and many people are. There is a lot of work to do, and a lot of hill to climb. It will take time. But remember, we are planning for our grandchildren. It is time to start, get busy, and get a steady pace of reform," says McDurmon of *The American Vision*.

"It begins with people caring about the problem. It advances when people get focused, study, and explain the problem. It succeeds when they take action on the problem. This is county rights in action. It will only work when you get involved. For people, can only be free if they will be responsible and courageous."

Corporations are no longer persons. We touched on this under taxation and in elections. Lobbyists to get pro-business laws passed should be deductible—lunches, jets, Super Bowl tickets, vacations in the Caribbean are not business expenses but bribes. No money should be given in coin or kind to anyone in government. No revolving door either; Trump wants a five-year hiatus for executive branch employees from leaving office to go and work for those wanting benefits from that office, and a lifetime ban from lobbying for foreign governments. It works both ways; another provision sets a two-year period during which appointees must avoid working on issues involving former employers or clients.

To fight the takeover of the experiment is going to take courage. To stand against the system is difficult. Prometheus in *Anthem* by Ayn Rand knew the costs of rebellion, be it violent or nonviolent.

> At first, man was enslaved by the gods. But he broke their chains. Then he was enslaved by the kings. But he broke their chains. He was enslaved by his birth, by his kin, by his race. But he broke their chains. He declared to all his brothers that a man has rights which neither god nor king nor other men can take away from him, no matter what their number, for his is the right of man, and there is no right on earth above this right. And he stood on the threshold of the freedom for which the blood of the centuries behind him had been spilled.
>
> But then he gave up all he had won, and fell lower than his savage beginning.
>
> What brought it to pass? What disaster took their reason away from men? What whip lashed them to their knees in shame and submission? The worship of the word "We."
>
> When men accepted that worship, the structure of centuries collapsed about them, the structure whose every beam had come from the thought of some one man, each in his day down the ages, from the depth of some one spirit, such spirit as existed but for its own sake. Those men who

survived—those eager to obey, eager to live for one another, since they had nothing else to vindicate them—those men could neither carry on, nor preserve what they had received. Thus did all thought, all science, all wisdom perish on earth. Thus did men—men with nothing to offer save their great numbers—lose the steel towers, the flying ships, the power wires, all the things they had not created and could never keep. Perhaps, later, some men had been born with the mind and the courage to recover these things which were lost; perhaps these men came before the Councils of Scholars. They were answered as I have been answered—and for the same reasons.

But I still wonder how it was possible, in those graceless years of transition, long ago, that men did not see whither they were going, and went on, in blindness and cowardice, to their fate. I wonder, for it is hard for me to conceive how men who knew the word "I," could give it up and not know what they lost. But such has been the story, for I have lived in the City of the damned, and I know what horror men permitted to be brought upon them.

Perhaps, in those days, there were a few among men, a few of clear sight and clean soul, who refused to surrender that word. What agony must have been theirs before that which they saw coming and could not stop! Perhaps they cried out in protest and in warning. But men paid no heed to their warning. And they, these few, fought a hopeless battle, and they perished with their banners smeared by their own blood. And they chose to perish, for they knew. To them, I send my salute across the centuries, and my pity.

Theirs is the banner in my hand. And I wish I had the power to tell them that the despair of their hearts was not to be final, and their night was not without hope. For the battle they lost can never be lost. For that which they died to save can never perish. Through all the darkness, through all the shame of which men are capable, the spirit of man will remain alive on this earth. It may sleep, but it will awaken. It may wear chains, but it will break through. And man will go on. Man, not men.

MART GRAMS

Today there seems to be problem after problem with solutions worse than the disease. Annie Holmquist for Intellectual Takeout believes we need true courage, the courage of Aristotle.

> . . . Like Tennyson's 600 in the *Charge of the Light Brigade*, there are (pardon the parody):
>
>> Riots to the right of them,
>> ISIS to the left of them,
>> Diving Wall Street in front of them.
>
> In the midst of such chaos and confusion, nothing is more needful than courageous individuals. But do we really have a correct idea of what courage is?
>
> Aristotle pondered a similar question in his famous work, Nicomachean Ethics. As he saw it, individuals often mistake the following five things for true courage:
>
> 1. Compulsion—Aristotle labels this as "political courage," wherein individuals are influenced to do brave acts by those in authority. Unfortunately, these brave acts are only performed out of a fear of the consequences administered by the authorities for *not* performing them!
>
> 2. Experience—The cocky overconfidence that comes to those who have had extensive practice navigating problems. Aristotle, however, notes that these individuals become even more cowardly than an average person when they meet with a danger or trial which they have no clue how to handle.
>
> 3. Anger—On this point, Aristotle says, "[A]nger is a painful state, the act of revenge is pleasant; but those who fight from these motives [i.e., to avoid pain or gain pleasure] may fight well, but are not courageous: for they do not act because it is noble to act so, or as reason bids, but are driven by their passions; though they bear some resemblance to the courageous man."
>
> 4. Optimism—Similar to those who base their courage on past experience, Aristotle declares that the individual with

this form of false courage is "confident because he thinks he is superior and will win without receiving a scratch."

5. Ignorance—This type of courage is exuded by those who display a "Mr. Magoo" approach to life; who boldly charge ahead simply because they fail to recognize danger for what it truly is.

So if these examples are not true courage, then what is? According to Aristotle, the foundation of true courage is found in someone who does the right thing *in spite of fear*:

"Courage then, as we have said, is observance of the mean with regard to things that excite confidence or fear, under the circumstances which we have specified, and chooses its course and sticks to its post because it is noble to do so, or because it is disgraceful not to do so."

The test of true courage is certainly coming to America in the near future.

Snowden said he decided to make what he was involved in public because of what he called "institutional momentum." Agencies created by Congress, our representatives in the Republic, were now acting on their own authority, doing what they thought best for us. With little congressional oversight or even knowledge of the actions of the agencies' heads, the momentum of doing A must allow B; thus, C and D are "necessary and proper" too! Hamilton's dream, curse, to have the aristocratic few care for us had emerged. Americans were never given the opportunity as self-rulers, to decide for themselves if they wanted more liberty or more security. We, the public, had been kicked away from the discussion table unable to determine, let alone know, our own fate.

It's is time to stand up and claim your rights under God. The deep state has a claim on the freedoms of We the People; however, we own it, we created it. Lincoln was adamant that this government, this experiment, "shall not perish from the earth." That this is a "government of the people, by the people, for the people." Time to take it back!

The method is ours to decide: secession, conventions, revolution. I am hoping the courage, liberty, and dignity of We the People is nonviolent. It may not be. The train of abuses Jefferson used as his justification is growing new cars daily. Adams Smith, Thomas Jefferson (writing months apart), James Madison, I, and now hopefully all of you believe in the great experiment. It is time to take Smith's hope and turn it into reality. It's not a failed experiment; Hamilton was wrong. America's dream is "allowing every man to pursue his own interest his own way, upon the liberal plan of equality, liberty and justice."

My final entreaty is best said by that sickly Frenchman stuck in the nonviolent yet self-destructing revolution of 1848 France, Bastiat.

> God has given to men all that is necessary for them to accomplish their destinies. He has provided a social form as well as a human form. And these social organs of persons are so constituted that they will develop themselves harmoniously in the clean air of liberty. Away, then, with quacks and organizers! A way with their rings, chains, hooks, and pincers! Away with their artificial systems! Away with the whims of governmental administrators, their socialized projects, their centralization, their tariffs, their government schools, their state religions, their free credit, their bank monopolies, their regulations, their restrictions, their equalization by taxation, and their pious moralizations!

> And now that the legislators and do-gooders have so futilely inflicted so many systems upon society, may they finally end where they should have begun: May they reject all systems, and try liberty; for liberty is an acknowledgment of faith in God and His works.

The Magna Carta

The Magna Carta (Great Charter) was wrested from King John by several barons of the realm, at Runnymede in 1215. One of the great documents of liberty, the Magna Carta rested on the feudal principle that the king and nobles had mutual contractual obligations. Its provisions limited the power of the crown and firmly planted the principle that the king, like other Englishmen, is subject to law. It became a symbol of political liberty and the foundation of constitutional government. Here are excerpts from thirteen of its sixty-three articles:

1. That the English church shall be free, and shall have her rights entire, and her liberties inviolate; and we will that it be thus observed; and our will is that it be observed in good faith by our heirs forever.

2. We also have granted to all the freemen of our kingdom, for us and for our heirs forever, all the underwritten liberties, to be had and holden by them and their heirs, of us and our heirs forever...

3. No scutage or aid shall be imposed in our kingdom, unless by the general council of our kingdom; except for ransoming our person, making our eldest son a knight and once for marrying our eldest daughter; and for these there shall be paid no more than a reasonable aid.

4. And for holding the general council of the kingdom concerning the assessment of aids, except in the three cases aforesaid, and for the assessing of scutage, we shall cause to be summoned the archbishops, bishops, abbots, earls, and greater barons of the realm, singly by our letters. And furthermore, we shall cause to be summoned generally, by our sheriffs and bailiffs all others who hold of us in chief, for a certain day, that is to say, forty days before their meeting at least, and to a certain place. And in all letters of such summons we will declare the cause of such summons. And summons being thus made, the business shall proceed on the day appointed, according to the advice of such as shall be present, although all that were summoned come not.

5. We will not in the future grant to any one that he may take aid of his own free tenants, except to ransom his body, and to make

his eldest son a knight, and once to marry his eldest daughter; and for this there shall be paid only a reasonable aid....

6. Nothing from henceforth shall be given or taken for a writ of inquisition of life or limb, but it shall be granted freely, and not denied...

7. No freeman shall be taken or imprisoned, or diseised [deprived], or outlawed, or banished, or in any way destroyed, nor will we pass upon him, nor will we send upon him, unless by the lawful judgment of his peers, or by the law of the land.

8. We will sell to no man, we will not deny to any man, either justice or right.

9. All merchants shall have safe and secure conduct to go out of, and to come into, England, and to stay there and to pass as well by land as by water, for buying and selling by the ancient and allowed customs, without any unjust tolls, except in time of war, or when they are of any nation at war with us....

10. It shall be lawful, for the time to come, for anyone to go out of our kingdom and return safely and securely by land or by water, saving his allegiance to us (unless in time of war, by some short space, for the common benefit of the realm).

11. All the aforesaid customs and liberties, which we have granted to be holden in our kingdom, as much as it belongs to us, all people of our kingdom, as well clergy as laity, shall observe, as far as they are concerned, towards their dependents.

12. And whereas, for the honor of God and the amendment of our kingdom, and for the better quieting the discord that has arisen between us and our barons, we have granted all these things aforesaid. Willing to render them firm and lasting, we do give and grant our subjects the underwritten security, namely, that the barons may choose five and twenty barons of the kingdom, whom they think convenient, who shall take care, with all their might, to hold and observe, and cause to be observed, the peace and liberties we have granted them, and by this our present Charter confirmed.

13. ...It is also sworn, as well on our part as on the part of the barons, that all the things aforesaid shall be observed in good faith, and without evil duplicity. Given under our hand, in the presence of the witnesses above named, and many others, in the

meadow called Runnymede, between Windsor and Staines, the 15th day of June, in the 17th year of our reign.

Declaration of Independence

IN CONGRESS, July 4, 1776.
The unanimous Declaration of the thirteen united States of America,

When in the Course of human events, it becomes necessary for one people to dissolve the political bands which have connected them with another, and to assume among the powers of the earth, the separate and equal station to which the Laws of Nature and of Nature's God entitle them, a decent respect to the opinions of mankind requires that they should declare the causes which impel them to the separation.

We hold these truths to be self-evident, that all men are created equal, that they are endowed by their Creator with certain unalienable Rights, that among these are Life, Liberty and the pursuit of Happiness.— That to secure these rights, Governments are instituted among Men, deriving their just powers from the consent of the governed,—That whenever any Form of Government becomes destructive of these ends, it is the Right of the People to alter or to abolish it, and to institute new Government, laying its foundation on such principles and organizing its powers in such form, as to them shall seem most likely to effect their Safety and Happiness. Prudence, indeed, will dictate that Governments long established should not be changed for light and transient causes; and accordingly all experience hath shewn, that mankind are more disposed to suffer, while evils are sufferable, than to right themselves by abolishing the forms to which they are accustomed. But when a long train of abuses and usurpations, pursuing invariably the same Object evinces a design to reduce them under absolute Despotism, it is their right, it is their duty, to throw off such Government, and to provide new Guards for their future security.—Such has been the patient sufferance of these Colonies; and such is now the necessity which constrains them to alter their former Systems of Government. The history of the present

King of Great Britain is a history of repeated injuries and usurpations, all having in direct object the establishment of an absolute Tyranny over these States. To prove this, let Facts be submitted to a candid world.

He has refused his Assent to Laws, the most wholesome and necessary for the public good. He has forbidden his Governors to pass Laws of immediate and pressing importance, unless suspended in their operation till his Assent should be obtained; and when so suspended, he has utterly neglected to attend to them. He has refused to pass other Laws for the accommodation of large districts of people, unless those people would relinquish the right of Representation in the Legislature, a right inestimable to them and formidable to tyrants only. He has called together legislative bodies at places unusual, uncomfortable, and distant from the depository of their public Records, for the sole purpose of fatiguing them into compliance with his measures. He has dissolved Representative Houses repeatedly, for opposing with manly firmness his invasions on the rights of the people. He has refused for a long time, after such dissolutions, to cause others to be elected; whereby the Legislative powers, incapable of Annihilation, have returned to the People at large for their exercise; the State remaining in the mean time exposed to all the dangers of invasion from without, and convulsions within. He has endeavoured to prevent the population of these States; for that purpose obstructing the Laws for Naturalization of Foreigners; refusing to pass others to encourage their migrations hither, and raising the conditions of new Appropriations of Lands. He has obstructed the Administration of Justice, by refusing his Assent to Laws for establishing Judiciary powers. He has made Judges dependent on his Will alone, for the tenure of their offices, and the amount and payment of their salaries. He has erected a multitude of New Offices, and sent hither swarms of Officers to harass our people, and eat out their substance. He has kept among us, in times of peace, Standing Armies without the Consent of our legislatures. He has affected to render the Military independent of and superior to the Civil power. He has combined with others to subject us to a jurisdiction foreign to our constitution, and unacknowledged by our laws; giving his Assent to their Acts of pretended Legislation: For Quartering large bodies of armed troops among us: For protecting them, by a mock Trial, from punishment for any Murders which they should commit on the Inhabitants of these States: For cutting off our

Trade with all parts of the world: For imposing Taxes on us without our Consent: For depriving us in many cases, of the benefits of Trial by Jury: For transporting us beyond Seas to be tried for pretended offences For abolishing the free System of English Laws in a neighbouring Province, establishing therein an Arbitrary government, and enlarging its Boundaries so as to render it at once an example and fit instrument for introducing the same absolute rule into these Colonies: For taking away our Charters, abolishing our most valuable Laws, and altering fundamentally the Forms of our Governments: For suspending our own Legislatures, and declaring themselves invested with power to legislate for us in all cases whatsoever. He has abdicated Government here, by declaring us out of his Protection and waging War against us. He has plundered our seas, ravaged our Coasts, burnt our towns, and destroyed the lives of our people. He is at this time transporting large Armies of foreign Mercenaries to complete the works of death, desolation and tyranny, already begun with circumstances of Cruelty & perfidy scarcely paralleled in the most barbarous ages, and totally unworthy the Head of a civilized nation. He has constrained our fellow Citizens taken Captive on the high Seas to bear Arms against their Country, to become the executioners of their friends and Brethren, or to fall themselves by their Hands. He has excited domestic insurrections amongst us, and has endeavoured to bring on the inhabitants of our frontiers, the merciless Indian Savages, whose known rule of warfare, is an undistinguished destruction of all ages, sexes and conditions.

In every stage of these Oppressions We have Petitioned for Redress in the most humble terms: Our repeated Petitions have been answered only by repeated injury. A Prince whose character is thus marked by every act which may define a Tyrant, is unfit to be the ruler of a free people.

Nor have We been wanting in attentions to our British brethren. We have warned them from time to time of attempts by their legislature to extend an unwarrantable jurisdiction over us. We have reminded them of the circumstances of our emigration and settlement here. We have appealed to their native justice and magnanimity, and we have conjured them by the ties of our common kindred to disavow these usurpations, which, would inevitably interrupt our connections and correspondence.

They too have been deaf to the voice of justice and of consanguinity. We must, therefore, acquiesce in the necessity, which denounces our Separation, and hold them, as we hold the rest of mankind, Enemies in War, in Peace Friends.

We, therefore, the Representatives of the united States of America, in General Congress, Assembled, appealing to the Supreme Judge of the world for the rectitude of our intentions, do, in the Name, and by Authority of the good People of these Colonies, solemnly publish and declare, That these United Colonies are, and of Right ought to be Free and Independent States; that they are Absolved from all Allegiance to the British Crown, and that all political connection between them and the State of Great Britain, is and ought to be totally dissolved; and that as Free and Independent States, they have full Power to levy War, conclude Peace, contract Alliances, establish Commerce, and to do all other Acts and Things which Independent States may of right do. And for the support of this Declaration, with a firm reliance on the protection of divine Providence, we mutually pledge to each other our Lives, our Fortunes and our sacred Honor.

Signed by ORDER and in BEHALF of the CONGRESS,
JOHN HANCOCK, PRESIDENT.

According to the authenticated list printed by order of Congress of January 18, 1777. Braces, spelling, and abbreviations of names conform to original printed list.

The Constitution of the United States

We the People of the United States, in Order to form a more perfect Union, establish Justice, insure domestic Tranquility, provide for the common defence, promote the general Welfare, and secure the Blessings of Liberty to ourselves and our Posterity, do ordain and establish this Constitution for the United States of America.

Article I

Section 1. All legislative Powers herein granted shall be vested in a Congress of the United States, which shall consist of a Senate and House of Representatives.

Section 2. The House of Representatives shall be composed of Members chosen every second Year by the People of the several States, and the Electors in each State shall have the Qualifications requisite for Electors of the most numerous Branch of the State Legislature.

No Person shall be a Representative who shall not have attained to the Age of twenty five Years, and been seven Years a Citizen of the United States, and who shall not, when elected, be an Inhabitant of that State in which he shall be chosen.

Representatives and direct Taxes shall be apportioned among the several States which may be included within this Union, according to their respective Numbers, which shall be determined by adding to the whole Number of free Persons, including those bound to Service for a Term of Years, and excluding Indians not taxed, three fifths of all other Persons. The actual Enumeration shall be made within three Years after the first Meeting of the Congress of the United States, and within every subsequent Term of ten Years, in such Manner as they shall by Law direct. The Number of Representatives shall not exceed one for every thirty Thousand, but each State shall have at Least one Representative; and until such enumeration shall be made, the State of New Hampshire shall be entitled to chuse three, Massachusetts eight, Rhode-Island and Providence Plantations one, Connecticut five, New-York six, New Jersey four, Pennsylvania eight, Delaware one, Maryland six, Virginia ten, North Carolina five, South Carolina five, and Georgia three.

When vacancies happen in the Representation from any State, the Executive Authority thereof shall issue Writs of Election to fill such Vacancies.

The House of Representatives shall chuse their Speaker and other Officers; and shall have the sole Power of Impeachment.

Section 3. The Senate of the United States shall be composed of two Senators from each State, chosen by the Legislature thereof for six Years; and each Senator shall have one Vote.

Immediately after they shall be assembled in Consequence of the first Election, they shall be divided as equally as may be into three Classes. The Seats of the Senators of the first Class shall be vacated at the Expiration of the second Year, of the second Class at the Expiration of the fourth Year, and of the third Class at the Expiration of the sixth Year, so that one third may be chosen every second Year; and if Vacancies happen by Resignation, or otherwise, during the Recess of the Legislature of any State, the Executive thereof may make temporary Appointments until the next Meeting of the Legislature, which shall then fill such Vacancies.

No Person shall be a Senator who shall not have attained to the Age of thirty Years, and been nine Years a Citizen of the United States, and who shall not, when elected, be an Inhabitant of that State for which he shall be chosen.

The Vice President of the United States shall be President of the Senate, but shall have no Vote, unless they be equally divided.

The Senate shall chuse their other Officers, and also a President pro tempore, in the Absence of the Vice President, or when he shall exercise the Office of President of the United States.

The Senate shall have the sole Power to try all Impeachments. When sitting for that Purpose, they shall be on Oath or Affirmation. When the President of the United States is tried, the Chief Justice shall preside: And no Person shall be convicted without the Concurrence of two thirds of the Members present.

Judgment in Cases of Impeachment shall not extend further than to removal from Office, and disqualification to hold and enjoy any Office of honor, Trust or Profit under the United States: but the Party convicted shall nevertheless be liable and subject to Indictment, Trial, Judgment and Punishment, according to Law.

Section 4. The Times, Places and Manner of holding Elections for Senators and Representatives, shall be prescribed in each State by the Legislature thereof; but the Congress may at any time by Law make or alter such Regulations, except as to the Places of chusing Senators.

The Congress shall assemble at least once in every Year, and such Meeting shall be on the first Monday in December, unless they shall by Law appoint a different Day.

Section 5. Each House shall be the Judge of the Elections, Returns and Qualifications of its own Members, and a Majority of each shall constitute a Quorum to do Business; but a smaller Number may adjourn from day to day, and may be authorized to compel the Attendance of absent Members, in such Manner, and under such Penalties as each House may provide.

Each House may determine the Rules of its Proceedings, punish its Members for disorderly Behaviour, and, with the Concurrence of two thirds, expel a Member.

Each House shall keep a Journal of its Proceedings, and from time to time publish the same, excepting such Parts as may in their Judgment require Secrecy; and the Yeas and Nays of the Members of either House on any question shall, at the Desire of one fifth of those Present, be entered on the Journal.

Neither House, during the Session of Congress, shall, without the Consent of the other, adjourn for more than three days, nor to any other Place than that in which the two Houses shall be sitting.

Section 6. The Senators and Representatives shall receive a Compensation for their Services, to be ascertained by Law, and paid out of the Treasury of the United States. They shall in all Cases, except Treason, Felony and Breach of the Peace, be privileged from Arrest during their Attendance at the Session of their respective Houses, and in going to and returning from the same; and for any Speech or Debate in either House, they shall not be questioned in any other Place.

No Senator or Representative shall, during the Time for which he was elected, be appointed to any civil Office under the Authority of the United States, which shall have been created, or the Emoluments whereof shall have been encreased during such time; and no Person holding any Office under the United States, shall be a Member of either House during his Continuance in Office.

Section 7. All Bills for raising Revenue shall originate in the House of Representatives; but the Senate may propose or concur with Amendments as on other Bills.

Every Bill which shall have passed the House of Representatives and the Senate, shall, before it become a Law, be presented to the President of the United States: If he approve he shall sign it, but if not he shall return it, with his Objections to that House in which it shall have originated, who shall enter the Objections at large on their Journal, and proceed to reconsider it. If after such Reconsideration two thirds of that House shall agree to pass the Bill, it shall be sent, together with the Objections, to the other House, by which it shall likewise be reconsidered, and if approved by two thirds of that House, it shall become a Law. But in all such Cases the Votes of both Houses shall be determined by yeas and Nays, and the Names of the Persons voting for and against the Bill shall be entered on the Journal of each House respectively. If any Bill shall not be returned by the President within ten Days (Sundays excepted) after it shall have been presented to him, the Same shall be a Law, in like Manner as if he had signed it, unless the Congress by their Adjournment prevent its Return, in which Case it shall not be a Law.

Every Order, Resolution, or Vote to which the Concurrence of the Senate and House of Representatives may be necessary (except on a question of Adjournment) shall be presented to the President of the United States; and before the Same shall take Effect, shall be approved by him, or being disapproved by him, shall be repassed by two thirds of the Senate and House of Representatives, according to the Rules and Limitations prescribed in the Case of a Bill.

Section 8. The Congress shall have Power To lay and collect Taxes, Duties, Imposts and Excises, to pay the Debts and provide for the common Defence and general Welfare of the United States; but all Duties, Imposts and Excises shall be uniform throughout the United States;

To borrow Money on the credit of the United States;

To regulate Commerce with foreign Nations, and among the several States, and with the Indian Tribes;

To establish an uniform Rule of Naturalization, and uniform Laws on the subject of Bankruptcies throughout the United States;

To coin Money, regulate the Value thereof, and of foreign Coin, and fix the Standard of Weights and Measures;

To provide for the Punishment of counterfeiting the Securities and current Coin of the United States;

To establish Post Offices and post Roads;

To promote the Progress of Science and useful Arts, by securing for limited Times to Authors and Inventors the exclusive Right to their respective Writings and Discoveries;

To constitute Tribunals inferior to the supreme Court;

To define and punish Piracies and Felonies committed on the high Seas, and Offences against the Law of Nations;

To declare War, grant Letters of Marque and Reprisal, and make Rules concerning Captures on Land and Water;

To raise and support Armies, but no Appropriation of Money to that Use shall be for a longer Term than two Years;

To provide and maintain a Navy;

To make Rules for the Government and Regulation of the land and naval Forces;

To provide for calling forth the Militia to execute the Laws of the Union, suppress Insurrections and repel Invasions;

To provide for organizing, arming, and disciplining, the Militia, and for governing such Part of them as may be employed in the Service of the United States, reserving to the States respectively, the Appointment of the Officers, and the Authority of training the Militia according to the discipline prescribed by Congress;

To exercise exclusive Legislation in all Cases whatsoever, over such District (not exceeding ten Miles square) as may, by Cession of particular States, and the Acceptance of Congress, become the Seat of the Government of the United States, and to exercise like Authority over all Places purchased by the Consent of the Legislature of the State in which the Same shall be, for the Erection of Forts, Magazines, Arsenals, dock-Yards, and other needful Buildings;—And

To make all Laws which shall be necessary and proper for carrying into Execution the foregoing Powers, and all other Powers vested by this Constitution in the Government of the United States, or in any Department or Officer thereof.

Section 9. The Migration or Importation of such Persons as any of the States now existing shall think proper to admit, shall not be prohibited by the Congress prior to the Year one thousand eight hundred and eight, but a Tax or duty may be imposed on such Importation, not exceeding ten dollars for each Person.

The Privilege of the Writ of Habeas Corpus shall not be suspended, unless when in Cases of Rebellion or Invasion the public Safety may require it.

No Bill of Attainder or ex post facto Law shall be passed.

No Capitation, or other direct, Tax shall be laid, unless in Proportion to the Census or enumeration herein before directed to be taken.

No Tax or Duty shall be laid on Articles exported from any State.

No Preference shall be given by any Regulation of Commerce or Revenue to the Ports of one State over those of another; nor shall Vessels bound to, or from, one State, be obliged to enter, clear, or pay Duties in another.

No Money shall be drawn from the Treasury, but in Consequence of Appropriations made by Law; and a regular Statement and Account of the Receipts and Expenditures of all public Money shall be published from time to time.

No Title of Nobility shall be granted by the United States: And no Person holding any Office of Profit or Trust under them, shall, without the Consent of Congress, accept of any present, Emolument, Office, or Title, of any kind whatever, from any King, Prince, or foreign State.

Section 10. No State shall enter into any Treaty, Alliance, or Confederation; grant Letters of Marque and Reprisal; coin Money; emit Bills of Credit; make any Thing but gold and silver Coin a Tender in Payment of Debts; pass any Bill of Attainder, ex post facto Law, or Law impairing the Obligation of Contracts, or grant any Title of Nobility.

No State shall, without the Consent of the Congress, lay any Imposts or Duties on Imports or Exports, except what may be absolutely necessary for executing it's inspection Laws: and the net Produce of all Duties and Imposts, laid by any State on Imports or Exports, shall be for the Use of the Treasury of the United States; and all such Laws shall be subject to the Revision and Controul of the Congress.

No State shall, without the Consent of Congress, lay any Duty of Tonnage, keep Troops, or Ships of War in time of Peace, enter into any Agreement or Compact with another State, or with a foreign Power, or engage in War, unless actually invaded, or in such imminent Danger as will not admit of delay.

Article II

Section 1. The executive Power shall be vested in a President of the United States of America. He shall hold his Office during the Term of four Years, and, together with the Vice President, chosen for the same Term, be elected, as follows:

Each State shall appoint, in such Manner as the Legislature thereof may direct, a Number of Electors, equal to the whole Number of Senators and Representatives to which the State may be entitled in the Congress: but no Senator or Representative, or Person holding an Office of Trust or Profit under the United States, shall be appointed an Elector.

The Electors shall meet in their respective States, and vote by Ballot for two Persons, of whom one at least shall not be an Inhabitant of the same State with themselves. And they shall make a List of all the Persons voted for, and of the Number of Votes for each; which List they shall sign and certify, and transmit sealed to the Seat of the Government of the United States, directed to the President of the Senate. The President of the Senate shall, in the Presence of the Senate and House of Representatives, open all the Certificates, and the

Votes shall then be counted. The Person having the greatest Number of Votes shall be the President, if such Number be a Majority of the whole Number of Electors appointed; and if there be more than one who have such Majority, and have an equal Number of Votes, then the House of Representatives shall immediately chuse by Ballot one of them for President; and if no Person have a Majority, then from the five highest on the List the said House shall in like Manner chuse the President. But in chusing the President, the Votes shall be taken by States, the Representation from each State having one Vote; A quorum for this purpose shall consist of a Member or Members from two thirds of the States, and a Majority of all the States shall be necessary to a Choice. In every Case, after the Choice of the President, the Person having the greatest Number of Votes of the Electors shall be the Vice President. But if there should remain two or more who have equal Votes, the Senate shall chuse from them by Ballot the Vice President.

The Congress may determine the Time of chusing the Electors, and the Day on which they shall give their Votes; which Day shall be the same throughout the United States.

No Person except a natural born Citizen, or a Citizen of the United States, at the time of the Adoption of this Constitution, shall be eligible to the Office of President; neither shall any Person be eligible to that Office who shall not have attained to the Age of thirty five Years, and been fourteen Years a Resident within the United States.

In Case of the Removal of the President from Office, or of his Death, Resignation, or Inability to discharge the Powers and Duties of the said Office, the Same shall devolve on the Vice President, and the Congress may by Law provide for the Case of Removal, Death, Resignation or Inability, both of the President and Vice President, declaring what Officer shall then act as President, and such Officer shall act accordingly, until the Disability be removed, or a President shall be elected.

The President shall, at stated Times, receive for his Services, a Compensation, which shall neither be increased nor diminished during the Period for which he shall have been elected, and he shall not receive within that Period any other Emolument from the United States, or any of them.

Before he enter on the Execution of his Office, he shall take the following Oath or Affirmation:—"I do solemnly swear (or affirm) that I will faithfully execute the Office of President of the United States, and will to the best of my Ability, preserve, protect and defend the Constitution of the United States."

Section 2. The President shall be Commander in Chief of the Army and

Navy of the United States, and of the Militia of the several States, when

called into the actual Service of the United States; he may require the Opinion, in writing, of the principal Officer in each of the executive Departments, upon any Subject relating to the Duties of their respective Offices, and he shall have Power to grant Reprieves and Pardons for Offences against the United States, except in Cases of Impeachment.

He shall have Power, by and with the Advice and Consent of the Senate, to make Treaties, provided two thirds of the Senators present concur; and

he shall nominate, and by and with the Advice and Consent of the Senate, shall appoint Ambassadors, other public Ministers and Consuls, Judges of the supreme Court, and all other Officers of the United States, whose Appointments are not herein otherwise provided for, and which shall be established by Law: but the Congress may by Law vest the Appointment of such inferior Officers, as they think proper, in the President alone, in the Courts of Law, or in the Heads of Departments.

The President shall have Power to fill up all Vacancies that may happen during the Recess of the Senate, by granting Commissions which shall expire at the End of their next Session.

Section 3. He shall from time to time give to the Congress Information of the State of the Union, and recommend to their Consideration such Measures as he shall judge necessary and expedient; he may, on extraordinary Occasions, convene both Houses, or either of them, and in Case of Disagreement between them, with Respect to the Time of Adjournment, he may adjourn them to such Time as he shall think proper; he shall receive Ambassadors and other public

Ministers; he shall take Care that the Laws be faithfully executed, and shall Commission all the Officers of the United States.

Section 4. The President, Vice President and all civil Officers of the United States, shall be removed from Office on Impeachment for, and Conviction of, Treason, Bribery, or other high Crimes and Misdemeanors.

Article III

Section 1. The judicial Power of the United States shall be vested in one supreme Court, and in such inferior Courts as the Congress may from time to time ordain and establish. The Judges, both of the supreme and inferior Courts, shall hold their Offices during good Behaviour, and shall, at stated Times, receive for their Services a Compensation, which shall not be diminished during their Continuance in Office.

Section 2. The judicial Power shall extend to all Cases, in Law and Equity, arising under this Constitution, the Laws of the United States, and Treaties made, or which shall be made, under their Authority;—to all Cases affecting Ambassadors, other public Ministers and Consuls;—to all Cases of admiralty and maritime Jurisdiction;—to Controversies to which the United States shall be a Party;—to Controversies between two or more States;—between a State and Citizens of another State,—between Citizens of different States,—between Citizens of the same State claiming Lands under Grants of different States, and between a State, or the Citizens thereof, and foreign States, Citizens or Subjects.

In all Cases affecting Ambassadors, other public Ministers and Consuls, and those in which a State shall be Party, the supreme Court shall have original Jurisdiction. In all the other Cases before mentioned, the supreme Court shall have appellate Jurisdiction, both as to Law and Fact, with such Exceptions, and under such Regulations as the Congress shall make.

The Trial of all Crimes, except in Cases of Impeachment, shall be by Jury; and such Trial shall be held in the State where the said Crimes shall have been committed; but when not committed within any State, the Trial shall be at such Place or Places as the Congress may by Law have directed.

Section 3. Treason against the United States, shall consist only in levying War against them, or in adhering to their Enemies, giving them Aid and Comfort. No Person shall be convicted of Treason unless on the Testimony of two Witnesses to the same overt Act, or on Confession in open Court.

The Congress shall have Power to declare the Punishment of Treason, but no Attainder of Treason shall work Corruption of Blood, or Forfeiture except during the Life of the Person attainted.

Article IV

Section 1. Full Faith and Credit shall be given in each State to the public Acts, Records, and judicial Proceedings of every other State. And the Congress may by general Laws prescribe the Manner in which such Acts, Records and Proceedings shall be proved, and the Effect thereof.

Section 2. The Citizens of each State shall be entitled to all Privileges and Immunities of Citizens in the several States.

A Person charged in any State with Treason, Felony, or other Crime, who shall flee from Justice, and be found in another State, shall on Demand of the executive Authority of the State from which he fled, be delivered up, to be removed to the State having Jurisdiction of the Crime.

No Person held to Service or Labour in one State, under the Laws thereof, escaping into another, shall, in Consequence of any Law or Regulation therein, be discharged from such Service or Labour, but shall be delivered up on Claim of the Party to whom such Service or Labour may be due.

Section 3. New States may be admitted by the Congress into this Union; but no new State shall be formed or erected within the Jurisdiction of any other State; nor any State be formed by the Junction of two or more States, or Parts of States, without the Consent of the Legislatures of the States concerned as well as of the Congress.

The Congress shall have Power to dispose of and make all needful Rules and Regulations respecting the Territory or other Property belonging to the United States; and nothing in this Constitution shall be so construed as to Prejudice any Claims of the United States, or of any particular State.

Section 4. The United States shall guarantee to every State in this Union a Republican Form of Government, and shall protect each of them against Invasion; and on Application of the Legislature, or of the Executive (when the Legislature cannot be convened), against domestic Violence.

Article V

The Congress, whenever two thirds of both Houses shall deem it necessary, shall propose Amendments to this Constitution, or, on the Application of the Legislatures of two thirds of the several States, shall call a Convention for proposing Amendments, which, in either Case, shall be valid to all Intents and Purposes, as Part of this Constitution, when ratified by the Legislatures of three fourths of the several States, or by Conventions in three fourths thereof, as the one or the other Mode of Ratification may be proposed by the Congress; Provided that no Amendment which may be made prior to the Year One thousand eight hundred and eight shall in any Manner affect the first and fourth Clauses in the Ninth Section of the first Article; and that no State, without its Consent, shall be deprived of its equal Suffrage in the Senate.

Article VI

All Debts contracted and Engagements entered into, before the Adoption of this Constitution, shall be as valid against the United States under this Constitution, as under the Confederation.

This Constitution, and the Laws of the United States which shall be made in Pursuance thereof; and all Treaties made, or which shall be made, under the Authority of the United States, shall be the supreme Law of the Land; and the Judges in every State shall be bound thereby, any Thing in the Constitution or Laws of any State to the Contrary notwithstanding.

The Senators and Representatives before mentioned, and the Members of the several State Legislatures, and all executive and judicial Officers, both of the United States and of the several States, shall be bound by Oath or Affirmation, to support this Constitution; but no religious Test shall ever be required as a Qualification to any Office or public Trust under the United States.

Article VII

The Ratification of the Conventions of nine States, shall be sufficient for the Establishment of this Constitution between the States so ratifying the Same.

The Word, "the," being interlined between the seventh and eighth Lines of the first Page, the Word "Thirty" being partly written on an Erazure in the fifteenth Line of the first Page, The Words "is tried" being interlined between the thirty second and thirty third Lines of the first Page and the Word "the" being interlined between the forty third and forty fourth Lines of the second Page.

Attest William Jackson Secretary

done in Convention by the Unanimous Consent of the States present the Seventeenth Day of September in the Year of our Lord one thousand seven hundred and Eighty seven and of the Independance of the United States of America the Twelfth In witness whereof We have hereunto subscribed our Names,

G. Washington

Presidt and deputy from Virginia

Attest: William Jackson, Secretary

The Preamble to the Bill of Rights

Congress of the United States begun and held at the City of New-York, on Wednesday the fourth of March, one thousand seven hundred and eighty nine.

THE Conventions of a number of the States, having at the time of their adopting the Constitution, expressed a desire, in order to prevent misconstruction or abuse of its powers, that further declaratory and restrictive clauses should be added: And as extending the ground of public confidence in the Government, will best ensure the beneficent ends of its institution.

RESOLVED by the Senate and House of Representatives of the United States of America, in Congress assembled, two thirds of both Houses concurring, that the following Articles be proposed to the Legislatures of the several States, as amendments to the Constitution of the United States, all, or any of which Articles, when ratified by three fourths of the said Legislatures, to be valid to all intents and purposes, as part of the said Constitution; viz.

ARTICLES in addition to, and Amendment of the Constitution of the United States of America, proposed by Congress, and ratified by the Legislatures of the several States, pursuant to the fifth Article of the original Constitution.

Note: The following text is a transcription of the first ten amendments to the Constitution in their original form. These amendments were ratified December 15, 1791, and form what is known as the "Bill of Rights."

Amendment I

Congress shall make no law respecting an establishment of religion, or prohibiting the free exercise thereof; or abridging the freedom of speech, or of the press; or the right of the people peaceably to assemble, and to petition the Government for a redress of grievances.

Amendment II

A well-regulated Militia, being necessary to the security of a free State, the right of the people to keep and bear Arms, shall not be infringed.

Amendment III

No Soldier shall, in time of peace be quartered in any house, without the consent of the Owner, nor in time of war, but in a manner to be prescribed by law.

Amendment IV

The right of the people to be secure in their persons, houses, papers, and effects, against unreasonable searches and seizures, shall not be violated, and no Warrants shall issue, but upon probable cause, supported by Oath or affirmation, and particularly describing the place to be searched, and the persons or things to be seized.

Amendment V

No person shall be held to answer for a capital, or otherwise infamous crime, unless on a presentment or indictment of a Grand Jury, except in cases arising in the land or naval forces, or in the Militia, when in actual service in time of War or public danger; nor shall any person be subject for the same offence to be twice put in jeopardy of life or limb; nor shall be compelled in any criminal case to be a witness against himself, nor be deprived of life, liberty, or property, without due process of law; nor shall private property be taken for public use, without just compensation.

Amendment VI

In all criminal prosecutions, the accused shall enjoy the right to a speedy and public trial, by an impartial jury of the State and district wherein the crime shall have been committed, which district shall have been previously ascertained by law, and to be informed of the nature and cause of the accusation; to be confronted with the witnesses against him; to have compulsory process for obtaining witnesses in his favor, and to have the Assistance of Counsel for his defence.

Amendment VII

In Suits at common law, where the value in controversy shall exceed twenty dollars, the right of trial by jury shall be preserved, and no fact tried by a jury, shall be otherwise re-examined in any Court of the United States, than according to the rules of the common law.

Amendment VIII

Excessive bail shall not be required, nor excessive fines imposed, nor cruel and unusual punishments inflicted.

Amendment IX

The enumeration in the Constitution, of certain rights, shall not be construed to deny or disparage others retained by the people.

Amendment X

The powers not delegated to the United States by the Constitution, nor prohibited by it to the States, are reserved to the States respectively, or to the people.

AMENDMENT XI

Passed by Congress March 4, 1794. Ratified February 7, 1795.

Note: Article III, section 2, of the Constitution was modified by amendment 11.

The Judicial power of the United States shall not be construed to extend to any suit in law or equity, commenced or prosecuted against one of the United States by Citizens of another State, or by Citizens or Subjects of any Foreign State.

AMENDMENT XII

Passed by Congress December 9, 1803. Ratified June 15, 1804.

Note: A portion of Article II, section 1 of the Constitution was superseded by the 12th amendment.

The Electors shall meet in their respective states and vote by ballot for President and Vice-President, one of whom, at least, shall not be an inhabitant of the same state with themselves; they shall name in their ballots the person voted for as President, and in distinct ballots the person voted for as Vice-President, and they shall make distinct lists of all persons voted for as President, and of all persons voted for as Vice-President, and of the number of votes for each, which lists they shall sign and certify, and transmit sealed to the seat of the government of the United States, directed to the President of the Senate;—the President of the Senate shall, in the presence of the Senate and House of Representatives, open all the certificates and the votes shall then be counted;—The person having the greatest number of votes for President, shall be the President, if such number be a majority of the whole number of Electors appointed; and if no person have such majority, then from the persons having the highest numbers not exceeding three on the list of those voted for as President, the House of Representatives shall choose immediately, by ballot, the President. But in choosing the President, the votes shall be taken by states, the representation from each state having one vote; a quorum for this purpose shall consist of a member or members from two-thirds of the states, and a majority of all the states shall be necessary to a choice. [And if the House of Representatives shall not choose a President whenever the right of choice shall devolve upon them, before the fourth day of March next following, then the Vice-President shall act as President, as in case of the death or other constitutional disability of the President. —]* The person having the greatest number of votes as Vice-President, shall be the Vice-President, if such number be a majority of the whole number of Electors appointed, and if no person have a majority, then from the two highest numbers on the list, the Senate shall choose the Vice-President; a quorum for the purpose shall consist of two-thirds of the whole number of Senators, and a majority of the whole number shall be necessary to a choice. But no person constitutionally ineligible to the office of President shall be eligible to that of Vice-President of the United States.

*Superseded by section 3 of the 20th amendment.

AMENDMENT XIII

Passed by Congress January 31, 1865. Ratified December 6, 1865.

Note: A portion of Article IV, section 2, of the Constitution was superseded by the 13th amendment.

Section 1. Neither slavery nor involuntary servitude, except as a punishment for crime whereof the party shall have been duly convicted, shall exist within the United States, or any place subject to their jurisdiction.

Section 2. Congress shall have power to enforce this article by appropriate legislation.

AMENDMENT XIV

Passed by Congress June 13, 1866. Ratified July 9, 1868.

Note: Article I, section 2, of the Constitution was modified by section 2 of the 14th amendment.

Section 1. All persons born or naturalized in the United States, and subject to the jurisdiction thereof, are citizens of the United States and of the State wherein they reside. No State shall make or enforce any law which shall abridge the privileges or immunities of citizens of the United States; nor shall any State deprive any person of life, liberty, or property, without due process of law; nor deny to any person within its jurisdiction the equal protection of the laws.

Section 2. Representatives shall be apportioned among the several States according to their respective numbers, counting the whole number of persons in each State, excluding Indians not taxed. But when the right to vote at any election for the choice of electors for President and Vice-President of the United States, Representatives in Congress, the Executive and Judicial officers of a State, or the members of the Legislature thereof, is denied to any of the male inhabitants of such State, being twenty-one years of age,* and citizens of the United States, or in any way abridged, except for participation in rebellion, or other crime, the basis of representation therein shall be reduced in the proportion which the number of such male citizens shall bear to the whole number of male citizens twenty-one years of age in such State.

Section 3. No person shall be a Senator or Representative in Congress, or elector of President and Vice-President, or hold any office, civil or military, under the United States, or under any State, who, having previously taken an oath, as a member of Congress, or as an officer of the United States, or as a member of any State legislature, or as an executive or judicial officer of any State, to support the Constitution of the United States, shall have engaged in insurrection or rebellion against the same, or given aid or comfort to the enemies thereof. But Congress may by a vote of two-thirds of each House, remove such disability.

Section 4. The validity of the public debt of the United States, authorized by law, including debts incurred for payment of pensions and bounties for services in suppressing insurrection or rebellion, shall not be questioned. But neither the United States nor any State shall assume or pay any debt or obligation incurred in aid of insurrection or rebellion against the United States, or any claim for the loss or emancipation of any slave; but all such debts, obligations and claims shall be held illegal and void.

Section 5. The Congress shall have the power to enforce, by appropriate legislation, the provisions of this article.
Changed by section 1 of the 26th amendment.

AMENDMENT XV
Passed by Congress February 26, 1869. Ratified February 3, 1870.
Section 1. The right of citizens of the United States to vote shall not be denied or abridged by the United States or by any State on account of race, color, or previous condition of servitude—
Section 2. The Congress shall have the power to enforce this article by appropriate legislation.

AMENDMENT XVI
Passed by Congress July 2, 1909. Ratified February 3, 1913.
Note: Article I, section 9, of the Constitution was modified by amendment 16.
The Congress shall have power to lay and collect taxes on incomes, from whatever source derived, without apportionment among the several States, and without regard to any census or enumeration.

AMENDMENT XVII
Passed by Congress May 13, 1912. Ratified April 8, 1913.
Note: Article I, section 3, of the Constitution was modified by the 17th amendment.
The Senate of the United States shall be composed of two Senators from each State, elected by the people thereof, for six years; and each Senator shall have one vote. The electors in each State shall have the qualifications requisite for electors of the most numerous branch of the State legislatures.
When vacancies happen in the representation of any State in the Senate, the executive authority of such State shall issue writs of election to fill such vacancies: *Provided*, That the legislature of any State may empower the executive thereof to make temporary appointments until the people fill the vacancies by election as the legislature may direct.
This amendment shall not be so construed as to affect the election or term of any Senator chosen before it becomes valid as part of the Constitution.

AMENDMENT XVIII

Passed by Congress December 18, 1917. Ratified January 16, 1919. Repealed by amendment 21.

Section 1. After one year from the ratification of this article the manufacture, sale, or transportation of intoxicating liquors within, the importation thereof into, or the exportation thereof from the United States and all territory subject to the jurisdiction thereof for beverage purposes is hereby prohibited.

Section 2. The Congress and the several States shall have concurrent power to enforce this article by appropriate legislation.

Section 3. This article shall be inoperative unless it shall have been ratified as an amendment to the Constitution by the legislatures of the several States, as provided in the Constitution, within seven years from the date of the submission hereof to the States by the Congress.

AMENDMENT XIX

Passed by Congress June 4, 1919. Ratified August 18, 1920.

The right of citizens of the United States to vote shall not be denied or abridged by the United States or by any State on account of sex.

Congress shall have power to enforce this article by appropriate legislation.

AMENDMENT XX

Passed by Congress March 2, 1932. Ratified January 23, 1933.

Note: Article I, section 4, of the Constitution was modified by section 2 of this amendment. In addition, a portion of the 12th amendment was superseded by section 3.

Section 1. The terms of the President and the Vice President shall end at noon on the 20th day of January, and the terms of Senators and Representatives at noon on the 3d day of January, of the years in which such terms would have ended if this article had not been ratified; and the terms of their successors shall then begin.

Section 2. The Congress shall assemble at least once in every year, and such meeting shall begin at noon on the 3d day of January, unless they shall by law appoint a different day.

Section 3. If, at the time fixed for the beginning of the term of the President, the President elect shall have died, the Vice President elect shall become President. If a President shall not have been chosen before the time fixed for the beginning of his term, or if the President elect shall have failed to qualify, then the Vice President elect shall act as President until a President shall have qualified; and the Congress may by law provide for the case wherein neither a President elect nor a Vice President shall have qualified, declaring who shall then act as President, or the manner in which one who is to act shall be selected, and such person shall act accordingly until a President or Vice President shall have qualified.

Section 4. The Congress may by law provide for the case of the death of any of the persons from whom the House of Representatives may choose a President whenever the right of choice shall have devolved upon them, and for the case of the death of any of the persons from whom the Senate may choose a Vice President whenever the right of choice shall have devolved upon them.

Section 5. Sections 1 and 2 shall take effect on the 15th day of October following the ratification of this article.

Section 6. This article shall be inoperative unless it shall have been ratified as an amendment to the Constitution by the legislatures of three-fourths of the several States within seven years from the date of its submission.

AMENDMENT XXI

Passed by Congress February 20, 1933. Ratified December 5, 1933.

Section 1. The eighteenth article of amendment to the Constitution of the United States is hereby repealed.

Section 2. The transportation or importation into any State, Territory, or Possession of the United States for delivery or use therein of intoxicating liquors, in violation of the laws thereof, is hereby prohibited.

Section 3. This article shall be inoperative unless it shall have been ratified as an amendment to the Constitution by conventions in the several States, as provided in the Constitution, within seven years from the date of the submission hereof to the States by the Congress.

AMENDMENT XXII

Passed by Congress March 21, 1947. Ratified February 27, 1951.

Section 1. No person shall be elected to the office of the President more than twice, and no person who has held the office of President, or acted as President, for more than two years of a term to which some other person was elected President shall be elected to the office of President more than once. But this Article shall not apply to any person holding the office of President when this Article was proposed by Congress, and shall not prevent any person who may be holding the office of President, or acting as President, during the term within which this Article becomes operative from holding the office of President or acting as President during the remainder of such term.

Section 2. This article shall be inoperative unless it shall have been ratified as an amendment to the Constitution by the legislatures of three-fourths of the several States within seven years from the date of its submission to the States by the Congress.

AMENDMENT XXIII
Passed by Congress June 16, 1960. Ratified March 29, 1961.

Section 1. The District constituting the seat of Government of the United States shall appoint in such manner as Congress may direct:
A number of electors of President and Vice President equal to the whole number of Senators and Representatives in Congress to which the District would be entitled if it were a State, but in no event more than the least populous State; they shall be in addition to those appointed by the States, but they shall be considered, for the purposes of the election of President and Vice President, to be electors appointed by a State; and they shall meet in the District and perform such duties as provided by the twelfth article of amendment.

Section 2. The Congress shall have power to enforce this article by appropriate legislation.

AMENDMENT XXIV
Passed by Congress August 27, 1962. Ratified January 23, 1964.

Section 1. The right of citizens of the United States to vote in any primary or other election for President or Vice President, for electors for President or Vice President, or for Senator or Representative in Congress, shall not be denied or abridged by the United States or any State by reason of failure to pay poll tax or other tax.

Section 2. The Congress shall have power to enforce this article by appropriate legislation.

AMENDMENT XXV
Passed by Congress July 6, 1965. Ratified February 10, 1967.

Note: Article II, section 1, of the Constitution was affected by the 25th amendment.

Section 1. In case of the removal of the President from office or of his death or resignation, the Vice President shall become President.

Section 2. Whenever there is a vacancy in the office of the Vice President, the President shall nominate a Vice President who shall take office upon confirmation by a majority vote of both Houses of Congress.

Section 3. Whenever the President transmits to the President pro tempore of the Senate and the Speaker of the House of Representatives his written declaration that he is unable to discharge the powers and duties of his office, and until he transmits to them a written declaration to the contrary, such powers and duties shall be discharged by the Vice President as Acting President.

Section 4. Whenever the Vice President and a majority of either the principal officers of the executive departments or of such other body as Congress may by law provide, transmit to the President pro tempore of the Senate and the Speaker of the House of Representatives their written declaration that the President is unable to discharge the powers and duties of his office, the Vice President shall immediately assume the powers and duties of the office as Acting President.

Thereafter, when the President transmits to the President pro tempore of the Senate and the Speaker of the House of Representatives his written declaration that no inability exists, he shall resume the powers and duties of his office unless the Vice President and a majority of either the principal officers of the executive department or of such other body as Congress may by law provide, transmit within four days to the President pro tempore of the Senate and the Speaker of the House of Representatives their written declaration that the President is unable to discharge the powers and duties of his office. Thereupon Congress shall decide the issue, assembling within forty-eight hours for that purpose if not in session. If the Congress, within twenty-one days after receipt of the latter written declaration, or, if Congress is not in session, within twenty-one days after Congress is required to assemble, determines by two-thirds vote of both Houses that the President is unable to discharge the powers and duties of his office, the Vice President shall continue to discharge the same as Acting President; otherwise, the President shall resume the powers and duties of his office.

AMENDMENT XXVI

Passed by Congress March 23, 1971. Ratified July 1, 1971.

Note: Amendment 14, section 2, of the Constitution was modified by section 1 of the 26th amendment.

Section 1. The right of citizens of the United States, who are eighteen years of age or older, to vote shall not be denied or abridged by the United States or by any State on account of age.

Section 2. The Congress shall have power to enforce this article by appropriate legislation.

AMENDMENT XXVII

Originally proposed Sept. 25, 1789. Ratified May 7, 1992.

No law, varying the compensation for the services of the Senators and Representatives, shall take effect, until an election of representatives shall have intervened.

Kentucky Resolution

RESOLUTIONS IN GENERAL ASSEMBLY

THE representatives of the good people of this commonwealth in general assembly convened, having maturely considered the answers of sundry states in the Union, to their resolutions passed at the last session, respecting certain unconstitutional laws of Congress, commonly called the alien and sedition laws, would be faithless indeed to themselves, and to those they represent, were they silently to acquiesce in principles and doctrines attempted to be maintained in all those answers, that of Virginia only excepted. To again enter the field of argument, and attempt more fully or forcibly to expose the unconstitutionality of those obnoxious laws, would, it is apprehended be as unnecessary as unavailing.

We cannot however but lament, that in the discussion of those interesting subjects, by sundry of the legislatures of our sister states, unfounded suggestions, and uncandid insinuations, derogatory of the true character and principles of the good people of this commonwealth, have been substituted in place of fair reasoning and sound argument. Our opinions of those alarming measures of the general government, together with our reasons for those opinions, were detailed with decency and with temper, and submitted to the discussion and judgment of our fellow citizens throughout the Union. Whether the decency and temper have been observed in the answers of most of those states who have denied or attempted to obviate the great truths contained in those resolutions, we have now only to submit to a candid world. Faithful to the true principles of the federal union, unconscious of any designs to disturb the harmony of that Union, and anxious only to escape the fangs of despotism, the good people of this commonwealth are regardless of censure or calumniation.

Least however the silence of this commonwealth should be construed into an acquiescence in the doctrines and principles advanced and attempted to be maintained by the said answers, or least those of our fellow citizens throughout the Union, who so widely differ from us on those important subjects, should be deluded by the expectation, that we shall be deterred from what we conceive our duty; or shrink from the principles contained in those resolutions: therefore.

RESOLVED, That this commonwealth considers the federal union, upon the terms and for the purposes specified in the late compact, as conducive to the liberty and happiness of the several states: That it does now unequivocally declare its attachment to the Union, and to that compact, agreeable to its obvious and real intention, and will be among the last to seek its dissolution: That if those who administer the general government be permitted to transgress the limits fixed by that compact, by a total disregard to the special delegations of power therein contained, annihilation of the state governments, and the erection upon their ruins, of a general consolidated government, will be the inevitable consequence: That the principle and construction contended for by sundry of the state legislatures, that the general government is the exclusive judge of the extent of the powers delegated to it, stop nothing short of despotism; since the discretion of those who administer the government, and not the constitution, would be the measure of their powers: That the several states who formed that instrument, being sovereign and independent, have the unquestionable right to judge of its infraction; and that a nullification, by those sovereignties, of all unauthorized acts done under colour of that instrument, is the rightful remedy: That this commonwealth does upon the most deliberate reconsideration declare, that the said alien and sedition laws, are in their opinion, palpable violations of the said constitution; and however cheerfully it may be disposed to surrender its opinion to a majority of its sister states in matters of ordinary or doubtful policy; yet, in momentous regulations like the present, which so vitally wound the best rights of the citizen, it would consider a silent acquiescence as highly criminal: That although this commonwealth as a party to the federal compact; will bow to the laws of the Union, yet it does at the same time declare, that it will not now, nor ever hereafter, cease to oppose in a constitutional manner, every attempt from what quarter soever offered, to violate that compact:

AND FINALLY, in order that no pretexts or arguments may be drawn from a supposed acquiescence on the part of this commonwealth in the constitutionality of those laws, and be thereby used as precedents for similar future violations of federal compact; this commonwealth does now enter against them, its SOLEMN PROTEST.

Approved December 3rd, 1799.

Virginia Resolution

RESOLVED, That the General Assembly of Virginia, doth unequivocably express a firm resolution to maintain and defend the Constitution of the United States, and the Constitution of this State, against every aggression either foreign or domestic, and that they will support the government of the United States in all measures warranted by the former.

That this assembly most solemnly declares a warm attachment to the Union of the States, to maintain which it pledges all its powers; and that for this end, it is their duty to watch over and oppose every infraction of those principles which constitute the only basis of that Union, because a faithful observance of them, can alone secure its existence and the public happiness.

That this Assembly doth explicitly and peremptorily declare, that it views the powers of the federal government, as resulting from the compact, to which the states are parties; as limited by the plain sense and intention of the instrument constituting the compact; as no further valid that they are authorized by the grants enumerated in that compact; and that in case of a deliberate, palpable, and dangerous exercise of other powers, not granted by the said compact, the states who are parties thereto, have the right, and are in duty bound, to interpose for arresting the progress of the evil, and for maintaining within their respective limits, the authorities, rights and liberties appertaining to them.

That the General Assembly doth also express its deep regret, that a spirit has in sundry instances, been manifested by the federal government, to enlarge its powers by forced constructions of the constitutional charter which defines them; and that implications have appeared of a design to expound certain general phrases (which having been copied from the very limited grant of power, in the former articles of confederation were the less liable to be misconstrued) so as to destroy the meaning and effect, of the particular enumeration which necessarily explains and limits the general phrases; and so as to consolidate the states by degrees, into one sovereignty, the obvious tendency and inevitable consequence of which would be, to transform the present republican system of the United States, into an absolute, or at best a mixed monarchy.

That the General Assembly doth particularly protest against the palpable and alarming infractions of the Constitution, in the two late cases of the "Alien and Sedition Acts" passed at the last session of Congress; the first of which exercises a power no where delegated to the federal government, and which by uniting legislative and judicial powers to those of executive, subverts the general principles of free government; as well as the particular organization, and positive provisions of the federal constitution; and the other of which acts, exercises in like manner, a power not delegated by the constitution, but on the contrary, expressly and positively forbidden by one of the amendments thereto; a power, which more than any other, ought to produce universal alarm, because it is levelled against that right of freely examining public characters and measures, and of free communication among the people thereon, which has ever been justly deemed, the only effectual guardian of every other right.

That this state having by its Convention, which ratified the federal Constitution, expressly declared, that among other essential rights, "the Liberty of Conscience and of the Press cannot be cancelled, abridged, restrained, or modified by any authority of the United States," and from its extreme anxiety to guard these rights from every possible attack of sophistry or ambition, having with other states, recommended an amendment for that purpose, which amendment was, in due time, annexed to the Constitution; it would mark a reproachable inconsistency, and criminal degeneracy, if an indifference were now shewn, to the most palpable violation of one of the Rights, thus declared and secured; and to the establishment of a precedent which may be fatal to the other.

That the good people of this commonwealth, having ever felt, and continuing to feel, the most sincere affection for their brethren of the other states; the truest anxiety for establishing and perpetuating the union of all; and the most scrupulous fidelity to that constitution, which is the pledge of mutual friendship, and the instrument of mutual happiness; the General Assembly doth solemnly appeal to the like dispositions of the other states, in confidence that they will concur with this commonwealth in declaring, as it does hereby declare, that the acts aforesaid, are unconstitutional; and that the necessary and proper measures will be taken by each, for co-operating with this state, in maintaining the Authorities, Rights, and Liberties, referred to the States respectively, or to the people.

That the Governor be desired, to transmit a copy of the foregoing Resolutions to the executive authority of each of the other states, with a request that the same may be communicated to the Legislature thereof; and that a copy be furnished to each of the Senators and Representatives representing this state in the Congress of the United States.

Agreed to by the Senate, December 24, 1798.

Gettysburg Address

November 19, 1963

The Battle of Gettysburg was the high point for the Confederacy during the Civil War. Never again would Southern troops penetrate so deeply into Union territory and never again would General Robert E. Lee be regarded as invincible. Lee was advancing with his Army of Northern Virginia through Pennsylvania, threatening Washington, DC. Then a Confederate infantry brigade stumbled onto a Union cavalry brigade near the town of Gettysburg. What begonias an unplanned skirmish turned into a three-day battle as more troops arrived to join in the battle, turning this chance encounter into what many feel is the greatest battle ever fought on American soil. On November 19, 1863, President Abraham Lincoln spoke at a ceremony at the battlefield. As is now clear, Lincoln was mistaken in his comment that the world would little note, nor long remember what was said there, for he gave one of the most stirring, most powerful—and shortest—speeches in U.S. history.

On June 1, 1865, Senator Charles Sumner commented on what is now considered the most famous speech by President Abraham Lincoln. In his eulogy on the slain president, he called it a monumental act. He said Lincoln was mistaken that the world will little note, nor long remember what we say here. Rather, the Bostonian remarked, the world noted at once what he said, and will never cease to remember it. The battle itself was less important than the speech.

"Fourscore and seven years ago our fathers brought forth on this continent a new nation, conceived in liberty and dedicated to the proposition that all men are created equal. Now we are engaged in a great civil war, testing whether that nation or any nation so conceived and so dedicated can long endure. We are met on a great battlefield of that war. We have come to dedicate a portion of that field as a final resting-place for those who here gave their lives that that nation might live. It is altogether fitting and proper that we should do this. But in a larger sense, we cannot dedicate, we cannot consecrate, we cannot hallow this ground. The brave men, living and dead who struggled here have consecrated it far above our poor power to add or detract. The world will little note nor long remember what we say here, but it can never forget what they did here. It is for us the living rather to be dedicated here to the unfinished work which they who fought here have thus far so nobly advanced. It is rather for us to be here dedicated to the great task remaining before us—that from these honored dead we take increased devotion to that cause for which they gave the last full measure of devotion—that we here highly resolve that these dead shall not have died in vain, that this nation under God shall have a new birth of freedom, and that government of the people, by the people, for the people shall not perish from the earth."

Second Inaugural Address of Abraham Lincoln

Saturday, March 4, 1865

Fellow-Countrymen:

At this second appearing to take the oath of the Presidential office there is less occasion for an extended address than there was at the first. Then a statement somewhat in detail of a course to be pursued seemed fitting and proper. Now, at the expiration of four years, during which public declarations have been constantly called forth on every point and phase of the great contest which still absorbs the attention and engrosses the energies of the nation, little that is new could be presented. The progress of our arms, upon which all else chiefly depends, is as well known to the public as to myself, and it is, I trust, reasonably satisfactory and encouraging to all. With high hope for the future, no prediction in regard to it is ventured.

On the occasion corresponding to this four years ago all thoughts were anxiously directed to an impending civil war. All dreaded it, all sought to avert it. While the inaugural address was being delivered from this place, devoted altogether to saving the Union without war, insurgent agents were in the city seeking to destroy it without war—seeking to dissolve the Union and divide effects by negotiation. Both parties deprecated war, but one of them would make war rather than let the nation survive, and the other would accept war rather than let it perish, and the war came.

One-eighth of the whole population were colored slaves, not distributed generally over the Union, but localized in the southern part of it. These slaves constituted a peculiar and powerful interest. All knew that this interest was somehow the cause of the war. To strengthen, perpetuate, and extend this interest was the object for which the insurgents would rend the Union even by war, while the Government claimed no right to do more than to restrict the territorial enlargement of it. Neither party expected for the war the magnitude or the duration which it has already attained. Neither anticipated that the cause of the conflict might cease with or even before the conflict itself should cease. Each looked for an easier triumph, and a result less fundamental and astounding. Both read the same Bible and pray to the same God, and each invokes His aid against the other. It may seem strange that any men should dare to ask a just God's assistance in wringing their bread from the sweat of other men's faces, but let us judge not, that we be not judged. The prayers of both could not be answered. That of neither has been answered fully. The Almighty has His own purposes. "Woe unto the world because of offenses; for it must needs be that offenses come, but woe to that man by whom the offense cometh." If we shall suppose that American slavery is one of those offenses which, in the providence of God, must needs come, but which, having continued through His appointed time, He now wills to remove, and that He gives to both North and South this terrible war as the woe due to those by whom the offense came, shall we discern therein any departure from those divine attributes which the believers in a living God always ascribe to Him? Fondly do we hope, fervently do we pray, that this mighty scourge of war may speedily pass away. Yet, if God wills that it continue until all the wealth piled by the bondsman's two hundred and fifty years of unrequited toil shall be sunk, and until every drop of blood drawn with the lash shall be paid by another drawn with the sword, as was said three thousand years ago, so still it must be said "the judgments of the Lord are true and righteous altogether."

With malice toward none, with charity for all, with firmness in the right as God gives us to see the right, let us strive on to finish the work we are in, to bind up the nation's wounds, to care for him who shall have borne the battle and for his widow and his orphan, to do all which may achieve and cherish a just and lasting peace among ourselves and with all nations.

BIBLIOGRAPHY

Arnn, Larry P. *The Founders' Key*. Nashville, Tennessee: Thomas Nelson, 2012.

Bastiat, Frederic. *The Law*. Baltimore, Maryland: Laissez-Faire Books, 2012.

Beck, Glenn. *The Original Argument*. New York: Simon and Schuster, Inc., 2011.

Bonner, William and Pierre Lemieux. *The Idea of America*. Baltimore, Maryland: Laissez-Faire Books, 2011.

Center for Civic Education. *We, the People*. Woodland Hills, California: Center for Civic Education, 1988.

Foundation for Economic Education (FEE) Atlanta, GA.

Gordon, David. *An Introduction to Economic Reasoning*. Auburn, Alabama: Mises Institute, 2000.

Gutzman, Kevin R. C. *The Politically Incorrect Guide to the Constitution*. Washington DC: Regnery Publishing, 2007.

Hayek, F. A. *The Road to Serfdom*. Chicago, Illinois: University of Chicago Press, 2007.

Hayek, F. A. *The Constitution of Liberty*. Chicago, Illinois: University of Chicago Press, 1960.

Hazlitt, Henry. *Economics in One Lesson*. Baltimore, Maryland: Laissez-Faire Books, 2012.

Heumer, Michael. Th*e Problem of Political Authority*. London, Palgrave MacMillan, 2013.

Higgs, Robert. *Against Leviathan*. Oakland, California: Independent Institute, 2004.

Hillsdale College Politics Faculty. *The U.S. Constitution: A Reader.* Hillsdale, Michigan: Hillsdale College, 2012.

Hoppe, Hans-Hermann. *Democracy: The God that Failed.* New Brunswick, New Jersey: Transaction Publishers, 2001.

John V. Denson, Ed. *Reassessing the Presidencxy: The Rise of the Executive State and the Decline of Freedom.* Auburn, Alabama: Mises Institute, 2001.

Knoebel, Charles Hirsschfeld and Edgar E. *The Modern World.* New York: Harcourt, Brace and Jovanovich, 1980.

Lee, Mike. *Written Out of History.* New York: Sentinel, 2017.

Lofgren, Mike. *The Deep State: The Fall of the Constitution and the Rise of a Shadow Government.* New York: Viking Press, 2016.

Manuel, Peter Marshall and David. *From Sea to Shining Sea.* Grand Rapids, Michigan: Fleming H. Revell, 1986.

———. *The Light and the Glory.* Grand Rapids, Michigan: Fleming H. Revell, 1977.

McClanahan, Brion. *How Alexander Hamilton Screwed up America.* Washington DC: Regnery History, 2017.

McCloskey, Deidre. *Bourgeois Dignity.* Chicago, IL: University Chicago Press, 2010.

———. *Bourgeois Equality.* Chicago, IL.: University Chicago Press, 2016.

Mises, Ludwig von. *Liberalism.* Indianapolis, Indiana: Liberty Fund, 2005.

Nock, Albert Jay. *Our Enemy, The State.* Caldwell, Idaho: Caxton Publishing, 1950.

Paul, Ron. *The Revolution at Ten Years.* Clute, Texas: Ron Paul Institute for Peace and Prosperity, 2017.

Pole, J. R. *The American Constitution: For and Against: The Federalist and Antifederalist Papers.* New York: Hill and Wang, 1987.

Rand, Ayn. *Anthem.* New York: Penguin, 1995.

Schlesinger, Arthur M., Jr. *The Imperial Presidency*. New York: Mariner Book, 1973.

Smith, Adam. *On the Wealth of Nations*. London, England: Ward, Locke and Co. Limited, 1795.

Spalding, Matthew. *We Still Hold These Truths*. Wilmington, Delaware: ISI Books, 2009.

Woods, Thomas E., Jr. *Nullification*. Washington DC: Regnery, 2010.

——. *Real Dissent*. CreateSpace, 2104.

INDEX

A

Adams, John, 60, 112, 115, 120, 123, 127–28, 133, 137, 159, 161, 205, 237, 316
Adams, John Quincy, 204–5
Adams, Sam, 31, 122, 137, 218
affirmative action, 342–44
Alinsky, Saul, 340, 430
American Revolution, 8, 54, 60, 108, 113, 115, 134, 146, 149, 205, 357, 451
Anti-Federalism, 8, 219
Aristotle, 20, 22, 25, 36, 40, 50, 61, 63, 86, 201–2, 241, 471–72
Arizona, 371, 405
Arouet, François-Marie. See Voltaire
Articles of Confederation, 140–42, 144, 151, 157–58, 161–66, 168, 171, 175, 179, 199–200, 216, 226–27, 249, 257, 389, 398
Assange, Julian, 317
Authorization for Use of Military Force (AUMF), 320

B

Beard, Charles, 378
Bellamy, Francis, 6, 301
Billaud-Varenne, Jacques Nicolas, 59
Bill of Responsibilities, 457

bill of rights, 3, 5–7, 11–12, 30, 65, 103, 110, 127, 130, 213, 215, 218, 220, 222–25, 227, 233–36, 245, 257, 267–68, 270–72, 276–77, 279, 282–84, 289, 296, 303, 307–9, 325, 406, 447–48, 452, 459, 493
Black, Hugo, 8, 272
branch
  executive, 69, 109, 113–14, 135–37, 166, 168, 179–81, 188, 190, 220, 232, 246, 250, 252, 273, 338, 434
  judicial, 135, 137, 141, 164, 166, 174, 193–95, 214, 232, 246–48, 256–57, 304, 390
  legislative, 83, 108, 135, 146, 164, 166, 169, 183, 187, 195, 220, 232, 245
Brandenburg, Clarence, 364
Bryant, Samuel, 31, 225
Burke, Edmund, 106, 193, 447
Bush, George W., 192, 240, 274–75

C

Caldwell, Matt, 403
Calhoun, John, 63
California, xiv, xvi, 302, 333–34, 343–44, 366, 378, 393, 431, 466, 513

capitalism, 68, 87, 91–92, 94–95, 152, 410
capital punishment, 324, 359, 455–56
Carter, Jimmy, 192, 451
Chandler, Robert, 430
Cheney, Dick, xix
Chicago, xi–xii, 90, 195, 298, 444, 513–14
Christianity, 285–86, 300
Christmas, 175, 290–91, 300–301
Citizens for Responsibility and Ethics in Washington (CREW), 376
Citizens United, 368, 460
Civil War, 53, 120, 152, 154, 212, 237, 244, 277, 280, 327–28, 333, 342, 347–48, 393–95, 440, 442, 451, 508, 510
classical liberalism, 52, 55, 87
classical republicanism, 74–75, 77, 80, 82, 410, 412, 419–20, 423, 439
clause
    commerce, 174, 264, 398–402, 404, 406, 463
    equal protection, 327–28, 333, 335–37, 350, 456
    establishment, 286–87, 289, 291, 293–94, 297–98, 301
    free exercise, 286–87, 289–90, 296, 341
Clay, Henry, 8, 240
Cleveland, Grover, 3, 63, 192, 240
Clinton, Bill, xix, 191–92, 274–75, 375, 430
Clinton, George, 31, 218, 225
Clinton, Hillary, xv, 258, 353, 361, 460
Columbia University, 378, 429–30
commerce
    interstate, 399, 403
    intrastate, 402–4
Common Sense (Paine), 60
commonwealth, 58, 113, 411, 447, 504–8
Communism, 57, 68, 89, 91
Confederation Congress, 144, 151, 153, 179, 216, 227, 416

CONOP 8888, 444–46
constitutionalism, 66, 233, 260
Continental Congress, 4, 123–24, 141–42, 144
Cowen, Tyler, xi, xiii

D

Declaration of Independence, 4–5, 12, 14, 20, 54, 122–25, 131, 142, 161, 218, 227, 269, 271, 351, 416, 476
Deep State: The Fall of the Constitution and the Rise of a Shadow Government (Lofgren), xix
democracy, 35, 56, 68, 71–72, 76, 81, 95, 99, 130, 135, 146, 212, 229–30, 247, 272, 346, 385, 419, 426, 448, 458, 461, 514
Democrats, 73, 152, 238–39, 261, 307
Dennis, Eugene, 363, 367–68
despotic, 56, 126, 360
Dingell, John, 460
discrimination, 92, 175, 298, 327–28, 333, 336–39, 341–42, 344, 347, 436
doctrine, xviii, 53, 72, 95, 101–2, 188–89, 297, 342, 504
Dyer, Mary, 359
dynamism, xii–xiii

E

economy, xiii, xix, 58, 82, 86, 89–90, 93, 107, 129, 186, 214, 238, 251, 305–6, 372, 397, 415, 421, 429
Eighth Amendment, 322, 324, 384, 455–56
Eisenhower, Dwight D., 191, 301
Elbridge Gerry, 31, 170, 211, 217, 226, 236, 388

126, 128, 201, 219, 227, 238, 267, 285, 298, 411, 444, 447

Lofgren, Mike, xix, 436

Louisiana, 294, 330–31, 335–36, 380

M

Madison, James, xvii, 5, 29–30, 55, 69, 72, 76, 80–82, 124, 150, 157–58, 160–61, 163, 169, 182, 192, 195, 199, 207, 211, 215–19, 224, 227–29, 232, 236–37, 240, 244, 250–51, 253–55, 262, 268, 276–77, 279, 283, 285–86, 304, 354–55, 387–88, 390, 393, 399, 402, 413–14, 447, 461, 465, 473

Magna Carta, 67, 98–100, 105, 108, 267–69, 304, 319, 322, 474

mandamus, 252–53

Marshall, John, 8, 162, 207, 237, 250–53, 264, 270, 307, 337, 390, 392–94, 467

Martin, Luther, 31, 218, 388

Marxism, 68

Maryland, 106–7, 157–58, 178, 207–8, 220, 235, 264, 279, 284, 290, 307, 330, 388, 390, 393, 395, 417, 481, 513

Mason, George, 31, 120, 124, 157, 161, 177, 211–13, 215, 226, 276, 406, 441, 443

Massachusetts, 106–7, 110, 115, 121–22, 133, 137–38, 147, 149, 212, 225, 234–35, 243, 283–84, 387–88, 394, 480

Massachusetts Constitution, 134, 137–38, 205

McClanahan, Brion, 8, 191

Mercer, John, 31, 226

Michigan, 343–44, 460

Mill, John Stuart, 90, 95

Milton, John, 16, 54

Mises, Ludwig, 68

monarchy, 52, 56, 60, 66, 71, 76, 102, 105, 123, 125, 163, 168, 220, 303

Montesquieu, Baron de, 52, 56, 76

Morris, Robert, 157, 301, 326

Motor Voter law, 430–31

Murray, Charles, 373–75

N

National Security Agency (NSA), 243, 316

National Security Council (NSC), 190

New Civics, 429–30

Newdow, Michael, 301

New England, 72, 107, 121, 255, 282–83, 419

New Hampshire, 106, 147–48, 220, 234–36, 284, 393, 404, 480

New Hampshire General Court, 403–4

New Jersey Plan, 166, 168

Nixon, Richard, 192, 270, 343

Norris, Chuck, 429–31, 447

North Carolina, 107, 147, 177, 220, 235, 284, 330–31, 348, 372, 386, 391, 466, 481

O

Obama, xx, 187–88, 191–92, 273–76, 320, 408–9, 429–30

Obama, Barack, xix–xx, 103, 187–88, 191–92, 240, 258, 273–76, 320, 408–10, 429–30, 447

Obamacare, 103, 245, 281–82, 329, 398, 400, 453, 455

Otis, James, 119–20, 310–11, 314

P

Paine, Thomas, 60, 85, 123, 161, 199, 347, 354

Parliament, 53–54, 96, 100–103, 105, 112, 114, 116–18, 121, 126, 136, 179, 200, 248, 268, 466

Paterson, William, 165–66

patriotism, 27, 74, 159, 221, 270, 423

Paul, Ron, xvii, 67, 124, 174, 226, 240, 267

peace, 15, 51, 75, 103, 118, 143, 146, 148, 151, 199, 204–5, 230, 250–51, 286, 342, 365, 388, 417, 475, 477, 479, 482, 486, 494, 511
    civil, 203–4
    international, 203–4

Peletier, Louis-Michel le, 59

Philadelphia, xii, xvi, 121–22, 152–53, 157–59, 162–63, 175, 192, 200, 225, 244, 258, 263, 269, 321, 354–55, 398

Philadelphia Convention, 120, 153, 158–59, 163, 217, 250, 263, 347, 389

Plato, 20, 40, 42, 50–51, 57, 61, 104

Pledge of Allegiance, 6, 64

Polk, James K., 3

powers
    absolute, 62, 355
    abuse of, 65, 108, 137–38, 270, 309
    division of, 69, 391–92
    executive, 180–81, 275, 356, 486
    implied, xviii, 174, 390
    judicial, 105, 246, 265, 489, 495, 507
    legislative, 109, 171, 181, 214, 276, 337, 477, 480
    separation of, 52, 68, 82, 135, 137–38, 193, 231, 414, 459

Preamble, 5, 74, 198, 203–4, 207, 209, 211, 227, 270

Progressivism, 57, 68, 89, 95, 340

R

Ramsay, David, 32

ratification, 81, 130, 160–61, 185, 199–200, 218, 221, 223–24, 227–28, 234, 237, 250, 257, 272, 283, 329–33, 417, 491–92, 499–500

rebellion, 19, 115, 125–26, 130, 147, 150–51, 153–55, 158, 267, 331, 438, 469, 485, 497

Reed, Phillip, 279

regulations
    federal, 403–4
    national, 463, 465

religious freedom, 103, 106, 282–83, 286, 288–89, 292

republican government, xvii, 29, 68, 71, 76, 82, 87, 160, 206, 217, 228–29, 260, 411, 414, 422, 443

republicanism, 76, 82, 133, 152, 155, 206, 217, 221, 231, 233, 261

Republicans, 152, 160, 205, 236, 239, 250, 259, 267, 307, 441

responsibilities, 6–7, 32, 45, 66, 68, 79–80, 98, 112, 126, 170, 179–80, 183, 189–90, 193, 210, 215, 245, 257, 264, 269, 271, 277, 306, 319, 324, 339, 348, 385–86, 415, 423–24, 440, 456–58

revolution, 12, 60, 65, 67, 74, 106, 109, 112, 120, 122, 124, 153, 156, 158, 221–22, 229, 231, 244, 248, 251, 273, 379, 387, 418, 439, 443, 472, 514
    right of, 64, 415

Revolutionary War, 12, 123, 133, 144–45, 147, 149, 151, 223, 249, 282, 347, 416–17

Rhode Island, 107, 162–63, 200, 220, 235, 283, 348, 422